KARL MARX
FREDERICK ENGELS
COLLECTED WORKS
VOLUME
19

KARL MARX
FREDERICK ENGELS

COLLECTED
WORKS

INTERNATIONAL PUBLISHERS

NEW YORK

KARL MARX
FREDERICK ENGELS

Volume
19

MARX AND ENGELS: 1861-64

INTERNATIONAL PUBLISHERS
NEW YORK

This volume has been prepared jointly by Lawrence &
Wishart Ltd., London, International Publishers Co. Inc.,
New York, and Progress Publishers, Moscow, in colla-
boration with the Institute of Marxism-Leninism,
Moscow.

Editorial commissions:

GREAT BRITAIN: Eric Hobsbawm, John Hoffman,
Nicholas Jacobs, Monty Johnstone, Martin Milligan,
Jeff Skelley, Ernst Wangermann.
USA: Louis Diskin, Philip S. Foner, James E. Jackson,
Leonard B. Levenson, Betty Smith, Dirk J. Struik,
William W. Weinstone.
USSR: for Progress Publishers—A. K. Avelichev,
N. P. Karmanova, V. N. Sedikh, M. K. Shcheglova;
for the Institute of Marxism-Leninism—
P. N. Fedoseyev, L. I. Golman, A. I. Malysh,
M. P. Mchedlov, A. G. Yegorov.

Library of Congress Cataloging in Publication Data

Marx, Karl, 1818-1883.
   Karl Marx, Frederick Engels: collected works.

   1. Socialism—Collected works. 2. Economics—
Collected works. I. Engels, Friedrich, 1820-1895.
Works, English. 1975. II. Title.
HX 39.5. A 16 1975   335.4   73-84671
ISBN 0-7178-0519-0   (v. 19)

HX
39.5
.A2/3
19
13 02/9
7w. 1984

Printed in the Union of Soviet Socialist Republics in 1983

Contents

KARL MARX AND FREDERICK ENGELS

WORKS

January 1861-June 1864

FROM THE PREPARATORY MATERIALS

APPENDICES

NOTES AND INDEXES

ILLUSTRATIONS

TRANSLATORS:

RODNEY LIVINGSTONE: Items 56, 73
HENRY MINS: Items 13, 14, 23, 24, 32, 36, 47-49, 52, 54,
 55, 57, 59, 61, 62, 65, 66, 68, 69, 72, 75-80
PETER and BETTY ROSS: Items 81, 82
SALO RYAZANSKAYA: Items 22, 58
VICTOR SCHNITTKE: Items 71, 74
BARRIE SELMAN: Item 67

Preface

Volume 19 of the *Collected Works* of Marx and Engels contains articles, letters and documents written between the end of January 1861 and the beginning of June 1864, except for Engels' articles for *The Volunteer Journal, for Lancashire and Cheshire,* which are published in Volume 18 with other works of his on military subjects.

The first half of the 1860s saw the continued rise of the bourgeois-democratic and national liberation movements that began in Europe and America after the world economic crisis of 1857. In Germany and Italy, which had yet to complete their bourgeois revolutions, the movement for national unity gained fresh impetus; in Russia peasant unrest continued, and revolutionary ideas spread in progressive circles after the abolition of serfdom in February 1861; in the USA civil war broke out between North and South (1861-65); there was growing opposition to the régime of the Second Empire in France; centrifugal tendencies intensified in the Austrian monarchy; in Mexico the bourgeois revolution triumphed; in China the Taiping peasant uprising entered its closing stage.

The industrial revolution in the economically advanced countries led to a great increase in the numerical strength of the proletariat and far-reaching changes in its composition and class-consciousness. The world economic crisis of 1857, the first of such magnitude in the history of capitalism, and the strikes that followed, vividly demonstrated the opposing economic and political interests of proletariat and bourgeoisie. The working-class movement began to pursue an independent struggle and this created conditions for its liberation from the ideological influence of the bourgeoisie. In the first half of the 1860s this showed itself in the growth of the British trade-union movement and the awakening of political activity of the British proletariat, in particular its demonstrations in defence of the national liberation movements and its opposition to the attempts by the British and French ruling classes to intervene in the US Civil War on behalf of the slave-owning Southern states. This process of working-class emancipation from bourgeois ideology was also expressed in the awakening of class consciousness among the French proletariat; in the attempts by the German workers to shake off the influence of the liberal bourgeoisie, and the foundation in 1863 of the General Association of German Workers; and in the active support by workers of various nationalities of the struggle for greater freedom and democracy in the USA (against the South in the Civil War) and of Garibaldi in Italy. The workers' realisation that their interests were in opposition to those of the ruling classes, an increased sense of proletarian solidarity, and the strengthening of international contacts, finally led to the foundation of the International Working Men's Association (the First International) on September 28, 1864.

Marx's and Engels' theoretical work and political activities during these years were many-sided. As before, Marx's main concern was political economy. From August 1861 to July 1863 he wrote *A Contribution to the Critique of Political Economy*; from the end of July or beginning of August 1863, to the summer of 1864, he worked on Book I of *Capital*—"The Process of Capitalist Production". Meanwhile, Engels continued with the theoretical development of the proletarian party's military strategy and tactics. At the same time they both pursued their interests in problems of philosophy and world history.

At the end of the 1850s, Marx and Engels began their attempts to restore old contacts—and to establish new ones—with German, French, Polish and Italian revolutionary democratic emigrants in London, and above all with the working-class and democratic movements in Britain, Germany, France, Austria and the USA. These efforts, both to consolidate the forces of the working class and to establish contacts with progressive democratic circles, were dictated by the general revolutionary upsurge.

Marx and Engels were above all guided by the objective interests of the proletariat: the bourgeois-democratic transformation of the countries of Europe and America, and the creation of legal conditions for the development of the working-class and democratic movement. The revolution of 1848-1849 had shown that in the more economically developed capitalist countries of Europe, the liberal bourgeoisie did not want, while the democratic and radical petty bourgeoisie proved unfit, to carry the bourgeois revolution through to the end. So in the 1860s the fulfilment of this historic task was becoming more and more the cause of the working class. Marx and Engels favoured the unification by revolutionary means of Germany and Italy, and the transition to revolutionary methods of conducting the US Civil War. They attached particular importance to the revolutionary movement in France and Russia, regarding Bonapartism and tsarism as the chief obstacles to the national liberation of the oppressed peoples of Europe.

The many-sided activity by Marx and Engels during this period is partly reflected in this volume. Their journalistic work is represented most fully. Until March 1862 Marx continued writing for the progressive American bourgeois newspaper, the *New York Tribune*; from October 1861 to December 1862 he contributed to the Viennese liberal newspaper *Die Presse*. Engels helped Marx in his work as correspondent for these newspapers; furthermore, as has been mentioned above, Engels wrote a great deal about military matters for the English magazine *The Volunteer Journal, for Lancashire and Cheshire,* and for the German newspaper *Allgemeine Militär-Zeitung.*

A theme central to the journalistic writings of Marx and Engels during these years was the US Civil War, which they saw as a crucial turning-point in the history of the USA, and of overall progressive significance. Their articles provided the first systematic account of its history, its political and social ramifications, its economic consequences, and the diplomatic struggles that resulted not only in America, but in Europe and especially in Britain. Most of the works on this subject were written by Marx and published in *Die Presse* and the *New-York Daily Tribune* in 1861-62.

For the American paper, Marx wrote mainly about the impact of the Civil War on Great Britain's economy, foreign policy and public opinion. *Die Presse,* which was read not only in Austria, but in Germany, carried articles mainly about the Civil War itself, its character, motive forces and historical significance. Marx endeavoured to give the European reader more exact information, based on American sources. He wrote to Engels on April 28, 1862 about the need to "disseminate correct views on this important matter in the land of the Teutons" (this edition, Vol. 41).

In the very first articles for European readers—"The North American Civil War" and "The Civil War in the United States"—and in his article for the *Tribune*, "The American Question in England", Marx demonstrated the groundlessness of the claims by the British bourgeois press (*The Times* and other newspapers) that the war between North and South was not a war over slavery, but over tariffs, the political rivalry of North and South for supremacy in the Union and the like. For Marx the conflict between the Northern and Southern states was the struggle between "two social systems"—slavery and wage labour (p. 50). He regarded the Civil War as an inevitable consequence of the long struggle of the industrial North and the slave-owning South, a struggle which "was the moving power of its [America's] history for half a century" (p. 11). Marx saw this war as a form of bourgeois-democratic revolution, the inevitability of which was conditioned by economic and political factors and, above all, by the "growth of the North-West, the immense strides its population has made from 1850 to 1860" (p. 10).

Analysis in depth of social-political relations in the United States throughout the first half of the 19th century enabled Marx to reveal in his articles the contradictory essence of American plantation slavery. A pre-capitalist form of exploitation, slavery was also closely linked with the world capitalist market; cotton produced by slave labour became one of the "monstrous pivots" of British industry (p. 19).

Studying the conditions under which plantation slavery and its primitive technology could exist, Marx wrote: "The cultivation of the Southern export articles, cotton, tobacco, sugar, etc., carried on by slaves, is only remunerative as long as it is conducted with large gangs of slaves, on a mass scale and on wide expanses of a naturally fertile soil, which requires only simple labour" (p. 39). Given the extensive nature of a plantation economy based on slave labour, unlimited reserves of free land were necessary, which resulted in the "continual expansion of territory and continual spread of slavery beyond its old limits" (p. 39).

Analysis of the economic structure of the plantation economy and the conditions for its survival enabled Marx to expose the groundlessness of the claims by the bourgeois press about the peaceful nature of the Secession (the withdrawal of the Southern states from the Union), and to rebuff attempts to portray the slave-owners of the South as defending the rights of individual states from the encroachments of the Federal Government. Marx stressed that it was the Southern Confederacy that "assumed the offensive in the Civil War" (p. 43). He repeatedly noted that the Secession was a form of aggression by the slave-owning planters against the lawful government, that the "war of the Southern Confederacy is in the true sense of the word a war of conquest for the spread and perpetuation of slavery" (p. 49). He warned against the real danger of slavery spreading all over the Republic: "The slave system would infect the whole Union" (p. 50).

Marx showed that the perpetuation and further spread of slavery would have fatal social consequences. "In the Northern States, where Negro slavery is in practice unworkable, the white working class would gradually be forced down to the level of helotry" (p. 50). In the Southern states, he pointed out, the numerically small slave-owning oligarchy was opposed by the disadvantaged "poor whites", whose numbers "have been constantly growing through concentration of landed property" (p. 40). These déclassé groups of the population, corrupted by the slave-owning ideology, could only be kept in subjection by flattery of their own hopes of obtaining new territory and by "the prospect of one day becoming slaveholders themselves" (41).

Marx and Engels repeatedly emphasised that the existence of slavery was retarding the development of the American working-class movement, was serving as a foundation for the intensified exploitation of the free workers of the North, and was a threat to the constitutional rights of the American workers.

Marx showed that although slavery partially facilitated the development of capitalism in the USA—as some of the bourgeoisie in the North were living off the trade in cotton and other products of slave labour—it was becoming more and more incompatible with the capitalist development of the Northern states. It was the problem of slavery, as Marx emphasised, that was at the root of the US Civil War: "The whole movement was and is based ... on the *slave question*. Not in the sense of whether the slaves within the existing slave states should be emancipated outright or not, but ... whether the vast Territories of the republic should be nurseries for free states or for slavery" (p. 42).

Using a wealth of factual material, Marx was already pointing out in his first articles on the US Civil War that the more advanced social system, namely, that of the Northern States, must win. While noting the progressive nature of the war as fought by the North, he also condemned the indecision and vacillation shown in the war by Union bourgeois circles in proclaiming the abolition of slavery. In his articles "The Dismissal of Frémont", "A Criticism of American Affairs" and others, Marx showed the reluctance of the bourgeois Republican Government to make it a popular and revolutionary war. This, in his opinion, showed up the limitations of American bourgeois democracy. The Lincoln government "fights shy of every step that could mislead the 'loyal' slaveholders of the border states" (p. 87), as a result of which the war as a struggle against slavery was being blunted (p. 227). It was this policy of the Northern government during the initial stages of the war that Marx saw as the main reason for the military failures of the Unionists, in spite of their superiority in economic potential and in manpower reserves.

In a series of articles written in 1862, Marx indicated the process of differentiation in the ruling Republican Party under the influence of the growth and consolidation of the forces favouring the immediate abolition of slavery ("Abolitionist Demonstrations in America", "The Election Results in the Northern States"). He noted changes in the balance of forces within the Republican Party, forced under pressure from the general public to take a more decisive stand over the emancipation of the slaves. After analysing the results of the voting in the states, Marx demonstrated that the failure of the Republicans at the elections was caused above all by the discontent of the farmers in the North with the former methods of conducting the war and by a shift to the left of the masses who followed the Republicans: "They came out emphatically for immediate emancipation, whether for its own sake or as a means of ending the rebellion" (p. 264). Summing up the first stage of the war, Marx wrote: "So far, we have only witnessed the first act of the Civil War—the *constitutional* waging of war. The second act, the *revolutionary* waging of war, is at hand" (p. 228).

Marx and Engels followed the increasingly revolutionary nature of the Civil War closely and noted the revolutionary-democratic measures to which the Lincoln government was compelled to resort and which ultimately led to the victory of the North. Marx attached special importance to two social measures: the Homestead Act, which gave a great many American farmers the chance of acquiring land, and the Proclamation that the black slaves of the rebellious planters were free. Marx valued the latter as "the most important document in American history since the establishment of the Union", pointing out that it was "tantamount to the tearing up of the old American constitution" (p. 250).

In the initial period of the war, Marx criticised Lincoln for vacillation and indecision, and for the bourgeois limitations of certain of his measures and legal enactments (see, e.g., p. 87). Items in the volume show, however, that the Lincoln government's revolutionary measures gradually changed the attitude of Marx and Engels to the President himself. In October 1862, Marx gave high praise to Lincoln's activity, declaring that "Lincoln's place in the history of the United States and of mankind will ... be next to that of Washington" (p. 250).

In their *New-York Daily Tribune* and *Die Presse* articles, the leaders of the proletariat tried to help the struggle of the revolutionary-democratic forces for a fuller and more consistent solution to the pressing historical tasks during the war. The consolidation of the forces of revolutionary democracy, which was pushing the bourgeois to the left, was regarded by Marx and Engels as an important task for the American working class. The farming and working-class population of the North played a major role in the struggle against slavery. Marx wrote: "New England and the Northwest, which have provided the main body of the army, are determined to force on the government a revolutionary kind of warfare and to inscribe the battle-slogan of 'Abolition of Slavery' on the star-spangled banner" (p. 228). Marx noted that although the consolidation of "the parties of the North which are consistent in point of principle", i.e. confirmed Abolitionists, takes place very slowly, they all nevertheless "are being pushed ... into the foreground by events" (p. 233).

Marx and Engels set great store by the participation of the Black masses in the liberation struggle and severely criticised the policy of the Northern states over the "Negro question". Fearing revolutionary disturbances, the American government could not at first make up its mind whether or not to admit Blacks into the army. The recruitment of Blacks into the army of the North would, in Marx's opinion, have had a tremendous influence on the course of the war; it would have considerably increased the North's chances by weakening the rear of the South. A single Black regiment, he wrote on August 7, 1862, "would have a remarkable effect on Southern nerves" (this edition, Vol. 41). Marx had a high estimation of the new officers brought into being in the course of the Civil War, since they were the ones actually solving the problem of abolition, declaring the slaves free and demanding that they be armed (see this volume, pp. 115-16).

Even early in the Civil War, Marx perceived the social-economic factors that subsequently, after the victory of the Republicans and the abolition of slavery, favoured the preservation of racial discrimination and of national and social oppression in the USA. Marx stressed the direct interest of the commercial and finance bourgeoisie in preserving the remnants of slave ownership. In his article, "The Election Results in the Northern States", he wrote that it was New York, "the seat of the American money market and full of holders of mortgages on Southern plantations", a city "actively engaged in the slave trade until recently", that had been, immediately before and during the Civil War, the main bulwark of the Democratic party (p. 263).

Much space in Marx's and Engels' articles on the Civil War is taken up by its military aspects. Engels pointed out the decisive role of the masses and the interrelation of economic, political and moral factors in the military operations. "The American Civil War," he wrote, "given the inventive spirit of the nation and the high technical level of engineering in America, would lead to great advances ... in the technical side of warfare..." (p. 289). At the same time, while acknowledging the role of war in technical development, Marx and Engels condemned the social role of the "human slaughter industry" (see letters from Marx to Engels, July 7, 1866, and Engels to Marx, July 12, 1866, this edition, Vol. 42).

In his article, "Artillery News from America", after analysing, on the evidence of individual operations, the forms and methods of conducting the war, Engels demonstrated the natural tendency of military equipment to become obsolete very quickly and the necessity for its continual improvement. Study of the Civil War enabled Engels to plot the main trends in the development of artillery, in the art of fortification and especially in the development of the navy, and to specify and elaborate certain points made in his earlier articles in The New American Cyclopaedia (see this edition, Vol. 18). Fundamentally significant, in particular, was Engels' forecast of the predominance in future naval armed forces of armoured vessels with gun turrets (p. 291).

In their jointly written articles, "The American Civil War", "The Situation in the American Theatre of War" and others, Marx and Engels developed the idea, important for military science, of the influence exerted by the character of a war on the methods by which it is conducted. Marx and Engels pointed out the negative role of the cadre officers under McClellan who were sympathetic to the South. Marx wrote that there was a strong *esprit de corps* among them and that they were more or less closely connected with their old comrades in the enemy camp. "In their view, the war must be waged in a strictly businesslike fashion, with constant regard to the restoration of the Union on its *old* basis, and therefore must above all be kept free from revolutionary tendencies and tendencies affecting matters of principle" (p. 179). Marx and Engels considered that the dismissal from the Northern army of reactionary officers sympathetic to the South was a military measure of the utmost priority. They also demonstrated that the strategic plan of the McClellan command (the North's "Anaconda Plan" envisaged a slowly contracting ring of troops round the rebellious slave-owning states) was not only intended to avoid a true revolutionary war of the people, but was untenable in military terms (pp. 193-95).

In the article "The American Civil War", Marx and Engels put forward their own strategic plan, taking into consideration the class content, the political and social aims of the war, and demanding revolutionary methods of conducting it. This consisted of a decisive blow by concentrated forces against the vitally important enemy centres and envisaged first and foremost the occupation of Georgia, as a result of which the territory of the Confederation would be cut into two parts (pp. 194-95). The subsequent course of the war showed that this plan was the only right one. A turning point in military operations occurred and the North achieved final victory in 1865, but only after the Northern command had carried out a similar plan (General Sherman's "march to the sea") in the second half of 1864 and had taken revolutionary measures the necessity of which Marx and Engels had been indicating all through 1861 and 1862.

The denunciation of bourgeois diplomacy and the reactionary designs of the ruling classes against the revolutionary democratic and national liberation movements were regarded by Marx and Engels as one of the most important tasks of the proletarian revolutionaries. The events of the US Civil War gave Marx the opportunity to denounce in his articles the foreign policy of the British ruling oligarchy which, in spite of Britain's declared neutrality, was secretly supporting the Southern rebels and was preparing an armed intervention to help the slave-owners. In connection with the seizure in November 1861 by an American warship of the British packet boat *Trent* with emissaries of the Confederacy on board, there was a real threat of armed conflict between Britain and the United States. In his articles "The

Anglo-American Conflict", "Controversy over the *Trent* Case", "The Washington Cabinet and the Western Powers" and others, Marx irrefutably demonstrated the groundlessness of the arguments put forward by British ruling circles and their allies on the continent, who were trying to use this incident as a pretext for unleashing a war on the side of the slave-owners.

Marx and Engels considered that the attitude of the European and American proletariat to the US Civil War should be determined by the prospects of the revolutionary movement in Europe and America and that the war against slavery in the USA would increase the political activity of the working class. Regarding an active influence on the foreign policy of the ruling classes as one of the most important tasks of the revolutionary proletariat, and as part of its general struggle for the liberation of the working people, Marx and Engels set great store by the demonstrations of the English workers against their government's intention to create a coalition of reactionary European states to provide armed help to the South. These demonstrations, in Marx's opinion, played a large part in educating the proletarian masses in the spirit of international solidarity and as a counterweight to the chauvinistic propaganda of the ruling classes, and, above all, of the Palmerston press. Marx demonstrated that the masses in Britain, France, Germany and, indeed, all Europe, considered the defence of the North as their cause, the cause of freedom "now to be defended sword in hand, from the sordid grasp of the slaveholder" (p. 29).

Marx's articles "The Opinion of the Newspapers and the Opinion of the People", "English Public Opinion", "A London Workers' Meeting", "Anti-Intervention Feeling" and others, taught the workers how to work out their own revolutionary line and stand up for it in international conflicts. Marx was particularly delighted by the actions of the British proletariat; he considered that "the English working class has won immortal historical honour for itself", having by means of mass protest meetings foiled the attempts of the ruling classes to organise an intervention on behalf of the South, although the continuation of the US Civil War and also the crisis in the cotton industry connected with it subjected "a million English workers to the most fearful sufferings and privations" (p. 297).

Marx described the appalling poverty of the Lancashire weavers left unemployed by the closure of many cotton mills. He denounced the attempts by the ruling classes (the articles "On the Cotton Crisis", "Workers' Distress in England", etc.) to attribute the stagnation in the British cotton industry exclusively to the cessation of the import of cotton from the USA as a result of the Civil War, to the protectionist measures of the North and to its blockade of the secessionist South. Marx showed that the disastrous plight of this industry was first and foremost caused by a crisis of overproduction (pp. 160-62, 239). He condemned the pathetic system of social charity in Britain (pp. 241-42). Marx wrote with indignation about the inhuman selfishness of the ruling classes, of the "strange dispute" between the landed and industrial aristocracy "as to which of them grinds the working class down the most, and which of them is least obliged to do something about the workers' distress" (p. 241).

The position of the British workers during the US Civil War, their demonstrations in defence of the Italian national liberation movement and their stand on other issues, enabled Marx to conclude that in the political life of Britain the actions of the working class were acquiring national significance for the first time since the defeat of Chartism. In his article, "Garibaldi Meetings.— The Distressed Condition of Cotton Workers", Marx wrote: "Anyone who has the slightest knowledge of English conditions and the attitude prevailing here knows, in addition, that any interference on the part of the present cabinet with the popular demonstrations can only end in the fall of the government" (p. 246).

Marx also noted that in its political demonstrations the working class was beginning to play an increasingly independent role, pursuing its aims and not acting simply as members of "the chorus" (p. 153). The demonstrations of the British proletariat in connection with international conflicts enabled Marx and Engels further to develop the theory of class struggle, to substantiate the position of the proletariat in problems of foreign policy and to define the strategic and tactical tasks of the proletarian party. Marx became still more convinced of his conclusion that even before the winning of political power, the working class, by influencing the foreign policy of the government of its own country, could compel it to renounce an aggressive course aimed at the enslavement of other peoples. As is known, this conclusion found expression in one of the first programme documents of the International, the Inaugural Address of the Working Men's International Association, written by Marx in October 1864 (see this edition, Vol. 20).

The problems of international relations and the colonial policy of the European powers are discussed in a group of articles about the beginning of the Anglo-French-Spanish intervention in Mexico in 1861. ("The Intervention in Mexico", "The Parliamentary Debate on the Address" and others). Marx disclosed the true aims of the participants in the "Mexican Expedition" and denounced its colonial character. Describing the intervention in Mexico as "one of the most monstrous enterprises ever chronicled in the annals of international history" (p. 71), Marx stressed that the real purpose of the intervention was to render assistance to the Mexican reactionaries in the struggle against the progressive Juárez government, to consolidate the anti-popular party of the clericals with the aid of French and Spanish bayonets, and once again to provoke a civil war. In articles filled with deep sympathy for the Mexican people and its liberation struggle, Marx sternly condemned the actions of the interventionists, who had perfidiously started a war against a peace-loving country under the false pretence of a struggle against anarchy. The articles on the intervention in Mexico are a vivid manifestation of the irreconcilable struggle waged by Marx and Engels against colonialism and national oppression, against exploitation and the enslavement of economically backward and dependent countries by European states more developed in the capitalist sense.

Interference by the "European armed Areopagus" in the internal affairs of American countries was seen by Marx as an attempt at the "transplantation of the Holy Alliance to the other side of the Atlantic" (p. 77).

Marx also pointed out another danger associated with the Anglo-French-Spanish intervention. For Palmerston and Napoleon III, the Mexican intervention was a means of provoking an armed conflict with the United States. In his articles "Progress of Feeling in England", "The Mexican Imbroglio" and others, Marx denounced the efforts of the British ruling circles to use the events in Mexico as a pretext, and the territory of Mexico as a base of operations, for the interference of Britain and France in the US Civil War on the side of the Southern slave-owning states. "Decembrist France, bankrupt, paralysed at home, beset with difficulty abroad, pounces upon an Anglo-American War as a real godsend and, in order to buy English support in Europe, will strain all her power to support 'Perfidious Albion' on the other side of the Atlantic" (p. 111).

In his articles "The London *Times* and Lord Palmerston", "The Intervention in Mexico" and others, Marx strips the mask off British diplomacy. Marx and Engels noted during this period an undoubted intensification of the counter-revolutionary role which bourgeois-aristocratic Britain had long played in international affairs. Britain's conversion in the 19th century into the "workshop of the world", and her efforts to preserve her industrial and colonial monopoly, inevitably made her ruling classes a bulwark of reaction not only in Europe but all over the world.

Exposing the aggressive foreign policy of the European powers—Britain, Austria and France—directed at the suppression of national liberation movements and the enslavement of other peoples, Marx demonstrated the grave consequences of the Palmerston government's colonial expansion for the peoples of China, India, Persia, Afghanistan and other countries (pp. 18-20, 23, 78, 209, 216).

Marx also paid attention to the social and political movements in these countries, especially in his article "Chinese Affairs", in which he discussed the causes and the contradictory nature of the Taiping movement. In this, Marx noted a combination of revolutionary tendencies—the striving for the overthrow of the reactionary system and the domination of the alien Manchurian dynasty—with conservative tendencies, the latter becoming especially pronounced in the last years of the Taiping state, within which a bureaucratic top layer had grown. Marx associated the conservative features of the movement with religious fanaticism, cruel customs inculcated in the army, the aggrandisement and even deification of the leaders, and "destruction without any nucleus of new construction" (p. 216).

A large part of the volume is made up of newspaper articles which Marx and Engels wrote on European problems. The articles about the economic position of Britain and France show that in analysing the internal and foreign policy of the European powers (and also of the USA), Marx and Engels were invariably guided by the principles of historical materialism.

In analysing the state of industry in Britain and its prospects of further development and influence on the world market, Marx took into account the situation that had developed in the cotton industry as a result of the blockade of the Southern states, the stopping of shipments of American cotton, and also the internal laws of capitalist production ("The Crisis in England", "British Commerce", "Economic Notes", "On the Cotton Crisis" and others). Marx noted the growth of economic contradictions between the metropolitan country and its colonies, the attempts of the latter to resort for the defence of their economy to protectionism, which they "find ... better suited to their interests" (p. 162).

Examining the condition of the British working class, Marx not only disclosed the horrors of unemployment among the cotton workers, but also described the ruthless capitalist exploitation of the workers, including children, in other branches of industry, and the inhuman working conditions in the baking industry (p. 254). He showed how in Britain, the country of machines and steam, there were branches of industry that had hardly experienced the influence of large-scale industry and in which obsolete techniques and heavy manual labour still predominated. Touching on the contradictory nature of technical progress under capitalism, Marx stressed that one of its positive sides was the supplanting of archaic, semi-artisan forms of production organisation. "The triumph of machine-made bread," he wrote, "will mark a turning point in the history of large-scale industry, the point at which it will storm the hitherto doggedly defended last ditch of medieval artisanship" (p. 255).

Marx drew on various examples to illustrate the disgraceful relics of domination by the landed aristocracy in the social life of England (his article "A Scandal"), and the true essence of bourgeois democracy. In his article "A Suppressed Debate on Mexico and the Alliance with France", he disclosed the voting procedure in the House of Commons, which allowed it not to put to the vote any motion that was "equally irksome to *both* oligarchical factions, the *Ins* and the *Outs* (those in office and those in opposition)..." (p. 223).

In his articles, "Economic Notes", "France's Financial Situation" and others, Marx analysed France's economic plight, revealing the causes of the financial, commercial and agricultural crisis and the growth of corruption; he demonstrated that the Bonapartist regime, with its predatory interference in the economy, was the cause of disruption in French finance and economy (pp. 83-84). In the autumn of 1861 Marx forecast that Napoleon III would seek a way out of his internal difficulties in foreign policy escapades (pp. 62-63, 83-84); the very next year, France took an active part in the punitive expedition against the Mexican Republic. In April 1861, in his article "An International *Affaire* Mirès", Marx explained the participation of France in the military intervention as a necessity for supporting "the gambling operations of certain *rouge-et-noir* politicians" (p. 198), i.e. the direct interest of the financial circles of the Second Empire, to extricate themselves by means of the Mexican escapade from the increasingly critical situation.

During the period covered by this volume, Marx and Engels wrote a number of articles about the struggle for national unity in Germany and in Italy ("German Movements", "A Meeting for Garibaldi", "Garibaldi Meetings.—The Distressed Condition of

Cotton Workers" and others), advocating its pursuit by revolutionary-democratic means. The struggle for unification in Germany and Italy by revolutionary means came up against resistance from reactionary forces in Germany itself, especially in Prussia and Austria, and also against countermeasures by the governments of other European powers, particularly Bonapartist France, which was endeavouring to keep Germany disunited and was actively obstructing the final unification of Italy. In his articles "The Strength of the Armies in Schleswig", "Artillery News from America", "England's Fighting Forces as against Germany", written in connection with the exacerbation of the conflict between Denmark and the German Confederation in 1863-1864, Engels analysed the military aspects of the country's unification from the viewpoint of the revolutionary camp's interests.

Marx and Engels also regarded the Polish national liberation movement as closely associated with that in Germany. Written in connection with the Polish national liberation uprising of 1863-64, the "Proclamation on Poland by the German Workers' Educational Society in London" disclosed the significance of the uprising for the future of Germany.

Marx's work on the theory of political economy is only indirectly represented in this volume in the articles on the economic position of Britain, France and the USA, and also in the manuscript, "Ground Rent". This is evidently a draft plan for one of the lectures on political economy that Marx delivered to the London German Workers' Educational Society at the end of the 1850s and the beginning of the 1860s. In it, Marx treated ground rent as the excess of the market price of the agricultural product over the cost of production. This definition echoes the corresponding formulations of the *Theories of Surplus-Value* (part of the above-mentioned manuscript of *A Contribution to the Critique of Political Economy* on which Marx worked from August 1861 to July 1863) and Volume III of *Capital*, which he began writing at the end of summer, 1864.

In addition to the above-mentioned articles on military matters by Engels, the present volume contains his unfinished manuscript "Kinglake on the Battle of the Alma". He attacks the nationalistic tendencies and prejudices typical of bourgeois military historiography, expressed in the exaggerated portrayal of the armed forces of one's own country and in minimising the fighting qualities of the armies of other states. Engels debunked the myth, created by British military writers, about the invincibility of the

British troops during the Crimean War. The ultimate aim of Kinglake's book, writes Engels, was the "glorification, carried to absurdity, of the English army", for the sake of which he filled his work with "embellishments, rodomontades and conjectures" (p. 274).

In his manuscript "The English Army", Engels, discussing the organisation, recruitment and training of the British armed forces, highlighted the conservative features of the British military system. He noted, in particular, the caste spirit prevalent in the officers' corps, the pernicious practice of selling commissions, the archaic forms of recruitment and the barbaric use of corporal punishment for breaches of discipline by the soldiers. Engels concluded that the customs of the British army were typical of the obsolescent régime of a bourgeois-aristocratic oligarchy and testified to the necessity for profound reforms, including radical military changes, in the country's social and political system.

The Appendices to this volume include applications by Marx for the restoration of his Prussian citizenship after the 1861 Amnesty. These steps were taken by him in connection with the rise of the working-class movement and the approaching revolutionary crisis in Germany, so that he could return at the necessary moment to active political work in his homeland. The Berlin Police President rejected Marx's applications (p. 353).

* * *

The volume contains 82 works by Marx and Engels, of which 52 were printed in *Die Presse* and 11 in the *New-York Daily Tribune.* Engels' article "England's Fighting Forces as against Germany" was published in the German *Allgemeine Militär-Zeitung*, and three more works by Engels, "Artillery News from America", "Kinglake on the Battle of the Alma" and "The English Army", also included in this volume, were intended for the same newspaper. Twenty-eight items are being published in English for the first time. Two items, "German Movements" and "British Commerce", have never been reproduced in English since their publication by the *New-York Daily Tribune.* English publications of individual articles by Marx and Engels in various editions, especially in the collection *The Civil War in the United States,* London, 1937 and New York, 1937, are mentioned in the notes.

Most of the articles in this volume were published unsigned in the *New-York Daily Tribune;* the articles in *Die Presse* were also published anonymously but, as a rule, with a special note "Orig.-Corr.", "Von unserem Londoner Correspondenten". The authorship of the unsigned articles is confirmed by the correspondence between Marx and Engels, by cross references and also by other documents.

When the articles were in preparation, the dates were checked and most of the sources used by the authors were identified. The results of this work will be found at the end of each article and in the editorial notes. Headings given by the editors of the volume are in square brackets.

Obvious errors discovered in the text, in personal and geographical names, figures, dates and so on, have been silently corrected, by reference to sources used by Marx and Engels. The personal and geographical names in the English texts are reproduced as spelled in the originals, which were checked with 19th-century reference books; in translated articles, the modern spelling is given. The use of English words in the German text is indicated in the footnotes. In quoting from newspapers and other sources, Marx sometimes gives a free rendering rather than the exact words. In this edition quotations are given in the form in which they occur in Marx's text.

The volume was compiled, the greater part of the texts prepared and the preface and notes written by Yevgenia Dakhina. The articles from the *New-York Daily Tribune* were prepared and notes to them written by Alexander Zubkov. The volume was edited by Valentina Smirnova except the articles "Kinglake on the Battle of the Alma", "The English Army" and "England's Fighting Forces as against Germany" which were prepared by Tatyana Vasilyeva and edited by Lev Golman. The name index and the index of periodicals were prepared by Tatyana Nikolayeva; the index of quoted and mentioned literature by Alexander Zubkov and the subject index by Marlen Arzumanov (Institute of Marxism-Leninism of the CC CPSU).

The translations were made by Henry Mins (International Publishers), Rodney Livingstone, Peter and Betty Ross and Barrie Selman (Lawrence & Wishart) and Salo Ryazanskaya and Victor Schnittke (Progress Publishers). Items 8, 10, 11, 19, 25-28, 30, 31, 33-35, 37, 40, 42, 46, 50 and 64 were reproduced from the collection *The Civil War in the United States,* International Publishers, N. Y., 1937. Items 6, 7, 15-17, 20, 39, 41, 43-45, 51, 53, 60 and 63 were reproduced from the collection *Marx and Engels on the United States,* Progress Publishers, Moscow, 1979. The translations, including those from the two collections, were checked with the German and edited for the present edition by James S. Allen (International Publishers), Nicholas Jacobs (Lawrence & Wishart) and Richard Dixon, Glenys Ann Kozlov, Tatiana Grishina and Victor Schnittke (Progress Publishers) and Norire Ter-Akopyan, scientific editor (USSR Academy of Sciences).

The volume was prepared for the press by editors Nadezhda Rudenko, Anna Vladimirova, and assistant editor Tatyana Bannikova.

KARL MARX
and
FREDERICK ENGELS

WORKS

January 1861-June 1864

New-York Daily Tribune.

| VOL.. XX........N⁰· 6.178. | NEW-YORK, TUESDAY. FEBRUARY 12. 1861. | PRICE TWO CENTS. |

Frederick Engels

GERMAN MOVEMENTS [1]

The year 1861, it appears, has not yet troubles enough to bear. We have our Secessionist Revolution in America; there is the Rebellion in China [2]; the advance of Russia in Eastern and Central Asia; the Eastern question, with its corollaries of the French occupation of Syria and the Suez Canal; the breaking up of Austria, with Hungary in almost open insurrection; the siege of Gaëta, [3] and Garibaldi's promise of liberating Venice on the first of March; and last, but not least, the attempt to restore Marshal MacMahon to his ancestral throne of Ireland. [4] But all this is not enough. We are now promised, besides, a fourth Schleswig-Holstein campaign. [5]

The King of Denmark, [a] in 1851, voluntarily entered into certain obligations to Prussia and Austria with regard to Schleswig. [b] He promised that the Duchy should not be incorporated with Denmark; that its Representative Assembly should remain distinct from that of Denmark; and that both the German and Danish nationalities in Schleswig should receive equal protection. Beside this, so far as regards Holstein, the rights of its Representative Assembly were expressly guaranteed. Upon these conditions, the federal troops which had occupied Holstein were withdrawn.

The Danish Government executed its promises in a most evasive way. In Schleswig, the southern half is exclusively German; in the northern half, all the towns are German, while the country people

---

[a] Frederick VII.— Ed.

[b] Frederik R., *Proclamation du roi de Danemark relative à l'organisation de la monarchie danoise y compris les Duchés de Schleswig, de Holstein et de Lauenbourg, signée le 28 janvier 1852.— Ed.*

speak a corrupted Danish dialect, and the written language, from
time immemorial, has almost everywhere been German. By the
consent of the population, a process of Germanization has been
going on there for centuries; so much so that, with the exception
of the most northerly border districts, even that portion of the
peasantry who speak a Danish dialect (which is, however, so far
distant from the written Danish as to be easily intelligible to the
German inhabitants of the South), understand the written High
German better than the written Danish language. After 1851, the
Government divided the country into a Danish, a German, and a
mixed district. In the German district, German; in the Danish
district, Danish was to be the exclusive official language of the
Government, the courts of law, the pulpit, and the schools. In the
mixed districts, both languages were to be equally admissible.
This looks fair enough, but the truth is that, in establishing the
Danish district, the written Danish language was forced upon a
population the great majority of whom did not even understand
it, and only desired to be governed, tried, educated, christened,
and married in the German language. However, the Government
now opened a regular crusade for the weeding out of all traces of
Germanism from the district, forbidding even private tuition in
families in any other than the Danish language; and sought at the
same time, by more indirect means, in the mixed district to give
the Danish language the preponderance. The opposition created
by these measures was very violent, and an attempt was made to
put it down by a series of petty acts of tyranny. In the small town
of Eckernförde, for instance, about $4,000 fines were at once
inflicted for the crime of unlawfully petitioning the Representative
Assembly; and all the parties fined were, as *convicts,* declared to be
deprived of their right of voting. Still, the population and the
Assembly persisted and now persist in their opposition.

In Holstein, the Danish Government found it impossible to
make the Representative Assembly vote any taxes unless they
granted concessions in a political and national sense. This they
would not do; neither would they do without the revenues of the
Duchy. In order, therefore, to manufacture some legal ground on
which to levy them, they convoked a Council of the Kingdom, an
assembly without any representative character, but supposed to
represent Denmark proper, Schleswig-Holstein, and Lauenburg.
Although the Holsteiners refused to attend, this body voted the
taxes for the whole monarchy, and, based upon this vote, the
Government assessed the taxes to be paid in Holstein. Thus
Holstein, which was to be an independent and separate Duchy,

was deprived of all political independence, and made subject to an Assembly preeminently Danish.

These are the grounds on which the German press, for five or six years past, have called on the German Governments to employ coercive measures against Denmark. The grounds, in themselves, are certainly good. But the German press—that press which was allowed to exist during the reactionary period after 1849—merely used Schleswig-Holstein as a means of popularity. It was indeed very cheap to hold forth in high indignation against the Danes, when the Governments of Germany allowed it—those Governments which at home tried to emulate Denmark in petty tyranny. War against Denmark was the cry when the Crimean war broke out. War against Denmark again, when Louis Napoleon invaded Austrian Italy. Now, then, they will have it all their own way. The "new era" in Prussia,[6] hitherto so coy when called upon by the liberal press, in this instance chimes in with it. The new King of Prussia proclaims to the world that he must bring this old complaint to a settlement;[a] the decrepit Diet at Frankfort puts all its clumsy machinery in motion for the salvation of German nationality,[b] and the liberal press—triumphs? No such thing. The liberal press, now at once put to the test, eats its words, cries out, Caution! discovers that Germany has no fleet wherewith to fight the ships of a naval power, and, especially in Prussia, shows all the symptoms of cowardice. What a few months ago was an urgent patriotic duty, is now all of a sudden an Austrian intrigue, which Prussia is warned not to give way to.

That the German Governments, in their sudden enthusiasm for the cause of Schleswig-Holstein, are in the least sincere, is, of course, out of the question. As the Danish *Dagbladet* says:

"We all know that it is one of the old tricks of the German Governments to take up the Schleswig-Holstein question as soon as they feel themselves to be in want of a little popularity, and to cover their own manifold sins by drawing bills upon the fanaticism against Denmark."

This has been decidedly the case in Saxony, and to a certain extent it is now the case in Prussia. But in Prussia the sudden starting of this question also signifies, evidently, an alliance with Austria. The Prussian Government behold Austria breaking to pieces from within, while she is menaced from without by a war

---

[a] William I [Speech to the Chambers, January 14, 1861], *The Times*, No. 23832, January 17, 1861.— *Ed.*

[b] A report on the subject appeared under the heading "Frankfort-on-the-Main, Thursday", *The Times*, No. 23833, January 18, 1861.— *Ed.*

with Italy. It certainly is not the interest of the Prussian Government to see Austria annihilated. At the same time, the Italian war, to which Louis Napoleon would not long remain an impartial spectator, would scarcely again come off without touching the territory of the German Confederation, in which case Prussia is bound to interfere. Then the war with France on the Rhine would certainly be combined with a Danish war on the Eider; and while the Prussian Government cannot afford to have Austria broken down, why wait till Austria is again defeated? Why not engage in the quarrel of Schleswig-Holstein, and thereby interest in the war all North Germany which would not fight for the defence of Venetia? If this be the reasoning of the Prussian Government, it is logical enough, but it was quite as logical in 1859, before Austria was weakened by Magenta and Solferino,[7] and by her internal convulsions. Why was it not then acted upon?

It is not at all certain that this great war will come off next Spring. But if it does come off, although neither party deserves any sympathy, it must have this result, that whichsoever be beaten in the beginning, there will be a revolution. If Louis Napoleon be defeated, his throne is sure to fall; and if the King of Prussia and the Emperor of Austria[a] be worsted, they will have to give way before a German revolution.

Written on January 23, 1861   Reproduced from the newspaper

First published in the *New-York Daily Tribune,* No. 6178, February 12, 1861 as a leader

---

[a] Francis Joseph.— *Ed.*

Karl Marx

THE AMERICAN QUESTION IN ENGLAND

London, Sept. 18, 1861

Mrs. Beecher Stowe's letter to Lord Shaftesbury,[8] whatever its intrinsic merit may be, has done a great deal of good, by forcing the anti-Northern organs of the London press to speak out and lay before the general public the ostensible reasons for their hostile tone against the North, and their ill-concealed sympathies with the South, which looks rather strange on the part of people affecting an utter horror of Slavery. Their first and main grievance is that the present American war is "not one for the abolition of Slavery," and that, therefore, the high-minded Britisher, used to undertake wars of his own, and interest himself in other people's wars only on the basis of "broad humanitarian principles," cannot be expected to feel any sympathy with his Northern cousins.

"In the first place [...]," says *The Economist*, "the assumption that the quarrel between the North and South is a quarrel between Negro freedom on the one side and Negro Slavery on the other, is as impudent as it is untrue."[a] "The North," says *The Saturday Review*, "does not proclaim abolition, and never pretended to fight for Anti-Slavery. The North has not hoisted for its *oriflamme* the sacred symbol of justice to the Negro; its *cri de guerre*[b] is not unconditional abolition."[c] "If," says *The Examiner*, "we have been deceived about the real significance of the sublime movement, who but the Federalists themselves have to answer for the deception?"[d]

---

[a] "American Complaints against England", *The Economist*, No. 942, September 14, 1861.— *Ed.*

[b] War-cry.— *Ed.*

[c] "Mrs. Beecher Stowe's Wounded Feelings", *The Saturday Review*, No. 307, September 14, 1861.— *Ed.*

[d] "Mrs. Stowe on the American War", *The Examiner*, No. 2798, September 14, 1861.— *Ed.*

Now, in the first instance, the premiss must be conceded. The war has not been undertaken with a view to put down Slavery, and the United States authorities themselves have taken the greatest pains to protest against any such idea. But then, it ought to be remembered that it was not the North, but the South, which undertook this war; the former acting only on the defense. If it be true that the North, after long hesitations, and an exhibition of forbearance unknown in the annals of European history, drew at last the sword, not for crushing Slavery, but for saving the Union, the South, on its part, inaugurated the war by loudly proclaiming "the peculiar institution" as the only and main end of the rebellion. It confessed to fight for the liberty of enslaving other people, a liberty which, despite the Northern protests, it asserted to be put in danger by the victory of the Republican party[9] and the election of Mr. Lincoln to the Presidential chair. The Confederate Congress boasted that its new-fangled constitution,[10] as distinguished from the Constitution of the Washingtons, Jeffersons, and Adams's,[11] had recognized for the first time Slavery as a thing good in itself, a bulwark of civilization, and a divine institution.[a] If the North professed to fight but for the Union, the South gloried in rebellion for the supremacy of Slavery. If Anti-Slavery and idealistic England felt not attracted by the profession of the North, how came it to pass that it was not violently repulsed by the cynical confessions of the South?

The Saturday Review helps itself out of this ugly dilemma by disbelieving the declarations of the seceders themselves. It sees deeper than this, and discovers "that Slavery had very little to do with Secession;" the declarations of Jeff. Davis and company to the contrary being mere "conventionalisms" with "about as much meaning as the conventionalisms about violated altars and desecrated hearths, which always occur in such proclamations."

The staple of argument on the part of the anti-Northern papers is very scanty, and throughout all of them we find almost the same sentences recurring, like the formulas of a mathematical series, at certain intervals, with very little art of variation or combination.

"Why," exclaims The Economist, "it is only yesterday, when the Secession movement first gained serious head, on the first announcement of Mr. Lincoln's election, that the Northerners offered to the South, if they would remain in the Union, every conceivable security for the performance and inviolability of the obnoxious institution—that they disavowed in the most solemn manner all

---

[a] Marx is giving the burden of the speech A. H. Stephens, Vice-President of the Confederacy, made at a meeting in Savannah on March 21, 1861.— Ed.

intention of interfering with it—that their leaders proposed compromise after compromise in Congress, all based upon the concession that Slavery should not be meddled with." "How happens it," says *The Examiner,* "that the North was ready to compromise matters by the largest concessions to the South as to Slavery? How was it that a certain geographical line was proposed in Congress within which Slavery was to be recognized as an essential institution? The Southern States were not content with this."

What *The Economist* and *The Examiner* had to ask was not only why the Crittenden [12] and other compromise measures were *proposed* in Congress, but why they were not *passed?* They affect to consider those compromise proposals as accepted by the North and rejected by the South, while, in point of fact, they were baffled by the Northern party, that had carried the Lincoln election. Proposals never matured into resolutions, but always remaining in the embryo state of *pia desideria,*[a] the South had of course never any occasion either of rejecting or acquiescing in. We come nearer to the pith of the question by the following remark of *The Examiner:*

"Mrs. Stowe says: 'The Slave party, finding they could no longer use the Union for their purposes, resolved to destroy it.' There is here an admission that up to that time the Slave party had used the Union for their purposes, and it would have been well if Mrs. Stowe could have distinctly shown where it was that the North began to make its stand against Slavery."

One might suppose that *The Examiner* and the other oracles of public opinion in England had made themselves sufficiently familiar with the contemporaneous history to not need Mrs. Stowe's information on such all-important points. The progressive abuse of the Union by the slave power, working through its alliance with the Northern Democratic party,[13] is, so to say, the general formula of the United States history since the beginning of this century. The successive compromise measures mark the successive degrees of the encroachment by which the Union became more and more transformed into the slave of the slave-owner. Each of these compromises denotes a new encroachment of the South, a new concession of the North. At the same time none of the successive victories of the South was carried but after a hot contest with an antagonistic force in the North, appearing under different party names with different watchwords and under different colors. If the positive and final result of each single contest told in favor of the South, the attentive observer of history could not but see that every new advance of the slave

---

[a] Pious wishes.— *Ed.*

power was a step forward to its ultimate defeat. Even at the times
of the Missouri Compromise the contending forces were so evenly
balanced that Jefferson, as we see from his memoirs,[a] apprehended
the Union to be in danger of splitting on that deadly antagonism.[14]
The encroachments of the slaveholding power reached their
maximum point, when, by the Kansas-Nebraska bill,[15] for the first
time in the history of the United States, as Mr. Douglas himself
confessed, every legal barrier to the diffusion of Slavery within the
United States territories was broken down, when, afterward, a
Northern candidate bought his Presidential nomination by pledg-
ing the Union to conquer or purchase in Cuba a new field of
dominion for the slaveholder[16]; when, later on, by the Dred Scott
decision,[17] diffusion of Slavery by the Federal power was
proclaimed as the law of the American Constitution, and lastly,
when the African slave-trade was de facto reopened on a larger
scale than during the times of its legal existence. But, concurrently
with this climax of Southern encroachments, carried by the
connivance of the Northern Democratic party, there were unmistakable signs of Northern antagonistic agencies having gathered
such strength as must soon turn the balance of power. The Kansas
war,[18] the formation of the Republican party, and the large vote
cast for Mr. Frémont during the Presidential election of 1856,[19]
were so many palpable proofs that the North had accumulated
sufficient energies to rectify the aberrations which United States
history, under the slaveowners' pressure, had undergone, for half
a century, and to make it return to the true principles of its
development. Apart from those political phenomena, there was
one broad statistical and economical fact indicating that the abuse
of the Federal Union by the slave interest had approached the
point from which it would have to recede forcibly, or *de bonne
grace*.[b] That fact was the growth of the North-West, the immense
strides its population had made from 1850 to 1860, and the new
and reinvigorating influence it could not but bear on the destinies
of the United States.

Now, was all this a secret chapter of history? Was "the
admission" of Mrs. Beecher Stowe wanted to reveal to *The
Examiner* and the other political illuminati[20] of the London press
the carefully hidden truth that "up to that time the Slave party
had used the Union for their purposes?" Is it the fault of the

---

    [a] Th. Jefferson, *Memoirs, Correspondence, and Private Papers...*, Vol. IV, London,
1829, p. 333.— *Ed.*
    [b] Of its own accord.— *Ed.*

American North that the English pressmen were taken quite unawares by the violent clash of the antagonistic forces, the friction of which was the moving power of its history for half a century? Is it the fault of the Americans that the English press mistake for the fanciful crotchet hatched in a single day what was in reality the matured result of long years of struggle? The very fact that the formation and the progress of the Republican party in America have hardly been noticed by the London press, speaks volumes as to the hollowness of its Anti-Slavery tirades. Take, for instance, the two antipodes of the London press, *The London Times* and *Reynolds's Weekly Newspaper,* the one the great organ of the respectable classes, and the other the only remaining organ of the working class. The former, not long before Mr. Buchanan's career drew to an end, published an elaborate apology for his Administration and a defamatory libel against the Republican movement. Reynolds, on his part, was, during Mr. Buchanan's stay at London,[a] one of his minions, and since that time never missed an occasion to write him up and to write his adversaries down. How did it come to pass that the Republican party, whose platform[b] was drawn up on the avowed antagonism to the encroachments of the Slaveocracy and the abuse of the Union by the slave interest, carried the day in the North? How, in the second instance, did it come to pass that the great bulk of the Northern Democratic party, flinging aside its old connexions with the leaders of Slaveocracy, setting at naught its traditions of half a century, sacrificing great commercial interests and greater political prejudices, rushed to the support of the present Republican Administration and offered it men and money with an unsparing hand?

Instead of answering these questions *The Economist* exclaims:

"Can we forget [...] that Abolitionists have habitually been as ferociously persecuted and maltreated in the North and West as in the South? Can it be denied that the testiness and half-heartedness, not to say insincerity, of the Government at Washington, have for years supplied the chief impediment which has thwarted our efforts for the effectual suppression of the slave trade on the coast of Africa; while a vast proportion of the clippers actually engaged in that trade have been built with Northern capital, owned by Northern merchants and manned by Northern seamen?"

This is, in fact, a masterly piece of logic. Anti-Slavery England cannot sympathize with the North breaking down the withering

---

[a] As US Minister to London in 1853-56.— *Ed.*

[b] The election platform of the Republicans was published in the article "The Platform" in the *New-York Daily Tribune,* No. 5950, May 19, 1860.— *Ed.*

influence of slaveocracy, because she cannot forget that the North, while bound by that influence, supported the slave-trade, mobbed the Abolitionists, and had its Democratic institutions tainted by the slavedriver's prejudices. She cannot sympathize with Mr. Lincoln's Administration, because she had to find fault with Mr. Buchanan's Administration. She must needs sullenly cavil at the present movement of the Northern resurrection, cheer up the Northern sympathizers with the slave-trade, branded in the Republican platform, and coquet with the Southern slaveocracy, setting up an empire of its own, because she cannot forget that the North of yesterday was not the North of to-day. The necessity of justifying its attitude by such pettifogging Old Bailey[21] pleas proves more than anything else that the anti-Northern part of the English press is instigated by hidden motives, too mean and dastardly to be openly avowed.

As it is one of its pet maneuvers to taunt the present Republican Administration with the doings of its Pro-Slavery predecessors, so it tries hard to persuade the English people that *The N. Y. Herald* ought to be considered the only authentic expositor of Northern opinion. *The London Times* having given out the cue in this direction, the *servum pecus*[a] of the other anti-Northern organs, great and small, persist in beating the same bush. So says *The Economist:*

"In the height of the strife, New-York papers and New-York politicians were not wanting who exhorted the combatants, now that they had large armies in the field, to employ them, not against each other, but against Great Britain—to compromise the internal quarrel, the slave question included, and invade the British territory without notice and with overwhelming force."

The Economist knows perfectly well that *The N. Y. Herald's* efforts, which were eagerly supported by *The London Times,* at embroiling the United States into a war with England,[b] only intended securing the success of Secession and thwarting the movement of Northern regeneration.

Still there is one concession made by the anti-Northern English press. *The Saturday* snob tells us:

"What was at issue in Lincoln's election, and what has precipitated the convulsion, was *merely the limitation of the institution of Slavery to States where that institution already exists.*"

And *The Economist* remarks:

---

a Crowd of slaves.— *Ed.*
b "Southampton, Friday", *The Times,* No. 24032, September 7, 1861.— *Ed.*

"It is true enough that it was the aim of the Republican party which elected Mr. Lincoln to prevent Slavery from spreading into the unsettled Territories.... It may be true that the success of the North, if complete and unconditional, would enable them to confine Slavery within the fifteen States which have already adopted it, and might thus lead to its eventual extinction—though this is rather probable than certain."

In 1859, on the occasion of John Brown's Harper's Ferry expedition,[22] the very same *Economist* published a series of elaborate articles with a view to prove that, by dint of an *economical law*, American Slavery was doomed to gradual extinction from the moment it should be deprived of its power of expansion.[a] That "economical law" was perfectly understood by the Slaveocracy.

"In 15 years more," said Toombs "without a great increase in Slave territory, either the slaves must be permitted to flee from the whites, or the whites must flee from the slaves."

The limitation of Slavery to its constitutional area, as proclaimed by the Republicans, was the distinct ground upon which the menace of Secession was first uttered in the House of Representatives on December 19, 1859. Mr. Singleton (Mississippi) having asked Mr. Curtis (Iowa), "if the Republican party would never let the South have another foot of slave territory while it remained in the Union," and Mr. Curtis having responded in the affirmative, Mr. Singleton *said this would dissolve the Union*. His advice to Mississippi was the sooner it got out of the Union the better— "gentlemen should recollect that [...] Jefferson Davis led our forces in Mexico, and [...] still he lives, perhaps to lead the Southern army."[b] Quite apart from the *economical law* which makes the diffusion of Slavery a vital condition for its maintenance within its constitutional areas, the leaders of the South had never deceived themselves as to its necessity for keeping up their *political* sway over the United States. *John Calhoun,* in the defense of his propositions to the Senate, stated distinctly on Feb. 19, 1847, "that the Senate was the only balance of power left to the South in the Government," and that the creation of new Slave States had become necessary "for the retention of the equipoise of power in the Senate."[c] Moreover, the Oligarchy of the 300,000

---

[a] "Harper's Ferry", "The Impending Crisis in the Southern States of America", "English Sympathy with the Slavery Party in America", *The Economist*, Nos. 845, 852, 853, November 5, December 24, 31, 1859.— *Ed.*

[b] O. Singleton [Speech in the House of Representatives on December 19, 1859], *New-York Daily Tribune*, No. 5822, December 20, 1859.— *Ed.*

[c] J. C. Calhoun [Speech in the Senate on February 19, 1847], *Congressional Globe: New Series: Containing Sketches of the Debates and Proceedings of the Second Session of Twenty-Ninth Congress*, Washington, 1847.— *Ed.*

slave-owners could not even maintain their sway at home save by constantly throwing out to their white plebeians the bait of prospective conquests within and without the frontiers of the United States. If, then, according to the oracles of the English press, the North had arrived at the fixed resolution of circumscribing Slavery within its present limits, and of thus extinguishing it in a constitutional way, was this not sufficient to enlist the sympathies of Anti-Slavery England?

But the English Puritans seem indeed not to be contented save by an explicit Abolitionist war.

"This," says *The Economist* "therefore, not being a war for the emancipation of the Negro race, [...] on what other ground can we be fairly called upon to sympathize so warmly with the Federal cause?" "There was a time," says *The Examiner*, "when our sympathies were with the North, thinking that it was really in earnest in making a stand against the encroachments of the Slave States," and in adopting "emancipation as a measure of justice to the black race."

However, in the very same numbers in which these papers tell us that they cannot sympathize with the North because its war is no Abolitionist war, we are informed that "the desperate expedient of proclaiming Negro emancipation and summoning the slaves to a general insurrection," is a thing "the mere conception of which [...] is repulsive and dreadful," and that "a compromise" would be "far preferable to success purchased at such a cost and *stained by such a crime.*" [a]

Thus the English eagerness for the Abolitionist war is all cant. The cloven foot peeps out in the following sentences:

"Lastly, [...]" says *The Economist*, "is the *Morrill Tariff*,[23] a title to our gratitude and to our sympathy, or is the certainty that, in case of Northern triumph, that Tariff should be extended over the whole Republic, a reason why we ought to be clamorously anxious for their success?" "The North Americans," says *The Examiner*, "are in earnest about nothing but a selfish protective Tariff. The Southern States were tired of being robbed of the fruits of their slave-labor by the protective tariff of the North."

The Examiner and *The Economist* comment each other. The latter is honest enough to confess at last that with him and his followers sympathy is a mere question of tariff, while the former reduces the war between North and South to a tariff war, to a war between Protection and Free-Trade. *The Examiner* is perhaps not aware that even the South Carolina Nullifiers of 1832,[24] as Gen. Jackson testifies, used Protection only as a pretext for secession; [b]

---

[a] "The Probable Continuance of the American Conflict", *The Economist*, No. 941, September 7, 1861.— *Ed.*

[b] *President Jackson's proclamation against the Nullification Ordinance of South Carolina*, December 11, 1832.— *Ed.*

but even *The Examiner* ought to know that the present rebellion did not wait upon the passing of the Morrill tariff for breaking out. In point of fact, the Southerners could not have been tired of being robbed of the fruits of their slave labor by the Protective tariff of the North, considering that from 1846-1861 a Free-Trade tariff had obtained.

The Spectator characterizes in its last number the secret thought of some of the Anti-Northern organs in the following striking manner:

"What, then, do the Anti-Northern organs really profess to think desirable, under the justification of this plea of deferring to the inexorable logic of facts?" They argue that disunion is desirable, just because, as we have said, it is the only possible step to a conclusion of this "causeless and fratricidal strife;" and next, of course, only as an afterthought, and as an humble apology for Providence and "justification of the ways of God to man," now that the inevitable necessity stands revealed—for further reasons discovered as beautiful adaptations to the moral exigencies of the country, when once the issue is discerned. It is discovered that it will be very much for the advantage of the States to be dissolved into rival groups. They will mutually check each other's ambition; they will neutralize each other's power, and if ever England should get into a dispute with one or more of them, more jealousy will bring the antagonistic groups to our aid. This will be, it is urged, a very wholesome state of things, for it will relieve us from anxiety and it will encourage political 'competition,' that great safeguard of honesty and purity, among the States themselves.

"Such is the case—very gravely urged—of the numerous class of Southern sympathizers now springing up among us. Translated into English—and we grieve that an English argument on such a subject should be of a nature that requires translating—it means that we deplore the present great scale of this "fratricidal" war, because it may concentrate in one fearful spasm a series of chronic petty wars and passions and jealousies among groups of rival States in times to come. The real truth is, and this very un-English feeling distinctly discerns this truth, though it cloaks it in decent phrases, that rival groups of American States could not live together in peace or harmony. The chronic condition would be one of malignant hostility rising out of the very causes which have produced the present contest. It is asserted that the different groups of States have different tariff interests. These different tariff interests would be the sources of constant petty wars if the States were once dissolved, and Slavery, the root of all the strife, would be the spring of innumerable animosities, discords and campaigns. No stable equilibrium could ever again be established among the rival States. And yet it is maintained that this long future of incessant strife is the providential solution of the great question now at issue—the only real reason why it is looked upon favorably being this, that whereas the present great-scale conflict may issue in a restored and stronger political unity, the alternative of infinitely multiplied small-scale quarrels will issue in a weak and divided continent, that England cannot fear.

"Now we do not deny that the Americans themselves sowed the seeds of this petty and contemptible state of feeling by the unfriendly and bullying attitude they have so often manifested to England, but we do say that the state of feeling on our part is petty and contemptible. We see that in a deferred issue there is no hope of a deep and enduring tranquillity for America, that it means a decline and fall of the American nation into quarrelsome clans and tribes, and yet we hold up our hands in horror at the present "fratricidal" strife because it holds out hopes of finality. We exhort them to look favorably on the indefinite future of small strifes, equally fratricidal and probably far more demoralizing, because the latter would draw out of our side the thorn of American rivalry."

Written on September 18, 1861

First published in the *New-York Daily Tribune*, No. 6403, October 11, 1861, reprinted in the *New-York Semi-Weekly Tribune*, No. 1710, October 15, 1861

Reproduced from the *New-York Daily Tribune*

Karl Marx
THE BRITISH COTTON TRADE[25]

London, Sept. 21, 1861

The continual rise in the prices of raw cotton begins at last to seriously react upon the cotton factories, their consumption of cotton being now 25 per cent less than the full consumption. This result has been brought about by a daily lessening rate of production, many mills working only four or three days per week, part of the machinery being stopped, both in those establishments where short time has been commenced and in those which are still running full time, and some mills being temporarily altogether closed. In some places, as at Blackburn, for instance, short time has been coupled with a reduction of wages. However, the short-time movement is only in its incipient state, and we may predict with perfect security that some weeks later the trade will have generally resorted to three days working per week, concurrently with a large stoppage of machinery in most establishments. On the whole, English manufacturers and merchants were extremely slow and reluctant in acknowledging the awkward position of their cotton supplies.

"The whole of the last American crop," they said, "has long since been forwarded to Europe. The picking of the new crop has barely commenced. Not a bale of cotton could have reached us more than has reached us, even if the war and the blockade[26] had never been heard of. The shipping season does not commence till far in November, and it is usually the end of December before any large exportations take place. Till then, it is of little consequence whether the cotton is retained on the plantations or is forwarded to the ports as fast as it is bagged. If the blockade ceases any time *before the end of this year,* the probability is that by March or April we shall have received just as full a supply of cotton as if the blockade had never been declared."[a]

---

[a] "The Probable Continuance of the American Conflict", *The Economist,* No. 941, September 7, 1861.— Ed.

In the innermost recesses of the mercantile mind the notion was cherished that the whole American crisis, and, consequently, the blockade, would have ceased before the end of the year, or that Lord Palmerston would forcibly break through the blockade. The latter idea has been altogether abandoned, since, beside all other circumstances, Manchester became aware that two vast interests, the monetary interest having sunk an immense capital in the industrial enterprises of Northern America, and the corn trade, relying on Northern America as its principal source of supply, would combine to check any unprovoked aggression on the part of the British Government. The hopes of the blockade being raised in due time, for the requirements of Liverpool or Manchester, or the American war being wound up by a compromise with the Secessionists, have given way before a feature hitherto unknown in the English cotton market, viz., American operations in cotton at Liverpool, partly on speculation, partly for reshipment to America. Consequently, for the last two weeks the Liverpool cotton market has been feverishly excited, the speculative investments in cotton on the part of the Liverpool merchants being backed by speculative investments on the part of the Manchester and other manufacturers eager to provide themselves with stocks of raw material for the Winter. The extent of the latter transactions is sufficiently shown by the fact that a considerable portion of the spare warehouse room in Manchester is already occupied by such stocks, and that throughout the week beginning with Sept. 15 and ending with Sept. 22, Middling Americans had increased 3/8d. per lb, and fair ones 5/8d.

From the outbreak of the American war the prices of cotton were steadily rising, but the ruinous disproportion between the prices of the raw material and the prices of yarns and cloth was not declared until the last weeks of August. Till then, any serious decline in the prices of cotton manufactures, which might have been anticipated from the considerable decrease of the American demand, had been balanced by an accumulation of stocks in first hands, and by speculative consignments to China and India. Those Asiatic markets, however, were soon overdone.

"Stocks," says The Calcutta Price Current of Aug. 7, 1861, "are accumulating, the arrivals since our last being no less than 24,000,000 yards of plain cottons. Home advices show a continuation of shipments in excess of our requirements, and so long as this is the case, improvement cannot be looked for.... The Bombay market, also, has been greatly oversupplied."

Some other circumstances contributed to contract the Indian market. The late famine in the north-western provinces has been

succeeded by the ravages of the cholera, while throughout Lower
Bengal an excessive fall of rain, laying the country under water,
seriously damaged the rice crops. In letters from Calcutta, which
reached England last week, sales were reported giving a net return
of $9^1/_4$d. per pound for 40s twist, which cannot be bought at
Manchester for less than $11^3/_8$d., while sales of 40-inch shirtings,
compared with present rates at Manchester, yield losses at $7^1/_2$d.,
9d., and 12d. per piece. In the China market, prices were also
forced down by the accumulation of the stocks imported. Under
these circumstances, the demand for the British cotton manufactures decreasing, their prices can, of course, not keep pace with
the progressive rise in the price of the raw material; but, on the
contrary, the spinning, weaving, and printing of cotton must, in
many instances, cease to pay the costs of production. Take, as an
example, the following case, stated by one of the greatest
Manchester manufacturers, in reference to coarse spinning:

	Per lb.	Margin.	Cost of spinning per lb
Sept. 17, 1860.			
Cost of cotton	$6^1/_4$d.	1d.	3d.
16s warp sold for	$10^1/_4$d.	..	..
Profit, 1d. per lb.			
Sept. 17, 1861.			
Cost of cotton	9d.	2d.	$3^1/_2$d.
16s warp sold for	11	..	..
Loss, $1^1/_2$d. per lb.			

The consumption of Indian cotton is rapidly growing, and with
a further rise in prices, the Indian supply will come forward at
increasing ratios; but still it remains impossible to change, at a few
months' notice, all the conditions of production and turn the
current of commerce. England pays now, in fact, the penalty for
her protracted misrule of that vast Indian empire. The two main
obstacles she has now to grapple with in her attempts at
supplanting American cotton by Indian cotton, is the want of
means of communication and transport throughout India, and the
miserable state of the Indian peasant, disabling him from
improving favorable circumstances. Both these difficulties the
English have themselves to thank for. English modern industry, in
general, relied upon two pivots equally monstrous. The one was
the *potato* as the only means of feeding Ireland and a great part of

the English working class. This pivot was swept away by the potato disease and the subsequent Irish catastrophe.[27] A larger basis for the reproduction and maintenance of the toiling millions had then to be adopted. The second pivot of English industry was the slave-grown cotton of the United States. The present American crisis forces them to enlarge their field of supply and emancipate cotton from slave-breeding and slave-consuming oligarchies. As long as the English cotton manufactures depended on slave-grown cotton, it could be truthfully asserted that they rested on a twofold slavery, the indirect slavery of the white man in England and the direct slavery of the black men on the other side of the Atlantic.

Written on September 21, 1861   Reproduced from the newspaper

First published in the *New-York Daily Tribune*, No. 6405, October 14, 1861

Karl Marx

THE LONDON *TIMES* AND LORD PALMERSTON [28]

London, Oct. 5, 1861

"English people participate in the government of their own country by reading *The Times* newspaper." This judgment, passed by an eminent English author[a] on what is called British self-government, is only true so far as the foreign policy of the Kingdom is concerned. As to measures of domestic reform, they were never carried by the support of *The Times,* but *The Times* never ceased attacking and opposing them until after it had become aware of its utter inability to any longer check their progress. Take, for instance, the Catholic Emancipation, the Reform bill, the abolition of the Corn laws, the Stamp Tax, and the Paper Duty.[29] When victory had unmistakably declared on the side of the Reformers, *The Times* wheeled round, deserted the reactionary camp, and managed to find itself, at the decisive moment, on the winning side. In all these instances, *The Times* gave not the direction to public opinion, but submitted to it, ungraciously, reluctantly, and after protracted, but frustrated, attempts at rolling back the surging waves of popular progress. Its real influence on the public mind is, therefore, confined to the field of foreign policy. In no part of Europe are the mass of the people, and especially of the middle-classes, more utterly ignorant of the foreign policy of their own country than in England, an ignorance springing from two great sources. On the one hand, since the glorious Revolution of 1688,[30] the aristocracy has always monopolized the direction of foreign affairs in England. On the

---

[a] R. Lowe, "The Part of *The Times* in the Government of the Country", *The Free Press,* No. 8, August 7, 1861.— *Ed.*

other hand, the progressive division of labor has, to a certain extent, emasculated the general intellect of the middle-class men by the circumscription of all their energies and mental faculties within the narrow spheres of their mercantile, industrial and professional concerns. Thus it happened that, while the aristocracy *acted* for them, the press *thought* for them in their foreign or international affairs; and both parties, the aristocracy and the press, very soon found out that it would be their mutual interest to combine. One has only to open Cobbett's Political Register to convince himself that, since the beginning of this century, the great London papers have constantly played the part of attorneys to the heaven-born managers of English foreign policy. Still, there were some intermediate periods to be run through before the present state of things had been brought about. The aristocracy, that had monopolized the management of foreign affairs, first shrunk together into an oligarchy, represented by a secret conclave, called the cabinet, and, later on, the cabinet was superseded by one single man, Lord Palmerston, who, for the last thirty years, has usurped the absolute power of wielding the national forces of the British Empire, and determining the line of its Foreign Policy. Concurrently with this usurpation, by the law of concentration, acting in the field of newspaper-mongering still more rapidly than in the field of cotton-spinning, *The London Times* had attained the position of being the national paper of England, that is to say, of representing the English mind to Foreign nations. If the monopoly of managing the Foreign affairs of the nation had passed from the aristocracy to an oligarchic conclave, and from an oligarchic conclave to one single man, *the* Foreign Minister of England, viz: Lord Palmerston, the monopoly of thinking and judging for the nation, on its own Foreign relations, and representing the public mind in regard to these relations, had passed from the press to one organ of the press, to *The Times.* Lord Palmerston, who secretly and from motives unknown to the people at large, to Parliament and even to his own colleagues, managed the Foreign affairs of the British Empire, must have been very stupid if he had not tried to possess himself of the one paper which had usurped the power of passing public judgment in the name of the English people on his own secret doings. *The Times,* in whose vocabulary the word virtue was never to be found, must, on its side, have boasted more than Spartan virtue not to ally itself with the absolute ruler in fact of the national power of the Empire. Hence, since the French *coup d'état,*[a]

---

[a] The reference is to the *coup d'état* in France on December 2, 1851.— *Ed.*

when the Government by faction was in England superseded by the Government by the coalition of factions,[31] and Palmerston, therefore, found no longer rivals endangering his usurpation, *The Times* became his mere slave. He had taken care to smuggle some of its virtue into the subordinate posts of the cabinet, and to cajole others by their admission into his social circle.[32] Since that time, the whole business of *The Times,* so far as the foreign affairs of the British Empire are concerned, is limited to manufacturing a public opinion to conform to Lord Palmerston's Foreign policy. It has to prepare the public mind for what he intends doing, and to make it acquiesce in what he has done.

The slavish drudgery which, in fulfilling this work, it has to undergo, was best exemplified during the last session of Parliament. That session proved anything but favorable to Lord Palmerston. Some independent members of the H. of C., Liberals and Conservatives, rebelled against his usurped dictatorship, and, by an exposure of his past misdeeds, tried to awaken the nation to a sense of the danger of continuing the same uncontrolled power in the same hands. Mr. Dunlop, opening the attack by a motion for a Select Committee on the Afghan Papers,[a] which Palmerston had laid on the table of the House in 1839, proved that Palmerston had actually forged these papers.[33] *The Times,* in its Parliamentary report, suppressed all the passages of Mr. Dunlop's speech which it considered most damaging to its master. Later on, Lord Montagu, in a motion for the publication of all papers relating to the Danish Treaty of 1852, accused Palmerston of having been the principal in the maneuvers intended to alter the Danish succession in the interest of a foreign power,[34] and of having misled the House of Commons by deliberate misstatements.[b] Palmerston, however, had come to a previous understanding with Mr. Disraeli to baffle Lord Montagu's motion by a count-out of the House, which in fact put a stop to the whole proceeding. Still, Lord Montagu's speech had lasted one hour and a half before it was cut off by the count-out. *The Times* having been informed by Palmerston that the count-out was to take place, its editor specially charged with the task of mutilating and cooking the Parliamentary reports had given himself a holiday, and thus

---

[a] A. M. Dunlop's speech in the House of Commons on March 19, 1861, *The Times,* No. 23885, March 20, 1861.— *Ed.*

[b] R. Montagu's speech in the House of Commons on June 18, 1861, *The Times,* No. 23963, June 19, 1861.— *Ed.*

Lord Montagu's speech appeared unmutilated in *The Times's* columns. When, on the following morning, the mistake was discovered, a leader was prepared telling John Bull that the count-out was an ingenious institution for suppressing bores, that Lord Montagu was a regular bore, and that the business of the nation could not be carried on if Parliamentary bores were not disposed of in the most unceremonious way.[a] Again Palmerston stood on his trial last session, when Mr. Hennessy moved for a production of the Foreign office dispatches during the Polish revolution of 1831.[b] Again *The Times* recurred, as in the case of Mr. Dunlop's motion, to the simple process of suppression. Its report of Mr. Hennessy's speech is quite an edition *in usum delphini*.[35] If one considers how much painstaking it must cause to run through the immense Parliamentary reports the same night they are forwarded to the newspaper office from the House of Commons, and in the same night mutilate, alter, falsify them so as not to tell against Palmerston's political purity, one must concede that whatever emoluments and advantages *The Times* may reap from its subserviency to the noble Viscount, its task is no pleasant one.

If, then, *The Times* is able by misstatement and suppression thus to falsify public opinion in regard to events that happened but yesterday in the British House of Commons, its power of misstatement and suppression in regard to events occurring on a distant soil, as in the case of the American war, must, of course, be unbounded. If in treating of American affairs it has strained all its forces to exasperate the mutual feelings of the British and Americans, it did not do so from any sympathy with the British Cotton Lords nor out of regard for any real or supposed English interest. It simply executed the orders of its master. From the altered tone of *The London Times* during the past week, we may, therefore, infer that Lord Palmerston is about to recede from the extremely hostile attitude he had assumed till now against the United States. In one of its to-day leaders, *The Times*, which for months had exalted the aggressive powers of the Secessionists, and expatiated upon the inability of the United States to cope with them, feels quite sure of the military superiority of the North.[c] That this change of tone is dictated by the master, becomes quite

---

a "We are at last enjoying...", *The Times*, No. 23963, June 19, 1861.— *Ed.*

b J. P. Hennessy's speech in the House of Commons on July 2, 1861, *The Times*, No. 23975, July 3, 1861.— *Ed.*

c "The time is now approaching...", *The Times*, No. 24056, October 5, 1861.— *Ed.*

evident from the circumstance that other influential papers, known to be connected with Palmerston, have simultaneously veered round. One of them, *The Economist,* gives rather a broad hint to the public-opinion-mongers that the time has come for "carefully watching" their pretended "feelings toward the United States."[a] The passage in *The Economist* which I allude to, and which I think worth quoting as a proof of the new orders received by Palmerston's pressmen, runs thus:

"On one point we frankly avow that the Northerners have a right to complain, and on one point also we are bound to be more upon our guard than perhaps we have uniformly been. Our leading journals have been too ready to quote and resent as embodying the sentiments and representing the position of the United States, newspapers notorious at all times for their disreputable character and feeble influence, and now more than suspected of being Secessionists at heart, of sailing under false colors, and professing extreme Northern opinions while writing in the interests and probably the pay of the South. Few Englishmen can, for example, with any decent fairness, pretend to regard *The N. Y. Herald* as representing either the character or views of the Northern section of the Republic. Again: we ought to be very careful lest our just criticism of the Unionists should degenerate by insensible gradation into approval and defense of the Secessionists. The tendency in all ordinary minds to *partisanship* is very strong. [...] Now, however warmly we may resent much of the conduct and the language of the North, [...] we must never forget that the Secession of the South was forced on with designs and inaugurated with proceedings which have our heartiest and most rooted disapprobation. We, of course, must condemn the protective tariff of the Union as an oppressive and benighted folly. [...] Of course, we reciprocate the wish of the South for low duties and unfettered trade. Of course, we are anxious that the prosperity of States which produce so much raw material and want so many manufactured goods should suffer no interruption or reverse. [...] But, at the same time, it is impossible for us to lose sight of the indisputable fact that the real aim and ultimate motive of secession was *not* to defend their right to hold slaves in their own territory (which the Northerners were just as ready to concede as they to claim), but to extend Slavery over a vast, undefined district, hitherto free from that curse, but into which the planters fancied they might hereafter wish to spread. This object we have always regarded as unwise, unrighteous and abhorrent. The state of society introduced in the Southern States by the institution of domestic servitude appears to English minds more and more detestable and deplorable the more they know of it. And the Southerners should be made aware that no pecuniary or commercial advantage which this country might be supposed to derive from the extended cultivation of the virgin soils of the planting States, and the new Territories which they claim, will ever in the slightest degree modify our views on these points, or interfere with the expression of those views, or warp or hamper our action whenever action shall become obligatory or fitting. [...][b] It is believed that they (the Secessionists) still entertain the extraordinary notion that by *starving* France and England—by the loss and suffering anticipated as the consequences of

---

a "English Feeling towards America", *The Economist,* No. 944, September 28, 1861.— *Ed.*

b Thus far from the article. "English Feeling towards America.".— *Ed.*

an entire privation of the American supply—they will compel those Governments to interfere on their behalf, and.force the United States to abandon the blockade.... There is not the remotest chance that either Power would feel justified for a moment in projecting such an act of decided and unwarrantable hostility against the United States.... We are less dependent on the South than the South is upon us, as they will ere long begin to discover. [...]ᵃ We, therefore, pray them to believe that Slavery, so long as it exists, must create more or less of a moral barrier between us, and that even tacit approval is as far from our thoughts as the impertinence of an open interference: that Lancashire is not England; and, for the honor and spirit of our manufacturing population be it said also, that even if it were, *Cotton would not be King.*" ᵇ

All I intended to show for the present was that Palmerston, and consequently the London press, working to his orders, is abandoning his hostile attitude against the United States. The causes that have led to this *revirement,*ᶜ as the French call it, I shall try to explain in a subsequent letter. Before concluding, I may still add that Mr. Forster, M.P. for Bradford, delivered last Tuesday,ᵈ in the theater of Bradford Mechanics' Institute,³⁶ a lecture "On the Civil War in America," in which he traced the true origin and character of that war, and victoriously refuted the misstatements of the Palmerstonian press.ᵉ

Written on October 5, 1861   Reproduced from the newspaper

First published in the *New-York Daily Tribune*, No. 6411, October 21, 1861

ᵃ "The Last Movements of the Northern and the Southern Confederation", *The Economist*, No. 943, September 21, 1861.— *Ed.*

ᵇ "English Feeling towards America".— *Ed.*

ᶜ Radical change.— *Ed.*

ᵈ October 1, 1861.— *Ed.*

ᵉ W. E. Forster's lecture "On the Civil War in America" was reported in *The Times*, No. 24054, October 3, 1861.— *Ed.*

Karl Marx

THE LONDON *TIMES* ON THE ORLEANS PRINCES
IN AMERICA

London, Oct. 12, 1861

On the occasion of the King of Prussia's[a] visit at Compiegne,[37] *The London Times* published some racy articles, giving great offense on the other side of the Channel.[b] The *Pays, Journal de l'Empire*, in its turn, characterized *The Times* writers as people whose heads were poisoned by gin, and whose pens were dipped into mud.[c] Such occasional exchanges of invective are only intended to mislead public opinion as to the intimate relations connecting Printing-House Square to the Tuileries.[38] There exists beyond the French frontiers no greater sycophant of the Man of December[d] than *The London Times*, and its services are the more invaluable, the more that paper now and then assumes the tone and the air of a Cato censor toward its Caesar. *The Times* had for months heaped insult upon Prussia. Improving the miserable Macdonald affair,[39] it had told Prussia that England would feel glad to see a transfer of the Rhenish Provinces from the barbarous sway of the Hohenzollern to the enlightened despotism of a Bonaparte.[e] It had not only exasperated the Prussian dynasty, but the Prussian people. It had written down the idea of an Anglo-Prussian alliance in case of a Prussian conflict with France. It had strained all its powers to convince Prussia that she had

---

[a] William I.— *Ed.*

[b] Marx refers to the following leading articles: "The popularity of a Government...", *The Times*, No. 24057, October 7, 1861; "The King of Prussia is welcomed to Compiègne...", *The Times*, No. 24058, October 8, 1861; "It is, perhaps, a mistake to attribute...", *The Times*, No. 24059, October 9, 1861.— *Ed.*

[c] "Paris, ·Thursday, Oct. 10, 7 A. M.", *The Times*, No. 24061, October 11, 1861.— *Ed.*

[d] Napoleon III.— *Ed.*

[e] "We trust we have now heard...", *The Times*, No. 23928, May 9, 1861, leading article.— *Ed.*

nothing to hope from England, and that the next best thing she could do would be to come to some understanding with France.[a] When at last the weak and trimming monarch of Prussia resolved upon the visit at Compiegne, *The Times* could proudly exclaim: *"quorum magna pars fui;"*[b] but now the time had also arrived for obliterating from the memory of the British the fact that *The Times* had been the pathfinder of the Prussian monarch. Hence the roar of its theatrical thunders. Hence the counter roars of the *Pays, Journal de l'Empire.*

The Times had now recovered its position of the deadly antagonist of Bonapartism, and, therefore, the power of lending its aid to the Man of December. An occasion soon offered. Louis Bonaparte is, of course, most touchy whenever the renown of rival pretenders to the French crown is concerned. He had covered himself with ridicule in the affair of the Duke d'Aumale's pamphlet[40] against Plon Plon,[c] and, by his proceedings, had done more in furtherance of the Orleanist cause than all the Orleanist partisans combined. Again, in these latter days, the French people were called upon to draw a parallel between Plon Plon and the Orleans princes.[d] When Plon Plon set out for America, there were caricatures circulated in the Faubourg St. Antoine representing him as a fat man in search of a crown, but professing at the same time to be a most inoffensive traveler, with a peculiar aversion to the smell of powder. While Plon Plon is returning to France with no more laurels than he gathered in the Crimea and in Italy, the Princes of Orleans cross the Atlantic to take service in the ranks of the National army. Hence a great stir in the Bonapartist camp. It would not do to give vent to Bonapartist anger through the venal press of Paris. The Imperialist fears would thus only be betrayed, the pamphlet scandal renewed, and odious comparisons provoked between exiled Princes who fight under the republican banner against the enslavers of working millions, with another exiled Prince, who had himself sworn in as an English special constable to share in the glory of putting down an English workingmen's movement.[41]

---

[a] "The tone in which the outrage on Captain Macdonald...", *The Times*, No. 23926, May 7, 1861, leading article; "We trust we have now heard...", *The Times*, No. 23928, May 9, 1861, leading article.— *Ed.*

[b] "Much of the credit for this belongs to me", Virgil, *Aeneid*, II, 6.— *Ed.*

[c] Joseph Charles Paul Bonaparte, Prince Napoléon.— *Ed.*

[d] François Ferdinand Philippe Louis Marie d'Orléans, Prince de Joinville; Robert Philippe Louis Eugène Ferdinand d'Orléans, duc de Chartres; Louis Philippe Albert d'Orléans, comte de Paris.— *Ed.*

Who should extricate the Man of December out of this dilemma? Who but *The London Times*? If the same *London Times*, which, on the 6th, 7th, 8th, and 9th of October, 1861, had roused the furies of the *Pays, Journal de l'Empire*, by its rather cynical strictures on the visit at Compiegne—if that very same paper should come out on the 12th of October, with a merciless onslaught on the Orleans Princes, because of their enlistment in the ranks of the National Army of the United States,[a] would Louis Bonaparte not have proved his case against the Orleans Princes? Would *The Times* article not be done into French, commented upon by the Paris papers, sent by the *Préfet de Police* to all the journals of all the departments, and circulated throughout the whole of France, as the impartial sentence passed by *The London Times*, the personal foe of Louis Bonaparte, upon the last proceedings of the Orleans Princes? Consequently, *The Times* of to-day has come out with a most scurrilous onslaught on these princes.

Louis Bonaparte is, of course, too much of a business man to share the judicial blindness in regard to the American war of the official public opinion-mongers. He knows that the true people of England, of France, of Germany, of Europe, consider the cause of the United States as their own cause, as the cause of liberty, and that, despite all paid sophistry, they consider the soil of the United States as the free soil of the landless millions of Europe, as their land of promise, now to be defended sword in hand, from the sordid grasp of the slaveholder. Louis Napoleon knows, moreover, that in France the masses connect the fight for the maintenance of the Union with the fight of their forefathers for the foundation of American independence, and that with them every Frenchman drawing his sword for the National Government appears only to execute the bequest of Lafayette.[42] Bonaparte, therefore, knows that if anything be able to win the Orleans Princes good opinions from the French people, it will be their enlistment in the ranks of the national army of the United States. He shudders at this very notion, and consequently *The London Times*, his censorious sycophant, tells to-day the Orleans princes that "they will derive no increase of popularity with the French nation from stooping to serve on this *ignoble field of action*." Louis Napoleon knows that all the wars waged in Europe between hostile nations since his *coup d'état*, have been mock wars, groundless, wanton, and carried on on false pretenses. The Russian war, and

---

a "Perhaps there is no position which an erring mortal...", *The Times*, No. 24062, October 12, 1861, leading article.— *Ed.*

the Italian war, not to speak of the piratical expeditions against China, Cochin-China,[43] and so forth, never enlisted the sympathies of the French people, instinctively aware that both wars were carried on only with the view to strengthening the chains forged by the *coup d'état*. The first grand war of contemporaneous history is the American war.

The peoples of Europe know that the Southern slaveocracy commenced that war with the declaration that the continuance of slaveocracy was no longer compatible with the continuance of the Union. Consequently, the people of Europe know that a fight for the continuance of the Union is a fight against the continuance of the slaveocracy—that in this contest the highest form of popular self-government till now realized is giving battle to the meanest and most shameless form of man's enslaving recorded in the annals of history.

Louis Bonaparte feels, of course, extremely sorry that the Orleans Princes should embark in just such a war, so distinguished, by the vastness of its dimensions and the grandeur of its ends, from the groundless, wanton and diminutive wars Europe has passed through since 1849. Consequently, *The London Times* must needs declare:

"To overlook the difference between a war waged by hostile nations, and this most groundless and wanton civil conflict of which history gives us any account, is a species of offense against public morals."[a]

The Times is, of course, bound to wind up its onslaught on the Orleans Princes because of their "stooping to serve on such an ignoble field of action." With a deep bow before the victor of Sevastopol and Solferino, "it is unwise," says *The London Times,* "to challenge a comparison between such actions as Springfield and Manassas,[44] and the exploits of Sevastopol and Solferino."

The next mail will testify to the premeditated use made of *The Times's* article by the Imperialist organs. A friend in times of need is proverbially worth a thousand friends in times of prosperity, and the secret ally of *The London Times* is just now very badly off.

A dearth of cotton, backed by a dearth of grain; a commercial crisis coupled with an agricultural distress, and both of them combined with a reduction of Custom revenues and a monetary embarrassment compelling the Bank of France to screw its rate of discount to six per cent, to enter into transactions with Rothschilds and Baring for a loan of two millions sterling on the London

---

a "Perhaps there is no position..."—*Ed.*

market, to pawn abroad French Government stock, and with all that to show but a reserve of 12,000,000 against liabilities amounting to more than 40,000,000. Such a state of economical affairs prepares just the situation for rival pretenders to stake double. Already there have been bread-riots in the Faubourg St. Antoine, and this of all times is therefore the most inappropriate time for allowing Orleans Princes to catch popularity. Hence the fierce forward rush of *The London Times*.

Written on October 12, 1861   Reproduced from the newspaper

First published in the *New-York Daily Tribune*, No. 6426, November 7, 1861

Die Presse.

№ 293.   Wien, Freitag den 25. October 1861.   14. Jahrgang

Karl Marx
THE NORTH AMERICAN CIVIL WAR [45]

London, October 20, 1861

For months the leading weekly and daily papers of the London press have been reiterating the same litany on the American Civil War. While they insult the free states of the North, they anxiously defend themselves against the suspicion of sympathising with the slave states of the South. In fact, they continually write two articles: one article, in which they attack the North, and another article, in which they excuse their attacks on the North. *Qui s'excuse s'accuse.*

In essence the extenuating arguments read: The war between the North and South is a tariff war. The war is, further, not for any principle, does not touch the question of slavery and in fact turns on Northern lust for sovereignty. Finally, even if justice is on the side of the North, does it not remain a vain endeavour to want to subjugate eight million Anglo-Saxons by force! Would not separation of the South release the North from all connection with Negro slavery and ensure for it, with its twenty million inhabitants and its vast territory, a higher, hitherto scarcely dreamt-of, development? Accordingly, must not the North welcome secession as a happy event, instead of wanting to overrule it by a bloody and futile civil war?

Point by point we will probe the plea of the English press.

The war between North and South—so runs the first excuse—is a mere tariff war, a war between a protectionist system and a free trade system, and Britain naturally stands on the side of free trade. Shall the slave-owner enjoy the fruits of slave labour in their entirety or shall he be cheated of a portion of these by the protectionists of the North? That is the question which is at issue in this war. It was reserved for *The Times* to make this brilliant discovery. *The Economist, The Examiner, The Saturday Review* and *tutti quanti*[a] expounded the theme further.[b] It is characteristic of this discovery that it was made, not in Charleston, but in London. Naturally, in America everyone knew that from 1846 to 1861 a free trade system prevailed, and that Representative Morrill carried his protectionist tariff through Congress only in 1861,[46] after the rebellion had already broken out. Secession, therefore, did not take place because the Morrill tariff had gone through Congress, but, at most, the Morrill tariff went through Congress because secession had taken place. When South Carolina had its first attack of secession in 1831,[47] the protectionist tariff of 1828 served it, to be sure, as a pretext, but only as a pretext, as is known from a statement of General Jackson.[c] This time, however, the old pretext has in fact not been repeated. In the Secession Congress at Montgomery[48] all reference to the tariff question was avoided, because the cultivation of sugar in Louisiana, one of the most influential Southern states, depends entirely on protection.

But, the London press pleads further, the war of the United States is nothing but a war for the forcible maintenance of the Union. The Yankees cannot make up their minds to strike fifteen stars from their standard.[49] They want to cut a colossal figure on the world stage. Yes, it would be different if the war was waged for the abolition of slavery! The question of slavery, however, as *The Saturday Review* categorically declares among other things, has absolutely nothing to do with this war.

It is above all to be remembered that the war did not originate with the North, but with the South. The North finds itself on the defensive. For months it had quietly looked on while the secessionists appropriated the Union's forts, arsenals, shipyards, customs houses, pay offices, ships and supplies of arms, insulted its flag and took prisoner bodies of its troops. Finally the secessionists resolved to force the Union government out of its passive attitude by a blatant act of war, and *solely for this reason* proceeded to the bombardment of Fort Sumter near Charleston. On April 11 (1861) their General Beauregard had learnt in a

---

[a] All such.— *Ed.*

[b] Marx means the articles "Few have pretended to give...", *The Times,* No. 24033, September 9, 1861, leading article; "American Complaints against England", *The Economist,* No. 942, September 14, 1861; "Mrs. Stowe on the American War", *The Examiner,* No. 2798, September 14, 1861; "Mrs. Beecher Stowe's Wounded Feelings", *The Saturday Review,* No. 307, September 14, 1861.— *Ed.*

[c] President Jackson's proclamation against the Nullification Ordinance of South Carolina, December 11, 1832 (see Note 24).— *Ed.*

meeting with Major Anderson, the commander of Fort Sumter, that the fort was only supplied with provisions for three days more and accordingly must be peacefully surrendered after this period. In order to forestall this peaceful surrender, the secessionists opened the bombardment early on the following morning (April 12), which brought about the fall of the fort in a few hours. News of this had hardly been telegraphed to Montgomery, the seat of the Secession Congress, when War Minister Walker publicly declared in the name of the new Confederacy: "No man can say where *the war opened today* will end."[a] At the same time he prophesied "that before the first of May the flag of the Southern Confederacy will wave from the dome of the old Capitol in Washington and within a short time perhaps also from the Faneuil Hall in Boston".[50] Only now ensued the proclamation in which Lincoln called for 75,000 men to defend the Union.[b] The bombardment of Fort Sumter cut off the only possible constitutional way out, namely the convocation of a general convention of the American people, as Lincoln had proposed in his inaugural address.[c] For Lincoln there now remained only the choice of fleeing from Washington, evacuating Maryland and Delaware and surrendering Kentucky, Missouri and Virginia, or of answering war with war.

The question of the principle of the American Civil War is answered by the battle slogan with which the South broke the peace. Stephens, the Vice-President of the Southern Confederacy, declared in the Secession Congress that what essentially distinguished the Constitution newly hatched at Montgomery from the Constitution of the Washingtons and Jeffersons was that now for the first time slavery was recognised as an institution good in itself, and as the foundation of the whole state edifice, whereas the revolutionary fathers, men steeped in the prejudices of the eighteenth century, had treated slavery as an evil imported from England and to be eliminated in the course of time.[d] Another matador of the South, Mr. Spratt, cried out: "For us it is a question of founding a great slave republic."[e] If, therefore, it was

---

[a] Quoted in the report "How the War News Is Received", *New-York Daily Tribune*, No. 6231, April 15, 1861.— *Ed.*

[b] A. Lincoln, *A Proclamation* [April 15, 1861], *New-York Daily Tribune*, same issue.— *Ed.*

[c] A. Lincoln, "The Inaugural Address" [March 4, 1861], *New-York Daily Tribune*, No. 6196, March 5, 1861.— *Ed.*

[d] Stephens's speech in Savannah on March 21, 1861.— *Ed.*

[e] Marx gives the English words "a great slave republic" in brackets after the German equivalent.— *Ed.*

indeed only in defence of the Union that the North drew the sword, had not the South already declared that the continuance of slavery was no longer compatible with the continuance of the Union?

Just as the bombardment of Fort Sumter gave the signal for the opening of the war, the election victory of the *Republican* Party of the North, the election of Lincoln as President, gave the signal for secession. On November 6, 1860, Lincoln was elected. On November 8, 1860, a message telegraphed from South Carolina said: "Secession is regarded here as a settled thing" [a]; on November 10 the legislature of Georgia occupied itself with secession plans, and on November 13 a special session of the legislature of Mississippi was convened to consider secession. But Lincoln's election was itself only the result of a split in the *Democratic* camp. During the election struggle the Democrats of the North concentrated their votes on *Douglas,* the Democrats of the South concentrated their votes on *Breckinridge,* and to this splitting of the Democratic votes the Republican Party owed its victory. Whence came, on the one hand, the preponderance of the *Republican* Party in the North? Whence, on the other, the disunion *within* the *Democratic* Party, whose members, North and South, had operated in conjunction for more than half a century?

Under the presidency of Buchanan the sway that the South had gradually usurped over the Union through its alliance with the Northern Democrats attained its zenith. The last Continental Congress of 1787 and the first Constitutional Congress of 1789-90 had legally excluded slavery from all Territories of the republic northwest of the Ohio.[b] (Territories, as is known, is the name given to the colonies lying within the United States itself which have not yet attained the level of population constitutionally prescribed for the formation of autonomous states.[51]) The so-called Missouri Compromise (1820), in consequence of which Missouri became one of the States of the Union as a slave state, excluded slavery from every remaining Territory north of 36°30' latitude and west of the Missouri.[52] By this compromise the area of slavery was advanced several degrees of longitude, whilst, on the other hand, a geographical boundary-line to its future spread

---

[a] Quoted in the report "Columbia, S. C. Thursday, Nov. 8, 1860", *New-York Daily Tribune,* No. 6098, November 9, 1860.— *Ed.*

[b] *An Ordinance for the government of the territory of the United States, north-west of the River Ohio,* adopted by the 1787 Congress, and *An Act to provide for the government of the territory north-west of the River Ohio,* adopted by the 1789-90 Congress.— *Ed.*

seemed quite definitely drawn. This geographical barrier, in its
turn, was thrown down in 1854 by the so-called Kansas-Nebraska
Bill, the initiator of which was St[ephen] A. Douglas, then leader
of the Northern Democrats. The Bill, which passed both Houses
of Congress, repealed the Missouri Compromise, placed slavery
and freedom on the same footing, commanded the Union
government to treat them both with equal indifference and left it
to the sovereignty of the people, that is, the majority of the
settlers, to decide whether or not slavery was to be introduced in a
Territory. Thus, for the first time in the history of the United
States, every geographical and legal limit to the extension of
slavery in the Territories was removed. Under this new legislation
the hitherto free Territory of New Mexico, a Territory five times
as large as the State of New York, was transformed into a slave
Territory, and the area[a] of slavery was extended from the border
of the Mexican Republic to 38° north latitude. In 1859 New
Mexico received a slave code that vies with the statute-books of
Texas and Alabama in barbarity. Nevertheless, as the census of
1860 proves,[b] among some 100,000 inhabitants New Mexico
does not count even half a hundred slaves. It had therefore
sufficed for the South to send some adventurers with a few slaves
over the border, and then with the help of the central government
in Washington and of its officials and contractors in New Mexico
to drum together a sham popular representation to impose slavery
and with it the rule of the slaveholders on the Territory.

However, this convenient method did not prove applicable in
other Territories. The South accordingly went a step further and
appealed from Congress to the Supreme Court of the United
States. This Court, which numbers nine judges, five of whom
belong to the South, had long been the most willing tool of the
slaveholders. It decided in 1857, in the notorious Dred Scott
case,[53] that every American citizen possesses the right to take with
him into any Territory any property recognised by the Constitution.[c] The Constitution, it maintained, recognises slaves as
property and obliges the Union government to protect this
property. Consequently, on the basis of the Constitution, slaves
could be forced to labour in the Territories by their owners, and

---

    [a] Marx uses the English word.— Ed.
    [b] Its data were cited in a report date-lined "New York, March 26", The Times,
No. 23903, April 10, 1861.— Ed.
    [c] The ruling of the US Supreme Court on the Dred Scott case was quoted in
the article "The Dred Scott Case Decided", New-York Daily Tribune, No. 4955,
March 7, 1857.— Ed.

so every individual slaveholder was entitled to introduce slavery into hitherto free Territories against the will of the majority of the settlers. The right to exclude slavery was taken from the Territorial legislatures and the duty to protect pioneers of the slave system was imposed on Congress and the Union government.

If the Missouri Compromise of 1820 had extended the geographical boundary-line of slavery in the Territories, if the Kansas-Nebraska Bill of 1854 had erased every geographical boundary-line and set up a political barrier instead, the will of the majority of the settlers, now the Supreme Court of the United States, by its decision of 1857, tore down even this political barrier and transformed all the Territories of the republic, present and future, from nurseries of free states into nurseries of slavery.

At the same time, under Buchanan's government the severer law on the surrendering of fugitive slaves enacted in 1850 was ruthlessly carried out in the states of the North.[54] To play the part of slave-catchers for the Southern slaveholders appeared to be the constitutional calling of the North. On the other hand, in order to hinder as far as possible the colonisation of the Territories by free settlers, the slaveholders' party frustrated all the so-called free-soil[a] measures, i. e., measures which were to secure for the settlers a definite amount of uncultivated state land free of charge.[55]

In the foreign, as in the domestic, policy of the United States, the interests of the slaveholders served as the guiding star: Buchanan had in fact obtained the office of President through the issue of the Ostend Manifesto, in which the acquisition of Cuba, whether by purchase or by force of arms, was proclaimed as the great task of national policy.[56] Under his government northern Mexico was already divided among American land speculators, who impatiently awaited the signal to fall on Chihuahua, Coahuila and Sonora.[57] The unceasing piratical expeditions of the filibusters against the states of Central America were directed no less from the White House at Washington. In the closest connection with this foreign policy, whose manifest purpose was conquest of new territory for the spread of slavery and of the slaveholders' rule, stood the *reopening of the slave trade,*[58] secretly supported by the Union government. St[ephen] A. Douglas himself declared in the American Senate on August 20, 1859: During the last year more Negroes have been imported from Africa than ever before in any single year, even at the time when the slave trade was still legal.

---

a Marx uses the English term.— *Ed.*

The number of slaves imported in the last year totalled fifteen thousand.[a]

Armed spreading of slavery abroad was the avowed aim of national policy; the Union had in fact become the slave of the 300,000 slaveholders who held sway over the South. A series of compromises, which the South owed to its alliance with the Northern Democrats, had led to this result. On this alliance all the attempts, periodically repeated since 1817, to resist the ever increasing encroachments of the slaveholders had hitherto come to grief. At length there came a turning point.

For hardly had the Kansas-Nebraska Bill gone through, which wiped out the geographical boundary-line of slavery and made its introduction into new Territories subject to the will of the majority of the settlers, when armed emissaries of the slavehold-ers, border rabble from Missouri and Arkansas, with bowie-knife in one hand and revolver in the other, fell upon Kansas and sought by the most unheard-of atrocities to dislodge its settlers from the Territory colonised by them. These raids were supported by the central government in Washington. Hence a tremendous reaction. Throughout the North, but particularly in the North-west,[59] a relief organisation was formed to support Kansas with men, arms and money.[60] Out of this relief organisation arose the *Republican Party*, which therefore owes its origin to the struggle for Kansas. After the attempt to transform Kansas into a *slave Territory* by force of arms had failed, the South sought to achieve the same result by political intrigues. Buchanan's government, in particular, exerted its utmost efforts to have Kansas included in the States of the Union as a *slave state* with a slave constitution imposed on it.[b] Hence renewed struggle, this time mainly conducted in Congress at Washington. Even St[ephen] A. Douglas, the chief of the Northern Democrats, now (1857-58) entered the lists against the government and his allies of the South, because imposition of a slave constitution could have been contrary to the principle of sovereignty of the settlers passed in the Nebraska Bill of 1854. Douglas, Senator for Illinois, a Northwestern state, would naturally have lost all his influence if he had wanted to concede to the South the right to steal by force of arms or through acts of Congress Territories colonised by the North. As the struggle for

---

[a] Douglas's statement, made at a reception in Washington on August 19, 1859, was reported in the article "Douglas Sure of the South", *New-York Daily Tribune*, No. 5720, August 23, 1859.— *Ed.*

[b] Its basic provisions were set forth in the article "The Great Swindle", *New-York Daily Tribune*, No. 5171, November 16, 1857.— *Ed.*

Kansas, therefore, called the *Republican Party* into being, it at the same time occasioned the first *split within the Democratic Party* itself. The Republican Party put forward its first platform for the presidential election in 1856. Although its candidate, John Frémont, was not victorious, the huge number of votes cast for him at any rate proved the rapid growth of the Party, particularly in the Northwest. At their second National Convention for the presidential elections (May 17, 1860), the Republicans again put forward their platform of 1856, only enriched by some additions.[a] Its principal contents were the following: Not a foot of fresh territory is further conceded to slavery. The filibustering policy abroad must cease. The reopening of the slave trade is stigmatised. Finally, free-soil[b] laws are to be enacted for the furtherance of free colonisation.

The vitally important point in this platform was that not a foot of fresh terrain was conceded to slavery; rather it was to remain once and for all confined within the boundaries of the states where it already legally existed. Slavery was thus to be formally interned; but continual expansion of territory and continual spread of slavery beyond its old limits is a law of life for the slave states of the Union.

The cultivation of the southern export articles, cotton, tobacco, sugar, etc., carried on by slaves, is only remunerative as long as it is conducted with large gangs of slaves, on a mass scale and on wide expanses of a naturally fertile soil, which requires only simple labour. Intensive cultivation, which depends less on fertility of the soil than on investment of capital, intelligence and energy of labour, is contrary to the nature of slavery. Hence the rapid transformation of states like Maryland and Virginia, which formerly employed slaves in the production of export articles, into states which raise slaves to export them into the deep South. Even in South Carolina, where the slaves form four-sevenths of the population, the cultivation of cotton has been almost completely stationary for years due to the exhaustion of the soil. Indeed, by force of circumstances South Carolina has already been transformed in part into a slave-raising state, since it already sells slaves to the sum of four million dollars yearly to the states of the extreme South and Southwest. As soon as this point is reached, the acquisition of new Territories becomes necessary, so that one section of the slaveholders with their slaves may occupy new fertile

---

[a] Both platforms were cited in the article "The Platform", *New-York Daily Tribune*, No. 5950, May 19, 1860.— *Ed.*
[b] Marx uses the English term.— *Ed.*

lands and that a new market for slave-raising, therefore for the sale of slaves, may be created for the remaining section. It is, for example, indubitable that without the acquisition of Louisiana, Missouri and Arkansas by the United States, slavery in Virginia and Maryland would have become extinct long ago. In the Secessionist Congress at Montgomery, Senator Toombs, one of the spokesmen of the South, strikingly formulated the economic law that commands the constant expansion of the territory of slavery.

"In fifteen years," said he, "without a great increase in slave territory, either the slaves must be permitted to flee from the whites, or the whites must flee from the slaves."

As is known, the representation of the individual states in the Congress House of Representatives depends on the size of their respective populations. As the populations of the free states grow far more quickly than those of the slave states, the number of Northern Representatives was bound to outstrip that of the Southern very rapidly. The real seat of the political power of the South is accordingly transferred more and more to the American Senate, where every state, whether its population is great or small, is represented by two Senators. In order to assert its influence in the Senate and, through the Senate, its hegemony over the United States, the South therefore required a continual formation of new slave states. This, however, was only possible through conquest of foreign lands, as in the case of Texas, or through the transformation of the Territories belonging to the United States first into slave Territories and later into slave states, as in the case of Missouri, Arkansas, etc. *John Calhoun,* whom the slaveholders admire as their statesman *par excellence,* stated as early as February 19, 1847, in the Senate, that the Senate alone placed a balance of power in the hands of the South, that extension of the slave territory was necessary to preserve this equilibrium between South and North in the Senate, and that the attempts of the South at the creation of new slave states by force were accordingly justified.

Finally, the number of actual slaveholders in the South of the Union does not amount to more than 300,000, a narrow oligarchy that is confronted with many millions of so-called poor whites,[a] whose numbers have been constantly growing through concentration of landed property and whose condition is only to be compared with that of the Roman plebeians in the period of

---

[a] Marx gives the English words "poor whites" in parenthesis after their German equivalent.— *Ed.*

Rome's extreme decline. Only by acquisition and the prospect of acquisition of new Territories, as well as by filibustering expeditions, is it possible to square the interests of these "poor whites" with those of the slaveholders, to give their restless thirst for action a harmless direction and to tame them with the prospect of one day becoming slaveholders themselves.

A strict confinement of slavery within its old terrain, therefore, was bound according to economic law to lead to its gradual extinction, in the political sphere to annihilate the hegemony that the slave states exercised through the Senate, and finally to expose the slaveholding oligarchy within its own states to threatening perils from the "poor whites". In accordance with the principle that any further extension of slave Territories was to be prohibited by law, the Republicans therefore attacked the rule of the slaveholders at its root. The Republican election victory was accordingly bound to lead to open struggle between North and South. And this election victory, as already mentioned, was itself conditioned by the split in the Democratic camp.

The Kansas struggle had already caused a split between the slaveholders' party and the Democrats of the North allied to it. With the presidential election of 1860, the same strife now broke out again in a more general form. The Democrats of the North, with Douglas as their candidate, made the introduction of slavery into Territories dependent on the will of the majority of the settlers. The slaveholders' party, with Breckinridge as their candidate, maintained that the Constitution of the United States, as the Supreme Court had also declared,[a] brought slavery legally in its train; in and of itself slavery was already legal in all Territories and required no special naturalisation. Whilst, therefore, the Republicans prohibited any extension of slave Territories, the Southern party laid claim to all Territories of the republic as legally warranted domains. What they had attempted by way of example with regard to Kansas, to force slavery on a Territory through the central government against the will of the settlers themselves, they now set up as law for all the Territories of the Union. Such a concession lay beyond the power of the *Democratic* leaders and would only have occasioned the desertion of their army to the Republican camp. On the other hand, Douglas's "settlers' sovereignty" could not satisfy the slaveholders' party. What it wanted to effect had to be effected within the next four years under the new President, could only be effected by the

---

[a] In its ruling on the Dred Scott case.— *Ed.*

resources of the central government and brooked no further delay. It did not escape the slaveholders that a new power had arisen, the *Northwest*, whose population, having almost doubled between 1850 and 1860, was already pretty well equal to the white population of the slave states—a power that was not inclined either by tradition, temperament or mode of life to let itself be dragged from compromise to compromise in the manner of the old Northeastern states. The Union was still of value to the South only so far as it handed over Federal power to it as a means of carrying out the slave policy. If not, then it was better to make the break now than to look on at the development of the Republican Party and the upsurge of the Northwest for another four years and begin the struggle under more unfavourable conditions. The slaveholders' party therefore played *va banque!* When the Democrats of the North declined to go on playing the part of the "poor whites" of the South, the South secured Lincoln's victory by splitting the vote, and then took this victory as a pretext for drawing the sword from the scabbard.

The whole movement was and is based, as one sees, on the *slave question*. Not in the sense of whether the slaves within the existing slave states should be emancipated outright or not, but whether the 20 million free men of the North should submit any longer to an oligarchy of 300,000 slaveholders; whether the vast Territories of the republic should be nurseries for free states or for slavery; finally, whether the national policy of the Union should take armed spreading of slavery in Mexico, Central and South America as its device.

In another article we will probe the assertion of the London press that the North must sanction secession as the most favourable and only possible solution of the conflict.

Written on October 20, 1861

First published in *Die Presse*, No. 293, October 25, 1861

Printed according to the newspaper

Karl Marx

THE CIVIL WAR IN THE UNITED STATES[61]

"Let him go, he is not worth your anger!"[a] Again and again English statesmanship cries—recently through the mouth of Lord John Russell[b]—to the North of the United States this advice of Leporello to Don Juan's deserted love. If the North lets the South go, it then frees itself from any association with slavery, from its historical original sin, and creates the basis of a new and higher development.

In reality, if North and South formed two independent countries, like, for example, England and Hanover, their separation would be no more difficult than was the separation of England and Hanover.[62] *"The South"*, however, is neither a territory closely sealed off from the North geographically, nor a moral unity. It is not a country at all, but a battle slogan.

The advice of an amicable separation presupposes that the Southern Confederacy, although it assumed the offensive in the Civil War, at least wages it for defensive purposes. It is believed that the issue for the slaveholders' party is merely one of uniting the territories it has hitherto dominated into an independent group of states and withdrawing them from the supreme authority of the Union. Nothing could be more false. *"The South needs its entire territory. It will and must have it."* With this battle-cry the secessionists fell upon Kentucky. By their "entire territory" they

---

[a] From Mozart's opera *Don Giovanni.—Ed.*

[b] Russell's speech in Newcastle on October 14, 1861. Reported in *The Times,* No. 24064, October 15, 1861.—*Ed.*

understand in the first place all the so-called *border states*[a]—
Delaware, Maryland, Virginia, North Carolina, Kentucky, Tennessee, Missouri and Arkansas. Besides, they lay claim to the entire
territory south of the line that runs from the nortwest corner
of Missouri to the Pacific Ocean. What the slaveholders, therefore,
call the South, embraces more than three-quarters of the territory
hitherto comprised by the Union. A large part of the territory
thus claimed is still in the possession of the Union and would first
have to be conquered from it. None of the so-called border states,
however, not even those in the possession of the Confederacy,
were ever *actual slave states.* Rather, they constitute the area of the
United States in which the system of slavery and the system of free
labour exist side by side and contend for mastery, the actual field
of battle between South and North, between slavery and freedom.
The war of the Southern Confederacy is, therefore, not a war of
defence, but a war of conquest, a war of conquest for the spread
and perpetuation of slavery.

The chain of mountains that begins in Alabama and stretches
northwards to the Hudson River—the spinal column, as it were,
of the United States—cuts the so-called South into three parts.
The mountainous country formed by the Allegheny Mountains
with their two parallel ranges, the Cumberland Range to the west
and the Blue Mountains[b] to the east, divides wedge-like the
lowlands along the western coast of the Atlantic Ocean from the
lowlands in the southern valleys of the Mississippi. The two
lowlands separated by the mountainous country, with their vast
rice swamps and far-flung cotton plantations, are the actual area
of slavery. The long wedge of mountainous country driven into
the heart of slavery, with its correspondingly clear atmosphere, an
invigorating climate and a soil rich in coal, salt, limestone, iron
ore, gold, in short, every raw material necessary for a many-sided
industrial development, is already for the most part free country.
In accordance with its physical constitution, the soil here can only
be cultivated with success by free small farmers. Here the slave
system vegetates only sporadically and has never struck root. In
the larger part of the so-called border states, the dwellers of these
highlands comprise the core of the free population, which sides
with the North if only for the sake of self-preservation.

Let us consider the contested territory in detail.

---

[a] Marx gives the English words "border states" in parenthesis after their
German equivalent.— *Ed.*

[b] Marx uses the English names: "Cumberland Range" and "Blue Mountains".— *Ed.*

Delaware, the most northeastern of the border states, is factually and morally in the possession of the Union. All the attempts of the secessionists at forming even one faction favourable to them have since the beginning of the war suffered shipwreck on the unanimity of the population. The slave element of this state has long been in process of dying out. From 1850 to 1860 alone the number of slaves diminished by half, so that with a total population of 112,218 Delaware now numbers only 1,798 slaves.[a] Nevertheless, Delaware is demanded by the Southern Confederacy and would in fact be militarily untenable for the North as soon as the South possessed itself of Maryland.

In *Maryland* itself the above-mentioned conflict between highlands and lowlands takes place. Out of a total population of 687,034 there are here 87,188 slaves. That the overwhelming majority of the population is on the side of the Union has again been strikingly proved by the recent general elections to the Congress in Washington. The army of 30,000 Union troops which holds Maryland at the moment, is intended not only to serve the army on the Potomac as a reserve, but, in particular, also to hold in check the rebellious slave-owners in the interior of the country. For here we observe a phenomenon similar to what we see in other border states where the great mass of the people stands for the North and a numerically insignificant slaveholders' party for the South. What it lacks in numbers, the slaveholders' party makes up in the means of power that many years' possession of all state offices, hereditary engagement in political intrigue and concentration of great wealth in few hands have secured for it.

Virginia now forms the great cantonment where the main army of secession and the main army of the Union confront each other. In the northwest highlands of Virginia the number of slaves is 15,000, whilst the twenty times as large free population consists mostly of free farmers. The eastern lowlands of Virginia, on the other hand, count well-nigh half a million slaves. Raising Negroes and the sale of the Negroes to the Southern states form the principal source of income of these lowlands. As soon as the ringleaders of the lowlands had carried through the secession ordinance by intrigues in the state legislature at Richmond[b] and had in all haste opened the gates of Virginia to the Southern army, northwest Virginia seceded from the secession, formed a

---

[a] Here and below Marx cites data of the 1860 US census contained in a report datelined "New York, March 26", *The Times,* No. 23903, April 10, 1861.— *Ed.*
[b] On April 17, 1861.— *Ed.*

new state, and under the banner of the Union now defends its
territory arms in hand against the Southern invaders.

Tennessee, with 1,109,847 inhabitants, 275,784 of whom are
slaves, finds itself in the hands of the Southern Confederacy,
which has placed the whole state under martial law and under a
system of proscription which recalls the days of the Roman
Triumvirates. When in the winter of 1861 the slaveholders
proposed a general convention of the people which was to vote for
secession or non-secession, the majority of the people rejected any
convention, in order to remove any pretext for the secession
movement. Later, when Tennessee was already militarily overrun
and subjected to a system of terror by the Southern Confederacy,
more than a third of the voters at the elections still declared
themselves for the Union. Here, as in most of the border states,
the mountainous country, *east Tennessee,* forms the real centre of
resistance to the slaveholders' party. On June 17, 1861, a General
Convention of the people of east Tennessee assembled in
Greeneville, declared itself for the Union, deputed the former
governor of the state, Andrew Johnson, one of the most ardent
Unionists, to the Senate in Washington and published a "declaration of grievances",[a] which lays bare all the means of deception,
intrigue and terror by which Tennessee was "voted out" of the
Union.[b] Since then the secessionists have held east Tennessee in
check by force of arms.

Similar relationships to those in West Virginia and east
Tennessee are found in the north of Alabama, in northwest
Georgia and in the north of North Carolina.

Further west, in the border state of *Missouri,* with 1,173,317
inhabitants and 114,965 slaves—the latter mostly concentrated in
the northwest of the state—the people's convention of August
1861 decided for the Union.[c] Jackson, the governor of the state
and the tool of the slaveholders' party, rebelled against the
legislature of Missouri, was outlawed and took the lead of the
armed hordes that fell upon Missouri from Texas, Arkansas and
Tennessee, in order to bring it to its knees before the Confederacy
and sever its bond with the Union by the sword. Next to Virginia,
Missouri is at the present moment the main theatre of the Civil
War.

---

[a] Marx uses the English expression and gives the German equivalent.— *Ed.*

[b] The resolutions of the Convention were reported by the *New-York Daily
Tribune,* No. 6308, July 4, 1861, in the item "The Knoxville (Tenn.) Whig...".—
Ed.

[c] The convention actually adopted this decision on March 9, 1861.— *Ed.*

New Mexico—not a state, but merely a Territory, into which 25 slaves were imported during Buchanan's presidency in order to send a slave constitution after them from Washington—had no craving for the South, as even the latter concedes. But the South has a craving for New Mexico and accordingly spewed an armed gang of adventurers from *Texas* over the border. New Mexico has implored the protection of the Union government against these liberators.

It will have been observed that we lay particular emphasis on the numerical proportion of slaves to free men in the individual border states. This proportion is in fact decisive. It is the thermometer with which the vital fire of the slave system must be measured. The soul of the whole secession movement is *South Carolina*. It has 402,541 slaves and 301,271 free men. *Mississippi*, which has given the Southern Confederacy its dictator, Jefferson Davis, comes second. It has 436,696 slaves and 354,699 free men. *Alabama* comes third, with 435,132 slaves and 529,164 free men.

The last of the contested border states, which we have still to mention, is *Kentucky*. Its recent history is particularly characteristic of the policy of the Southern Confederacy. Among its 1,135,713 inhabitants Kentucky has 225,490 slaves. In three successive general elections by the people—in the winter of 1861, when elections to a congress of the border states were held; in June 1861, when elections to the Congress in Washington took place; finally, in August 1861, in elections to the legislature of the State of Kentucky—an ever increasing majority decided for the Union. On the other hand, Magoffin, the Governor of Kentucky, and all the high officials of the state are fanatical supporters of the slaveholders' party, as is Breckinridge, Kentucky's representative in the Senate in Washington, Vice-President of the United States under Buchanan and candidate of the slaveholders' party in the presidential elections of 1860. Too weak to win over Kentucky for secession, the influence of the slaveholders' party was strong enough to make this state amenable to a declaration of neutrality on the outbreak of war. The Confederacy recognised the neutrality as long as it served its purposes, as long as the Confederacy itself was engaged in crushing the resistance in east Tennessee. Hardly was this end attained when it knocked at the gates of Kentucky with the butt of a gun to the cry of: "*The South needs its entire territory*. It will and must have it!"

From the southwest and southeast its corps of free-booters simultaneously invaded the "neutral" state. Kentucky awoke from its dream of neutrality, its legislature openly sided with the Union, surrounded the traitorous Governor with a committee of public safety, called the people to arms, outlawed Breckinridge and ordered the secessionists to evacuate the invaded territory immediately. This was the signal for war. An army of the Southern Confederacy is moving on Louisville, while volunteers from Illinois, Indiana and Ohio flock hither to save Kentucky from the armed missionaries of slavery.

The attempts of the Confederacy to annex Missouri and Kentucky, for example, against the will of these states, prove the hollowness of the pretext that it is fighting for the rights of the individual states against the encroachments of the Union. On the individual states that it considers to belong to the "South" it confers, to be sure, the right to secede from the Union, but by no means the right to remain in the Union.

Even the slave states proper, however much external war, internal military dictatorship and slavery give them everywhere for the moment a semblance of harmony, are nevertheless not without oppositional elements. A striking example is *Texas*, with 180,388 slaves out of 601,039 inhabitants. The law of 1845,[a] by virtue of which Texas became a State of the Union as a slave state, entitled it to form not merely one, but five states out of its territory. The South would thereby have gained ten new votes instead of two in the American Senate, and an increase in the number of its votes in the Senate was a major object of its policy at that time. From 1845 to 1860, however, the slaveholders found it impracticable to cut up Texas, where the German population plays an important part, into even two states without giving the party of free labour the upper hand over the party of slavery in the second state.[63] This furnishes the best proof of the strength of the opposition to the slaveholding oligarchy in Texas itself.

Georgia is the largest and most populous of the slave states. It has 462,230 slaves out of a total of 1,057,327 inhabitants, therefore nearly half the population. Nevertheless, the slaveholders' party has not so far succeeded in getting the Constitution imposed on the South at Montgomery[b] sanctioned by a general vote of the people in Georgia.

In the State Convention of *Louisiana*, meeting on March 21, 1861, at New Orleans, Roselius, the political veteran of the state, declared:

---

[a] *Joint Resolution for annexing Texas to the United States* [1845].— Ed.

[b] *Constitution of the Confederate States of America* (*New-York Daily Tribune*, No. 6206, March 16, 1861).— Ed.

"The Montgomery Constitution is not a constitution, but a conspiracy. It does not inaugurate a government of the people, but *an odious and unmitigated oligarchy.* The people were not permitted to have any say in this matter. The Convention at Montgomery has dug the grave of political liberty, and now we are called upon to attend its funeral." [a]

Indeed, the oligarchy of three hundred thousand slaveholders utilised the Congress of Montgomery not only to proclaim the separation of the South from the North. It exploited it at the same time to reshape the internal constitutions of the slave states, to subjugate completely the section of the white population that had still preserved some independence under the protection and the democratic Constitution of the Union. Between 1856 and 1860 the political spokesmen, jurists, moralists and theologians of the slaveholders' party had already sought to prove, not so much that Negro slavery is justified, but rather that colour is a matter of indifference and the working class is everywhere born to slavery.

One sees, therefore, that the war of the Southern Confederacy is in the true sense of the word a war of conquest for the spread and perpetuation of slavery. The greater part of the border states and Territories are still in the possession of the Union, whose side they have taken first through the ballot-box and then with arms. The Confederacy, however, counts them for the *"South"* and seeks to conquer them from the Union. In the border states which the Confederacy has occupied for the time being, it is holding the relatively free highlands in check by martial law. Within the actual slave states themselves it is supplanting the hitherto existing democracy by the unrestricted oligarchy of the 300,000 slaveholders.

Were it to relinquish its plans of conquest, the Southern Confederacy would relinquish its capacity to live and the purpose of secession. Secession, indeed, only took place because within the Union the transformation of the border states and Territories into slave states seemed no longer attainable. On the other hand, were it to cede the contested territory peacefully to the Southern Confederacy, the North would surrender to the slave republic more than three-quarters of the entire territory of the United States. The North would lose the whole of the Gulf of Mexico and the Atlantic Ocean, except the narrow strip from Penobscot Bay to Delaware Bay, and would even cut itself off from the Pacific Ocean. Missouri, Kansas, New Mexico, Arkansas and Texas would draw California after them.[64] Incapable of wresting the mouth of

---

[a] Reported in the *New-York Daily Tribune*, No. 6217, March 29, 1861.— *Ed.*

the Mississippi from the hands of the strong, hostile slave republic
in the South, the great agricultural states in the basin between the
Rocky Mountains and the Alleghenies, in the valleys of the
Mississippi, the Missouri and the Ohio, would be compelled by
their economic interests to secede from the North and enter the
Southern Confederacy. These northwestern states,[65] in their turn,
would draw after them into the same whirlpool of secession all the
Northern states lying further east, with perhaps the exception of
the states of New England.[66]

What would in fact take place would be not a dissolution of the
Union, but a *reorganisation* of it, a *reorganisation on the basis of
slavery*, under the recognised control of the slaveholding oligarchy.
The plan of such a reorganisation has been openly proclaimed by
the principal speakers of the South at the Congress of Montgomery and explains the paragraph of the new Constitution which
leaves it open to every state of the old Union to join the new
Confederacy. The slave system would infect the whole Union. In
the Northern states, where Negro slavery is in practice impossible,
the white working class would gradually be forced down to
the level of helotry.[67] This would fully accord with the loudly
proclaimed principle that only certain races are capable of
freedom, and as the actual labour is the lot of the Negro in the
South, so in the North it is the lot of the German and the
Irishman, or their direct descendants.

The present struggle between the South and North is, therefore,
nothing but a struggle between two social systems, the system of
slavery and the system of free labour. The struggle has broken out
because the two systems can no longer live peacefully side by side
on the North American continent. It can only be ended by the
victory of one system or the other.

If the border states, the disputed areas in which the two systems
have hitherto contended for domination, are a thorn in the flesh
of the South, there can, on the other hand, be no mistake that, in
the course of the war up to now, they have constituted the chief
weakness of the North. One section of the slaveholders in these
districts simulated loyalty to the North at the bidding of the
conspirators in the South; another section found that in fact it was
in accordance with their real interests and traditional ideas to go
with the Union. The two sections have equally crippled the North.
Anxiety to keep the "loyal" slaveholders of the border states in
good humour; fear of throwing them into the arms of secession,
in a word, tender regard for the interests, prejudices and
sensibilities of these ambiguous allies, has smitten the Union

government with incurable weakness since the beginning of the war, driven it to half measures, forced it to dissemble away the principle of the war, and to spare the foe's most vulnerable spot, the root of the evil— *slavery itself*.

When, only recently, Lincoln pusillanimously revoked[a] Frémont's Missouri proclamation on the emancipation of Negroes belonging to the rebels,[68] this was done solely out of regard for the loud protest of the "loyal" slaveholders of Kentucky. However, a turning point has already been reached. With Kentucky, the last border state has been pushed into the series of battlefields between South and North. With the real war for the border states in the border states themselves, the question of winning or losing them is withdrawn from the sphere of diplomatic negotiations and parliamentary discussions. One section of slaveholders will throw off the mask of loyalty; the other will content itself with the prospect of a financial compensation such as Great Britain gave the West Indian planters.[69] Events themselves drive to the promulgation of the decisive slogan— *emancipation of the slaves*.

That even the most hardened Democrats and diplomats of the North feel themselves drawn to this point, is shown by some announcements of very recent date. In an open letter, General Cass, Secretary of State for War under Buchanan and hitherto one of the most ardent allies of the South, declared emancipation of the slaves the *conditio sine qua non* of the Union's salvation.[b] In his last *Review* for October, Dr. *Brownson,* the spokesman of the Catholic party of the North, on his own admission the most energetic adversary of the emancipation movement from 1836 to 1860, publishes an article *for* Abolition.

"If we have opposed Abolition heretofore," he says among other things, "because we would preserve the Union, we must *a fortiori* now oppose slavery whenever, in our judgement, its continuance becomes incompatible with the maintenance of the Union, or of our nation as a free republican state."[c]

Finally, the *World,* a New York organ of the diplomats of the Washington Cabinet, concludes one of its latest blustering articles against the Abolitionists with the words:

---

[a] In a letter to Frémont of September 11, 1861, (*New-York Daily Tribune,* No. 6380, September 15, 1861).— *Ed.*

[b] Cass's statement was quoted in a leading article in the *New-York Daily Tribune,* No. 6381, September 16, 1861.— *Ed.*

[c] Marx presumably quotes from the leading article in the *New-York Daily Tribune,* No. 6401, October 9, 1861, which contains this passage from the article in *Brownson's Quarterly Review.— Ed.*

"On the day when it shall be decided that either slavery or the Union must go down, on that day sentence of death is passed on slavery. If the North cannot triumph *without* emancipation, it will triumph *with* emancipation."

Written about October 20, 1861   Printed according to the news-
                                                  paper
First published in *Die Presse*, No. 306,
November 7, 1861

Karl Marx

THE CRISIS IN ENGLAND[70]

Today, as fifteen years ago, England faces a catastrophe that threatens to strike at the root of her entire economic system. As is known, the *potato* formed the exclusive food of Ireland and a not inconsiderable section of the English working people when the potato blight of 1845 and 1846 struck the root of Irish life with decay. The results of this great catastrophe are known. The Irish population declined by two million, of whom one part died of starvation and the other fled across the Atlantic Ocean. At the same time, this dreadful misfortune helped the English Free Trade party to triumph; the English landed aristocracy was compelled to sacrifice one of its most lucrative monopolies, and the abolition of the Corn Laws[a] assured a broader and sounder basis for the reproduction and maintenance of the working millions.

What the *potato* was to Irish agriculture, *cotton* is to the dominant branch of Great Britain's industry. On its manufacture depends the subsistence of a mass of people greater than the total number of inhabitants of Scotland and than two-thirds of the present number of inhabitants of Ireland. For according to the census of 1861, the population of Scotland consisted of 3,061,117 persons, that of Ireland now only 5,764,543,[b] whilst more than four millions in England and Scotland live directly or indirectly by the cotton industry. Now the cotton plant is not, indeed, diseased. Just as little is its production the monopoly of a few regions of the earth. On the contrary, no other plant that yields clothing material

---

a "An Act to Amend the Laws Relating to the Importation of Corn" [1846].— *Ed.*

b *Population of the United Kingdom according to the Census of 1861 (The Times,* No. 23992, July 23, 1861).— *Ed.*

thrives in equally extensive areas of America, Asia and Africa. The cotton monopoly of the slave states of the American Union is not a natural, but an historical monopoly. It grew and developed simultaneously with the monopoly of the English cotton industry on the world market. In the year 1793, shortly after the time of the great mechanical inventions in England, a Quaker[71] of Connecticut, Ely Whitney, invented the cotton gin,[a] a machine for cleaning cotton, which separates the cotton fibre from the cotton seed. Prior to this invention, a day of a Negro's most intensive labour barely sufficed to separate a pound of cotton fibre from the cotton seed. After the invention of the cotton gin, an old Negrowoman could comfortably supply fifty pounds of cotton daily, and gradual improvements have subsequently doubled the efficiency of the machine. The fetters on the cultivation of cotton in the United States were now burst asunder. Hand in hand with the English cotton industry, it grew swiftly to a great commercial power. Now and then in the course of development, England seemed to take fright at the monopoly of American cotton, as at a spectre that threatened danger. Such a moment occurred, for example, at the time when the emancipation of the Negroes in the English colonies was purchased for £20,000,000.[72] It was a matter for misgiving that the industry in Lancashire and Yorkshire should rest on the sovereignty of the slave-whip in Georgia and Alabama, whilst the English nation imposed on itself so great a sacrifice to abolish slavery in its own colonies. Philanthropy, however, does not make history, least of all commercial history. Similar doubts arose as often as a cotton crop failure occurred in the United States and as, in addition, such a natural phenomenon was exploited by the slaveholders to artificially raise the price of cotton still higher through combination. The English cotton spinners and weavers then threatened rebellion against "King Cotton". Manifold projects for procuring cotton from Asiatic and African sources came to light. This was the case, for example, in 1850.[b] However, the following good crop in the United States triumphantly dispelled such yearnings for emancipation. Indeed, in the last few years the American cotton monopoly attained dimensions scarcely dreamt of before, partly in consequence of the free trade legislation, which repealed the hitherto existing differential tariff on the cotton grown by slaves; partly in

---

[a] Marx uses the English term.— *Ed.*

[b] This may refer to articles on cotton cultivation published in *The Economist*, Nos. 370, 371 and 372, September 28, October 5 and 12, 1850.— *Ed.*

consequence of the simultaneous giant strides made by the English cotton industry and American cotton cultivation during the last decade. In the year 1857 the consumption of cotton in England already amounted to nearly 1,500 million pounds.

Now, all of a sudden, the American Civil War menaces this great pillar of English industry. Whilst the Union blockades the harbours of the Southern states, in order to cut off the secessionists' chief source of income by preventing the export of their cotton crop of this year, the Confederacy lends compelling force to this blockade with the decision not to export a bale of cotton of its own accord, but rather to compel England to come and fetch her cotton from the Southern harbours herself. England is to be driven to the point of forcibly breaking through the blockade, of then declaring war on the Union and so of throwing her sword into the scale of the slave states.

From the beginning of the American Civil War the price of cotton in England rose continuously; for a considerable time, however, to a less degree than was to be expected. On the whole, the English commercial world appeared to look down very phlegmatically on the American crisis. The cause of this cold-blooded way of viewing things was unmistakable. The whole of the last American crop was long ago in Europe. The yield of a new crop is never shipped before the end of November, and this shipment seldom attains considerable dimensions before the end of December. Till then, therefore, it remained pretty much a matter of indifference whether the cotton bales were held back on the plantations or forwarded to the harbours of the South immediately after their packing. Should the blockade cease at any time before the end of the year, England could safely count on receiving her customary cotton imports in March or April, quite as if the blockade had never taken place. The English commercial world, in large measure misled by the English press, succumbed, however, to the delusion that a spectacle of about six months' war would end with recognition of the Confederacy by the United States. But at the end of August, North Americans appeared in the market of Liverpool to buy cotton, partly for speculation in Europe, partly for reshipment to North America. This unheard-of event opened the eyes of the English. They began to understand the seriousness of the situation. The Liverpool cotton market has since been in a state of feverish excitement; the prices of cotton were soon driven 100 per cent above their average level; the speculation in cotton assumed the same wild features that characterised the speculation in railways in 1845.[73] The spinning and weaving mills in Lancashire and other seats of the British cotton industry limited their labour time to three days a week; a number of mills stopped their machines altogether; the disastrous reaction on other branches of industry was not wanting, and at this moment all England trembles at the approach of the greatest economic catastrophe that has yet threatened her.

The consumption of *Indian* cotton is naturally increasing, and the rising prices will ensure further increase of importation from the ancient home of cotton. Nevertheless, it remains impossible radically to change the conditions of production and the course of trade at, so to speak, a few months' notice. England is, in fact, now expiating her long mismanagement of India. Her present spasmodic attempts to replace American cotton by Indian encounter two great obstacles: the lack of means of communication and transport in India, and the miserable condition of the Indian peasant, which prevents him from taking advantage of the momentarily favourable circumstances. But, apart from this, apart from the process of improvement that Indian cotton has still to go through to be able to take the place of American, even under the most favourable circumstances it will be *years* before India can produce for export the requisite quantity of cotton. It is statistically established, however, that in *four months* the stocks of cotton in Liverpool will be exhausted. They will hold out even as long as this only if the limitation of the labour time to three days a week and the complete stoppage of a part of the machinery is effected by the British cotton spinners and weavers to a still greater extent than hitherto. Such a procedure is already exposing the factory districts to the greatest social sufferings. But if the American blockade continues over January! What then?

Written about November 1, 1861

First published in *Die Presse* No. 305, November 6, 1861

Printed according to the newspaper

Karl Marx

BRITISH COMMERCE

London, Nov. 2, 1861

The English Board of Trade Returns for the nine months ending Sept. 30, 1861, show in exports a large diminution, and in imports a still larger increase. A comparison between the export lists of the last three years gives the following general result:

Value of Exports for the nine months ending Sept. 30.

1859 .... £98,037,311
1860 101,724,346
1861 .... 93,795,332 [a]

Consequently the exports of this year, if compared to the corresponding period of 1860, have decreased by £7,929,014; of which total decrease the by far larger portion, viz.: £5,671,730, is accounted for by the sudden contraction of the American trade. The rates in which the general loss derived from this source has affected the different branches of British industry may be seen from the annexed table:

Value of Exports to the United States in the nine months ending Sept. 30.

	1859. £	1860. £	1861. £
Beer and ale	78,060	76,843	25,642
Coals and culm	144,556	156,665	200,244
Cottons	2,753,782	2,776,472	1,130,973
Earthenware and porcelain	448,661	518,778	191,606

---

[a] Here and below the tables are quoted from "The Board of Trade Returns", *The Economist*, No. 949, November 2, 1861.— *Ed.*

Haberdashery and millinery	1,204,085	1,083,438	542,312
Linens	1,486,276	1,337,778	493,654
Hardwares and cutlery	865,066	776,772	446,095
Metals—Iron—Pig	205,947	165,052	79,086
Bar, bolt, and rod	642,822	546,493	148,587
Railway of all kinds	744,505	665,619	168,657
Cast	16,489	17,056	9,239
Wrought of all kinds	357,162	378,842	125,752
Steel, unwrought	372,465	457,490	216,246
Copper, sheets and nails	99,422	44,971	10,005
Lead, pig	53,451	66,015	1,451
Tin plates	935,692	833,644	274,488
Oil Seed	122,570	72,915	1,680
Salt	63,876	84,818	59,809
Silk stuffs, handkerchiefs, and ribbons	197,605	102,393	88,360
Other silk articles	129,557	93,227	22,984
Soda	439,584	399,153	142,311
Spirits, (British)	53,173	56,423	12,430
Woolens—Cloths of all kinds	586,701	535,130	250,023
Mixed stuffs, flannels, blankets, etc.	1,732,224	1,612,284	652,399
Worsted Stuffs	1,052,053	840,507	377,597
Total	15,785,784	13,698,778 [74]	5,671,730

Beyond the diminution due to the decrease of the American trade, the general exports show, moreover, a decline of £2,257,284. The greater part of this loss was incurred during the month of September, when the high price of cotton, and the consequent rise in cotton manufactures and yarns, had begun to powerfully react on the markets of British North America,[a] East India, and Australia. During the whole period of nine months ended September, 1861, Turkey and Germany were, next to the United States, the countries foremost in restraining their absorption of British merchandise. The export trade to France has not grown in any observable degree, the only striking instance of increase being limited to an agricultural article, viz., sheeps' and lambs' wool. During the first nine months of 1860, England exported to France 4,735,150 pounds of wool, worth £354,047.[b]

---

[a] Canada.— Ed.

[b] The figures here and below are quoted from the Accounts relating to Trade and Navigation for the Nine Months ended September 30, 1861 (The Economist, No. 949, November 2, 1861).— Ed.

During the corresponding period of this year, that export has risen to 8,716,082 pounds, valued at £642,468. The only other remarkable feature in the export returns refers to Italy. British exports to the new kingdom are evidently enlarging, which fact will go a great length in accounting for English sympathies with Italian liberty.[75] Thus, for instance, the export of British cottons to Sardinia, Tuscany, Naples, and Sicily, has increased from £756,892 in 1860, to £1,204,287 in 1861; the export of cotton yarns from £348,158 in 1860 to £538,373 in 1861; the export of irons from £120,867 in 1860, to £160,912 in 1861.

The import tables extend only to the first *eight months* of the current year. Their general result is shown by the subsequent figures:

Real Value of Imports.

1859	£ 88,993,762
1860	106,894,278
1861	114,588,107

The principal part of that increase of imports is due to a large addition in the purchase of foreign wheat, which, from £6,796,131 in the first eight months of 1860, had risen to £13,431,487 in the corresponding period of 1861. As to raw cotton, the quantity imported had, during the period referred to, only slightly fallen off, while the price of the article had largely increased, as will be seen from the annexed figures:

Quantity of Cotton imported (during the first eight months).

	Cwts.[a]	Value.
1859	8,023,082	£24,039,197
1860	10,616,347	28,940,676
1861	9,616,087	30,809,279

There exist no general politics at the present moment in England. Everything and everybody are absorbed in the industrial question and the American crisis. I called your attention in a former letter to the feverish state of the Liverpool cotton market.[b] For the last two weeks it has exhibited, in fact, all the symptoms of the railway mania in 1845.[76] Surgeons, dentists, physicians, barristers, cooks, workingmen, clerks and lords, comedians and parsons, soldiers and sailors, newspaper writers and boarding-

---

a The figures in this column are given for the period of nine months.— *Ed.*
b See this volume, pp. 17-20.— *Ed.*

school mistresses, males and females, all were speculating in cotton. Many of the lots purchased, sold and resold amounted to only one, two, three, or four bales. More considerable quantities remained in the same warehouses, although changing their proprietors twenty times. One who had purchased cotton at 10 o'clock offered it for sale at 11 o'clock, and realized a profit of $1/_2$d. on one pound. Many lots circulated in this way through several hands in 12 hours. This week, however, a sort of reaction has taken place, due to the single circumstance that a shilling is a round number, being composed of 12d., and that most people had resolved upon selling out so soon as the price of the pound of cotton should have been pushed to one shilling; consequently, there set in suddenly a great increase in the offers of cotton, and hence a reaction in its price. This, however, can be only transitory.

The British mind once become familiar with the idea that a pound of cotton may cost 15d., the temporary barrier to speculation will break down, and the speculating mania reappear with redoubled fury. There is one thing favorable to the United States in this movement. It is hostile to the breaking-of-blockade party. Already there have been published protests on the part of the speculators, in which it is reasonably said that any warlike movement by the British Government would be an act of direct injustice to those merchants who, on the faith of the British Government's adherence to its recognized and avowed principle of non-interference, had made their calculations, speculated at home, sent out their orders abroad and purchased cotton on an estimate of the price which it would reach under the operation of natural, probable and foreseeable courses.

This day's *Economist* publishes a very foolish article, in which, from statistics given as to the population and the area of the United States, he arrives at the conclusion that there would be room enough for the establishment of at least seven vast empires, and that, consequently, "the dream of universal dominion" ought to be banished from the hearts of the Unionists.[a] The only rational inference which *The Economist* might have drawn from its own statistical statements, viz., that the Northerners, even if they liked to do so, could not desist from their claims without sacrificing to Slavery the vast States and Territories "in which Slavery still lingers, but cannot maintain itself as a permanent institution"— this only rational conclusion he successfully contrives not even to touch upon.

[a] "Motives of the Federalists in Coercing the Secessionists", *The Economist*, No. 949, November 2, 1861.— *Ed.*

Apart from its own commercial difficulties, England is simultaneously bothered by the critical state of the French finances. The maneuvers of the Bank of France to stay the bullion drain to England by accommodation bills, obtained from the Rothschilds and other great firms, have, as was to be foreseen, resulted in a but temporary mitigation of her embarrassments. She has now successively applied for succor to the banks at Berlin, Hamburg, and St. Petersburg; but all these tentatives, instead of procuring relief, have only betrayed despair. The straits to which the French Government is actually put appear from two measures recurred to in the course of a fortnight. The interest on the Treasury bills, in order to keep them afloat, had to be raised to $7 \frac{1}{2}$ per cent, while Victor Emmanuel was commanded to partially postpone the instalments of the new Italian loan, of which French capitalists hold a very large amount. He, of course, acceded to the application of his patron.

In the Tuileries there are now two opposite influences, proposing two opposite nostrums for the temporary cure of the financial disease. The real Bonapartists, Persigny, and the Crédit Mobilier,[77] cherish a project by which to subject the Bank of France to the direct and complete control of the Government, to convert her into a mere dependency on the Treasury, and to use the power thus obtained for the unrestricted emission of inconvertible State paper money. The other party, represented by Fould, and other renegades of former regimes, propose a new loan, whose amount is variously estimated by the most modest at £16,000,000, by the more daring at £30,000,000.

Written on November 2, 1861

First published in the *New-York Daily Tribune*, No. 6440, November 23, 1861

Reproduced from the newspaper

Karl Marx

ECONOMIC NOTES[78]

London, November 3

At the present moment general politics are non-existent in England. The interest of the country is absorbed in the French financial, commercial and agricultural crisis, the British industrial crisis, the dearth of cotton and the American question.

Competent circles here are not for a moment deceived concerning the Bank of France's bill-jobbing with a few big houses on both sides of the Channel being a palliative of the weakest sort.[a] All that could be achieved and has been achieved thereby was a *momentary* abatement of the drain of gold to England. The repeated attempts of the Bank of France to raise metallic auxiliary troops in Petersburg, Hamburg and Berlin damage its credit, without filling its coffers. The raising of the rate of interest on treasury bills, in order to keep them in currency, and the necessity of securing a remission of the payments for the new Italian loan from Victor Emmanuel—both are held here to be serious symptoms of French financial sickness. It is known, moreover, that at the present moment two projects contend in the Tuileries for precedence. The full-blooded Bonapartists, with Persigny and Péreire (of the Crédit Mobilier)[b] at their head, want to make the Bank of France completely subject to governmental authority, to reduce it to a mere office of the Finance Ministry, and to use the institution, thus transformed, as an assignat factory.

It is known that this principle was originally at the bottom of the organisation of the Crédit Mobilier. The less adventurous party,

---

[a] See this volume, p. 61.— *Ed.*

[b] The Crédit Mobilier bank was founded by the brothers Émile and Isaac Péreire. Marx presumably means the latter.— *Ed.*

represented by Fould and other renegades of Louis Philippe's time, proposes a *new national loan,* which is to amount to 400 million francs, according to some; to 700 million, according to others. *The Times,* in a leading article today, probably reflects the view of the City [79] when it states that France is completely paralysed by her economic crisis and robbed of her European influence.[a] Nevertheless, *The Times* and the City are wrong. Should the December power [80] succeed in outlasting the winter without great internal storms, it will then blow the war trumpet in the spring. The internal distress will not thereby be remedied, but its voice will be drowned.

In an earlier letter [b] I pointed out that the cotton swindle in Liverpool during the last few weeks fully reminds one of the maddest days of the railway mania of 1845. Dentists, surgeons, barristers, cooks, widows, workers, clerks and lords, comedians and clergymen, soldiers and tailors, journalists and persons letting apartments, man and wife, all speculated in cotton. Quite small quantities of from 1 to 4 bales were bought, sold and sold again. More considerable quantities lay for months in the same warehouse, although they changed owners twenty times. Whoever had bought cotton at 10 o'clock, sold it again at 11 o'clock with an addition of a halfpenny a pound. Thus the same cotton often circulated from hand to hand six times in ten hours. This week, however, there came a lull, and for no more rational reason than that a pound of cotton (namely, middling Orleans cotton) had risen to a shilling, that 12 pence make a shilling and are therefore a round figure. So everyone had purposed selling out, as soon as this maximum was reached. Hence sudden increase of the supply, and consequent reaction. As soon as the English make themselves conversant with the possibility that a pound of cotton can rise *above* a shilling, the St. Vitus's dance will return more madly than ever.

The last official monthly report of the *Board of Trade* [c] on British exports and imports [d] has by no means dispelled the gloomy feeling. The *export tables* cover the nine months' period from January to September 1861. In comparison with the same period of 1860, they show a falling-off of about £8,000,000. Of this,

---

[a] "To those who concern themselves with French politics...", *The Times,* No. 24080, November 2, 1861.— *Ed.*

[b] See this volume, pp. 53-56.— *Ed.*

[c] Marx uses the English name.— *Ed.*

[d] *Accounts relating to Trade and Navigation for the Nine Months ended September 30, 1861 (The Economist,* No. 949, November 2, 1861, Supplement).— *Ed.*

£5,671,730 fall to exports to the United States alone, whilst the remainder is distributed over British North America,[a] the East Indies, Australia, Turkey and Germany. Only in Italy is an increase shown. Thus, for example, the export of British cotton commodities to Sardinia, Tuscany, Naples and Sicily has risen from £756,892 for the year 1860 to £1,204,287 for the year 1861; the export of British cotton yarn from £348,158 to £538,373; the export of iron from £120,867 to £160,912, etc. These figures are not without weight in the scale of British sympathy for Italian freedom.[81]

Whilst the export trade of Great Britain has thus declined by nearly £8,000,000 her *import trade* has risen in still higher proportion, a circumstance that by no means facilitates the adjustment of the balance. This rise in imports stems, in particular, from the increase in wheat imports. Whereas for the first *eight* months of 1860 the value of the wheat imported amounted to only £6,796,131, for the same period of the present year it totals £13,431,487.

The most remarkable phenomenon revealed by the *import tables* is the rapid increase of *French imports* which have now attained a volume of nearly £18,000,000 (yearly), whilst English exports to France are not much bigger than, perhaps, those to Holland. Continental politicians have hitherto overlooked this entirely new phenomenon of modern commercial history. It proves that the economic dependence of France on England is, perhaps, six times as great as the economic dependence of England on France, if, that is, one not only considers the English export and import tables, but also compares them with the French export and import tables. It then follows that England has now become the principal export market for France, whereas France has remained a quite secondary export market for England. Hence, despite all chauvinism and all Waterloo[82] rodomontade, the nervous dread of a conflict with "perfidious Albion".[83]

Finally, one more important fact emerges from the latest English export and import tables. Whilst in the first *nine* months of this year English exports to the *United States* declined by more than 65 per cent[b] in comparison with the same period of 1860, the port of New York alone has *increased* its exports to England by

---

[a] Canada.— *Ed.*

[b] The original mistakenly says 25 per cent. Marx took the figure from *The Economist,* No. 949, November 2, 1861, where an error had been made in the calculation.— *Ed.*

£6,000,000 during the first *eight* months of the present year. During this period the export of American gold to England had almost ceased, while now, on the contrary, gold has been flowing for weeks from England to New York. It is in fact England and France whose crop failures cover the North American deficit, while the Morrill tariff [84] and the economy inseparable from a civil war have simultaneously decimated the consumption of English and French manufactures in North America. And now one may compare these statistical facts with the jeremiads of *The Times* on the financial ruin of North America!

Written on November 3, 1861

First published in *Die Presse*, No. 308, November 9, 1861

Printed according to the newspaper

Karl Marx

INTERVENTION IN MEXICO [85]

London, November 7

The Times of today has a leading article[a] in its well-known, confusedly kaleidoscopic, affectedly humorous style, on the French government's invasion of Dappenthal and on Switzerland's protest against this violation of territory.[86] The oracle of Printing House Square[87] recalls how, at the time of most acute struggle between English manufacturers and landowners, little children employed in the factories were led to throw needles into the most delicate parts of the machinery to upset the motion of the whole powerful automaton. The machinery is Europe, the little child is Switzerland and the needle that she throws into the smoothly running automaton is—Louis Bonaparte's invasion of her territory or, rather, her outcry at his invasion. Thus the needle is suddenly transformed into the outcry at the needle's prick and the metaphor into a piece of buffoonery at the expense of the reader who expects a metaphor. The Times is further enlivened by its own discovery that Dappenthal consists of a single village called Cressonnières. It ends its short article with a complete contradiction of its beginning. Why, it exclaims, make so much ado about this infinitely small Swiss bagatelle, when every quarter of Europe will be ablaze next spring? One may not forget that, shortly before, Europe was a well regulated automaton. The whole article appears sheer nonsense and yet it has its sense. It is a declaration that Palmerston has given carte blanche in the Swiss incident to his ally on the other side of the Channel. The explanation of this

---

[a] "Some of our middle-aged readers may recollect the time...", The Times, No. 24083, November 6, 1861.— Ed.

declaration is found in the dry notice in the *Moniteur*[a] that on October 31 England, France and Spain concluded a convention on joint *intervention in Mexico*.[88] The article of *The Times* on Dappenthal and the note of the *Moniteur* on Mexico stand as close together as the Canton of Waadt and Vera Cruz lie far apart.

It is credible that Louis Bonaparte counted on intervention in Mexico among the many possibilities which he continually has ready to divert the French people. Surely Spain, whose cheap successes in Morocco and St. Domingo [89] have gone to her head, dreams of a Restoration in Mexico. But it is certain that France's project had not yet matured and that both France and Spain were opposed to a crusade against Mexico under *English* command.

On September 24, Palmerston's private *Moniteur*, the *Morning Post*, announced the details of an agreement that England, France and Spain had reached for joint intervention in Mexico.[b] The following day the *Patrie* denied the existence of any such agreement. On September 27 *The Times* refuted the *Patrie*, without naming it. According to *The Times'* article, Lord Russell had *communicated* the English decision on intervention to the French government, whereupon M. Thouvenel had answered that the Emperor of the French had arrived at a like conclusion. It was now the turn of Spain. In a semi-official organ the Spanish government declared that it purposed an intervention in Mexico, but by no means an intervention alongside of England. It rained *dementis*. *The Times* had categorically announced that "the full assent of the American President had been given to the planned expedition". Hardly had the report reached the other side of the Atlantic Ocean when all the organs of the American government branded it as a lie, since President Lincoln was going with and not against Mexico. From all this it follows that the plan of intervention in its present form originated in the Cabinet of St. James.[90]

No less puzzling and contradictory than the statements concerning the origin of the convention were the statements concerning its points at issue. One organ of Palmerston, the *Morning Post*, announced that Mexico was not an organised state, with an established government, but a mere robbers' nest. It was to be treated as such. "The expedition had only one object—the satisfaction of the Mexican state's creditors in England, France and

---

a "Bulletin", *Le Moniteur universel*, No. 309, November 5, 1861.— *Ed.*

b Here and below Marx draws on the press review published in *The Free Press*, No. 10, October 2, 1861 ("The Projected Intervention in Mexico").— *Ed.*

Spain. To this end the combined forces would occupy the principal ports of Mexico, collect the import and export duties on her coast and hold this "material guarantee" [a] till all debt claims were satisfied.

The other organ of Palmerston, *The Times,* declared, on the contrary, that England was "steeled against plunderings on the part of bankrupt Mexico by long experience". It was not a question of the private interests of the creditors, but "they hope that the mere presence of a combined squadron in the Gulf of Mexico and the seizure of certain ports, will urge the Mexican government to *new* exertions in keeping the internal peace, and will compel the malcontents to confine themselves to some form of opposition more constitutional than brigandage".

According to this, the expedition would therefore take place to support the official government of Mexico. At the same time, however, *The Times* intimates that "the City of Mexico was sufficiently healthy, should it be necessary to penetrate so far".

The most original means of consolidating a government indisputably consists in the sequestration of its revenues and its territories by force. On the other hand, mere occupation of the ports and collection of the duties in them can only cause the Mexican government to set up a more inland-lying line of custom houses. Import duties on foreign commodities, export duties on American commodities would in this way be doubled; the intervention would in fact satisfy the claims of European creditors by extortions from European-Mexican trade. The Mexican government can become solvent only by internal consolidation, but it can consolidate itself at home only so long as its independence is respected abroad.

If the expedition's ostensible ends are so contradictory, then the ostensible means to these ostensible ends are still more contradictory. The English government organs themselves admit that if one thing or another would be attainable by a unilateral intervention of France or England or Spain, everything becomes unattainable by a *joint* intervention of these states.

One may recall that the Liberal Party in Mexico under Juárez, the official President of the republic, has now the upper hand at almost all points; that the Catholic Party under General Márquez has suffered defeat after defeat, and that the robber band organised by it has been driven back to the sierras of Queretaro and is dependent on an alliance with Mejía, the Indian chief there. The last hope of the Catholic Party was *Spanish* intervention.

---

^a The phrase occurs in an item published in the column "Great Britain" in the *New-York Daily Tribune,* No. 6462, December 19, 1861.— *Ed.*

"The only point," says *The Times*, "on which there may possibly be a difference between ourselves and our allies, regards the *government of the republic*. England will be content to see it remain in the hands of the Liberal Party, while France and Spain are suspected of a partiality for the ecclesiastical rule which has recently been overthrown. It would be strange, if France were, in both the old and the new world, to make herself the protector of priests and bandits. Just as in Italy the partisans of Francis II at Rome are being equipped for their work of making Naples ungovernable, so in Mexico the highways, indeed, the streets of the capital, are infested with robbers, whom the church party openly declares to be its friends."

And just for this reason England strengthens the Liberal government; in undertaking a crusade against it with France and Spain she seeks to suppress anarchy by supplying the clerical party lying at its last gasp with fresh allied troops from Europe!

Save during the short winter months the coasts of Mexico, pestilential as they are, can only be held by conquest of the country itself. But a third English government organ, *The Economist*, declares the conquest of Mexico to be impossible.

"If it is desired," says this paper, "to thrust upon her a British prince with an English army, then the fiercest wrath of the United States is excited. France's jealousy would make such a conquest impossible, and a motion to this effect would be rejected almost unanimously by an English parliament the moment it was submitted to it. England, for her part, cannot entrust the government of Mexico to France. Of Spain there can be no question whatever." [a]

The whole expedition is therefore a mystification, the key to which the *Patrie* gives in these words:

"The convention recognises the necessity of installing in Mexico a strong government that can maintain tranquillity and order there." [b]

The question is simply one of applying to the states of America through a new Holy Alliance the principle according to which the Holy Alliance held itself called on to interfere in the internal governmental affairs of the countries of Europe.[91] The first plan of this sort was drawn up by Chateaubriand for the Bourbons of Spain and France at the time of the Restoration.[92] It was frustrated by *Canning* and *Monroe*, the President of the United States, who declared any European interference in the internal affairs of American states to be forbidden. Since then the American Union has constantly asserted the Monroe Doctrine[93] as an international law. The present Civil War, however, created the right situation for securing to the European monarchies an

---

[a] "The Case of Mexico", *The Economist*, No. 947, October 19, 1861.— *Ed.*

[b] Marx presumably quotes this passage (*La Patrie*, October 29, 1861) from a reprint in the *New-York Daily Tribune*, No. 6434, November 16, 1861.— *Ed.*

intervention precedent on which they can build later. That is the real object of the English-French-Spanish intervention. Its immediate result can only be and is only intended to be the *restoration* of the anarchy just dying out in Mexico.

Apart from all standpoints of international law in general, the affair has the great significance for Europe that by concessions in the domain of Continental politics England has purchased the support of Louis Bonaparte in the Mexican expedition.

Written on November 6-7, 1861

First published in *Die Presse*, No. 311, November 12, 1861

Printed according to the newspaper

Karl Marx

THE INTERVENTION IN MEXICO

London, Nov. 8, 1861

The contemplated intervention in Mexico by England, France, and Spain, is, in my opinion, one of the most monstrous enterprises ever chronicled in the annals of international history. It is a contrivance of the true Palmerston make, astounding the uninitiated by an insanity of purpose and an imbecility of the means employed which appear quite incompatible with the known capacity of the old schemer.

It is probable that, among the many irons which, to amuse the French public, Louis Bonaparte is compelled to always keep in the fire, a Mexican Expedition may have figured. It is sure that Spain, whose never overstrong head has been quite turned by her recent cheap successes in Morocco and St. Domingo, dreams of a restoration in Mexico. But, nevertheless, it is certain that the French plan was far from being matured, and that both France and Spain strove hard against a joint expedition to Mexico under English leadership.

On Sept. 24, Palmerston's private Moniteur, *The London Morning Post,* first announced in detail the scheme for the joint intervention, according to the terms of a treaty just concluded, as it said, between England, France, and Spain.[a] This statement had hardly crossed the Channel, when the French Government, through the columns of the Paris *Patrie,* gave it the lie direct. On Sept. 27, *The London Times,* Palmerston's national organ, first broke its silence

---

[a] Here and below Marx makes use of the press review from the article "The Projected Intervention in Mexico", *The Free Press,* No. 10, October 2, 1861.— *Ed.*

on the scheme in a leader contradicting, but not quoting, the
Patrie. The Times even stated that Earl Russell had communicated
to the French Government the resolution arrived at on the part of
England of interfering in Mexico, and that M. de Thouvenel
replied that the Emperor of the French had come to a similar
conclusion. Now it was the turn of Spain. A semi-official paper of
Madrid, while affirming Spain's intention to meddle with Mexico,
repudiated at the same time the idea of a joint intervention with
England. The *dementis* were not yet exhausted. *The Times* had
categorically asserted that "the full assent of the American
President had been given to the Expedition." All the American
papers taking notice of *The Times* article, have long since
contradicted its assertion.

It is, therefore, certain, and has even been expressly admitted by
The Times, that the joint intervention in its present form is of
English—i.e., Palmerstonian—make. Spain was cowed into adherence by the pressure of France; and France was brought round by
concessions made to her in the field of European policy. In this
respect, it is a significant coincidence that *The Times* of November 6, in the very number in which it announces the conclusion
at London of a convention for the joint interference in Mexico,[a]
simultaneously publishes a leader, pooh-poohing and treating with
exquisite contumely the protest of Switzerland against the recent
invasion of her territory—viz., the Dappenthal—by a French
military force.[b] In return for his fellowship in the Mexican
expedition, Louis Bonaparte has obtained *carte blanche* for his
contemplated encroachments on Switzerland and, perhaps, on
other parts of the European continent. The transactions on these
points between England and France have lasted throughout the
whole of the months of September and October.

There exist in England no people desirous of an intervention in
Mexico save the Mexican bondholders, who, however, had never
to boast the least sway over the national mind. Hence the difficulty
of breaking to the public the Palmerstonian scheme. The next best
means was to bewilder the British elephant by contradictory
statements, proceeding from the same laboratory, compounded of
the same materials, but varying in the doses administered to the
animal.

---

[a] "Paris, Tuesday, Nov. 5, 7 A.M.", *The Times,* No. 24083, November 6,
1861.— *Ed.*
[b] "Some of our middle-aged readers may recollect the time...", *The Times,*
No. 24083, November 6, 1861.— *Ed.*

The Morning Post, in its print of September 24, announced that there would be "no territorial war on Mexico," that the only point at issue was the monetary claims on the Mexican exchequer; that "it would be impossible to deal with Mexico as an organized and established Government," and that, consequently, "the principal Mexican ports would be temporarily occupied and their customs revenues sequestered." [a]

The Times of September 27 declared, on the contrary, that "to dishonesty, to repudiation, to the legal and irremediable plunder of our countrymen by the default of a bankrupt community, we were steeled by long endurance," and that, consequently, "the private robbery of the English bondholders" lay not, as *The Post* had it,[b] at the bottom of the intervention. While remarking, *en passant,* that "the City of Mexico was sufficiently healthy, should it be necessary to penetrate so far," *The Times* hoped, however, that "the mere presence of a combined squadron in the Gulf, and the seizure of certain ports, will urge the Mexican Government to *new* exertions in keeping the peace, and will convince the malcontents that they must confine themselves to some form of opposition more constitutional than brigandage."

If, then, according to *The Post,* the expedition was to start because there "exists no Government in Mexico," it was, according to *The Times,* only intended as encouraging and supporting the *existing* Mexican Government. To be sure! The oddest means ever hit upon for the consolidation of a Government consists in the seizure of its territory and the sequestration of its revenue.

The Times and *The Morning Post* having once given out the cue, John Bull was then handed over to the minor ministerial oracles, systematically belaboring him in the same contradictory style for four weeks, until public opinion had at last become sufficiently trained to the idea of a joint intervention in Mexico, although kept in deliberate ignorance of the aim and purpose of that intervention. At last, the transactions with France had drawn to an end; the *Moniteur* announced that the convention between the three interfering powers had been concluded on October 31;[c] and the *Journal des Débats,* one of whose coproprietors is appointed to the command of one of the vessels of the French squadron, informed the world that no permanent territorial conquest was intended;

---

[a] Here and below Marx draws on the press review given in the article "The Projected Intervention in Mexico", *The Free Press,* No. 10, October 2, 1861.— *Ed.*
[b] *The Morning Post.— Ed.*
[c] "Bulletin", *Le Moniteur universel,* No. 309, November 5, 1861.— *Ed.*

that Vera Cruz and other points on the coast were to be seized, an advance to the capital being agreed upon in case of non-compliance by the constituted authorities in Mexico with the demands of the intervention; that, moreover, a strong government was to be imported into the Republic.[a]

The Times, which ever since its first announcement on September 27,[b] seemed to have forgotten the very existence of Mexico, had now again to step forward. Everybody ignorant of its connection with Palmerston, and the original introduction in its columns of his scheme, would be induced to consider the to-day's leader of *The Times* as the most cutting and merciless satire on the whole adventure. It sets out by stating that "the expedition is a *very remarkable* one" [later on it says *a curious one*].

"Three States are combining to coerce a fourth into good behavior, *not so much by way of war as by authoritative interference in behalf of order.*" [c]

Authoritative interference in behalf of order! This is literally the Holy Alliance[94] slang, and sounds very *remarkable* indeed on the part of England, glorying in the non-intervention principle! And why is "the way of war, and of declaration of war, and all other behests of international law," supplanted by "an authoritative interference in behalf of order?" Because, says *The Times,* there "exists no Government in Mexico." And what is the professed aim of the expedition? "To address demands to the constituted authorities at Mexico."

The only grievances complained of by the intervening Powers, the only causes which might give to their hostile procedure the slightest shade of justification, are easily to be summed up. They are the monetary claims of the bondholders and a series of personal outrages said to have been committed upon subjects of England, France and Spain. These were also the reasons of the intervention as originally put forth by *The Morning Post,* and as some time ago officially indorsed by Lord John Russell in an interview with some representatives of the Mexican bondholders in England. The to-day's *Times* states:

"England, France, and Spain have concerted an expedition to bring Mexico to the *performance of her specific engagements,* and to *give protection to the subjects of the respective crowns.*"

---

a "France. Paris, 3 novembre", *Journal des Débats,* November 6, 1861.— *Ed.*

b "The assurance, in spite of the denial of the *Patrie...*", *The Times,* No. 24049, September 27, 1861, leading article.— *Ed.*

c "In a very short time...", *The Times,* No. 24085, November 8, 1861.— *Ed.*

However, in the progress of its article, *The Times* veers round, and exclaims:

"We shall, no doubt, succeed *in obtaining* at least *a recognition of our pecuniary claims;* in fact, *a single British frigate could have obtained that amount of satisfaction at any moment.* We may trust, too, that the more scandalous of the outrages committed will be expiated by more immediate and substantial atonements; but *it is clear that, if only this much was to be brought about, we need not have resorted to such extremities as are now proposed.*"

The Times, then, confesses in so many words that the reasons originally given out for the expedition are shallow pretexts; that for the attainment of redress nothing like the present procedure was needed; and that, in point of fact, the "recognition of monetary claims, and the protection of European subjects" have nothing at all to do with the present joint intervention in Mexico. What, then, is its real aim and purpose?

Before following *The Times* in its further explanations, we will, *en passant,* note some more *"curiosities"* which it has taken good care not to touch upon. In the first instance, it is a real "curiosity" to see Spain—Spain out of all other countries—turn crusader for the sanctity of foreign debts! Last Sunday's[a] *Courrier du Dimanche* already summons the French Government to improve the opportunity, and compel Spain, "into the eternally delayed performance of her old standing engagements to French bondholders."

The second still greater "curiosity" is, that the very same Palmerston who, according to Lord John Russell's recent declaration, is about invading Mexico to make its Government pay the English bondholders, has himself, voluntarily, and despite the Mexican Government, *sacrificed* the treaty rights of England and the security mortgaged by Mexico to her British creditors.[b]

By the treaty concluded with England in 1826, Mexico became bound to not allow the establishment of Slavery in any of the territories constituting her then empire.[c] By another clause of the same treaty, she tendered England, as a security for the loans obtained from British capitalists, the mortgage of 45,000,000 acres of the public lands in Texas. It was Palmerston who, ten or twelve years later,[d] interfered as the mediator for Texas against Mexico. In the treaty then concluded by him with Texas, he sacrificed not

---

a November 3, 1861.— *Ed.*

b *The Times,* No. 24049, September 27, 1861.— *Ed.*

c Here and below Marx draws on documents cited in the article "Annexation of the Texas, a Case of War between England and the United States", *The Portfolio; Diplomatic Review* (new series), London, 1844, Vol. III, No. XI.— *Ed.*

d In 1840.— *Ed.*

only *the Anti-Slavery cause,* but also the *mortgage on the public lands,* thus robbing the English bondholders of their security. The Mexican Government protested at the time, but meanwhile, later on, Secretary John C. Calhoun could permit himself the jest of informing the Cabinet of St. James that its desire "of seeing Slavery abolished in Texas would be" best realized by annexing Texas to the United States. The English bondholders lost, in fact, any claim upon Mexico, by the voluntary sacrifice on the part of Palmerston of the mortgage secured to them in the treaty of 1826.

But, since *The London Times* avows that the present intervention has nothing to do either with monetary claims or with personal outrages, what, then, in all the world, is its real or pretended aim?

"An authoritative interference in behalf of Order."[a]

England, France, and Spain, planning a new Holy Alliance, and having formed themselves into an armed areopagus for the restoration of order all over the world, "Mexico," says *The Times,* "*must be rescued from anarchy,* and put in the way of self-government and peace. A strong and stable government must be established" there by the invaders, and that government is to be extracted from "some Mexican party."

Now, does any one imagine that Palmerston and his mouthpiece, *The Times,* really consider the joint intervention as a means to the professed end, viz: The extinction of anarchy, and the establishment in Mexico of a strong and stable government? So far from cherishing any such chimerical creed, *The Times* states expressly in its first leader of September 27:

"The only point on which there may possibly be a difference between ourselves and our allies, regards *the government of the Republic.* England will be content to see it *remain* in the hands of the *liberal party which is now in power,* while France and Spain are suspected of a partiality for the *ecclesiastical rule which has recently been overthrown....* It would, indeed, be strange, if France were, in both the old and new world, to make herself the protector of priests and bandits."

In its to-day's leader, *The Times* goes on reasoning in the same strain, and resumes its scruples in this sentence:

"It is *hard to suppose* that the intervening powers could all concur in the absolute preference of either of the two parties between which Mexico is divided, and *equally hard to imagine* that a compromise would be found practicable between enemies so determined."

Palmerston and *The Times,* then, are fully aware that there "exists a government in Mexico," that "the Liberal party,"

---

[a] *The Times,* No. 24085, November 8, 1861.— *Ed.*

ostensibly favored by England, "is now in power," that "the ecclesiastical rule has been overthrown;" [a] that Spanish intervention was the last forlorn hope of the priests and bandits; and, finally, that Mexican anarchy was dying away. They know, then, that the joint intervention, with no other avowed end save the rescue of Mexico from anarchy, will produce just the opposite effect, weaken the Constitutional Government, strengthen the priestly party by a supply of French and Spanish bayonets, rekindle the embers of civil war, and, instead of extinguishing, restore anarchy to its full bloom.

The inference The Times itself draws from those premises is really "remarkable" and "curious."

Although, it says, "these considerations may induce us to look with some anxiety to the results of the expedition, they do not militate against the expediency of the expedition itself." [b]

It does, consequently, not militate against the expediency of the expedition itself, that the expedition militates against its only ostensible purpose. It does not militate against the means that it baffles its own avowed end.

The greatest "curiosity" pointed out by The Times, I have, however, still kept in petto.

"If," says it, "President Lincoln should accept the invitation, which is provided for by the convention, to participate in the approaching operations, the character of the work would become more curious still."

It would, indeed, be the greatest "curiosity" of all if the United States, living in amity with Mexico, should associate with the European order-mongers, and, by participating in their acts, sanction the interference of a European armed Areopagus with the internal affairs of American States. The first scheme of such a transplantation of the Holy Alliance to the other side of the Atlantic was, at the time of the restoration, drawn up for the French and Spanish Bourbons by Chateaubriand.[95] The attempt was baffled by an English Minister, Mr. Canning, and an American President, Mr. Monroe. The present convulsion in the United States appeared to Palmerston an opportune moment for taking up the old project in a modified form. Since the United States, for the present, must allow no foreign complication to interfere with their war for the Union, all they can do is to protest. Their best well-wishers in Europe hope that they will protest, and thus,

---

[a] The Times, No. 24049, September 27, 1861.— Ed.
[b] Here and below, The Times, No. 24085, November 8, 1861.— Ed.

before the eyes of the world, firmly repudiate any complicity in one of the most nefarious schemes.

This military expedition of Palmerston's, carried out by a coalition with two other European powers, is started during the prorogation, without the sanction, and against the will of the British Parliament. The first extra Parliamentary war of Palmerston's was the Afghan war softened and justified by the production of *forged papers*.[a][96] Another war of that sort was his Persian war of 1856-1857.[97] He defended it at the time on the plea that "the principle of the previous sanction of the House did not apply to *Asiatic* wars."[b] It seems that it does neither apply to *American* wars. With the control over foreign wars, Parliament will lose all control over the national exchequer, and Parliamentary government turn to a mere farce.

Written on November 8, 1861   Reproduced from the newspaper

First published in the *New-York Daily Tribune*, No. 6440, November 23, 1861

---

a *Correspondence Relating to Persia and Afghanistan*, London, 1839.— *Ed.*
b H. J. Palmerston's speech in the House of Commons on July 16, 1857, *Hansard's Parliamentary Debates*, Third series, Vol. CXLVI, London, 1857.— *Ed.*

Karl Marx

MONSIEUR FOULD [98]

Paris, November 16

Art experts in the field of high political comedy find a source of the purest pleasure in the French *Moniteur* of November 14. As in the ancient classical drama, Fate invisibly, irresistibly enmeshes the heroes—Fate in the form of a thousand million-franc deficit. As in ancient drama, the dialogue is only between two persons, Oedipus-Bonaparte and Teiresias-Fould. The tragedy turns into comedy, however, since Teiresias says only what Oedipus has whispered to him in advance.[a]

One of the most characteristic tricks of Bonapartist comedy is to put its old, worn *dramatis personae* on stage over and over again as brand-new heroes. Billault comes on in place of Persigny, and then Persigny comes on in place of Billault! And likewise in the Decembrist press![b] Grandguillot, Cassagnac, Limayrac are tossed to and fro between the *Constitutionnel,* the *Pays* and the *Patrie.* Monsieur Véron, the "Bourgeois de Paris",[c] is replaced by Cesena as director of the *Constitutionnel,* Cesena by Cucheval, Cucheval by Cassagnac, Cassagnac by Renée, Renée by Grandguillot, and after six years Véron comes on again in his old spot—as a brand-new hero.

Likewise under the constitutional system Thiers became new as soon as Guizot was worn out, and Molé new as soon as Thiers was worn out, and then the round was repeated. However, these

---

[a] An allusion to Napoleon III's message to Fould and the latter's "Mémoire à l'Empereur", both published in *Le Moniteur universel,* No. 318, November 14, 1861.— *Ed.*

[b] The press of Louis Bonaparte, who staged a *coup d'état* on December 2, 1851.— *Ed.*

[c] An allusion to L. Véron's book *Mémoires d'un bourgeois de Paris.—Ed.*

different men represented different parties and tendencies. If they pushed one another out, in order to follow one another, and followed one another in order to push one another out again, then their toing and froing only showed the oscillations in the balance of the parties that in general formed the *pays légal*[a] under Louis Philippe. But Billault or Persigny, Walewski or Thouvenel, Laroquette or Fould, Grandguillot or Limayrac? It is what the English call "a distinction without a difference".[b] They all represent the same thing—the *coup d'état*. They do not represent different interests and parties among the people. They only represent different facial features of the Emperor. They are only different masks, behind which the same head is hidden.

The Times, whose weak point is comparisons, compares Louis Bonaparte with Louis XVI and Fould with Turgot.[c] Fould and Turgot! It is like trying to compare M. Vaillant with Carnot, because both of them were Ministers of War. Turgot was the head of the new economic school of the eighteenth century, the Physiocratic School.[99] He was one of the intellectual heroes who overthrew the old regime, while Louis XVI was the incarnation of that old regime. But who is Fould? Fould, a member of the dynastic opposition [100] under Louis Philippe, was always passed over on principle despite the most obtrusive solicitation, whenever the dynastic opposition was in a position to nominate a Finance Minister. Fould was held to be a *"financier dangereux"*, a reputation he had earned owing to his various unlucky financial operations. He needed only to defend a proposal, and the Chambers rejected it. Then came the provisional government. It had hardly been proclaimed, when Fould rushed to Ledru-Rollin, offered his services as Finance Minister and—proposed *national bankruptcy*. The courtship was unsuccessful, and the rejected suitor got his revenge by writing the pamphlet, *Pas d'assignats!* Finally Fould recognised in Louis Bonaparte the man who was foolhardy enough to hand the French treasury over to Mr. Fould.

Fould was closely involved in the manoeuvres that ensured the "nephew's"[d] election to the presidency on December 10, 1848. Fould was a very active friend and made the financial preparations for the *coup d'état*. December 2, 1851 was not only the victory of

---

[a] The section of the people having the right to vote.— *Ed.*

[b] Marx uses the English phrase and gives the German translation in brackets.— *Ed.*

[c] "The hour of reckoning has at length overtaken France...", *The Times*, No. 24091, November 15, 1861, leading article.— *Ed.*

[d] Louis Bonaparte's.— *Ed.*

Louis Bonaparte but also the victory of Fould. Fould became all-powerful. Fould became Minister of State. Fould could raise even his *menus plaisirs*[a] to the level of affairs of state. He seized hold of the dictatorship of the theatre along with the dictatorship of finances. Like other notorious men of *haute finance*,[b] Fould shared a passion for the dollar with a passion for the heroines of the wings. Fould became a sultan of the wings. Fould, with Péreire, is the inventor of imperialist finance. He is the direct cause of nine-tenths of the current deficit. Finally, in 1860, the great Fould withdrew into private life, to reappear in 1861 as "a new man" ("a brand new man")[c] in the imperialist finance comedy. Fould appears again as Turgot, Fould as Marquis Posa! *Applaudite, amici!*[101]

Written on November 16, 1861

First published in *Die Presse*, No. 318, November 19, 1861

Printed according to the newspaper

Published in English for the first time

---

[a] Lesser pleasures.— *Ed.*
[b] High finance.— *Ed.*
[c] Marx uses the English phrase "a new man" and adds "a brand new man" in German in brackets.— *Ed.*

Karl Marx

FRANCE'S FINANCIAL SITUATION

The *Times,* which at first praised the imperialist *coup d'éclat*[a] moderately and then lauded it in hyperboles, makes a sudden switch today from panegyrics to criticism.[b] The way in which this manoeuvre is executed is typical of the Leviathan of the English press:

"We will leave to others the task of congratulating Caesar on his admission that he is a finite and fallible being, and that, indisputably reigning by the power of the sword, he does not pretend to rule by virtue of Divine right. We had rather inquire what have been the financial results of ten years of Imperial sway, which are better worth thinking of than the phrases in which those results have been made known.... The Executive did what it pleased; the Ministers were responsible to the Emperor alone; the state of the finances was entirely concealed from the public and the Chambers. The annual form of voting a budget, instead of a check, was a mask; instead of a protection, a delusion. What, then, have the French people achieved by placing their liberties and their possessions at the disposal of a single man?... M. Fould himself admits that between 1851 and 1858 extraordinary credits have been opened to the amount of 2,800,000,000 francs, and that the deficit for the present year amounts to no less than 1,000,000,000 francs.

"We do not know how these sums were raised, but assuredly it has not been by taxation. We are told that four millions paid by the Bank of France for the renewal of its privileges have been spent, that five millions and a half of the Army Dotation Fund have been borrowed, and that securities of different kinds have been thrown into circulation. *As to the present state of affairs,* our Correspondent in Paris assures us *that there is not money in the Treasury to pay the half-yearly dividends due next month.* Such is the disastrous, the disgraceful state of French Finance, after ten years of brilliant and successful Imperialism, and it is only now, at a moment when it is unable to discharge its current obligations, that the French Government has taken the nation in some degree into its confidence and shown it a little of the reality that

---

[a] Glorious exploit.— *Ed.*

[b] "The extraordinary frankness of M. Fould...", *The Times,* No. 24093, November 18, 1861, leading article.— *Ed.*

has lain hidden behind the glamorous phantasmagoria of the financial prosperity of which it has been so often assured. Nay, at this very moment the *Revue des Deux Mondes* is being prosecuted for making statements with regard to the financial position of France, the only fault of which is that they are far too rosy."

The Times goes on to enquire into the causes of this collapse. During the imperialist decade France's exports have more than doubled. Agriculture has developed along with industry, and the railway system with both. The credit system, only incipient before 1848, has shot up in all directions. All these developments did not arise from any decree of the Emperor's, but from the revolutionary changes in the world market since the discovery of gold in California and Australia. Then what has caused the catastrophe?

The Times mentions the extraordinary expenditures on the army and navy, the natural fruit of Louis Bonaparte's efforts to play Napoleon in Europe. It mentions the wars, and finally the gigantic outlays on public works in order to occupy the entrepreneurs and the proletariat and keep them in good humour.

"But," it continues, "all this is insufficient to account for this frightful deficit, the largest of which the history of mankind furnishes us with an example.... To the aggressive military and naval armaments, public works, and occasional wars, has been added a *shameless and universal system of pillage*. A shower of gold has descended upon the *Empire* and its supporters. The enormous fortunes suddenly and unaccountably acquired have been the cause of scandal and wonder till scandal grew dumb and wonder weak from the frequency, indeed the universality, of the phenomenon. Modern France has taught us better to understand those passages in Juvenal's satires which treat suddenly acquired wealth as a crime against the people.[a] The splendid mansions, the brilliant equipages, the enormous wastefulness of men who till the *coup d'état* notoriously starved, have been in every one's mouth. The Court has been conducted on a scale of almost incredible wastefulness. New palaces have arisen as by the wand of an enchanter, and the splendours of the *ancien régime*[b] have been surpassed. Extravagance has had no limits but public money and public credit; the one is gone and the other shattered. *This is what ten years of Imperialism have done for France.*"

The most important question for Europe is without doubt whether the imperialist finance system *can be converted* into a constitutional finance system, as the correspondence between Louis Bonaparte and Fould contemplates.[c] What is involved here is not the momentary intentions of persons. It is the economic *conditions for the life* of the restored empire. The financial fraud

---

[a] Juvenal, *Satires*, XIV, 173-78.— *Ed.*

[b] The political and social system of France before the revolution of 1789.— *Ed.*

[c] This refers to Napoleon III's message to A. Fould and the latter's "Mémoire à l'Empereur...", published in *Le Moniteur universel*, No. 318, November 14, 1861.— *Ed.*

system could only be converted into a prosaic finance system by eliminating corruption as a general means of government; by reducing the army and navy to a peace footing, and therefore by *abandoning the Napoleonic character* of the present regime; finally, by complete renunciation of the plan followed hitherto of binding a part of the middle class and of the city proletariat to the existing government by means of great government construction projects and other public works. Would not meeting all these conditions mean: *Et propter vitam vivendi perdere causas?*[a] Is it actually believed that the modest system of Louis Philippe can be brought into being again under Napoleonic auspices? As little as that the July monarchy could be established under the *drapeau blanc.*[102]

We therefore called the *coup d'éclat* of November 14 a comedy[b] from the outset, and did not doubt for a moment that this comedy had only two aims in view: remedying the immediate difficulty and—getting through the winter. Once these two goals had been achieved, the war bugles would blow in the spring and the attempt would be undertaken to make the war pay its own way this time. It should not be forgotten that up to now—and this was a necessary consequence of a merely *simulated* Napoleonism—Decembrist France has paid for all its glory out of the French state treasury.

After a brief period of wavering, the English press has arrived at the same conclusions with respect to the *seriousness* of the November 14 promises and the *possibility* of their being carried out.

Thus, *The Times* of to-day says in the leader cited above:

"The Emperor gives up the power of originating extraordinary credits. This is exactly one of those pieces of self-denying virtue which usually precede, but seldom survive, a new French loan."

And its Stock Exchange article says:

"Whether the financial sanctity suddenly adopted at the crisis of the Treasury sickness will outlast the fit for a long time after the Exchequer has been replenished and a new loan secured, is now the question.... Public opinion, it is asserted, will force the Emperor, whether he will or not, to carry out Fould's programme. Would it not be more correct to say that every one is prepared to accept this self-delusion, while army and navy contractors and speculators firmly rely on it that in the spring, after the present danger has been weathered, the *Moniteur* will find sufficient reasons, in 'the changed circumstances of Europe', or the necessity of rectifying something that somewhere threatens French honour, the Catholic faith, or the civilisation and liberty of the human race, for a recurrence to the old financial system, which can never be permanently abandoned in any

---

[a] "And for life's sake, destroy the very basis of life" (Juvenal, *Satires*, VIII, 84).— *Ed.*

[b] See this volume, pp. 79-81.— *Ed.*

country under military dictatorship, and unpossessed of constitutional rights that are universal and inviolable?"[a]

The Economist expresses itself similarly. It concludes its analysis with the following words:

"Despite the decree, *political risk* must still be the first thought of a man who looks to his dynasty as something which any incidental failure may uproot."[b]

So far, Louis Bonaparte has only exposed Europe to dangers because he himself has been continually exposed to danger in France. Is it believed that his danger to Europe will decrease to the same extent as the danger to himself in France increases? Only if the internal danger is given time to explode.

Written on November 18, 1861

First published in *Die Presse*, No. 322, November 23, 1861

Printed according to the newspaper

Published in English for the first time

---

[a] "Money-Market and City Intelligence", *The Times*, No. 24093, November 18, 1861.— *Ed.*

[b] "The Constitutional Change in France", *The Economist*, No. 951, November 16, 1861.— *Ed.*

Karl Marx

THE DISMISSAL OF FRÉMONT[103]

Frémont's dismissal from the post of Commander-in-Chief in Missouri forms a turning point in the history of the development of the American Civil War. Frémont has two great sins to expiate. He was the first candidate of the Republican Party for the presidential office (1856), and he is the first general of the North to have threatened the slaveholders with emancipation of slaves (August 30, 1861).[a] He remains, therefore, a rival of candidates for the presidency in the future and an obstacle to the makers of compromises in the present.

During the last two decades the singular practice developed in the United States of not electing to the presidency any man who occupied an authoritative position in his own party. The names of such men, it is true, were utilised for election demonstrations, but as soon as it came to actual business, they were dropped and replaced by unknown mediocrities of merely local influence. In this manner Polk, Pierce, Buchanan, etc., became Presidents. Likewise Abraham Lincoln. General Andrew Jackson was in fact the last President of the United States who owed his office to his personal importance, whilst all his successors owed it, on the contrary, to their personal unimportance.

In the election year 1860, the most distinguished names of the Republican Party were Frémont and Seward. Known for his adventures during the Mexican War,[104] for his intrepid exploration of California and his candidacy of 1856, Frémont was too striking a figure even to come under consideration as soon as it was no longer a question of a Republican demonstration, but of a

---

^a See this volume, pp. 51-52.— *Ed.*

Republican success. He did not, therefore, stand as a candidate. It was otherwise with Seward, a Republican Senator in the Congress of Washington, Governor of the State of New York and, since the rise of the Republican Party, unquestionably its leading orator. It required a series of mortifying defeats to induce Mr. Seward to renounce his own candidacy and to give his oratorical patronage to the then more or less unknown Abraham Lincoln. As soon, however, as he saw his attempt to stand as a candidate fail, he imposed himself as a Republican Richelieu on a man whom he considered a Republican Louis XIII. He contributed towards making Lincoln President, on condition that Lincoln made him Secretary of State, an office which is in some measure comparable with that of a British Prime Minister. As a matter of fact, Lincoln was hardly President-elect, when Seward secured the Secretaryship of State. Immediately a singular change took place in the attitude of the Demosthenes of the Republican Party, whom the prophesying of the "irrepressible conflict"[a] between the system of free labour and the system of slavery had made famous.[b] Although elected on November 6, 1860, Lincoln took up office as President only on March 4, 1861. In the interval, during the winter session of Congress, Seward made himself the central figure of all attempts at compromise; the Northern organs of the South, such as the *New-York Herald,* for example, whose *bête noire* Seward had been till then, suddenly extolled him as the statesman of reconciliation and, indeed, it was not his fault that peace at any price was not achieved. Seward manifestly regarded the post of Secretary of State as a mere preliminary step, and busied himself less with the "irrepressible conflict" of the present than with the presidency of the future. He has provided fresh proof that virtuosos of the tongue are dangerously inadequate statesmen. Read his state dispatches! What a repulsive mixture of magniloquence and petty-mindedness, of simulated strength and real weakness!

For Seward, therefore, Frémont was the dangerous rival who had to be ruined; an undertaking that appeared so much the easier since Lincoln, in accordance with his legal tradition, has an aversion for all genius, anxiously clings to the letter of the Constitution and fights shy of every step that could mislead the "loyal" slaveholders of the border states. Frémont's character

---

[a] Marx gives the English phrase.— *Ed.*
[b] W. H. Seward [Speech at Rochester, October 25, 1858], *New-York Daily Tribune,* No. 5466, October 28, 1858.— *Ed.*

8*

offered another hold. He is manifestly a man of pathos, somewhat pompous and haughty, and not without a touch of the melodramatic. First the government attempted to drive him to voluntary retirement by a succession of petty chicaneries. When this did not succeed, it deprived him of his command at the very moment when the army he himself had organised came face to face with the enemy in southwest Missouri and a decisive battle was imminent.

Frémont is the idol of the states of the Northwest, which sing his praises as the "pathfinder".[a] They regard his dismissal as a personal insult. Should the Union government meet with a few more mishaps like those of Bull Run and Ball's Bluff,[105] it has itself given the opposition, which will then rise up against it and smash the hitherto prevailing diplomatic system of waging war, its leader in John Frémont. We shall return later to the indictment of the dismissed general[b] published by the War Department in Washington.

Written about November 19, 1861

First published in *Die Presse*, No. 325, November 26, 1861

Printed according to the newspaper

---

    [a] Marx uses the English word.— *Ed.*
    [b] The reference is to Brigadier General A. Thomas's report on the investigation of General Frémont's activity as Commander of the Western military area, published in the *New-York Daily Tribune*, No. 6419, October 30, 1861.— *Ed.*

Karl Marx

THE *TRENT* CASE [106]

London, November 28

The conflict of the English mail ship *Trent* with the North American warship *San Jacinto* in the narrow passage of the Old Bahama Channel is the lion among the events of the day. In the afternoon of November 27 the mail ship *La Plata* brought the news of the incident to Southampton, whence the electric telegraph at once flashed it to all parts of Great Britain. The same evening the London Stock Exchange was the stage of stormy scenes similar to those at the time of the announcement of the Italian war. Quotations for government stock sank $^3/_4$ to 1 per cent. The wildest rumours circulated in London. The American Ambassador, *Adams,* was said to have been given his passports, an embargo to have been imposed on all American ships in the Thames, etc. At the same time a protest meeting of merchants was held at the Stock Exchange in Liverpool, to demand measures from the British Government for the satisfaction of the violated honour of the British flag. Every sound-minded Englishman went to bed with the conviction that he would go to sleep in a state of peace but wake up in a state of war.

Nevertheless, the fact is well-nigh categorically established that the conflict between the *Trent* and the *San Jacinto* brings *no war* in its train. The semi-official press, like *The Times* and *The Morning Post,* strikes a peaceful note and pours juridically cool deductions on the flickerings of passion.[a] Papers like the *Daily Telegraph,* which at the faintest *mot d'ordre*[b] roar for the British

---

[a] The reference is to the leading articles "It requires a strong effort...", *The Times,* No. 24102, November 28, 1861 and "The Government of the United States has taken a step...", *The Morning Post,* No. 27440, November 28, 1861.— *Ed.*

[b] Watchword.— *Ed.*

lion, are true models of moderation. Only the Tory opposition press, *The Morning Herald* and *The Standard,* hits out. These facts force every expert to conclude that the ministry has already decided not to make a *casus belli* out of the "untoward event".[a]

It must be added that the event, if not the details of its enactment, was anticipated. On October 12, Messrs. Slidell, Confederacy emissary to France, and Mason, Confederacy emissary to England, together with their secretaries Eustis and MacFarland, had run the blockade of Charleston on the steamship *Theodora* and sailed for Havana, there to seek the opportunity of a passage to Europe under the British flag. In England their arrival was expected daily. North American warships had set out from Liverpool to intercept the gentlemen, with their dispatches, on this side of the Atlantic Ocean. The British ministry had already submitted the question whether the North Americans were entitled to take such a step to its official jurisconsults for their opinion. Their answer is said to have been in the affirmative.

The legal question turns in a narrow circle. Since the foundation of the United States, North America has adopted *British* maritime law in all its rigour. A major principle of this maritime law is that all *neutral merchantmen* are subject to *search* by the belligerent parties.

"This right," said Lord Stowell in a judgment which has become famous, "offers the sole security that no contraband is carried on neutral ships."[b]

The greatest American authority, *Kent,* states in the same sense:

"The right of self-preservation gives belligerent nations this right. The doctrine of the *English* admiralty on the right of visitation and search ... has been recognised in its fullest extent by the courts of justice in this country."[c]

It was not opposition to the right of search, as is sometimes erroneously suggested, that brought about the Anglo-American War of 1812 to 1814.[107] Rather, America declared war because England *unlawfully* presumed to search even American *warships,* on the pretext of catching deserters from the British Navy.

The *San Jacinto,* therefore, had the right to search the *Trent* and to confiscate any contraband stowed aboard her. That *dispatches* in the possession of Mason, Slidell and Co. come under

---

[a] Marx uses the English expression here and below, and gives the German translation in brackets in the first case.— *Ed.*

[b] Quoted from the leading article "It requires a strong effort...", *The Times,* No. 24102, November 28, 1861.— *Ed.*

[c] Ibidem; *The Times* quotes from J. Kent's book *Commentaries on American Law* — *Ed.*

the category of contraband even *The Times, The Morning Post,* etc., admit. There remains the question whether Messrs. Mason, Slidell and Co. were themselves contraband and might consequently be confiscated! The point is a ticklish one and differences of opinion prevail among the doctors of law. *Pratt,* the most distinguished British authority on "Contraband", in the section *"Quasi-Contraband—Dispatches, Passengers"* specifically refers to "communication of information and orders from a belligerent government to its officers abroad, or the conveyance of military passengers".[a] Messrs. Mason and Slidell, if not officers, were just as little ambassadors, since their governments are recognised neither by Britain nor by France. What are they, then? In justification of the very broad conceptions of contraband asserted by Britain in the Anglo-French wars,[108] *Jefferson* already remarks in his memoirs that contraband, by its nature, precludes any exhaustive definition and necessarily leaves great scope for arbitrariness.[b] In any event, however, one sees that from the standpoint of English law the *legal* question dwindles to a Duns Scotus controversy,[109] the explosive force of which will not go beyond exchange of diplomatic notes.

The *political* aspect of the North American procedure was estimated quite correctly by *The Times* in these words:

> "Even Mr. Seward himself must know that the voices of the Southern commissioners, sounding from their captivity, are a thousand times more eloquent in London and in Paris than they would have been if they had been heard in St. James's and the Tuileries."[c]

And is not the Confederacy already represented in London by Messrs. Yancey and Mann?

We regard this latest operation of Mr. Seward as a characteristic act of tactlessness by self-conscious weakness simulating strength. If the naval incident hastens Seward's removal from the Washington Cabinet, the United States will have no reason to record it as an "untoward event" in the annals of its Civil War.

Written on November 28, 1861

First published in *Die Presse,* No. 331, December 2, 1861

Printed according to the newspaper

---

a F. Th. Pratt, *Law of Contraband of War...,* London, 1856, pp. LIV-LV.— *Ed.*

b Th. Jefferson, *Memoirs, Correspondence, and Private Papers...,* Vol. III, London, 1829, p. 488.— *Ed.*

c "It requires a strong effort...".— *Ed.*

Karl Marx

THE ANGLO-AMERICAN CONFLICT [110]

London, November 29

The law officers of the Crown[a] had yesterday to give their opinion on the naval incident in the Bahama Channel.[b] Their records of the case consisted of the written reports of the British officers who have remained on board the *Trent* and of the oral testimony of Commodore Williams, who was on board the *Trent* as Admiralty agent, but disembarked from the steamer *La Plata* on November 27 at Southampton, whence he was immediately summoned by telegraph to London. The law officers of the Crown acknowledged the right of the *San Jacinto* to visit and search the *Trent*. Since Queen Victoria's proclamation of neutrality on the outbreak of the American Civil War[c] expressly lists *dispatches* among articles of contraband,[d] there could be no doubt on this point either. There remained, then, the question whether Messrs. Mason, Slidell and Co. were themselves contraband and therefore confiscable. The law officers of the Crown appear to hold this view, for they have dropped the *material* legal question entirely. According to the report of *The Times*,[e] their opinion blames the commander of the *San Jacinto*[f] only for an *error in procedure*. Instead of Messrs. Mason, Slidell and Co., he should have taken

---

[a] The Attorney-General and the Solicitor-General. At the time, the posts were held by R. Palmer and W. Atherton.— *Ed.*

[b] See this volume, pp. 89-91.— *Ed.*

[c] Victoria, R. *A Proclamation* [May 13, 1861], *The Times*, No. 23933, May 15, 1861.— *Ed.*

[d] See this volume, pp. 105-107.— *Ed.*

[e] "Wherever two or three men met together yesterday...", *The Times*, No. 24103, November 29, 1861, leading article.— *Ed.*

[f] Ch. Wilkes.— *Ed.*

the *Trent* herself in tow as a prize, brought her to the nearest American port and there submitted her to the judgment of a North American prize court.[111] This is incontestably the procedure corresponding to British and therefore to North American maritime law.

It is equally incontestable that the British frequently violated this rule during the anti-Jacobin war and proceeded in the summary fashion of the *San Jacinto*. However that may be, the whole conflict is reduced by this opinion of the law officers of the Crown to a *technical error* and consequently deprived of any immediate import. Two circumstances make it easy for the Union government to accept this point of view and therefore to afford formal satisfaction. In the first place, Captain Wilkes, the commander of the *San Jacinto,* could have received no direct instructions from Washington. On the voyage home from Africa to New York, he called on November 2 at Havana, which he left again on November 4, whilst his encounter with the *Trent* took place on the high seas on November 8. Captain Wilkes's stay of only two days in Havana did not permit any exchange of notes between him and his government. The consul of the Union[a] was the only American authority with whom he could deal. In the second place, however, he had obviously lost his head, as his failure to insist on the surrender of the dispatches proves.

The importance of the incident lies in its moral effect on the English people and in the political capital that can easily be made out of it by the British cotton friends of secession. Characteristic of the latter is the Liverpool protest meeting organised by them and previously mentioned by me.[b] The meeting took place on November 27 at three in the afternoon, in the cotton auction-rooms of the Liverpool Exchange, an hour after the alarming telegram from Southampton had arrived.

After vain attempts to press the chairmanship on Mr. Cunard, the owner of the Cunard steamships laying between Liverpool and New York, and other high trade officials, a young merchant named *Spence,* notorious for a work he wrote in support of the slave republic,[c] took the chair. Contrary to the rules of English meetings, he, the chairman, himself proposed the motion to

"call upon the government to assert the dignity of the British flag by requiring prompt reparation for this outrage".[d]

---

[a] Charles J. Helm.— *Ed.*
[b] See this volume, p. 89.— *Ed.*
[c] J. Spence, *The American Union...*, London, 1861.— *Ed.*
[d] "Liverpool, Wednesday", *The Times*, No. 24102, November 28, 1861.— *Ed.*

Tremendous applause, clapping and cheers upon cheers! The main argument of the opening speaker for the slave republic was that slave ships had hitherto been protected by the American flag from the right of search claimed by Britain. And then this philanthropist launched a furious attack on the slave trade! He admitted that England had brought about the war of 1812-14 with the United States by insisting on searching Union warships for deserters from the British Navy.

"But," he continued with wonderful dialectic, "there is a difference between the right of search to recover deserters from the British Navy and the right to seize passengers, like Mr. Mason and Mr. Slidell, men of the highest respectability, regardless of the fact that they were protected by the British flag!"

He played his highest trump, however, at the close of his diatribe.

"The other day," he bellowed, "while I was on the European Continent, I heard observations made as to our conduct in regard to the United States which made me blush. What is the feeling of every intelligent man upon the Continent? That we would slavishly submit to any outrage and suffer every indignity offered to us by the Government of the United States. What could I reply to this? I could only blush. But the pitcher goes so often to the well that it is broken at last. Our patience had been exercised long enough—as long as it was possible to control it. At last we have arrived at facts [!]: this is a very hard and startling fact [!] and it is the duty of every Englishman to apprise the Government of how strong and unanimous is the feeling of this great community of the outrage offered to our flag."

This senseless rigmarole was greeted with a peal of applause. Opposing voices were howled down and hissed down and stamped down. To the remark of a Mr. Campbell that the whole meeting was "irregular", the inexorable Spence replied: "So may it be, but the fact that we have met to consider is rather an irregular fact." To the proposal of a Mr. Turner to adjourn the meeting to the following day, in order that "the city of Liverpool can have its say and not a clique of cotton brokers usurp its name", cries of "Collar him, throw him out!" resounded from all sides. Unperturbed, Mr. Turner repeated his motion, which, however, was not put to the vote, again contrary to all the rules of English meetings. Spence triumphed. But, as a matter of fact, nothing has done more to cool London's temper than the news of Mr. Spence's triumph.

Written on November 29, 1861   Printed   according   to   the   news-
                                           paper
First published in *Die Presse*, No. 332,
December 3, 1861

Karl Marx

THE NEWS AND ITS EFFECT IN LONDON

London, Nov. 30, 1861

Since the declaration of war against Russia I never witnessed an excitement throughout all the strata of English society equal to that produced by the news of the *Trent* affair, conveyed to Southampton by the *La Plata* on the 27th inst. At about 2 o'clock p.m., by means of the electric telegraph, the announcement of the "untoward event" was posted in the news-rooms of all the British Exchanges. All commercial securities went down, while the price of saltpeter went up. Consols declined $^3/_4$ per cent, while at Lloyds[112] war risks of five guineas were demanded on vessels from New-York. Late in the evening the wildest rumors circulated in London, to the effect that the American Minister[a] had forthwith been sent his passports, that orders had been issued for the immediate seizure of all American ships in the ports of the United Kingdom, and so forth. The cotton friends of Secession at Liverpool improved the opportunity for holding, at ten minutes' notice, in the cotton salesroom of the Stock Exchange, an indignation meeting, under the presidency of Mr. Spence, the author of some obscure pamphlet in the interest of the Southern Confederacy.[b] Commodore Williams, the Admiralty Agent on board the *Trent,* who had arrived with the *La Plata,* was at once summoned to London.

On the following day, the 28th of November, the London press exhibited, on the whole, a tone of moderation strangely contrasting with the tremendous political and mercantile excitement of the previous evening. The Palmerston papers, *Times, Morning Post,*

---

[a] Ch. Adams.— *Ed.*
[b] J. Spence, *The American Union...*, London, 1861.— *Ed.*

Daily Telegraph, Morning Advertiser, and *Sun,* had received orders to calm down rather than to exasperate. *The Daily News,* by its strictures on the conduct of the *San Jacinto,* evidently aimed less at hitting the Federal Government than clearing itself of the suspicion of "Yankee prejudices," while *The Morning Star,* John Bright's organ, without passing any judgment on the policy and wisdom of the "act," pleaded its lawfulness. There were only two exceptions to the general tenor of the London press. The Tory-scribblers of *The Morning Herald* and *The Standard,* forming in fact one paper under different names, gave full vent to their savage satisfaction of having at last caught the "republicans" in a trap, and finding a *casus belli,* ready cut out. They were supported by but one other journal, *The Morning Chronicle,* which for years had tried to prolong its checkered existence by alternately selling itself to the poisoner Palmer and the Tuileries.[113] The excitement on the Exchange greatly subsided in consequence of the pacific tone of the leading London papers. On the same 28th of Nov., Commander Williams attended at the Admiralty, and reported the circumstances of the occurrence in the old Bahama Channel. His report, together with the written depositions of the officers on board the *Trent,* were at once submitted to the law officers of the Crown,[a] whose opinion, late in the evening, was officially brought under the notice of Lord Palmerston, Earl Russell and other members of the Government.

On the 29th of November there was to be remarked some slight change in the tone of the ministerial press. It became known that the law officers of the Crown, on a technical ground, had declared the proceedings of the frigate *San Jacinto illegal,* and that later in the day, the Cabinet, summoned to a general council, had decided to send by next steamer to Lord Lyons instructions to conform to the opinion of the English law officers. Hence the excitement in the principal places of business, such as the Stock Exchange, Lloyd's, the Jerusalem, the Baltic,[114] etc., set in with redoubled force, and was further stimulated by the news that the projected shipments to America of saltpeter had been stopped on the previous day, and that on the 29th a general order was received at the Custom-House prohibiting the exportation of this article to any country except under certain stringent conditions. The English funds further fell $^3/_4$, and at one time a real panic prevailed in all the stock markets, it having become impossible to transact any business in some securities, while in all descriptions a

---

a R. Palmer and W. Atherton.— *Ed.*

severe depression of prices occurred. In the afternoon a recovery in the stock market was due to several rumors, but principally to the report that Mr. Adams had expressed his opinion that the act of the *San Jacinto* would be disavowed by the Washington Cabinet. On the 30th of November (to-day) all the London papers, with the single exception of *The Morning Star*, put the alternative of reparation by the Washington Cabinet or—*war*.

Having summed up the history of the events from the arrival of the *La Plata* to the present day, I shall now proceed to recording opinions. There were, of course, two points to be considered—on the one hand the law, on the other hand the policy, of the seizure of the Southern Commissioners[a] on board an English mail steamer.

As to the legal aspect of the affair, the first difficulty mooted by the Tory press and *The Morning Chronicle* was that the United States had never recognized the Southern Secessionists as belligerents, and, consequently, could not claim belligerent rights in regard to them.

This quibble was at once disposed of by the Ministerial press itself.

"We," said *The Times*, "have already recognized these Confederate States as a belligerent power, and we shall, when the time comes, recognize their Government. Therefore we have imposed on ourselves all the duties and inconveniences of a power neutral between two belligerents."[b]

Hence, whether or not the United States recognize the Confederates as belligerents, they have the right to insist upon England submitting to all the duties and inconveniences of a neutral in maritime warfare.

Consequently, with the exceptions mentioned, the whole London press acknowledges the right of the *San Jacinto* to overhaul, visit, and search the *Trent*, in order to ascertain whether she carried goods or persons belonging to the category of "contraband of war." *The Times's* insinuation that the English law of decisions[115] "was given *under circumstances very different from* those which now occur;" that "steamers did not then exist," and mail vessels, "carrying letters wherein all the nations of the world have immediate interest, were unknown;" that "we (the English) were *fighting for existence*, and did in those days *what we should not* allow others to do," was not seriously thrown out. Palmerston's private

---

[a] J. Mason and J. Slidell.— *Ed.*
[b] "It requires a strong effort...", *The Times*, No. 24102, November 28, 1861, leading article.— *Ed.*

Moniteur, *The Morning Post,* declared on the same day that mail
steamers were simple merchantmen, not sharing the exemption
from the right of search of men-of-war and transports.[a] The *right
of search,* on the part of the *San Jacinto,* was in point of fact,
conceded by the London press as well as the law officers of the
Crown. The objection that the *Trent,* instead of sailing from a
belligerent to a belligerent port, was, on the contrary, bound from
a neutral to a neutral port, fell to the ground by Lord Stowell's
decision that the right of search is intended to ascertain the
destination of a ship.[b]

In the second instance, the question arose whether by firing a
round shot across the bows of the *Trent,* and subsequently
throwing a shell, bursting close to her, the *San Jacinto* had not
violated the usages and courtesies appurtenant to the exercise of
the right of visitation and search. It was generally conceded by the
London press that, since the details of the event have till now been
only ascertained by the depositions of one of the parties
concerned, no such minor question could influence the decision to
be arrived at by the British Government.

The right of search, exercised by the *San Jacinto,* thus being
conceded, what had she to look for? For *contraband of war,*
presumed to be conveyed by the *Trent.* What is contraband of
war? Are the *dispatches* of a belligerent Government contraband of
war? Are the *persons* carrying those dispatches contraband of war?
And, both questions being answered in the affirmative, do those
dispatches and the bearers of them continue to be contraband of
war, if found on a merchant ship bound from a neutral port to a
neutral port? The London press admits that the decisions of the
highest legal authorities on both sides of the Atlantic are so
contradictory, and may be claimed with such appearance of justice
for both the affirmative and the negative, that, at all events, a
prima facie[c] case is made out for the *San Jacinto.*

Concurrently with this prevalent opinion of the English press,
the English Crown lawyers have altogether dropped the material
question, and only taken up the formal question. They assert that
the law of nations was not violated in *substance,* but in *form* only.
They have arrived at the conclusion that the *San Jacinto* failed in
seizing, on her own responsibility, the Southern Commissioners,

---

    [a] "The Government of the United States has taken a step...", *The Morning Post,*
No. 27440, November 28, 1861.— *Ed.*

    [b] "It requires a strong effort...".— *Ed.*

    [c] Plausible.— *Ed.*

instead of taking the *Trent* to a Federal port and submitting the question to a Federal Prize-Court, no armed cruiser having a right to make himself a Judge at sea. A violation in the *procedure* of the San Jacinto is, therefore, all that is imputed to her by the English Crown lawyers, who, in my opinion, are right in their conclusion. It might be easy to unearth precedents, showing England to have similarly trespassed on the formalities of maritime law; but violations of law can never be allowed to supplant the law itself.

The question may now be mooted, whether the reparation demanded by the English Government—that is, the restitution of the Southern Commissioners—be warranted by an injury which the English themselves avow to be of *form* rather than of *substance?* A lawyer of the Temple,[116] in the to-day's *Times,* remarks, in respect to this point:

"If the case is not so clearly in our favor as that a decision in the American Court condemning the vessel would have been liable to be questioned by us as manifestly contrary to the laws of nations, then the irregularity of the American Captain[a] in allowing the *Trent* to proceed to Southampton, clearly redounded to the advantage of the British owners and the British passengers. Could we in such a case find a ground of international quarrel in an error of procedure which in effect told in our own favor?"[b]

Still, if the American Government must concede, as it seems to me, that Capt. Wilkes has committed a violation of maritime law, whether formal or material, their fair fame and their interest ought alike to prevent them from nibbling at the terms of the satisfaction to be given to the injured party. They ought to remember that they do the work of the Secessionists in embroiling the United States in a war with England, that such a war would be a godsend to Louis Bonaparte in his present difficulties, and would, consequently, be supported by all the official weight of France; and, lastly, that, what with the actual force under the command of the British on the North American and West Indian stations, what with the forces of the Mexican Expedition,[c] the English Government would have at its disposal an overwhelming maritime power.

As to the policy of the seizure in the Bahama Channel, the voice not only of the English but of the European press is unanimous in expressions of bewilderment at the strange conduct of the

---

[a] Ch. Wilkes.— *Ed.*

[b] Justitia, "To the Editor of *The Times*", *The Times,* No. 24104, November 30, 1861.— *Ed.*

[c] See pp. 71-78 of this volume.— *Ed.*

American Government, provoking such tremendous international dangers, for gaining the bodies of Messrs. Mason, Slidell & Co., while Messrs. Yancey and Mann are strutting in London. *The Times* is certainly right in saying:

"Even Mr. Seward himself must know that the voices of these Southern Commissioners, sounding from their captivity, are a thousand times more eloquent in London and in Paris than they would have been if they had been heard at St. James's and the Tuileries." [a]

The people of the United States having magnanimously submitted to a curtailment of their own liberties in order to save their country, will certainly be no less ready to turn the tide of popular opinion in England by openly avowing, and carefully making up for, an international blunder the vindication of which might realize the boldest hopes of the rebels.

Written on November 30, 1861   Reproduced from the newspaper

First published in the *New-York Daily Tribune*, No. 6462, December 19, 1861

---

[a] "It requires a strong effort...", *The Times*, No. 24102, November 28, 1861, leading article.— *Ed.*

Karl Marx

THE PRINCIPAL ACTORS IN THE *TRENT* DRAMA [117]

London, December 4

At the present moment it is of interest to get acquainted in some measure with the leading figures in the *Trent* drama. On one side stands the active hero, Captain *Wilkes,* the commander of the *San Jacinto;* on the other, the passive heroes, *J. M. Mason* and *John Slidell.* Captain Charles Wilkes is a direct descendant of the brother of the celebrated English demagogue, [John] Wilkes, who threatened for a moment to shake the throne of George III.[118] The struggle with the North American colonies saved the Hanoverian dynasty at that time from the outbreak of an English revolution, symptoms of which were alike perceptible in the cry of a Wilkes and the letters of a Junius. Captain Wilkes, born in New York in 1798, forty-three years in the service of the American navy, commanded the squadron that from 1838 to 1842 explored the North and South Pacific Ocean by order of the Union government. He has published a report on this expedition in five volumes.[a] He is also the author of a work on *Western America,* which contains some valuable information on California and the Oregon district.[b] It is now certain that Wilkes improvised his *coup de main*[c] independently and without instructions from Washington.

The two intercepted commissioners of the Southern Confederacy—Messrs. *Mason* and *Slidell*—form a contrast in every respect. *Mason,* born in 1798, is descended from one of those old

---

[a] Ch. Wilkes, *Narrative of the United States Exploring Expedition...,* Vols. I-V, Philadelphia, 1845.— *Ed.*

[b] Ch. Wilkes, *Western America, including California and Oregon...,* Philadelphia, 1849.— *Ed.*

[c] An impetuous and unexpected attack.— *Ed.*

aristocratic families of Virginia that fled from England after the Royalists had been defeated at the battle of Worcester.[119] The grandsire of our hero[a] belongs to the circle of men who, along with Washington, Jefferson, etc., are designated by the Americans as "the revolutionary fathers".[b] John Slidell is neither, like Mason, of aristocratic lineage, nor, like his colleague, a slaveholder by birth. His native town is New York, where his grandfather and his father lived as honest tallow-chandlers.[c] Mason, after he had occupied himself for some years with the study of law, stepped on the political stage. He figured repeatedly since 1826 as a member of the House of Representatives of Virginia; made his appearance in 1837 in the House of Representatives of the American Congress for a session; but his importance only dates from 1847. In that year Virginia elected him to the American Senate, in which he held his seat until the spring of 1861. Slidell, who is now sixty-eight years old, was obliged to leave New York as a young man in consequence of adultery and a duel, in short, of a scandal. He betook himself to New Orleans, where he lived first by gambling, later by practising law. Having become first a member of the legislature of Louisiana, he soon made his way to the House of Representatives and finally to the Senate of the American Congress. As a director of election rogueries during the presidential election of 1844 and, later, as a participant in a swindle in state lands, he had even somewhat shocked the sort of morals that prevail in Louisiana.

Mason inherited influence; Slidell acquired it. The two men found and supplemented each other in the American Senate, the bulwark of the slave oligarchy. In accordance with the American Constitution, the Senate elects a special Committee of Foreign Relations, which plays about the same role as the Privy Council[d] [120] formerly played in England, before the so-called Cabinet, a quantity theoretically unknown to the English Constitution, usurped the Privy Council's functions. Mason was for a long time chairman of this committee; Slidell, a prominent member of it.

Mason, firmly convinced that every Virginian is a demi-god and every Yankee a plebeian rascal, never sought to conceal his contempt for his Northern colleagues. Haughty, overbearing,

---

[a] G. Mason.— Ed.

[b] Marx uses the English expression and gives the German translation in parenthesis.— Ed.

[c] Marx uses the English words "tallow-chandlers" and gives the German translation in parenthesis.— Ed.

[d] Marx gives the English name in brackets after its German equivalent.— Ed.

insolent, he knew how to knit his brows in a somber, Zeus-like frown and in fact transported to the Senate the manners native to the plantation. A fanatical eulogist of slavery, a shameless slanderer of the North and particularly of the Northern working class, a blusterer against England, Mason wearied the Senate with the prolix importunity of a persistent flow of speech that vainly sought to hide its complete vacuity under a hollow pomp. As a sort of demonstration, he went around in recent years in Virginian home-made gray linen; but, and this is characteristic of the man, the gray coat was adorned with loud buttons, all of which came from a state of New England, from Connecticut.

Whilst Mason played the *Jupiter Tonans*[a] of the slave oligarchy on the proscenium, Slidell worked behind the scenes. With a rare talent for intrigue, tireless perseverance and an unscrupulous lack of regard, but at the same time wary, covert, never strutting, but always insinuating himself, Slidell was the soul of the Southern conspiratorial conclave. One may judge the man's repute from the fact that when in 1845, shortly before the outbreak of war with Mexico, he was sent there as Ambassador, Mexico refused to treat with such an individual.[121] Slidell's intrigues made Polk President. He was one of the most pernicious counsellors of President Pierce and the evil genius of Buchanan's administration. The two, Mason and Slidell, were the chief sponsors of the law on runaway slaves[122]; they brought about the bloodbath in Kansas,[123] and both were wirepullers for the measures whereby Buchanan's administration smuggled all the means to secession into the hands of the South, whilst it left the North defenceless.[124]

As early as 1855 Mason declared on a public occasion in South Carolina that "for the South only one way lies open—immediate, absolute and eternal separation".[b] In March 1861 he declared in the Senate that "he owed the Union government no *allegiance*",[c] but retained his seat in the Senate and continued to draw his senatorial salary as long as the safety of his person allowed—a spy in the supreme council of the nation and a fraudulent parasite on the public exchequer.

Mason's great-grandmother was a daughter of the celebrated Sir William Temple. He is therefore a distant relative of Palmerston.

---

[a] Jupiter the thunderer.— *Ed.*

[b] J. M. Mason [Statement urging the separation of the South], *New-York Times,* October 14, 1856.— *Ed.*

[c] J. M. Mason [Speech in the Senate on March 11, 1861], *The New-York Daily Tribune,* No. 6202, March 12, 1861. In quoting, Marx uses the English word "allegiance" and gives the translation in brackets.— *Ed.*

Mason and Slidell appeared to the people of the North not merely as their political opponents, but as their *personal enemies*. Hence the general jubilation over their capture, which in its first days even overwhelmed regard for the danger threatening from England.

Written on December 4, 1861

First published in *Die Presse*, No. 337, December 8, 1861

Printed according to the newspaper

Karl Marx

[CONTROVERSY OVER THE *TRENT* CASE] [125]

London, December 7

The Palmerston press—and on another occasion I will show that in foreign affairs Palmerston's control over nine-tenths of the English press is just as *absolute* as Louis Bonaparte's over nine-tenths of the French press[a]—the Palmerston press feels that it works among "pleasing hindrances".[b] On the one hand, it admits that the law officers of the Crown[c] have reduced the accusation against the United States to a *mere mistake in procedure*, to a *technical error*. On the other hand, it boasts that on the basis of such a legal quibble a *compelling ultimatum* has been presented to the United States, such as can only be justified by a gross violation of law, but not by a formal error in the exercise of a recognised right. Accordingly, the Palmerston press now pleads the question of *material* right again. The great importance of the case appears to demand a brief examination of the question of *material* right.

By way of introduction, it may be observed that not a single English paper ventures to reproach the *San Jacinto* for the visitation and search of the *Trent*. This point, therefore, falls outside the controversy.

First, we again call to mind the relevant passage in Queen Victoria's proclamation of neutrality of May 13, 1861. The passage reads:

"*Victoria R.*

"As we are at peace with the United States ... we warn all our beloved subjects ... to abstain from contravening our Proclamation ... by breaking the legally

---

[a] See this volume, pp. 127-30.— *Ed.*
[b] Heinrich Heine, "Neuer Frühling", Prolog.— *Ed.*
[c] R. Palmer and W. Atherton.— *Ed.*

recognised blockade or by *carrying officers* ... *dispatches* ... or any other contraband of war. All persons so offending will be liable to the various penalties imposed in that behalf by the English municipal law and by the law of nations.... Such persons will in no way receive our *protection* against the consequences of their conduct but will, on the contrary, incur our displeasure."[a]

This proclamation of Queen Victoria, therefore, in the first place declares *dispatches* to be contraband and makes the ship that carries such contraband liable to the "penalties of the law of nations". What are these penalties?

Wheaton, an American writer on international law whose authority is recognised on both sides of the Atlantic Ocean alike, says in his *Elements of International Law,* p. 565[b]:

"The carrying of dispatches of the enemy subjects the *neutral* vessel in which they are transported to *capture* and *confiscation.* The consequences of such a service are infinitely beyond the effect of conveying ordinary contraband.... As Sir W. Scott, the *English* judge, says, the carrying of military stores is necessarily of limited nature, while the carrying of dispatches is an act that may defeat the entire plan of campaign of the other belligerent.... The confiscation of the noxious article, which constitutes the usual penalty for contraband, would be ridiculous when applied to dispatches. There would be no freight dependent on their transportation. Therefore, their confiscation does not affect the shipowner and hence does not punish the ship carrying them. The vehicle, in which they are carried, must, therefore, be *confiscated.*"

Walker, in his *Introduction to American Law,* says:

"Neutrals may not be concerned in bearing *hostile dispatches,* under the penalty of confiscation of the vehicle, and of the cargo also."

Kent, who is accounted a decisive authority in English courts, states in his *Commentaries:*

"If, on search of a ship, it is found that she carries *enemy dispatches,* she incurs the penalty of capture and of confiscation by judgment of a prize court."

Dr. Robert Phillimore, Advocate of Her Majesty in Her Office of Admiralty,[c] says in his latest work on international law, p. 370:

"Official communications from an official person[d] on the affairs of a belligerent Government are such *dispatches* as impress an hostile character upon the carriers of them. The mischievous consequences of such a service cannot be estimated, and extend far beyond the effect of any Contraband that can be conveyed, for it is manifest that by the carriage of such dispatches the most important plans of a

---

a Here and below Marx quotes from the article "The Capture of Mason and Slidell", *New-York Daily Tribune,* No. 6435, November 18, 1861.— *Ed.*

b Here and below Marx gives the English titles of the books and the German translation in brackets.— *Ed.*

c Marx gives the English designation and supplies the German translation in brackets.— *Ed.*

d Marx gives the English words "official" and, below, "carriers" in brackets after their German equivalents.— *Ed.*

Belligerent may be forwarded or obstructed.... The penalty is confiscation of the ship which conveys the dispatches and of the cargo."[a]

Two points are therefore established. Queen Victoria's proclamation of May 13, 1861, subjects *English* ships that carry dispatches of the Confederacy to the penalties of international law. International law, according to its English and American interpreters, imposes the *penalty* of capture and confiscation on such ships.

Palmerston's organs consequently *lied* on orders from above—and we were naive enough to believe their lie—in affirming that the captain of the *San Jacinto* had neglected to seek for *dispatches* on the *Trent* and therefore had of course found none; and that the *Trent* had consequently become shot-proof through this oversight. The American journals of November 17 to 20, which *could not* yet have been aware of the English lie, *unanimously* state, on the contrary, that the dispatches *had been seized* and were already in print for submission to Congress in Washington. This changes the whole state of affairs. Because of these dispatches, the *San Jacinto* had the right to take the *Trent* in tow and every American prize court had the duty to confiscate her and her cargo. With the *Trent*, her passengers also naturally came within the pale of American jurisdiction.

Messrs. Mason, Slidell and Co., as soon as the *Trent* had touched at Monroe, came under American jurisdiction as rebels. If, therefore, instead of towing the *Trent* herself to an American port, the captain of the *San Jacinto* contented himself with seizing the dispatches and their bearers, he in no way worsened the position of Mason, Slidell and Co., whilst, on the other hand, his *error in procedure* benefited the *Trent,* her cargo and her passengers. And it would be indeed unprecedented if Britain wished to declare war on the United States because Captain Wilkes committed an *error in procedure* harmful to the United States, but profitable to Britain.

The question whether Mason, Slidell and Co. were themselves contraband, was only raised and could only be raised because the Palmerston journals had broadcast the *lie* that Captain Wilkes had neither searched for dispatches, nor seized dispatches. For in this case Mason, Slidell and Co. in fact constituted the sole objects on the ship *Trent* that could possibly fall under the category of contraband. Let us, however, disregard this aspect for the moment. Queen Victoria's proclamation designates *"officers"*[b] of a belligerent party as contraband. Are *"officers"* merely military

---

- [a] R. Phillimore, *Commentaries upon International Law.*— *Ed.*
- [b] Here and further on Marx uses the English word.— *Ed.*

officers? Were Mason, Slidell and Co. *"officers"* of the Confederacy? *"Officers,"* says *Samuel Johnson* in his dictionary of the English language, are "men employed by the public",[a] that is, in German: *öffentliche Beamte. Walker* gives the same definition. (See his dictionary, 1861 edition.)

According to the usage of the English language, therefore, Mason, Slidell and Co., these emissaries, *id est,* officials of the Confederacy, come under the category of "officers", whom the royal proclamation declares to be *contraband.* The *Trent* captain *knew* them in this capacity and therefore rendered himself, his ship and his passengers confiscable. If, according to Phillimore and all other authorities, a ship becomes confiscable as the carrier[b] of an enemy dispatch because it violates neutrality, in a still higher degree is this true of the *person* who carries the dispatches. According to *Wheaton,* even an enemy *ambassador,* so long as he is *in transitu,* may be intercepted. In general, however, the basis of all international law is that any member of the belligerent party may be regarded and treated as "belligerent" by the opposing party.

"So long as a man," says *Vattel,* "continues to be a citizen of his own country, he is the enemy of all those with whom his nation is at war."[c]

One sees, therefore, that the law officers of the English Crown reduced the point of contention to a mere *error in procedure,* not an error *in re,*[d] but an error *in forma,*[e] because, actually, no *violation of material right* is to hand. The Palmerston organs chatter about the question of material right again because a mere error in procedure, *in the interest of the "Trent"* at that, gives no plausible pretext for a haughty-toned ultimatum.

Meanwhile, important voices have been raised in this sense from diametrically opposite sides: on the one side, Messrs. *Bright* and *Cobden;* on the other, *David Urquhart.* These men are enemies on grounds of principle and personally: the first two, peaceable cosmopolitans; the third, the *"last of the Englishmen"*[126]; the former always ready to sacrifice all international law to international trade; the other hesitating not a moment: *"Fiat justitia, pereat mundus",*[f] and by "justice" he understands "English" justice. The

---

[a] Marx gives the definition in English.— *Ed.*
[b] Marx uses the English word and gives the German translation in brackets.— *Ed.*
[c] E. de Vattel, *Le Droit des gens...,* Tome II, livre III, chapitre V, § 71.— *Ed.*
[d] In substance.— *Ed.*
[e] In form.— *Ed.*
[f] Let justice be done, though the world perish.— *Ed.*

voices of *Bright* and *Cobden* are important because they represent a powerful section of middle-class interests and are represented in the ministry by Gladstone, Milner Gibson and also, more or less, by Sir Cornewall Lewis. The voice of Urquhart is important because international law is his life-study and everyone recognises him as an *incorruptible* interpreter of this international law.

The usual newspaper sources will communicate Bright's speech in support of the United States and Cobden's letter, which is conceived in the same sense.[a] Therefore I will not dwell on them.

Urquhart's organ, *The Free Press*, states in its latest issue, published on December 4:

> "'We must bombard New York!' Such were the frantic sounds which met the ears of every one who traversed the streets of London on the evening of this day week, on the arrival of the intelligence of a trifling warlike incident. The act was one which, *in every war*, England has committed *as a matter of course*—namely, the seizure on board of a neutral of the persons and property of her enemies."

The Free Press further argues that, in 1856 at the Congress of Paris, Palmerston, without any authority from the Crown or Parliament, sacrificed English maritime law *in the interest of Russia*, and then says:

> "In order to justify this sacrifice, Palmerston's organs stated at that time that if we *maintained the right of visitation and search*, we should assuredly be *involved in a war with the United States* on the occasion of the first war in Europe. And now he calls on us through the same organs of public opinion to bombard New York because the United States act on those laws which are theirs no less than our own."[b]

With regard to the utterances of the "organs of public opinion", *The Free Press* remarks:

> "The bray of Baron Munchausen's thawing post-horn was nothing to the clangour of the British press on the capture of Messrs. Mason and Slidell."[c]

Then humorously, it places side by side, in "strophe" and "antistrophe", the contradictions by which the English press seeks to convict the United States of a "breach of law".

Written on December 7, 1861

First published in *Die Presse*, No. 340, December 11, 1861

Printed according to the newspaper

---

[a] J. Bright's speech and R. Cobden's letter were reported in the note, "Mr. Bright on America", *The Times*, No. 24109, December 6, 1861.—*Ed.*

[b] Here and above Marx quotes from the article, "'We must bombard New York!' Such were...", *The Free Press*, No. 12, December 4, 1861.—*Ed.*

[c] "'Public Opinion' on the *San Jacinto* Affair", *The Free Press*, same issue.—*Ed.*

Karl Marx

PROGRESS OF FEELING IN ENGLAND

London, Dec. 7, 1861

The friends of the United States on this side of the Atlantic anxiously hope that conciliatory steps will be taken by the Federal Government. They do so not from a concurrence in the frantic crowing of the British press over a war incident, which, according to the English Crown lawyers themselves, resolves itself into a mere error of procedure, and may be summed up in the words that there has been a breach of international law, because Capt. Wilkes, instead of taking the *Trent,* her cargo, her passengers, and the Commissioners,[a] did only take the Commissioners. Nor springs the anxiety of the well-wishers of the Great Republic from an apprehension lest, in the long run, it should not prove able to cope with England, although backed by the civil war; and, least of all, do they expect the United States to abdicate, even for a moment, and in a dark hour of trial, the proud position held by them in the council of nations. The motives that prompt them are of quite a different nature.

In the first instance, the business next in hand for the United States is to crush the rebellion and to restore the Union. The wish uppermost in the minds of the Slaveocracy and their Northern tools was always to plunge the United States into a war with England. The first step of England as soon as hostilities broke out would be to recognize the Southern Confederacy, and the second to terminate the blockade. Secondly, no general, if not forced, will accept battle at the time and under the conditions chosen by his enemy.

---

[a] J. Mason and J. Slidell.— *Ed.*

"A war with America," says *The Economist,* a paper deeply in Palmerston's confidence, "must always be one of the most lamentable incidents in the history of England; but if it is to happen, *the present is certainly the period at which it will do us the minimum of harm, and the only moment* in our *joint annals at which it would confer on us an incidental and partial compensation.*" a

The very reasons accounting for the eagerness of England to seize upon any decent pretext for war at this "only moment" ought to withhold the United States from forwarding such a pretext at this "only moment." You go not to war with the aim to do your enemy *"the minimum of harm,"* and, even to confer upon him by the war, *"an incidental and partial compensation."* The opportunity of the moment would all be on one side, on the side of your foe. Is there any great strain of reasoning wanted to prove that an internal war raging in a State is the least opportune time for entering upon a foreign war? At every other moment the mercantile classes of Great Britain would have looked upon a war against the United States with the utmost horror. Now, on the contrary, a large and influential party of the mercantile community has for months been urging on the Government to violently break the blockade, and thus provide the main branch of British industry with its raw material. The fear of a curtailment of the English export trade to the United States has lost its sting by the curtailment of that trade having already actually occurred. "They" (the Northern States), says *The Economist,* "are wretched customers, instead of good ones." The vast credit usually given by English commerce to the United States, principally by the acceptance of bills drawn from China and India, has been already reduced to scarcely a fifth of what it was in 1857. Last, not least, Decembrist France, bankrupt, paralyzed at home, beset with difficulty abroad, pounces upon an Anglo-American war as a real godsend, and, in order to buy English support in Europe, will strain all her power to support "Perfidious Albion" on the other side of the Atlantic. Read only the French newspapers. The pitch of indignation to which they have wrought themselves in their tender care for the "honor of England," their fierce diatribes as to the necessity on the part of England to revenge the outrage on the Union Jack, their vile denunciations of everything American, would be truly appalling, if they were not ridiculous and disgusting at the same time. Lastly, if the United States give way in this instance, they will not derogate one iota of their dignity. England has reduced her complaint to a mere *error of procedure, a technical blunder* of which

---

a "The Effect of an American War upon English Commerce", *The Economist,* No. 954, December 7, 1861.— *Ed.*

she has made herself systematically guilty in all her maritime wars, but against which the United States have never ceased to protest, and which President Madison, in his message inaugurating the war of 1812,[a] expatiated upon as one of the most shocking breaches of international law. If the United States may be defended in paying England with her own coin, will they be accused for magnanimously disavowing, on the part of a single American captain,[b] acting on his own responsibility, what they always denounced as a systematic usurpation on the part of the British Navy! In point of fact, the gain of such a procedure would be all on the American side. England, on the one hand, would have acknowledged the right of the United States to capture and bring to adjudication before an American prize court every English ship employed in the service of the Confederation. On the other hand, she would, once for all, before the eyes of the whole world, have practically resigned a claim which she was not brought to desist from either in the peace of Ghent, in 1814,[c] or the transactions carried on between Lord Ashburton and Secretary Webster in 1842.[127] The question then comes to this: Do you prefer to turn the "untoward event" to your own account, or, blinded by the passions of the moment, turn it to the account of your foes at home and abroad?

Since this day week, when I sent you my last letter,[d] British consols have again lowered, the decline, compared with last Friday, amounting to 2 per cent, the present prices being $89^3/_4$ to $^7/_8$ for money and 90 to $90^1/_8$ for the new account on the 9th of January. This quotation corresponds to the quotation of the British consols during the first two years of the Anglo-Russian war.[e] This decline is altogether due to the warlike interpretation put upon the American papers conveyed by the last mail, to the exacerbating tone of the London press, whose moderation of two days' standing was but a feint, ordered by Palmerston, to the dispatch of troops for Canada, to the proclamation forbidding the export of arms and materials for gunpowder[f] and lastly, to the

----

[a] J. Madison, *To the Senate and House of Representatives of the United States* [Washington, June 1, 1812].— *Ed.*

[b] Ch. Wilkes.— *Ed.*

[c] *A Treaty of Peace and Amity between his Britannic Majesty and the United States of America; signed at Ghent, December 24, 1814.*— *Ed.*

[d] See this volume, pp. 95-100.— *Ed.*

[e] The Crimean War of 1853-56.—*Ed.*

[f] Victoria, R., *A Proclamation* [December 4, 1861], *The Times*, No. 24108, December 5, 1861.— *Ed.*

daily ostentatious statements concerning the formidable preparations for war in the docks and maritime arsenals.

Of one thing you may be sure, Palmerston wants a legal pretext for a war with the United States, but meets in the Cabinet councils with a most determinate opposition on the part of Messrs. Gladstone and Milner Gibson, and, to a less degree, of Sir Cornwall Lewis. "The noble viscount" is backed by Russell, an abject tool in his hands, and the whole Whig Coterie. If the Washington Cabinet should furnish the desired pretext, the present Cabinet will be sprung, to be supplanted by a Tory Administration. The preliminary steps for such a change of scenery have been already settled between Palmerston and Disraeli. Hence the furious war-cry of *The Morning Herald* and *The Standard,* those hungry wolves howling at the prospect of the long-missed crumbs from the public almoner.

Palmerston's designs may be shown up by calling into memory a few facts. It was he who insisted upon the proclamation, acknowledging the Secessionists as belligerents, on the morning of the 14th of May, after he had been informed by telegraph from Liverpool that Mr. Adams would arrive at London on the night of the 13th May. He, after a severe struggle with his colleagues, dispatched 3,000 men to Canada, an army ridiculous, if intended to cover a frontier of 1,500 miles, but a clever sleight-of-hand if the rebellion was to be cheered, and the Union to be irritated. He, many weeks ago, urged Bonaparte to propose a joint armed intervention "in the internecine struggle," supported that project in the Cabinet council, and failed only in carrying it by the resistance of his colleagues. He and Bonaparte then resorted to the Mexican intervention as a *pis aller.*[a] That operation served two purposes, by provoking just resentment on the part of the Americans, and by simultaneously furnishing a pretext for the dispatch of a squadron, ready, as *The Morning Post* has it, "to perform whatever duty the hostile conduct of the Government of Washington may require us to perform in the waters of the Northern Atlantic."[b] At the time when that expedition was started, *The Morning Post,* together with *The Times* and the smaller fry of Palmerston's press slaves, said that it was a very fine thing, and a philanthropic thing into the bargain, because it would expose the slaveholding Confederation to two fires—the Anti-

---

[a] The last means.— *Ed.*

[b] "We are glad to be able to inform our readers...", *The Morning Post,* No. 27442, November 30, 1861.— *Ed.*

Slavery North and the Anti-Slavery force of England and France. And what says the very same *Morning Post,* this curious compound of Jenkins and Rhodomonte, of plush and swash, in its to-day's issue, on occasion of Jefferson Davis's address?[a] Hearken to the Palmerston oracle:

"We must look to this intervention as one that may be in operation during a considerable period of time; and while the Northern Government is too distant to admit of its attitude entering materially into this question, the Southern Confederation, on the other hand, stretches for a great distance along the frontier of Mexico, so as to render its friendly disposition to the authors of the insurrection of no slight consequence. The Northern Government has invariably railed at our neutrality, but the Southern with statesmanship and moderation has recognized in it all that we could do for either party; and whether with a view to our transactions in Mexico, or to our relations with the Cabinet at Washington, the *friendly forbearance* of the Southern Confederacy is an important point in our favor."[b]

I may remark that the *Nord* of December 3—a Russian paper, and consequently a paper initiated into Palmerston's designs— insinuates that the Mexican expedition was from the first set on foot, not for its ostensible purpose, but for a war against the United States.[c]

Gen. Scott's letter had produced such a beneficent reaction in public opinion, and even on the London Stock Exchange, that the conspirators of Downing street and the Tuileries[128] found it necessary to let loose the *Patrie,* stating with all the airs of knowledge derived from official sources that the seizure of the Southern Commissioners from the *Trent* was directly authorized by the Washington Cabinet.

Written on December 7, 1861   Reproduced from the newspaper

First published in the *New-York Daily Tribune,* No. 6467, December 25, 1861

---

[a] J. Davis, "*To the Congress of the Confederate States.* Richmond, Nov. 18, 1861", *New-York Daily Tribune,* No. 6441, November 25, 1861.— *Ed.*

[b] "The principal intelligence conveyed by the Edinburgh...", *The Morning Post,* No. 27448, December 7, 1861.— *Ed.*

[c] "Résumé politique", *Le Nord,* No. 337, December 3, 1861.— *Ed.*

Karl Marx

THE CRISIS OVER THE SLAVERY ISSUE [129]

London, December 10

The United States has evidently entered a critical stage with regard to the *slavery question,* the question underlying the whole Civil War. General Frémont has been dismissed for declaring the slaves of *rebels* free.[a] A directive to General Sherman, the commander of the expedition to South Carolina, was a little later published by the Washington Government, which goes further than Frémont, for it decrees that fugitive slaves even of *loyal* slave-owners should be welcomed and employed as workers and paid a wage, and under certain circumstances armed, and consoles the "loyal" owners with the prospect of receiving compensation later.[b] Colonel Cochrane has gone even further than Frémont, he demands the arming of all slaves as a military measure.[c] The Secretary of War Cameron publicly approves of Cochrane's "views".[d] The Secretary of the Interior,[e] on behalf of the government, then repudiates the Secretary of War. The Secretary of War expresses his "views" even more emphatically at a public meeting stating that he will vindicate these views in his report to Congress.[f] General Halleck, Frémont's successor in Missouri, and General Dix in east Virginia have driven fugitive Negroes from their military camps and forbidden them to appear in future in the vicinity of the positions held by their armies. General Wool at the same time has received the black "contraband" with open

---

[a] See this volume, pp. 86-88. Frémont's proclamation was published in the *New-York Daily Tribune,* No. 6366, September 1, 1861.— *Ed.*

[b] The directive was discussed in the item "Instructions to Gen. Sherman", *New-York Daily Tribune,* No. 6445, November 29, 1861.— *Ed.*

[c] Cochrane's message to soldiers, *New-York Daily Tribune,* No. 6433, November 15, 1861.— *Ed.*

[d] Cameron's speech to soldiers, *New-York Daily Tribune,* same issue.— *Ed.*

[e] C. B. Smith.— *Ed.*

[f] The Smith-Cameron polemic was discussed in a report from Washington and published in *The Times,* No. 24111, December 9, 1861.— *Ed.*

arms at Fort Monroe.[130] The old leaders of the *Democratic* Party,
Senator Dickinson and Croswell (a former member of the so-called
Democratic regency[131]), have published open letters in which they
express their agreement with Cochrane and Cameron,[a] and
Colonel *Jennison* in Kansas has surpassed all his military predecessors by an address to his troops which contains the following
passage:

> "No temporising with rebels and those sympathising with them.... I have told
> General Frémont that I would not have drawn my sword had I thought that slavery
> would outlast this struggle. The slaves of rebels will always find protection in this
> camp and we will defend them to the last man and the last bullet. I want no men
> who are *not Abolitionists,*[b] I have no use for them and I hope that there are no such
> people among us, for everyone knows that slavery is the basis, the centre and the
> vertex of this infernal war.... Should the government disapprove of my action it can
> take back my patent, but in that case I shall act on my own hook even if in the
> beginning I can only count on six men."[c]

The slavery question is being solved in practice in the border
slave states even now, especially in *Missouri* and to a lesser extent
in Kentucky, etc. A large-scale dispersal of slaves is taking place.
For instance 50,000 slaves have disappeared from Missouri, some
of them have run away, others have been transported by the
slave-owners to the more distant southern states.

It is rather strange that a most important and significant event is
not mentioned in any English newspaper. On November 18,
delegates from 45 North Carolina counties met on Hatteras
Island, appointed a provisional government, revoked the Ordinance of Secession and proclaimed that North Carolina was
returning to the Union. The counties of North Carolina represented at this convention have been called together to elect their
Representatives to Congress at Washington.[d]

Written on December 10, 1861

First published in *Die Presse*, No. 343,
December 14, 1861

Printed according to the newspaper

---

[a] Croswell's letter in the *New-York Daily Tribune*, No. 6441, November 25,
1861. In a postscript to it Dickinson declared himself in agreement with
Croswell.— *Ed.*

[b] Marx gives the beginning of this sentence in English in brackets, after the
German equivalent. In the same manner he gives the phrase "on my own hook"
further in this paragraph.— *Ed.*

[c] Jennison's address was reproduced in the item "Camp Jennison. Kansas City,
Tuesday, Nov. 12, 1861", *New-York Daily Tribune*, No. 6441, November 25,
1861.— *Ed.*

[d] These events were reported in the item "Hatteras Inlet, N.C., Nov. 18, 1861",
New-York Daily Tribune, No. 6438, November 21, 1861.— *Ed.*

Karl Marx

AMERICAN MATTERS

London, December 13

The news of the fate of the *Harvey Birch* and the visit of the cruiser *Nashville* in Southampton harbour reached New York on November 29, but does not seem to have provoked the sensation that was every bit as expected in certain circles here as it was feared in others, hostile to the war.[132] This time, one wave broke on another. For New York was stirred up by the campaign for the election of the Mayor on December 3. The Washington correspondent of *The Times*, Mr. Russell, who spoils his Celtic talent by affecting English ways, pretends to shrug his shoulders in wonder at this excitement over the mayoral election.[a] Of course, Mr. Russell is flattering the illusion of the London cockney that the election of the Mayor in New York is the same kind of old-fashioned tomfoolery as the election of a Lord Mayor in London. It is well known that the Lord Mayor of London has nothing to do with the greater part of London. He is the nominal ruler of the City, a story-book character who strives to prove his reality by producing good turtle soups at banquets and bad judgments in cases of violation of police regulations. A Lord Mayor of London is a government figure only in the imagination of Paris writers of vaudeville and *faits divers*.[b] The Mayor of New York, on the contrary, is a real power. At the beginning of the secession movement the then Mayor, the notorious *Fernando Wood*, was on the point of proclaiming New York an independent city republic,[133] in collusion, of course, with Jefferson Davis. His plan

---

[a] [W. H. Russell] "Washington, Nov. 29", *The Times*, No. 24115, December 13, 1861.— *Ed.*

[b] Local news items.— *Ed.*

foundered owing to the energy of the Republican Party of the Empire City.[134]

On November 27, Charles Sumner of Massachusetts, a member of the American Senate, where he had been beaten with a stick by a Southern senator[a] at the time of the Kansas affair,[135] delivered a brilliant speech before a large meeting in Cooper Union[136] in New York on the origin and secret motives of the slaveholder rebellion.[b] After his speech the meeting adopted the following resolution:

"The doctrine enunciated by General Frémont, with respect to the emancipation of the slaves of rebels, and the more recent utterances of General Burnside, Senator Wilson,[c] George Bancroft (the famous historian), Colonel Cochrane and Simon Cameron, foreshadowing the eventual rooting out of slavery as the cause of the rebellion, indicate a moral, political, and military necessity. In the judgment of this meeting, the public sentiment of the North is now fully in sympathy with any practicable scheme which may be presented for the extirpation of this national evil, and it regards such a result as the only consistent issue of this contest between civilisation and barbarism."[d]

The *New-York Tribune* comments, in particular, on Sumner's address:

"The allusion of Mr. Sumner to the coming discussions of Congress on the subject of slavery will kindle a hope that that body will at last understand where Southern weakness and Northern strength really lie, and will seize the instrumentality by which alone the rebellion is to be brought to a speedy and final extirpation."[e]

A private letter from *Mexico* states among other things:

"The English ambassador[f] pretends to be a warm friend of the administration of President Juárez. Persons well acquainted with the Spanish intrigues assure us that General Marquez has been instructed by Spain to bring the scattered forces of the Clerical party together again, its Mexican as well as Spanish elements. This party is then to take advantage of the opportunity soon to be offered to beg Her Catholic Majesty[g] to provide a king for the Mexican throne. An uncle of the

---

[a] P. S. Brooks.— *Ed.*

[b] Sumner's speech was published in the *New-York Daily Tribune*, No. 6444, November 28, 1861.— *Ed.*

[c] Presumably Henry Wilson.— *Ed.*

[d] "The Sentiment of the Cooper Institute Meeting Last Night", *New-York Daily Tribune*, No. 6444, November 28, 1861.— *Ed.*

[e] "It is certainly an indicative and important fact...", *New-York Daily Tribune*, same issue, leading article.— *Ed.*

[f] Th. Murphy.— *Ed.*

[g] Isabella II.— *Ed.*

Queen [a] is said to have been selected for the position already. As he is an old man, he would soon leave the stage in the natural course of events, and since any clause concerning the nomination of his successor is to be avoided, Mexico would thus revert to Spain—so that the same policy would triumph in Mexico as in Haiti."[137]

Written on December 13, 1861

First published in *Die Presse,* No. 346, December 17, 1861

Printed according to the newspaper

Published in English for the first time

---

[a] Francisco de Paula Antonio de Borbón.— *Ed.*

10*

Karl Marx

A SLANDER TRIAL

London, December 19

The ancient Egyptians are known to have developed the *division of labour* to a high degree, so far as it extended to the whole of society and not to the individual workshop. With them almost every particular part of the body had its own special physician, whose therapy was confined by law to this particular region. Theft was the occupation of a special trade, the head of which was an officially recognised person. But how inadequate the ancient Egyptian division of labour appears when compared to that of modern England! The strange nature of some trades in London amazes us no less than the extent to which they are carried on.

One of these curious industries is *espionage*. It divides into two big branches, *civil* espionage and *political* espionage. We leave the latter entirely out of account here. Civil espionage is again broken down into two large subdivisions— *official* and *private* espionage.

The *official* sort is carried on, on the one hand, by detectives, who are paid either by the government or the municipal authorities, and on the other hand, by common informers, who spy on their own and are paid by jobwork[a] by the police.

The business of private espionage breaks down into many subtypes, which may be united under two major headings. One comprises *non-commercial* private relations, the other *commercial*. Under the first heading, in which espionage on marital infidelity plays an important part, the establishment of *Mr. Field* has won European fame. The business of *commercial* espionage will be better understood from the following incident.

Last Tuesday[b] the Court of Exchequer [138] dealt with a suit for

---

[a] Marx uses the English words "detectives", "common informers" and "jobwork" and gives the German translation in brackets.— *Ed.*

[b] December 17.— *Ed.*

slander, in which a local weekly paper, *Lloyd's Weekly News,* was the defendant and Stubbs and Comp. the plaintiff. Stubbs and Comp. publish a weekly under the title of *Stubbs' Gazette,* the organ of *Stubbs' Trade Protection Company.* The paper is sent privately to subscribers, who pay 3 guineas a year, but is not sold by single copies, as other newspapers are, in stationers'[a] shops, on the street, at railway stations, and so on. Actually, it is a proscription list of bad debtors, whatever their position in life. Stubbs' "Protection Company" spies out the solvency of private individuals, *Stubbs' Gazette* records them in black and white. The number of subscribers runs to 20,000.

Well, *Lloyd's Weekly News* had published an article in which the following statement appeared: "It is the duty of every honourable man to put an end to this disgraceful system of *espionage.*" Stubbs demanded judicial revenge for this slander.

After the attorney for the plaintiff, Serjeant Shee, had poured out the stream of his Irish eloquence, the plaintiff Stubbs underwent a cross examination[b] (in effect, the cross fire to which the witnesses are subjected during the hearing) by Serjeant Ballantine, the attorney for *Lloyd's Weekly News.* The following comical dialogue ensued.[c]

Ballantine: "Do you ask your subscribers for information?"

Stubbs: "I invite the subscribers to send me the names of persons they consider to be swindlers. We then investigate these cases. I do not investigate them myself. I have agents in London and other large cities. I have 9 or 10 agents in London, who get a yearly salary."

Ballantine: "What do these gentlemen receive for hunting out information?"

Stubbs: "From 150 to 200 pounds sterling."

Ballantine: "And a new suit? Well, when one of these well-paid gentlemen catches a swindler, what happens then?"

"We publish his name."

Ballantine: "When he is a thorough swindler?"

"Yes."

"But if he is only half a swindler?"

"Then we enter it in our register."

---

[a] Marx uses the English word.— *Ed.*
[b] Marx uses the English words "serjeant", "cross examination" and, below, "solicitor".— *Ed.*
[c] Marx draws on a report published in *The Times,* No. 24119, December 18, 1861.— *Ed.*

"Until he is in full bloom, and then you publish it?"

"Yes."

"Do you publish autographs of swindlers?"

"Yes."

"And you go to even greater expense for the benefit of trade. You publish photographs of swindlers?"

"Yes."

"Do you not have a secret police agency? Are you not connected with Mr. Field?"

"I am glad to be able to say No!"

"What is the difference?"

"I decline to answer that."

"What do you mean by your 'legal agents'?"

"That concerns collection of debts. I mean by it solicitors (something between attorney and bailiff) who take care of subscribers' business according to the conditions stated in the prospectus."

"So, you are a collector of debts, too?"

"I collect debts through 700 solicitors."

"Good Lord, you have 700 solicitors, and the world still exists! Do you keep the solicitors or do the solicitors keep you?"

"They keep themselves."

"Have you had other court cases?"

"Yes, half a dozen."

"Did you ever contest them?"

"Yes."

"Was the decision ever in your favour?"

"Once."

"What do you mean by the heading in your paper, 'Addresses Wanted', followed by a long list of names?"

"Absconding debtors whose whereabouts neither we nor our subscribers could trace."

"How is your business organised?"

"Our central office is in London, with branch offices in Birmingham, Glasgow, Edinburgh and Dublin. My father left me the business. He carried it on in Manchester originally."

Attorney Ballantine in his plea pounced mercilessly on Stubbs, whose "smiling and self-complacent attitude during his testimony proved at any rate that he had no more idea than a dung-beetle of the filth of the material he moved in". English trade must have sunk deep indeed, if it needed such a protector. This unworthy spy system would give Stubbs a fearful weapon for extortion, etc.

The Lord Chief Baron,[139] who was sitting as judge,[a] threw his summing-up into the balance for the defence. He concluded with the words:

"The jury owe much to the freedom of the press; but juries are not independent because the press is free, but the press is free because the juries are independent. You must consider whether the incriminated article goes beyond the bounds of honest criticism. Stubbs is a public character and as such is subject to criticism. Should you believe that *Lloyd's Weekly News* has gone beyond the bounds of honest criticism, then it is up to you to award the plaintiff *appropriate* damages."

The jurors withdrew to the jury room to deliberate. After debating for a quarter of an hour they reappeared in the courtroom with the verdict: Plaintiff Stubbs is in the right; damages for his wounded honour — *one farthing.* The farthing is the smallest English coin, corresponding to the French centime and the German pfennig. Stubbs left Guildhall amidst the loud laughter of the large audience, escorted by a number of admirers, from whose urgent ovations only speedy flight could save his modest dignity.

Written on December 19, 1861

First published in *Die Presse*, No. 353, December 24, 1861

Printed according to the newspaper

Published in English for the first time

---

[a] J. F. Pollock, the Chief Justice of the Court of Exchequer. Marx gives the English title: "Lord Chief Baron".— *Ed.*

Karl Marx

THE WASHINGTON CABINET
AND THE WESTERN POWERS [140]

One of the most striking surprises of a war so rich in surprises as the Anglo-French-Turkish-Russian [a] was incontestably the declaration on maritime law agreed at Paris in the spring of 1856.[141] When the war against Russia began, England suspended her most formidable weapons against Russia: confiscation of enemy-owned goods on neutral ships and privateering. At the conclusion of the war, England broke these weapons in pieces and sacrificed the fragments on the altar of peace. Russia, the ostensibly vanquished party, received a concession that, by a series of "armed neutralities",[142] wars and diplomatic intrigues, she had tried in vain to extort since Catherine II. England, the ostensible victor, renounced, on the other hand, the great means of attack and defence that had grown up out of her sea power and that she had maintained for a century and a half against a world in arms.

The humanitarian grounds that served as a pretext for the Declaration of 1856 vanish before the most superficial examination. Privateering is no greater *barbarism* than the action of volunteer corps or guerillas in land warfare. The privateers are the guerillas of the sea. Confiscation of the private goods of a belligerent nation also occurs in land warfare. Do military requisitions, for example, hit only the cash-box of the enemy government and not the property of private persons also? The nature of land warfare safeguards enemy possessions that are on neutral soil, therefore under the sovereignty of a neutral power. The nature of sea warfare obliterates these barriers, since the sea,

---

[a] The Crimean War.— *Ed.*

as the common highway of the nations, cannot fall to the sovereignty of any neutral power.

As a matter of fact, however, the Declaration of 1856 veils under its philanthropic phrases a great inhumanity. In principle it transforms war from a war of peoples into a war of governments. It endows property with an inviolability that it denies to persons. It emancipates trade from the terrors of war and thereby makes the classes carrying on trade and industry callous to the terrors of war. For the rest, it is self-understood that the humanitarian pretexts of the Declaration of 1856 were only addressed to the European gallery, just like the religious pretexts of the Holy Alliance.

It is a well-known fact that Lord *Clarendon,* who signed away Britain's maritime rights at the Congress of Paris, acted, as he subsequently confessed in the Upper House, without the fore-knowledge or instructions of the Crown. His sole authority consisted in a *private letter* from Palmerston. Up to the present Palmerston has not dared to demand the sanction of the British Parliament for the Declaration of Paris and its signature by Clarendon. Apart from the debates on the contents of the Declaration, there was fear of debates on the Constitutional question whether, independently of Crown and Parliament, a British minister might usurp the right to sweep away the old basis of English sea power with a stroke of the pen. That this ministerial *coup d'état* did not lead to stormy interpellations, but, rather, was silently accepted as a *fait accompli,* Palmerston owed to the influence of the Manchester school.[143] It found to be in accordance with the interests represented by it, and therefore also with philanthropy, civilisation and progress, an innovation which would allow English commerce to continue to pursue its business with the enemy undisturbed on neutral ships, whilst sailors and soldiers fought for the honour of the nation. The Manchester men were jubilant over the fact that by an unconstitutional *coup de main* the minister had bound England to international concessions whose attainment in the constitutional parliamentary way was wholly improbable. Hence the present indignation of the Manchester party in England over the disclosures of the Blue Book submitted by Seward to the Congress in Washington!

As is known, the United States was the only great power that refused to accede to the Paris Declaration of 1856. If they had renounced privateering, then they would have to create a great state navy. Any weakening of their means of war at sea simultaneously threatened them with the dreadful prospect of having to maintain a standing land army on the European scale. Nevertheless, President Buchanan stated that he was ready to accept the Declaration of Paris provided that the same inviolability would be assured to all property, enemy or neutral, found on ships, with the exception of contraband of war. His proposal was rejected. From Seward's Blue Book it now appears that Lincoln, immediately after his assumption of office, offered England and France the adhesion of the United States to the Declaration of Paris, so far as it abolishes privateering, on condition that the prohibition of privateering should be extended to the parts of the United States in revolt, that is, the Southern Confederacy. The answer that he received amounted in practice to recognition of the belligerent rights of the Southern Confederacy.[a]

"Humanity, progress and civilisation" whispered to the Cabinets of St. James's and the Tuileries that the prohibition of privateering would extraordinarily reduce the chances of secession and therefore of dissolution of the United States. The Confederacy was therefore recognised in all haste as a belligerent party, in order afterwards to reply to the Cabinet at Washington that England and France could naturally not recognise the proposal of one belligerent party as a binding law for the other belligerent party. The same "noble uprightness" inspired all the diplomatic negotiations of England and France with the Union government since the outbreak of the Civil War, and had the *San Jacinto* not held up the *Trent* in the Bahama Channel, any other incident would have sufficed to provide a pretext for the conflict that Lord Palmerston aimed at.

Written about December 20, 1861   Printed according to the news-
                                          paper
First published in *Die Presse*, No. 354,
December 25, 1861

---

[a] The reference is to Queen Victoria's proclamation of neutrality of May 13, 1861 (see this volume, pp. 92).— *Ed.*

Karl Marx

THE OPINION OF THE NEWSPAPERS
AND THE OPINION OF THE PEOPLE [144]

London, December 25

Continental politicians, who imagine that in the London press they possess a thermometer for the temper of the English people, inevitably draw false conclusions at the present moment. With the first news of the *Trent* case the English national pride flared up and the call for war with the United States resounded from almost all sections of society.[a] The London press, on the other hand, affected moderation and even *The Times* doubted whether a *casus belli* existed at all.[b] Whence this phenomenon? Palmerston was uncertain whether the Crown lawyers were in a position to contrive any legal pretext for war. For, a week and a half before the arrival of the *La Plata* at Southampton, agents of the Southern Confederacy had turned to the English Cabinet from Liverpool, denounced the intention of American cruisers to put out from *English* ports and intercept Messrs. Mason, Slidell, etc., on the high seas, and demanded the intervention of the English government. In accordance with the opinion of its Crown lawyers, the latter refused the request. Hence, in the beginning, the peaceful and moderate tone of the London press in contrast to the warlike impatience of the people. So soon, however, as the Crown lawyers—the Attorney-General and the Solicitor-General,[c] both themselves members of the Cabinet[d]—had worked out a *technical* pretext for a quarrel with the United States, the relationship

---

a See this volume, pp. 89-94.— *Ed.*
b The reference is to the article "It requires a strong effort...", *The Times,* No. 24102, November 28, 1861.— *Ed.*
c Marx gives the titles in English.— *Ed.*
d W. Atherton and R. Palmer.— *Ed.*

between the people and the press turned into its opposite. The war fever increased in the press in the same measure as the war fever abated in the people. At the present moment a war with America is just as unpopular with all sections of the English people, the friends of cotton and the country squires excepted, as the war-howl in the press is overwhelming.

But now, consider the London press! At its head stands *The Times,* whose leading editor, *Bob Lowe,* was formerly a demagogue in Australia, where he agitated for separation from England. He is a subordinate member of the Cabinet, a kind of minister for education, and a mere creature of Palmerston. *Punch* is the court jester of *The Times* and transforms its *sesquipedalia verba*[a] into flat jokes and spiritless caricatures. A principal editor of *Punch* was accommodated by Palmerston with a seat on the Board of Health[b] and an annual salary of a thousand pounds sterling.

The *Morning Post* is in part Palmerston's private property. Another part of this singular institution is sold to the French Embassy. The rest belongs to the *haute volée*[c] and supplies the most precise reports for court flunkeys and ladies' tailors. Among the English people the *Morning Post* is accordingly notorious as the *Jenkins* (the stock figure for the lackey) of the press.

The *Morning Advertiser* is the joint property of the "licensed victuallers",[d] that is, of the public houses, which, besides beer, may also sell spirits. It is, further, the organ of the English *Pietists*[145] and ditto of the sporting characters, that is, of the people who make a business of horse-racing, betting, boxing and the like. The editor of this paper, Mr. *Grant,* previously employed as a stenographer by the newspapers and quite uneducated in a literary sense, has had the honour to get invited to Palmerston's private *soirées.* Since then he has been enthusiastic for the "truly English minister"[146] whom, on the outbreak of the Russian war, he had denounced as a "Russian agent". It must be added that the pious patrons of this liquor-journal stand under the ruling rod of the Earl of Shaftesbury and that Shaftesbury is Palmerston's son-in-law. Shaftesbury is the pope of the Low Churchmen,[147] who

---

a Words of a foot and a half long (Horace, *Art of Poetry,* 97).— *Ed.*
b Marx uses the English name and gives the German translation in brackets.— *Ed.*
c High society.— *Ed.*
d Here and below Marx uses the English expressions "licensed victuallers", "sporting characters", "Low Churchmen", "truly English minister" (he translates the last phrase into German in brackets).— *Ed.*

blend the *spiritus sanctus*[a] with the profane spirit of the honest *Advertiser*.

The *Morning Chronicle! Quantum mutatus ab illo!*[b] For well-nigh half a century the great organ of the Whig Party and the not unfortunate rival of *The Times*, its star paled after the Whig war.[148] It went through metamorphoses of all sorts, turned itself into a penny paper[c] and sought to live by "sensations",[149] thus, for example, by taking the side of the poisoner, *Palmer*. It subsequently sold itself to the French Embassy, which, however, soon regretted throwing away its money. It then threw itself into anti-Bonapartism, but with no better success. Finally, it found the long missing buyer in Messrs. Yancey and Mann—the agents of the Southern Confederacy in London.

The *Daily Telegraph* is the private property of a certain *Levy*. His paper is stigmatised by the English press itself as *Palmerston's* mob paper. Besides this function it conducts a *chronique scandaleuse*.[d] It is characteristic of this *Telegraph* that, on the arrival of the news about the *Trent*, by *ordre* from above it declared *war to be impossible*. In the dignity and moderation dictated to it, it seemed so strange to itself that since then it has published half-a-dozen articles about this instance of moderation and dignity displayed by it. As soon, however, as the *ordre* to change its line reached it, the *Telegraph* has sought to compensate itself for the constraint put upon it by outbawling all its comrades in howling loudly for war.

The *Globe* is the ministerial evening paper which receives official subsidies from all Whig ministries.

The Tory papers, *The Morning Herald* and *The Evening Standard*, both belonging to the same *boutique*, are governed by a double motive: on the one hand, hereditary hate for "the *revolted* English colonies"[e]; on the other hand, a chronic ebb in their finances. They know that a war with America must shatter the present coalition Cabinet and pave the way for a Tory Cabinet. With the Tory Cabinet official subsidies for *The Herald* and *The Standard* would return. Accordingly, hungry wolves cannot howl louder for prey than these Tory papers for an American war with its ensuing shower of gold!

---

[a] Holy Spirit.— *Ed.*

[b] How changed from what he once was! (Virgil, *Aeneid*, II, 274).— *Ed.*

[c] Marx uses the English expression "penny paper" and, below, "mob paper", the latter with the German translation in brackets.— *Ed.*

[d] Chronicle of scandal.— *Ed.*

[e] An allusion to the leading article "Let those who believe...", *The Times*, No. 24122, December 21, 1861.— *Ed.*

Of the London daily press, *The Daily News* and *The Morning Star* are the only papers left that are worth mentioning; both work counter to the trumpeters of war. *The Daily News* is restricted in its movement by a connection with Lord John Russell; *The Morning Star* (the organ of Bright and Cobden) is diminished in its influence by its character as a "peace-at-any-price paper".

Most of the London weekly papers are mere echoes of the daily press, therefore overwhelmingly warlike. *The Observer* is in the ministry's pay. *The Saturday Review* strives for *ésprit* and believes it has attained it by affecting a cynical elevation above "humanitarian" prejudices.[a] To show *"ésprit"*, the corrupt lawyers, parsons and schoolmasters that write this paper have smirked their approbation of the slaveholders since the outbreak of the American Civil War. Naturally, they subsequently blew the war-trumpet with *The Times*. They are already drawing up plans of campaign against the United States displaying a hair-raising ignorance.

The Spectator, The Examiner and, particularly, *MacMillan's Magazine* must be mentioned as more or less respectable exceptions.

One sees: On the whole, the London press—with the exception of the cotton organs, the provincial papers form a commendable contrast—represents nothing but Palmerston and again Palmerston. Palmerston wants war; the English people don't want it. Imminent events will show who will win in this duel, Palmerston or the people. In any case, he is playing a more dangerous game than Louis Bonaparte at the beginning of 1859.[150]

Written on December 25, 1861

First published in *Die Presse*, No. 359, December 31, 1861

Printed according to the newspaper

---

[a] An allusion to the article "Unblessed Peacemakers", *The Saturday Review*, No. 320, December 14, 1861.— *Ed.*

Karl Marx

FRENCH NEWS HUMBUG.—
ECONOMIC CONSEQUENCES OF WAR [151]

London, December 31

The belief in miracles seems to be withdrawn from one sphere only in order to settle in another. If it is driven out of nature, it now rises up in politics. At least, that is the view of the Paris newspapers and their confederates in the telegraph agencies and the newspaper-correspondence shops. Thus, Paris evening papers of yesterday announce: Lord Lyons has stated to Mr. Seward that he will wait until the evening of December 20, but then depart for London, in the event of the Cabinet at Washington refusing to surrender the prisoners.[a] Therefore, the Paris papers already knew *yesterday* the steps that Lord Lyons took *after* receiving the dispatches transmitted to him on the *Europa*. Up to *today*, however, news of the arrival of the *Europa* in New York has not yet reached Europe. The *Patrie* and its associates, *before* they are informed of the arrival of the *Europa* in America, publish in Europe news of the events that ensued on the heels of the *Europa*'s arrival in the United States. The *Patrie* and its associates manifestly believe that legerdemain requires no magic. One journal over here remarks in its stock exchange article that these Paris inventions, quite like the provocatory articles in some English papers, serve not only the political speculations of certain persons in power, but just as much the *stock exchange speculations* of certain private individuals.

---

[a] J. Mason and J. Slidell. Marx cites the statement according to *The Times*, No. 24130, December 31, 1861.— *Ed.*

The Economist, hitherto one of the loudest bawlers of the war party, publishes in its last number a *letter from a Liverpool merchant* and a leading article in which the English public is warned not on any account to underestimate the dangers of a war with the United States.[a] England imported grain worth £15,380,901 during 1861; of the whole amount nearly £6,000,000 fell to the United States.[b] England would suffer more from the inability to buy American grain than the United States would suffer from the inability to sell it. The United States would have the advantage of *prior information.* If they decided for war, then telegrams would fly forthwith from Washington to San Francisco, and the American ships in the Pacific Ocean and the China seas would commence war operations many weeks before England could bring the news of the war to India.

Since the outbreak of the Civil War the American-Chinese trade, and the American-Australian trade quite as much, has diminished to an enormous extent. So far, however, as it is still carried on, it buys its cargoes in most cases with English letters of credit, therefore with English capital. English trade from India, China and Australia, always very considerable, has, on the contrary, grown still more since the interruption of the trade with the United States. American privateers would therefore have a great field for privateering; English privateers, a relatively insignificant one. English investments of capital in the United States are greater than the whole of the capital invested in the English cotton industry. American investments of capital in England are nil. The English navy eclipses the American, but not nearly to the same extent as during the war of 1812 to 1814.[152]

If at that time the American privateers already showed themselves far superior to the English, then how about them now? An effective blockade of the North American ports, particularly in winter, is quite out of the question. In the inland waters between Canada and the United States—and superiority here is decisive for the land warfare in Canada—the United States would, with the opening of the war, hold absolute sway.

In short, the Liverpool merchant comes to the conclusion:

"Nobody in England dares to recommend war for the sake of mere cotton. It would be cheaper for us to feed the whole of the cotton districts for three years at

---

a "The Mercantile Realities of an American War", signed "A Liverpool Merchant", and the article "Operation of a War with America on England" published in *The Economist,* No. 957, December 28, 1861.— *Ed.*

b "The Board of Trade Tables", *The Economist,* same issue.— *Ed.*

state expense than to wage war with the United States on their behalf for one year."

Ceterum censeo[a] that the *Trent* case will not lead to war.

Written on December 31, 1861

First published in *Die Presse*, No. 4, January 4, 1862

Printed according to the newspaper

---

[a] "Ceterum censeo Carthaginem esse delendam" ("By the way, I believe that Carthage should be destroyed", Plutarch, *Life of Cato the Elder*)—the words with which Cato, Roman soldier and statesman (234-149 B.C.) usually concluded, refrain-like, his speeches in the Senate. Here the phrase means, roughly: "I repeat".— *Ed.*

Karl Marx

A PRO-AMERICA MEETING [153]

London, January 1

The anti-war movement among the *English people* gains from day to day in energy and extent. Public meetings in the most diverse parts of the country insist on settlement *by arbitration* of the dispute between England and America. Memoranda in this sense rain on the chief of the Cabinet,[a] and the independent *provincial press* is almost unanimous in its opposition to the war-cry of the London press.

Subjoined is a detailed report of the meeting held last Monday[b] in *Brighton*, since it emanated from the working class, and the two principal speakers, Messrs. *Coningham* and *White*, are influential members of Parliament who both sit on the *ministerial* side of the House.

Mr. *Wood* (a worker) proposed the first motion, to the effect

"that the dispute between England and America arose out of a misinterpretation of international law, but not out of an intentional insult to the British flag; that accordingly this meeting is of the opinion that the whole question in dispute should be referred to a neutral power for decision by arbitration; that under the existing circumstances a war with America is not justifiable, but rather merits the condemnation of the English people".

In support of his motion Mr. Wood, among other things, remarked:

"It is said that this new insult is merely the last link in a chain of insults that America has offered to England. Suppose this to be true, what would it prove in regard to the cry for war at the present moment? It would prove that so long as America was undivided and strong, we submitted quietly to her insults; but now, in

---

[a] H. J. Palmerston.— *Ed.*
[b] December 30, 1861.— *Ed.*

the hour of her peril, we take advantage of a position favourable to us, to revenge the insult. Would not such a procedure brand us as cowards in the eyes of the civilised world?"

Mr. *Coningham:*

"...At this moment there is developing in the midst of the Union an avowed *policy of emancipation (Applause),* and I express the earnest hope that no intervention on the part of the English government will be permitted *(Applause)....* Will you, freeborn Englishmen, allow yourselves to be embroiled in an anti-republican war? For that is the intention of *The Times* and of the party that stands behind it.... I appeal to the workers of England, who have the greatest interest in the preservation of peace, to raise their voices and, in case of need, their hands for the prevention of so great a crime *(Loud applause)...* The Times* has exerted every endeavour to excite the warlike spirit of the land and by bitter scorn and slanders to engender a hostile mood among the Americans.... I do not belong to the so-called peace party.[154] *The Times* favoured the policy of Russia and put forth (in 1853) all its powers to mislead our country into looking on calmly at the military encroachments of Russian barbarism in the East. I was amongst those who raised their voices against this false policy. At the time of the introduction of the *Conspiracy Bill,* whose object was to facilitate the extradition of political refugees, no expenditure of effort seemed too great to *The Times,* to force this Bill through the Lower House. I was one of the 99 members of the House who withstood this encroachment on the liberties of the English people and brought about the minister's downfall [155] *(applause).* This minister is now at the head of the Cabinet. I prophesy to him that should he seek to embroil our country in a war with America without good and sufficient reasons, his plan will fail ignominiously. I promise him a fresh ignominious defeat, a worse defeat than was his lot on the occasion of the Conspiracy Bill *(Loud applause)....* I do not know the official communication that has gone to Washington; but the opinion prevails that the Crown lawyers[a] have recommended the government to take its stand on the quite narrow legal ground that the Southern commissioners might not be seized without the ship that carried them. Consequently the handing over of Slidell and Mason is to be demanded as the *conditio sine qua non.*

"Suppose the people on the other side of the Atlantic Ocean does not permit its government to hand them over. Will you go to war for the bodies of these two envoys of the slavedrivers?... There exists in this country an anti-republican war party. Remember the last Russian war. From the secret dispatches published in Petersburg it was clear beyond all doubt that the articles published by *The Times* in 1855 were written by a person who had access to the secret Russian state papers and documents. At that time Mr. Layard read the striking passages in the Lower House,[b] and *The Times,* in its consternation, immediately changed its tone and blew the war-trumpet next morning[c]... *The Times* has repeatedly attacked the Emperor Napoleon and supported our government in its demand for unlimited credits for land fortifications and floating batteries. Having done this and raised the alarm cry against France, does *The Times* now wish to leave our coast exposed to the French emperor by embroiling our country in a trans-Atlantic war...? It is to be feared that

---

[a] W. Atherton and R. Palmer.— *Ed.*

[b] A. H. Layard [Speech in the House of Commons on March 31, 1854], *Hansard's Parliamentary Debates,* Third series, Vol. CXXXII, London, 1854.— *Ed.*

[c] "To whatever quarter...", *The Times,* No. 21704, April 1, 1854, leading article.— *Ed.*

the present great preparations are intended by no means only for the *Trent* case but for the eventuality of a recognition of the government of the slave states. If England does this, then she will cover herself with everlasting shame."

Mr. *White:*

"It is due to the working class to mention that they are the originators of this meeting and that all the expenses of organising it are borne by their committee.... The present government never had the good judgment to deal honestly and frankly with the people.... I have never for a moment believed that there was the remotest possibility of a war developing out of the *Trent* case. I have said to the face of more than one member of the government that not a single member of the government believed in the possibility of a war on account of the *Trent* case. Why, then, these massive preparations? I believe that England and France have reached an understanding to recognise the independence of the Southern states next spring. By then Great Britain would have a fleet of superior strength in American waters. Canada would be completely equipped for defence. If the Northern states are then inclined to make a *casus belli* out of the recognition of the Southern states, Great Britain will then be prepared...."

The speaker then went on to develop the dangers of a war with the United States, called to mind the sympathy that America showed on the death of General Havelock, the assistance that the American sailors rendered to the English ships in the unlucky Peiho engagement,[156] etc. He closed with the remark that the Civil War would end with the abolition of slavery and England must therefore stand unconditionally on the side of the North.

The original motion having been unanimously adopted, a memorandum for Palmerston was submitted to the meeting, debated and adopted.

Written on January 1, 1862   Printed according to the news-

First published in *Die Presse*, No. 5,   paper
January 5, 1862

Karl Marx

ENGLISH PUBLIC OPINION

London, Jan. 11, 1862

The news of the pacific solution of the *Trent* conflict [157] was, by the bulk of the English people, saluted with an exultation proving unmistakably the unpopularity of the apprehended war and the dread of its consequences. It ought never to be forgotten in the United States that at least the *working classes* of England, from the commencement to the termination of the difficulty, have never forsaken them. To them it was due that, despite the poisonous stimulants daily administered by a venal and reckless press, not one single public war meeting could be held in the United Kingdom during all the period that peace trembled in the balance. The only war meeting convened on the arrival of the *La Plata*, in the cotton salesroom of the Liverpool Stock Exchange, was a corner meeting where the cotton jobbers had it all to themselves. Even at Manchester, the temper of the working classes was so well understood that an insulated attempt at the convocation of a war meeting was almost as soon abandoned as thought of.

Wherever public meetings took place in England, Scotland, or Ireland, they protested against the rabid war-cries of the press, against the sinister designs of the Government, and declared for a pacific settlement of the pending question. In this regard, the two last meetings held, the one at Paddington, London, the other at Newcastle-upon-Tyne, are characteristic. The former meeting applauded Mr. Washington Wilkes's argumentation that England was not warranted in finding fault with the seizure of the Southern Commissioners [a]; while the Newcastle meeting almost unanimously carried the resolution—firstly, that the Americans

---

[a] J. Mason and J. Slidell.— *Ed.*

had only made themselves guilty of a *lawful* exercise of the right of search and seizure; secondly, that the captain of the *Trent*[a] ought to be punished for his violation of English neutrality, as proclaimed by the Queen.[b] In ordinary circumstances, the conduct of the British workingmen might have been anticipated from the natural sympathy the popular classes all over the world ought to feel for the only popular Government in the world.

Under the present circumstances, however, when a great portion of the British working classes directly and severely suffers under the consequences of the Southern blockade; when another part is indirectly smitten by the curtailment of the American commerce, owing, as they are told, to the selfish "protective policy" of the Republicans; when the only remaining democratic weekly, *Reynolds's* paper, has sold itself to Messrs. Yancey and Mann, and week after week exhausts its horse-powers of foul language in appeals to the working classes to urge the Government, for their own interests, to war with the Union—under such circumstances, simple justice requires to pay a tribute to the sound attitude of the British working classes, the more so when contrasted with the hypocritical, bullying, cowardly, and stupid conduct of the official and well-to-do John Bull.

What a difference in this attitude of the people from what it had assumed at the time of the Russian complication![c] Then *The Times, The Post,* and the other Yellowplushes of the London press, whined for peace, to be rebuked by tremendous war meetings all over the country. Now they have howled for war, to be answered by peace meetings denouncing the liberticide schemes and the Pro-Slavery sympathy of the Government. The grimaces cut by the augurs of public opinion at the news of the pacific solution of the *Trent* case are really amusing.

In the first place, they must needs congratulate themselves upon the dignity, common sense, good will, and moderation, daily displayed by them for the whole interval of a month. They *were* moderate for the first two days after the arrival of the *La Plata,* when Palmerston felt uneasy whether any legal pretext for a quarrel was to be picked. But hardly had the crown lawyers[d] hit upon a legal quibble, when they opened a charivari unheard of since the anti-Jacobin war.[158] The dispatches of the English

---

ᵃ Moir.— *Ed.*

ᵇ Victoria, R., *A Proclamation* [May 13, 1861], *The Times,* No. 23933, May 15, 1861.— *Ed.*

ᶜ I.e., of the Crimean War.— *Ed.*

ᵈ R. Palmer and W. Atherton.— *Ed.*

Government left Queenstown in the beginning of December. No official answer from Washington could possibly be looked for before the commencement of January. The new incidents arising in the interval told all in favor of the Americans. The tone of the Transatlantic Press, although the Nashville affair[159] might have roused its passions, was calm. All facts ascertained concurred to show that Capt. Wilkes had acted on his own hook. The position of the Washington Government was delicate. If it resisted the English demands, it would complicate the civil war by a foreign war. If it gave way, it might damage its popularity at home, and appear to cede to pressure from abroad. And the Government thus placed, carried, at the same time, a war which must enlist the warmest sympathies of every man, not a confessed ruffian, on its side.

Common prudence, conventional decency, ought, therefore, to have dictated to the London press, at least for the time separating the English demand from the American reply, to anxiously abstain from every word calculated to heat passion, breed ill-will, complicate the difficulty. But no! That "inexpressibly mean and groveling" press, as William Cobbett, and he was a *connoisseur,* calls it, really boasted of having, when in fear of the compact power of the United States, humbly submitted to the accumulated slights and insults of Pro-Slavery Administrations for almost half a century, while now, with the savage exultation of cowards, they panted for taking their revenge on the Republican Administration, distracted by a civil war. The record of mankind chronicles no self-avowed infamy like this.

One of the yellow-plushes, Palmerston's private *Moniteur—The Morning Post*—finds itself arraigned on a most ugly charge from the American papers. John Bull has never been informed—on information carefully withheld from him by the oligarchs that lord it over him—that Mr. Seward, without awaiting Russell's dispatch, had disavowed any participation of the Washington Cabinet in the act of Capt. Wilkes. Mr. Seward's dispatch arrived at London on December 19. On the 20th December, the rumor of this "secret" spread on the Stock Exchange. On the 21st, the yellow-plush of *The Morning Post* stepped forward to gravely herald that "the dispatch in question does not in any way whatever refer to the outrage on our mail packet."[a]

In *The Daily News, The Morning Star,* and other London

---

[a] "In the present state of the public mind...", *The Morning Post,* No. 27460, December 21, 1861, leading article.— *Ed.*

journals, you will find yellow-plush pretty sharply handled, but you will not learn from them what people out of doors say. They say that *The Morning Post* and *The Times,* like the *Patrie* and the *Pays,* duped the public not only to politically mislead them, but to fleece them in the monetary line on the Stock Exchange, in the interest of their patrons.

The brazen *Times,* fully aware that during the whole crisis it had compromised nobody but itself, and given another proof of the hollowness of its pretensions of influencing the real people of England, plays to-day a trick which here, at London, only works upon the laughing muscles, but on the other side of the Atlantic, might be misinterpreted.[a] The "popular classes" of London, the "mob", as the yellow-plush call them, have given unmistakable signs—have even hinted in newspapers—that they should consider it an exceedingly seasonable joke to treat Mason (by the by, a distant relative of Palmerston, since the original Mason had married a daughter of Sir W. Temple), Slidell & Co. with the same demonstrations Haynau received on his visit at Barclay's brewery.[160] *The Times* stands aghast at the mere idea of such a shocking incident, and how does it try to parry it? It admonishes the people of England not to overwhelm Mason, Slidell & Co. with any sort of public *ovation! The Times* knows that its to-day's article will form the laughing-stock of all the tap-rooms of London. But never mind! People on the other side of the Atlantic may, perhaps, fancy that the magnanimity of *The Times* has saved them from the affront of public ovations to Mason, Slidell & Co., while, in point of fact, *The Times* only intends saving those gentlemen from public insult!

So long as the *Trent* affair was undecided, *The Times, The Post, The Herald, The Economist, The Saturday Review,* in fact the whole of the fashionable, hireling press of London, had tried its utmost to persuade John Bull that the Washington Government, even if it willed, would prove unable to keep the peace, because the Yankee mob would not allow it, and because the Federal Government was a mob Government. Facts have now given them the lie direct. Do they now atone for their malignant slanders against the American people? Do they at least confess the errors which yellow-plush, in presuming to judge of the acts of a free people, could not but commit? By no means. They now unanimously discover that the American Government, in not anticipating England's demands,

---

[a] "A turn of the wheel, which the American Cabinet has managed to make...", *The Times,* No. 24140, January 11, 1862, leading article.— *Ed.*

and not surrendering the Southern traitors as soon as they were caught, missed a great occasion, and deprived its present concession of all merit. Indeed, yellow plush! Mr. Seward disavowed the act of Wilkes before the arrival of the English demands, and at once declared himself willing to enter upon a conciliatory course[a]; and what did you do on similar occasions? When, on the pretext of impressing English sailors on board American ships—a pretext not at all connected with maritime belligerent rights, but a downright, monstrous usurpation against all international law—the *Leopard* fired its broadside at the *Chesapeake*, killed six, wounded twenty-one of her sailors, and seized the pretended Englishmen on board the *Chesapeake*, what did the English Government do? That outrage was perpetrated on the 20th of June, 1807. The real satisfaction, the surrender of the sailors, &c., was only offered on November 8, 1812, five years later. The British Government, it is true, disavowed at once the act of Admiral Berkeley, as Mr. Seward did in regard to Capt. Wilkes; but, to punish the Admiral, it removed him from an inferior to a superior rank. England, in proclaiming her Orders in Council,[161] distinctly confessed that they were outrages on the rights of neutrals in general, and of the United States in particular; that they were forced upon her as measures of retaliation against Napoleon, and that she would feel but too glad to revoke them whenever Napoleon should revoke his encroachments on neutral rights.[b] Napoleon did revoke them, as far as the United States were concerned, in the Spring of 1810. England persisted in her avowed outrage on the maritime rights of America. Her resistance lasted from 1806 to 23d of June, 1812—after, on the 18th of June, 1812, the United States had declared war against England. England abstained, consequently, in this case for six years, not from atoning for a confessed outrage, but from discontinuing it. And this people talk of the magnificent occasion missed by the American Government! Whether in the wrong or in the right, it was a cowardly act on the part of the British Government to back a complaint grounded on pretended technical blunder, and a mere error of procedure, by an ultimatum, by a demand for the surrender of the prisoners. The American Government might have reasons to accede to that demand; it could have none to anticipate it.

---

[a] "New York, Dec. 28", *The Times*, No. 24139, January 10, 1862.—*Ed.*
[b] *Order in Council. At the Court at the Queen's Palace, the 11th of November, 1807, present, the King's most Excellent Majesty in Council.*—*Ed.*

By the present settlement of the *Trent* collision, the question underlying the whole dispute, and likely to again occur—the belligerent rights of a maritime power against neutrals—has not been settled. I shall, with your permission, try to survey the whole question in a subsequent letter. For the present, allow me to add that, in my opinion, Messrs. Mason and Slidell have done great service to the Federal Government. There was an influential war party in England, which, what for commercial, what for political reasons, showed eager for a fray with the United States. The *Trent* affair put that party to the test. It has failed. The war passion has been discounted on a minor issue, the steam has been let off, the vociferous fury of the oligarchy has raised the suspicions of English democracy, the large British interests connected with the United States have made a stand, the true character of the civil war has been brought home to the working classes, and last, not least, the dangerous period when Palmerston rules single-headed without being checked by Parliament, is rapidly drawing to an end. That was the only time in which an English war for the slaveocrats might have been hazarded. It is now out of question.

Written on January 11, 1862   Reproduced from the newspaper

First published in the *New-York Daily*
Tribune, No. 6499, February 1, 1862

Karl Marx

MORE ON SEWARD'S SUPPRESSED DISPATCH [162]

London, January 14

The defunct *Trent* case is resurrected, this time, however, as a *casus belli* not between England and the United States, but between the English people and the English government. The new *casus belli* will be decided in Parliament, which assembles next month. Without doubt you have already taken notice of the polemic of *The Daily News*[a] and *The Star* against *The Morning Post* over the suppression and denial of Seward's peace dispatch of November 30,[b] which on December 19 was read to Lord John Russell by the American Ambassador, Mr. Adams. Permit me, now, to return to this matter. With the assurance of *The Morning Post* that Seward's dispatch had not the remotest bearing on the *Trent* affair,[c] stock exchange securities fell and property worth millions changed hands, was lost on the one side, won on the other. In commercial and industrial circles, therefore, the wholly unjustifiable semi-official lie of *The Morning Post* disclosed by the publication of Seward's dispatch of November 30 arouses the most tremendous indignation.

On the afternoon of January 9 the peace news reached London. The same evening *The Evening Star* (the evening edition of *The Morning Star*) interpellated the government concerning the suppression of Seward's dispatch of November 30. The following morning, January 10, *The Morning Post* replied as follows:

[a] The reference is to the leading article in *The Daily News*, No. 4890, January 11, 1862 ("As the rising of the sun after a night of troublous watchings...").— *Ed.*

[b] Seward's dispatch was published in the item "Southampton, Jan. 12", *The Times*, No. 24141, January 13, 1862.— *Ed.*

[c] "In the present state of the public mind...", *The Morning Post*, No. 27460, December 21, 1861, leading article.— *Ed.*

"It is asked why nothing has been heard sooner of Mr. Seward's dispatch, which reached Mr. Adams some time in December. The explanation of this is very simple. It is that the dispatch received by Mr. Adams was *not communicated*[a] *to our government*." [b]

On the evening of the same day *The Star* gave the lie to the *Post* completely and declared its "rectification" to be a miserable subterfuge. The dispatch, it wrote, had in fact not been *"communicated"* to Lord Palmerston and Lord Russell by Mr. Adams, but had been *"read out"*.

Next morning, Saturday, January 11, *The Daily News* entered the lists and proved from *The Morning Post's* article of December 21 that the *Post* and the government had been fully acquainted with Seward's dispatch at that time and deliberately falsified it. The government now prepared to retreat. On the evening of January 11 the semi-official *Globe* declared that Mr. Adams had, to be sure, communicated Seward's dispatch to the government on December 19; this, however, "contained no offer by the Washington Cabinet" any more than "a direct apology for the outrage on the British flag". This shamefaced admission of a deliberate deception of the English people for three weeks only fanned the flame higher, instead of quenching it. A cry of anger resounded through all the organs of the industrial districts of Great Britain, which yesterday finally found its echo even in the Tory newspapers. The whole question, one should note, was placed on the order of the day, not by politicians, but by the commercial public. Today's *Morning Star* remarks on the subject:

"Lord John Russell is undoubtedly an accomplice in that suppression of the truth; he allowed the *Morning Post's* lie to circulate uncontradicted, but he is incapable of having dictated that mendacious and incalculably pernicious article which appeared in *The Morning Post* on the 21st of December. This could only be done by *one* man. The Minister who fabricated the Afghan war is alone capable of having suppressed Mr. Seward's message of peace.[163] The foolish leniency of the House of Commons condoned the one offence. Will not Parliament and people unite in the infliction of punishment for the other?"

Written on January 14, 1862   Printed according to the news-
                                                paper
First published in *Die Presse*, No. 17,
January 18, 1862

---

[a] Marx gives the English words "not communicated" in brackets after the German translation.— *Ed.*

[b] "We have it in our power to state...", *The Morning Post*, No. 27476, January 10, 1862, leading article.— *Ed.*

Karl Marx

A COUP D'ÉTAT BY LORD JOHN RUSSELL[164]

London, January 17

Lord John Russell's position during the recent crisis was a thoroughly vexatious one, even for a man whose whole parliamentary life proves that he has seldom hesitated to sacrifice real power for official position. No one forgot that Lord John Russell had lost the Premiership to Palmerston, but no one seemed to remember that he had gained the Foreign Office from Palmerston. All the world considered it a self-evident axiom that Palmerston directed the Cabinet in his own name and foreign policy under the name of Russell. On the arrival of the first peace news from New York,[a] Whigs and Tories vied with one another in trumpet-blasts to the greater glory of Palmerston's statesmanship, whilst the Foreign Secretary, Lord John Russell, was not even a candidate for praise as his assistant. He was absolutely ignored. Hardly, however, had the scandal over the *suppressed* American dispatch of November 30[b] broken out, when Russell's name was resurrected from the dead.

Attack and defence now made the discovery that the *responsible* Foreign Secretary was called Lord *John Russell!* But now even Russell's patience gave way. Without waiting for the opening of Parliament and contrary to every ministerial convention, he published forthwith in the official *Gazette* of January 14 his own

---

a "New York, Dec. 27, Evening", *The Times*, No. 24138, January 9, 1861.— *Ed.*
b See this volume, pp. 143-44.— *Ed.*

correspondence with Lord Lyons.[a] This correspondence proves that Seward's dispatch of November 30 was read by Mr. Adams to Lord John Russell on December 19; that Russell expressly acknowledged this dispatch as an *apology* for the act of Captain Wilkes, and that Mr. Adams, after Russell's disclosures, considered a peaceful outcome of the dispute as certain. After this *official* disclosure, what becomes of the *Morning Post* of December 21, which denied the arrival of any dispatch from Seward relating to the *Trent* case[b]; what becomes of the *Morning Post* of January 10, which blamed Mr. Adams for the suppression of the dispatch,[c] what becomes of the entire war racket of the Palmerston press from December 19, 1861, to January 8, 1862? Even more! Lord John Russell's dispatch to Lord Lyons of December 19, 1861, proves that the English Cabinet presented *no war ultimatum;* that Lord Lyons did *not* receive instructions to leave Washington seven days after delivering "this ultimatum"; that Russell ordered the ambassador to avoid every semblance of a threat, and, finally, that the English Cabinet had decided to make a *definitive decision* only *after receipt* of the American answer. The whole of the policy trumpeted by the Palmerston press, which found so many servile echoes on the Continent, is therefore a mere chimera. It has never been carried out in real life. It only proves, as a London paper states today, that Palmerston "sought to thwart the declared and binding policy of the *responsible* advisers of the Crown".

That Lord John Russell's *coup de main* struck the Palmerston press like a bolt from the blue, one fact proves most forcibly. *The Times* of yesterday *suppressed* the Russell correspondence and made no mention of it whatever. Only today a reprint from the *London Gazette* figures in its columns, introduced and prefaced by a leading article that carefully avoids the real issue, *the issue between the English people and the English Cabinet,* and touches on it merely in the ill-humoured phrase that "Lord John Russell has exerted all his ingenuity to extract an *apology* out of Seward's dispatch of November 30".[d] On the other hand, the wrathful *Jupiter Tonans*[e]

---

[a] "Foreign Office, January 14, 1862. Copies of Correspondence...", *The London Gazette*, No. 22589, January 14, 1862.— *Ed.*

[b] "In the present state of the public mind...", *The Morning Post*, No. 27460, December 21, 1861, leading article.— *Ed.*

[c] "We have it in our power to state...", *The Morning Post*, No. 27476, January 10, 1862, leading article.— *Ed.*

[d] "The following additional correspondence...", *The Times*, No. 24144, January 16, 1862, leading article.— *Ed.*

[e] Jupiter the thunderer.— *Ed.*

of Printing House Square[165] lets off steam in a second leading article, in which Mr. Gilpin, a member of the ministry, the President of the Board of Trade[a] and a partisan of the Manchester school,[166] is declared to be unworthy of his place in the ministry.[b] For last Tuesday,[c] at a public meeting in Northampton, whose parliamentary representative he is, Gilpin, a former bookseller, a demagogue and an apostle of moderation, whom nobody will take for a hero, criminally urged the English people to prevent by public demonstrations an untimely recognition of the Southern Confederacy, which he inconsiderately stigmatised as an offspring of slavery. As if, *The Times* indignantly exclaims, as if Palmerston and Russell— *The Times* now remembers the existence of Lord John Russell once more—had not fought all their lives to put down slavery![d] It was surely an indiscretion, a *calculated* indiscretion on the part of Mr. Gilpin, to call the English people into the lists against the pro-slavery longings of a ministry to which he himself belongs. But Mr. Gilpin, as already mentioned, is no hero. His whole career evidences little capacity for martyrdom. His indiscretion occurred on the *same day* as Lord John Russell carried out his *coup de main.* We may therefore conclude that the Cabinet is not a "happy family"[e] and that its individual members have already familiarised themselves with the idea of "separation".

No less noteworthy than the English ministerial sequel to the *Trent* drama is its *Russian epilogue.* Russia, which during the entire racket stood silently in the background with folded arms, now springs to the proscenium, claps Mr. Seward on the shoulders— and declares that the moment for the definitive regulation of the maritime rights of neutrals has at last arrived. Russia, as is known, considers herself called on to put the urgent questions of civilisation on the agenda of world history at the right time and in the right place. Russia becomes unassailable by the maritime powers the moment the latter give up, with their belligerent rights against neutrals, their power over Russia's export trade. The Paris Convention of April 16, 1856, which is in part a *verbatim* copy of

---

[a] Marx gives the English name.— *Ed.*
[b] "The true and just instinct of the House of Commons...", *The Times,* same issue.— *Ed.*
[c] January 14.— *Ed.*
[d] "Mr. Gilpin, M. P., and Lord Henley, M. P., on America and England", *The Times,* No. 24143, January 15, 1862.— *Ed.*
[e] Marx uses the English phrase.— *Ed.*

the *Russian* "Armed" Neutrality Treaty of 1780 against England,[a] is meanwhile not yet *law* in England. What a trick of destiny if the *Anglo-American* dispute ended with the British Parliament and the British Crown sanctioning a concession that two British ministers made to Russia on their own authority at the end of the *Anglo-Russian* war.

Written on January 16-17, 1862

First published in *Die Presse*, No. 20, January 21, 1862

Printed according to the newspaper

---

[a] Here Marx probably drew on the excerpts from documents on the law of the sea published in *The Free Press*, No. 1, January 1, 1862.— *Ed.*

Karl Marx

STATISTICAL OBSERVATIONS
ON THE RAILWAY SYSTEM

The English railways are a generation old, 30 years. Except for the national debt, no other branch of the national wealth has developed so rapidly to such an enormous size. According to a recently published Blue Book, the capital invested in the railways until 1860 came to £348,130,127, of which £190,791,067 were raised by common stock, £67,873,840 by preferred stock, £7,576,878 by bonds, and £81,888,546 by current loans. The total capital amounts to about half the national debt and is five times the yearly revenue from all the real estate in Great Britain. This parvenu form of wealth, the most colossal offspring of modern industry, a remarkable economic hybrid whose feet are rooted in the earth and whose head lives on the Stock Exchange, has given aristocratic landowning a powerful rival, and the middle class an army of new auxiliary troops.

In 1860, the steel rails stretched for 22,000 English miles, counting double-track and branch lines. On average, therefore, 733 miles of track have been laid every year over the last 30 years. This sort of average figure, however, is even more deceptive in this branch of industry than in any other, as regards expressing the actual living process. Some years of the railway mania,[167] such as 1844 and 1845, conquered the bulk of the territory at the double. The other years fill things out gradually, connect the major lines, branch out, expand relatively slowly. During these years the production of railways falls below the average level.

An enormous amount of work precedes the laying of the rails. According to the data provided by Robert Stephenson as early as

1854 some 70 miles of railway tunnels had been driven through, there were 25,000 railway bridges and numerous viaducts, one of which, near London, was more than 11 miles long. The earthworks, 70,000 cubic yards per mile, would fill an area of 550 million cubic yards. Piled up in the form of a pyramid, the diameter would be half an (English) mile and the height a mile and a half, a mountain of earth beside which St. Paul's Cathedral would shrink to Lilliputian size. But since the time of Robert Stephenson's estimate the length of railways has increased by a third.

The "eternal way", as the English have baptised the railway, is not immortal by any means. It is subject to constant metabolism. The iron, which is continually being lost by wear, oxidation, and new manufacture, has constantly to be replaced. It has been calculated that a locomotive wears off 2.2 pounds in a run of 60 miles, every empty car $4^1/_2$ ounces, every ton of freight an ounce and a half, and that the railways like the London-North Western Line will last about 20 years. The yearly total of iron worn off is estimated at half a pound per yard; 24,000 tons of iron are required for replacements over the whole system in its present extent every year and 240,000 tons for the annual installation. But the rails form the bones and need to be replaced much more slowly than the wooden supports of the rails. The wood part of the apparatus of the network requires an annual input of 300,000 trees, which need an area of 6,000 acres to grow in.

When the railway is completed, it needs locomotives, coal, water, railway cars, and finally working personnel to operate it. The number of locomotives was 5,801 in 1860, or more than one locomotive for every two miles. Like most machines in their infancy, locomotives were at first clumsy-looking, awkward in motion, still bound up to a certain extent in reminiscences of the old-fashioned instrument they replaced, and relatively cheap. The first English locomotive, four-wheeled, weighing barely 6 tons and priced at £550, has gradually been replaced by steam engines priced at £3,000, which pull 30 passenger cars, each weighing $5^1/_2$ tons, at 30 miles an hour, or 500 tons of goods at 20 miles per hour. Like their predecessors, the horses, individual locomotives have their own names and have attained varying degrees of fame for their names.

The *Liverpool,* belonging to the North Western Line, pours out 1,140 horsepower at full load. A monster like this consumes a ton of coal and 1,000 to 1,500 gallons of water daily. The organism of these iron horses is extremely delicate. It has no less than 5,416 parts, which are assembled as carefully as the parts of a watch. A railway train going 50 (English) miles per hour has a sixth of the velocity of a cannon ball. Reckoning the average cost of a locomotive at £2,200, the outlay on 5,801 locomotives comes to over £12,700,000. Every minute of the year 4 to 5 tons of coal turn 20 to 25 tons of water into steam. Stephenson remarks that the water thus converted into steam would be an adequate daily water supply for the entire population of Liverpool. The quantity of fuel consumed is almost as much as Britain's total coal exports four years ago, more than half the entire consumption of London.

The 5,801 locomotives are followed, as baggage, by 15,076 passenger cars and 180,574 goods wagons, which represent a total capital of £20 million. A train made up of all the locomotives and cars would take the entire line from Brighton to Aberdeen, over 600 miles.

More than 7,000 trains run every day, over seven trains every minute throughout the twenty-four hours. Last year passengers and goods travelled over 100 million miles, more than four thousand times the circumference of the earth. Every second of the year over 3 miles of railway are covered by trains. Twelve millions cattle, sheep, and pigs made railway journeys; 90 million tons of goods and minerals were transported. The minerals came to twice the quantity of all the other goods.

The gross revenue totalled £28 million. The production costs, apart from the wear of the railway itself, came to 41 per cent of the revenue for the Midland Company, 42 per cent for the Yorkshire and Lancashire railway line, 46 per cent for the West Midland Line and 55 to 56 per cent for the Great Northern Line; the average outlay for all the lines came to £13,187,368, or 47 per cent of revenue.

The London and North Western Line ranks first in size. Originally limited to the London and Birmingham Line, the Grand Junction, the Manchester and Liverpool Line, it now extends with its branch lines from London to Carlisle and from Peterborough to Leeds in the east and to Holyhead in the west. Its management controls over a thousand miles of railways and is at the head of an industrial army of about 20,000 men. Construction of the railway line costs over £36 million. Every hour of the day and night its gross revenue is £500; its weekly law costs are £1,000. The net yield of this railway, as of most of the others, fell relatively as their extent increased to cover less populous and less industrial districts. Their shares, issued at £100, gradually sank from £240 to £92-93, and dividends from 10 per cent to $3^3/_4$ per cent. As the scale of operations grew enormously, for this as well as other railways, control by the shareholders decreased, the management gained greater power and mismanagement ensued.

Written not later than January 20, 1862

First published in *Die Presse*, No. 22, January 23, 1862

Printed according to the newspaper

Published in English for the first time

Karl Marx

A LONDON WORKERS' MEETING [168]

London, January 28

The working class, so preponderant a part of a society that within living memory has no longer possessed a *peasantry,* is known not to be represented in Parliament. Nevertheless, it is not without political influence. No important innovation, no decisive measure has ever been carried through in this country without pressure from without,[a] whether it was the opposition that required such pressure against the government or the government that required the pressure against the opposition. By pressure from without the Englishman understands great, extra-parliamentary popular demonstrations, which naturally cannot be staged without the lively participation of the working class. *Pitt* understood how to use the masses against the Whigs in his anti-Jacobin war. The Catholic emancipation, the Reform Bill, the abolition of the Corn Laws, the Ten Hours Bill, the war against Russia, the rejection of Palmerston's Conspiracy Bill,[169] all were the fruit of stormy extra-parliamentary demonstrations, in which the working class, sometimes artificially incited, sometimes acting spontaneously, played the principal part only, as a *persona dramatis,* only as the chorus or, according to circumstances, performed the noisy part. So much the more striking is the attitude of the English working class in regard to the American Civil War.

The misery that the stoppage of the factories and the shortening of the labour time, *motivated* by the blockade of the slave states, has produced among the workers in the northern manufacturing districts is incredible and in daily process of growth. The other

---

[a] Marx uses the English words "pressure from without" and gives the German translation in brackets. He also uses the English phrase further in the text.— *Ed.*

component parts of the working class do not suffer to the same extent; but they suffer severely from the reaction of the crisis in the cotton industry on the other industries, from the curtailment of the export of their own products to the North of America in consequence of the Morrill tariff [170] and from the loss of this export to the South in consequence of the blockade. At the present moment, English interference in America has accordingly become a knife-and-fork question [171] for the working class. Moreover, no means of inflaming its wrath against the United States is scorned by its "natural superiors".[a] The sole great and widely circulating workers' organ still existing, *Reynolds's Newspaper*, has been purchased expressly in order that for six months it might reiterate weekly in raging diatribes the *ceterum censeo*[b] of English intervention. The working class is accordingly fully conscious that the government is only waiting for the intervention cry from below, the pressure from without, to put an end to the American blockade and English misery. Under these circumstances, the persistence with which the working class keeps silent, or breaks its silence only to raise its voice against intervention and *for* the United States, is admirable. This is a new, brilliant proof of the indestructible staunchness of the English popular masses, of that staunchness which is the secret of England's greatness and which, to speak in the hyperbolic language of Mazzini, made the common English soldier seem a demi-god during the Crimean War and the Indian insurrection.

The following report on a great *workers' meeting* that took place yesterday in Marylebone, the most populous district of London, may serve to characterise the "policy" of the working class:

Mr. *Steadman,* the chairman, opened the meeting with the remark that the question was one of a decision on the part of the English people in regard to the *reception of Messrs. Mason and Slidell.*

"It has to be considered whether these gentlemen were coming here to free the slaves from their chains or to forge a new link for these chains."

Mr. *Yates:*

"On the present occasion the working class dare not keep silent. The two gentlemen who are sailing across the Atlantic Ocean to our country are the agents of slaveholding and tyrannical states. They are in open rebellion against the lawful Constitution of their country and come here to induce our government to recognise the independence of the slave states. It is the duty of the working class to

---

[a] Marx uses the English phrase and gives the German translation in brackets.— *Ed.*

[b] See p. 133, footnote *a.— Ed.*

pronounce its opinion now, if the English government is not to believe that we regard its foreign policy with indifference. We must show that the money expended by this people on the emancipation of slaves cannot be allowed to be uselessly squandered.[172] Had our government acted honestly, it would have supported the Northern states heart and soul in suppressing this fearful rebellion."

After a detailed defence of the Northern states and the observation that "Mr. Lovejoy's violent tirade against England[a] was called forth by the slanders of the English press", the speaker proposed the following motion:

"This meeting resolves that the agents of the rebels, Mason and Slidell, now on the way from America to England, are absolutely unworthy of the moral sympathies of the working class of this country, since they are slaveholders as well as the confessed agents of the tyrannical faction that is at this very moment in rebellion against the American republic and the sworn enemy of the social and political rights of the working class in all countries."

Mr. *Whynne* supported the motion. It was, however, self-understood that every personal insult to Mason and Slidell must be avoided during their stay in London.

Mr. *Nichols,* a resident "*of the extreme North* of the United States", as he announced, who was in fact sent to the meeting by Messrs. Yancey and Mann as the *advocatus diaboli,*[b] protested against the motion.

"I am here, because here freedom of speech prevails. With us at home, the government has permitted no man to open his mouth for three months. Liberty has been crushed not only in the South, but also in the North. The war has many opponents in the North, but they dare not speak. No less than two hundred newspapers have been suppressed or destroyed by the mob. The Southern states have the same right to secede from the North as the United States had to separate from England."

Despite the eloquence of Mr. Nichols, the first motion was carried unanimously. He now sprang up afresh:

"If they reproached Messrs. Mason and Slidell with being slaveholders, the same thing would apply to Washington and Jefferson, etc."

Mr. *Beales* refuted Nichols in a detailed speech and then brought forward a second motion:

"In view of the ill-concealed efforts of *The Times* and other misleading journals to misrepresent English public opinion on all American affairs; to embroil us in

---

[a] In his speech in Congress on January 14, 1862, Lovejoy called on the government to declare war on England after the suppression of the Southern rebellion.— *Ed.*

[b] *Advocatus diaboli* (the devil's advocate)—a participant in the canonisation procedure of the Catholic Church whose task is to point out defects in the character of the person for whom the honour is sought; figuratively, an implacable accuser.— *Ed.*

war with millions of our kinsmen on any pretext whatever, and to take advantage of the perils currently threatening the republic to defame democratic institutions, this meeting regards it as the very special duty of the workers, since they are not represented in the Senate of the nation, to declare their sympathy with the United States in their titanic struggle for the maintenance of the Union; to denounce the shameful dishonesty and advocacy of slaveholding on the part of *The Times* and kindred aristocratic journals; to express themselves most emphatically in favour of the strictest policy of non-intervention in affairs of the United States and in favour of the settlement of all matters that may be in dispute by commissioners or arbitration courts nominated by both sides; to denounce the war policy of the organ of the stock exchange swindlers[a] and to express the warmest sympathy with the strivings of the Abolitionists for a final solution of the slave question."

This motion was unanimously adopted, as well as the final motion

"to forward to the American government *per medium* of Mr. Adams a copy of the resolutions framed, as an expression of the feelings and opinions of the working class of England".

Written on January 28, 1862

First published in *Die Presse,* No. 32, February 2, 1862

Printed according to the newspaper

---

[a] *The Economist.—Ed.*

Karl Marx

ANTI-INTERVENTION FEELING[173]

London, January 31

Liverpool's commercial greatness derives its origin from the *slave trade*. The sole contributions with which Liverpool has enriched the poetic literature of England are odes to the slave trade. Fifty years ago *Wilberforce* could set foot on Liverpool soil only at the risk of his life. As in the preceding century the slave trade, so in the present century the trade in the product of slavery—cotton— formed the material basis of Liverpool's greatness. No wonder, therefore, that Liverpool is the centre of the English friends of secession. It is in fact the *sole* city in the United Kingdom where during the recent crisis it was possible to organise a quasi-public meeting in favour of a war with the United States.[a] And what does Liverpool say now? Let us hearken to one of its great daily organs, the *Daily Post.*

In a leading article entitled "The Cute Yankees"[b] it is stated among other things:

"The Yankees, with their usual adroitness, have converted an apparent loss into a real gain and made England subservient to their advantage.... Great Britain has in fact displayed her power, but to what end? Since the foundation of the United States the Yankees have always claimed for a neutral flag the privilege that passengers sailing under it are protected from any intervention and attack by the belligerents. We contested this privilege to the limit during the Anti-Jacobin War, the Anglo-American War of 1812 to 1814, and again, more recently, in 1842, during the negotiations between Lord Ashburton and the Secretary of State, Daniel Webster.[174] Now our opposition must cease. *The Yankee principle has triumphed.* Mr. Seward registers the fact and declares that we have given way in principle and that

---

a See this volume, pp. 93-94, 95.— *Ed.*

b *The Daily Post*, No. 2061, January 13, 1862. Marx gives the title in English and supplies the German translation in brackets.— *Ed.*

through the *Trent* case the United States have obtained a concession from us to secure which they had hitherto exhausted every means of diplomacy and of war in vain."

More important still is the *Daily Post*'s admission of the shift in public opinion even in Liverpool.

"The Confederates", it says, "have certainly done nothing to forfeit the good opinion entertained of them. Quite the contrary. They have fought manfully and made dreadful sacrifices. If they do not obtain their independence everyone must admit that they deserve it. Public opinion, however, has now run counter to their claims. They are no longer the fine fellows[a] they were four weeks ago. They are now pronounced a very sorry set. ...A reaction has indeed commenced. The anti-slavery people, who shrank into their shoes during the recent popular excitement, now come forth to thunder big words against man-selling and the rebellious slave-owners.... Are not even the walls of our town posted with large placards full of denunciations and angry invectives against Messrs. Mason and Slidell, the authors of the accursed Fugitive Slave Law? The Confederates have lost by the *Trent* affair. It was to be their gain; it has turned out to be their ruin. The sympathy of this country will be withdrawn from them, and they will have to realise as soon as possible their peculiar situation. They have been very ill-used but they will have no redress."

After this admission by such a friend of secession as the Liverpool daily paper it is easy to explain the altered language that some important organs of Palmerston now suddenly make use of before the opening of Parliament. Thus *The Economist* of last Saturday has an article entitled, "Shall the Blockade be Respected?"[b]

It proceeds in the first place from the *axiom* that the blockade is a mere *paper blockade* and that its violation is therefore permitted by international law. France demanded the blockade's forcible removal. The practical decision of the question lay accordingly in the hands of England, who had great and pressing motives for such a step. In particular she was in need of American cotton. One may remark incidentally that it is not quite clear how a "mere paper blockade" can prevent the shipping of cotton.

"But nevertheless," cries *The Economist,* "England *must* respect the blockade." Having motivated this judgment with a series of sophisms, it finally comes to the gist of the matter.[c]

---

[a] Marx quotes in German but gives a number of phrases in English in brackets after their German equivalents: "fine fellows", "a very sorry set", "they will have no redress".— *Ed.*

[b] *The Economist,* No. 961, January 25, 1862.— *Ed.*

[c] Marx has: "des Pudels Kern", an allusion to the saying, "Das also war des Pudels Kern", in Goethe's *Faust* (Der Tragödie erster Theil, "Studierzimmer").— *Ed.*

"In a case of this kind," it says, "the government would have to have the whole country behind it. The great body of the British people are not yet *prepared* for any interposition which would even have the semblance of aiding the establishment of a slave republic. The social system of the Confederacy is based on slavery; the Federalists have done what they could to persuade us that slavery lay at the root of the Secession movement, and that they, the Federalists, were hostile to slavery; and slavery is our especial horror and detestation.... The real error of the popular sentiment is here. The dissolution, not the restoration, of the Union, independence, not the defeat of the South, is the only sure path to the emancipation of the slaves. We hope soon to make this clear to our readers. But *it is not clear yet. The majority of Englishmen still think otherwise;* and as long as they persist in this prejudice, any intervention on the part of our government which should place us in active opposition to the North, and inferential alliance with the South, would scarcely be supported by the hearty cooperation of the British nation."

In other words: the attempt at such intervention would cause the downfall of the ministry. And this also explains why *The Times* pronounces itself so decidedly against any intervention and for England's neutrality.

Written on January 31, 1862

First published in *Die Presse*, No. 34, February 4, 1862

Printed according to the newspaper

Karl Marx

ON THE COTTON CRISIS [175]

Some days ago[a] the annual meeting of the *Chamber of Commerce of Manchester* took place. It represents Lancashire, the greatest industrial district of the United Kingdom and the chief seat of British cotton manufacture. The chairman of the meeting, Mr. E. Potter, and the principal speakers at it, Messrs. Bazley and Turner, represent Manchester and a part of Lancashire in the Lower House. From the proceedings of the meeting, therefore, we learn *officially* what attitude the great centre of the English cotton industry will adopt in the "Senate of the nation" in face of the American crisis.[b]

At the meeting of the Chamber of Commerce *last year* Mr. Ashworth, one of England's biggest cotton barons, had celebrated with Pindaric extravagance the unexampled expansion of the cotton industry during the last decade.[c] In particular he stressed that even the commercial crises of 1847 and 1857 had produced no falling off in the export of English cotton yarns and textile fabrics. He explained the phenomenon by the wonder-working powers of the free trade system introduced in 1846.[d] Even then it sounded strange that this system, though unable to spare England the crises of 1847 and 1857, should be able to withdraw a

---

[a] January 30, 1862.— *Ed.*

[b] Below Marx makes use of the article "Indian Import Duties and the American Question", published in *The Times*, No. 24157, January 31, 1862.— *Ed.*

[c] The meeting was held on January 30, 1860. A report on it appeared in *The Times*, No. 23530, on January 31, 1860, under the title "Manchester Chamber of Commerce".— *Ed.*

[d] The system was introduced by "An Act to Amend the Laws Relating to the Importation of Corn".— *Ed.*

particular branch of English industry—the cotton industry—from the influence of those crises. But what do we hear to-day? All the speakers, Mr. Ashworth included, confess that since 1858 an unprecedented glutting of the Asian markets has taken place and that in consequence of steadily continuing *overproduction* on a mass scale the present stagnation was bound to occur, even without the American Civil War, the Morrill tariff[176] and the blockade. Whether without these aggravating circumstances the falling off in last year's exports would have been as much as £6,000,000, naturally remains an open question, but does not appear improbable when we hear that the principal markets of Asia and Australia are stocked with English cotton manufactures for twelve months.

Thus, according to the admission of the Manchester Chamber of Commerce, which in *this* matter speaks with authority, the crisis in the English cotton industry has so far been the result not of the American blockade, but of English overproduction. But what would be the consequences of a continuation of the American Civil War? To this question we again receive an unanimous answer: Measureless suffering for the working class and ruin for the smaller manufacturers.

"It is said in London," observed Mr. Cheetham, "that we have still plenty of cotton to go on with; but it is not a question of cotton, but a question of *price,* and at present prices the capital of the millowners is being destroyed."

The Chamber of Commerce, however, declares itself to be decidedly *against any intervention* in the United States, although most of its members are sufficiently swayed by *The Times* to consider the dissolution of the Union to be unavoidable.

"The last thing," says Mr. Potter, "that we could recommend is intervention. The last place whence such a proposal could issue is Manchester. Nothing will tempt us to suggest anything that is morally wrong."

Mr. *Bazley:*

"Our attitude to the American quarrel must be one of strict non-intervention. The people of that vast country must be allowed to settle their own affairs."

Mr. *Cheetham:*

"The leading opinion in this district is wholly opposed to any intervention in the American dispute. It is necessary to make this clear, because strong pressure would be put by the other side upon the Government if there was any doubt of it."

What, then, does the Chamber of Commerce recommend? The English government ought to remove all the obstacles of an administrative character that still impede cotton cultivation in *India.* In particular, it ought to lift the import duty of 10 per cent with which English cotton yarns and textile fabrics are burdened in India. The régime of the East India Company[177] had hardly been done away with, East India had hardly been incorporated in the British Empire, when Palmerston introduced this import duty on *English* manufactures through Mr. Wilson, and that at the same time as he sold Savoy and Nice for the Anglo-French commercial treaty.[178] Whilst the French market was opened to English industry to a certain extent, the East Indian market was closed to it to a greater extent.

With reference to the above, Mr. Bazley remarked that since the introduction of this duty great quantities of English machinery had been exported to Bombay and Calcutta and factories had been erected there in the English style. These were preparing to snatch the best Indian cotton from them. If 15 per cent for freight are added to the 10 per cent import duty, the rivals artificially called into being through the initiative of the English government enjoy a protective duty of 25 per cent.

In general, bitter resentment was expressed at the meeting of magnates of English industry at the protectionist tendency that was developing more and more in the colonies, in Australia in particular. The gentlemen forget that for a century and a half the colonies protested in vain against the "colonial system" of the mother country. At that time the colonies demanded free trade. England insisted on prohibition. Now England preaches free trade, and the colonies find protection against England better suited to their interests.

Written in early February 1862

First published in *Die Presse*, No. 38, February 8, 1862

Printed according to the newspaper

Karl Marx

ENGLISH [179]

"Eccentricity" or "individuality" are the marks of insular John Bull in the minds of continentals. On the whole, this notion confuses the Englishman of the past with the Englishman of the present. Intense class development, extreme division of labour and what is called "public opinion", manipulated by the Brahmins of the press, have, on the contrary, produced a monotony of character that would make it impossible for a Shakespeare, for example, to recognise his own countrymen. The differences no longer belong to the individuals but to their "profession" and class. Apart from his profession, in everyday life one "respectable" Englishman is so like another that even Leibniz could hardly discover a difference, a *differentia specifica*, between them.[a] The individuality, so highly praised, is banished from every sphere of politics and society and finds its last refuge in the crotchets and whims of private life, asserting itself there now and then *sans-gêne*[b] and with unconscious humour. Hence it is chiefly in the *courts of justice*—those great public arenas in which private whims clash with one another—that the Englishman still appears as a being *sui generis.*[c]

This is the preface to a diverting courtroom scene that took place a few days ago in the Court of Exchequer.[d] The *dramatis personae* were, on one side, Sir Edwin Landseer, the greatest

---

[a] See G. W. Leibniz, *Nouveaux essais sur l'entendement humain.* Livre deuxième "Des idées", chapitre XXVII "Ce que c'est qu'identité ou diversité."— *Ed.*
[b] Brusquely.— *Ed.*
[c] Unique of its kind.— *Ed.*
[d] Marx uses the English name.— *Ed.*

English painter of the present time, and, on the other, Messrs. Haldane, first-rate London tailors; Sir Edwin was the defendant, Messrs. Haldane the plaintiffs. The *corpus delicti* consisted of an overcoat and a frock-coat, valued at £12, for which the painter refused to pay. Sergeant[a] Ballantine pleaded for Landseer, Mr. Griffiths for Haldane.

Haldane testifies: Sir Edwin Landseer ordered the two coats. They had been sent to him to try on and he had complained about the height of the collars. They were altered. Now he complained that he could not wear them without feeling hot and uncomfortable in them. In addition, they rubbed against the hair of his head. To please the defendant, various alterations were made. Finally, the plaintiffs refused to make any more alterations unless they were specially paid for. At that point Landseer sent the two coats back by his servant. The plaintiffs then sent him the following letter: [b]

"We beg respectfully to send you two coats, having again altered them according to the direction you last gave. The many alterations you speak of as being unsuccessful arise from your own fault. The coats when first tried on fitted remarkably well, but if you will place your body into the most unreasonable positions it will require something more than human science to fit you. (Laughter.) We have most unwillingly made the alterations you have required, believing them to be unnecessary and contrary to the rules of our craft, and we now find it impossible to please you. With reference to your demand that we should take the coats back, we cannot think of doing so. We therefore annex the enclosed statement and request prompt payment."

Sergeant *Ballantine:* You would not assert that the coats fit now? *Haldane:* That is what I assert.

Ballantine: Were they not better before they were altered? *Haldane:* Yes.

B.: Coats are not your speciality. You are big in the trousers field, aren't you?

H.: Well, we are better known for trousers.

B.: But not for coats? Did not Mr. Alfred Montgomery, who introduced Sir Edwin Landseer to you, warn him about your coats?

H.: Yes, he did.

B.: Did not you or your brother tell Sir Edwin that you would rather make the coats for nothing than not make them at all?

H.: We said nothing of the sort.

B.: What do you mean by "weakening" the collar?

---

[a] Here and below Marx uses the English word.— *Ed.*

[b] Quoted from the report "Court of Exchequer, Feb. 1" published in *The Times*, No. 24159, February 3, 1862.— *Ed.*

H.: Sir Edwin complained that the coat collar irritated his neck. So we weakened the collar, that is, we reduced it to a smaller size.

B.: And how much are you charging for this reduction?

H.: Two or three pounds.

Sergeant *Ballantine:* Sir Edwin Landseer considered it necessary to complain of Haldane's insulting letter. Mr. Montgomery advised Sir Edwin to entrust the lower part of his body to the Haldane firm, but by no means the upper portion. Although Sir Edwin is a great artist, he is a mere child in these things and so took the risk, and the jury sees what the consequences were. The plaintiff, whom the jurors have just seen on the witness stand, is also a great artist. But would a great artist ever remodel his work? He must stand or fall on his feeling of its excellence; but Haldane did not stand up for the excellence of his work. He acceded to alterations so long as they corresponded to his own principles. And then to ask two or three pounds for his botching! I have the honour of addressing a tribunal that wears coats; I ask it whether there is any greater torture in the world than a stiff collar on the neck? I hear that when Sir Edwin put on one of these coats, his neck was in a vice and England was in danger of losing one of its greatest artists. Sir Edwin consents to put the coats in question on before the court, and the gentlemen of the jury can then decide for themselves. I now call Sir Edwin as a witness, and he will tell you the story of the two coats.

Sir Edwin Landseer: ... When I put the coats on—the collar was like this. (At this point Sir Edwin turned around and to loud laughter presented his back to the jurors, leaving the impression in their minds that he had suddenly suffered an apoplectic fit.) ... I offered to leave the decision to the arbitration of any tailor; but all the same any one must know best how his coat fits or where his shoe pinches.

Mr. *Griffiths:* What did Mr. Montgomery say when he introduced you to the Haldane firm?

He said to me: "Sir Edwin, you are usually not so fortunate with your trousers as your coats."

Griffiths: Would you try the coats on here?

Why not? (Puts one of the coats on.) Now look! (Laughter.)

Baron *Martin* (the judge): There is a tailor among the jurors. Will the gentleman be good enough to look carefully at the *corpus delicti?*

The aforesaid tailor leaves the jury box and goes over to Sir Edwin, has him put on the frock-coat and the overcoat, examines them expertly and shakes his head.

Griffiths: Sir Edwin, do you consider the frock-coat too tight?
Yes! (Laughter.)
Too narrow? I ask.
Well, I would have to take it off, if I had to eat luncheon *in it.*
Ballantine: Then, Sir Edwin, you need not be stuck in it any longer. Emancipate yourself from it.
I am much obliged to you. (Takes the coats off.)
After moving pleas by the two attorneys and a comical summing-up by the judge, who stressed in particular that English comfort should not be sacrificed to the artistic ideals of the firm of Haldane, the jury found for Sir Edwin Landseer.

Written about February 3, 1862

First published in *Die Presse*, No. 39, February 9, 1862

Printed according to the newspaper

Published in English for the first time

Karl Marx

THE PARLIAMENTARY DEBATE
ON THE ADDRESS [180]

London, February 7

The opening of Parliament was a lusterless ceremony. The absence of the Queen and the reading of the Speech from the Throne[a] by the Lord Chancellor[b] banished every theatrical effect. The Speech from the Throne itself is short without being striking. It recapitulates the *faits accomplis*[c] of foreign politics and, for an estimation of these facts, refers to the documents submitted to Parliament.[d] Only one remark created a certain sensation, the one in which the Queen "trusts[e] there is no reason to apprehend any disturbance of the peace of Europe". It in fact implies that European peace is relegated to the domain of hope and faith.

In accordance with parliamentary practice, the gentlemen who moved the Reply to the Speech from the Throne in the two Houses had already been commissioned by the ministers with this business three weeks before. In conformity with the usual procedure, their Reply consists of a broad echo of the Speech from the Throne and of fulsome praises that the ministers bestow upon themselves in the name of Parliament. When Sir *Francis Burdett* anticipated the official movers of the Address in 1811 and seized the opportunity to subject the Speech from the Throne to a

---

[a] Victoria [Speech from the Throne on the opening of Parliament], *The Times*, No. 24163, February 7, 1862.— *Ed.*

[b] R. Bethell.— *Ed.*

[c] Accomplished facts.— *Ed.*

[d] The reference is to *Convention, conclue à Londres, le 31 octobre 1861, entre l'Espagne, la France et la Grande-Bretagne pour combiner une action commune contre le Mexique* and *Convention entre la Grande-Bretagne et le Maroc relative à un emprunt à faire à Londres par le Maroc; signée à Tanger, le 24 octobre 1861.—Ed.*

[e] Marx uses the English word and gives the German translation in brackets.— *Ed.*

cutting criticism,[a] Magna Charta[181] itself appeared to be imper-
illed. Since that time no further enormity of the kind has
happened.

The interest of the debate on the Speech from the Throne is
therefore limited to the "hints" of the official Opposition clubs
and the "counter-hints" of the ministers. This time, however, the
interest was more academic than political. It was a question of the
best funeral oration on Prince Albert, who during his life found
the yoke of the English oligarchy by no means light. According to
the *vox populi,* Derby and Disraeli have borne off the academic
palm, the first as a natural speaker, the other as a rhetorician.

The "business" part of the debate turned on the *United States,
Mexico,* and *Morocco.*

With regard to the *United States,* the *Outs* (those out of office)
eulogised the policy of the *Ins*[b] (the *beati possidentes*[c]). *Derby,* the
Conservative leader in the House of Lords, and *Disraeli,* the
Conservative leader in the Lower House, opposed not the Cabinet,
but each other.

Derby in the first place gave vent to his dissatisfaction[d] over the
absence of *"pressure from without".*[e] He "admired", he said, the
stoical and dignified bearing of the factory workers. As far as the
millowners were concerned, however, he ought to exclude them
from his commendation. For them the American disturbance had
come in extraordinarily handy, since overproduction and glutting of
all markets had in any case imposed on them a restriction of trade.

Derby went on to make a violent attack on the Union
government, "which had exposed itself and its people to the most
undignified humiliation" and had not acted like "gentlemen",
because it had not taken the initiative and voluntarily surrendered
Mason, Slidell and company and made amends. His seconder in
the Lower House, Mr. *Disraeli,* at once grasped how very
damaging Derby's onslaught was to the Conservatives' aspirations
to the Ministry. He therefore declared to the contrary:

"When I consider the great difficulties which the statesmen of North America
have had to encounter ... I would venture to say they have met these manfully and
courageously." [f]

---

[a] In his speech in the House of Commons of February 12, 1811.— *Ed.*
[b] Marx uses the English words "Ins" and "Outs" here and below.— *Ed.*
[c] Blessed possessors.— *Ed.*
[d] E. Derby [Speech in the House of Lords on February 6, 1862], *The Times,*
No. 24163, February 7, 1862.— *Ed.*
[e] Marx uses the English phrase.— *Ed.*
[f] B. Disraeli [Speech in the House of Commons, February 6, 1862], *The Times,*
same issue.— *Ed.*

On the other hand—with the consistency customary to him—
Derby protested against the "new doctrines" of maritime law.
England had at all times upheld belligerents' rights against the
pretensions of neutrals. Lord Clarendon, it was true, had made a
"dangerous" concession at Paris in 1856.[182] Happily, this had not
yet been ratified by the Crown, so that "it did not alter the state of
international law". Mr. *Disraeli,* on the contrary, manifestly in
collusion with the ministry here, avoided touching on this point at
all.

Derby approved of the non-intervention policy of the ministry.
The time to recognise the Southern Confederacy had not *yet*
come, but he demanded authentic documents for the purpose of
judging "how far the blockade is effective and therefore legally
binding". Lord *John Russell,* on the other hand, declared that the
Union government had employed a sufficient number of ships in
the blockade, but had not everywhere carried this out consistently.
Mr. *Disraeli* will permit himself no judgment on the nature of the
blockade, but demands ministerial papers for enlightenment. He
gives such emphatic warning against any premature recognition of
the Confederacy since England is compromising herself at the
present moment by threatening an American state (Mexico), the
independence of which she herself was the first to recognise.

After the *United States,* it was *Mexico's* turn. No member of
Parliament condemned a war without declaration of war,[183] but
they condemned interference in the internal affairs of a country
under the shibboleth of a "non-intervention policy", and the
coalition of England with France and Spain in order to intimidate
a semi-defenceless country. As a matter of fact, the *Outs* merely
indicated that they reserve Mexico to themselves for party
manoeuvres. *Derby* demands documents on both the Convention
between the three powers and the mode of carrying it out. He
approves of the Convention because—in his view—the right way
was for each of the contracting parties to enforce its claims *independently* of the others. Certain public rumours caused him to fear
that at least one of the powers—Spain—purposed operations going
beyond the provisions of the treaty. As if Derby really believed
the great power, Spain, capable of the audacity of acting *counter* to
the will of England and France! Lord *John Russell* answered: The
three powers pursued *the same* aim and would anxiously avoid
hindering the Mexicans from regulating their own political affairs.

In the Lower House, Mr. *Disraeli* defers any judgment prior to
scrutinising the documents submitted. However, he finds "the
announcement of the government *suspicious"*. The independence

of Mexico was first recognised by England. This recognition recalls a notable policy—the anti-Holy-Alliance policy—and a notable man, *Canning.* What singular occasion, then, drove England to strike the first blow against this independence? Moreover, the intervention has changed its pretext within a very short time. Originally it was a question of satisfaction for wrong done to English subjects. Now there are rumours about the introduction of new governmental principles and the setting up of a new dynasty. Lord *Palmerston* refers to the papers submitted, to the Convention that prohibits the "subjugation" of Mexico by the Allies or the imposition of a form of government distasteful to the people. At the same time, however, he opens a diplomatic loophole. He has it from hearsay that a party in Mexico desires the transformation of the republic into a monarchy. The strength of this party he does not know. He, "for his part, only wishes that there shall be established *some form of government* in Mexico with which foreign governments may treat". He wishes, therefore, to establish a "new" form of government. He declares the *non-existence of the present government.* He claims for the alliance of England, France and Spain the prerogative of the Holy Alliance to decide over the existence or non-existence of foreign governments. "That is the utmost," he adds modestly, "which the government of Great Britain is desirous of obtaining." Nothing more!

The last "open question" of foreign policy concerned *Morocco.* The English government has concluded a convention with Morocco in order to enable her to pay off her debt to Spain, a debt with which Spain could never have saddled Morocco without England's leave. Certain persons, it appears, have advanced Morocco money with which to pay her instalments to Spain, thus depriving the latter of a pretext for further occupation of Tetuan and resumption of war.[184] The British government has in one way or another guaranteed these persons the interest on their loan and, in its turn, takes over the administration of Morocco's customs houses as security. Derby found this manner of ensuring the independence of Morocco *"rather strange"*,[a] but elicited no answer from the ministers. In the Lower House Mr. *Disraeli* went into the transaction further: it was "to some extent unconstitutional", since the ministry had saddled England with new financial obligations behind Parliament's back. *Palmerston* simply referred him to the "documents" submitted.

---

[a] Marx uses the English words "rather strange" and gives the German translation in brackets.— *Ed.*

Home affairs were hardly mentioned. Derby merely warned members, out of regard "for the state of mind of the Queen", not to raise "disturbing" controversial questions like parliamentary reform. He is ready to pay his tribute of admiration regularly to the English working class, on condition that it suffers its exclusion from popular representation with the same restraint and stoicism as it suffers the American blockade.

It would be a mistake to infer from the idyllic opening of Parliament an idyllic future. Quite the contrary! Dissolution of Parliament or dissolution of the ministry is the motto of this year's session. Opportunity to substantiate these alternatives will be found later.

Written on February 7, 1862

First published in *Die Presse*, No. 42, February 12, 1862

Printed according to the newspaper

Karl Marx

THE MEXICAN IMBROGLIO [185]

London, Feb. 15, 1862

The Blue Book on the intervention in Mexico,[a] just published, contains the most damning exposure of modern English diplomacy with all its hypocritical cant, ferocity against the weak, crawling before the strong, and utter disregard of international law. I must reserve for another letter the task of forwarding, by a minute analysis of the dispatches exchanged between Downing street and the British representatives of Mexico, the irrefragable proof that the present imbroglio is of English origin, that England took the initiative in bringing about the intervention, and did so on pretexts too flimsy and self-contradictory to even veil the real but unavowed motives of her proceedings. This infamy of the means employed in starting the Mexican intervention is only surpassed by the anile imbecility with which the British government affect to be surprised at and slink out of the execution of the nefarious scheme planned by themselves. It is the latter part of the business I propose dealing with for the present.[b]

On the 13th December, 1861, Mr. Istúriz, the Spanish Ambassador at London, submitted to John Russell a note including the instructions sent by the Captain-General of Cuba[c] to the Spanish commanders, at the head of the expedition to Mexico. John Russell shelved the note and kept silent. On the 23d December, Mr. Istúriz addresses him a new note, professing to explain the

---

[a] *Correspondence Respecting the Affairs of Mexico.* Presented to both Houses of Parliament by Command of Her Majesty, 3 parts, London, 1862.— *Ed.*

[b] Here and below Marx draws on material published under the heading "Papers Relating to Mexican Affairs" in *The Times*, No. 24168, February 13, 1862.— *Ed.*

[c] F. Serrano y Dominguez.— *Ed.*

reasons that had induced the Spanish expedition to leave Cuba before the arrival of the English and French forces. John Russell again shelves the note and persists in his taciturn attitude. Mr. Istúriz, anxious to ascertain whether that protracted restraint of speech so unusual in the verbose upshoot of the house of Bedford, means possibly mischief, urges a personal interview, which is granted to him, and takes place on the 7th of January. John Russell had now for more than a month been fully acquainted with the onesided opening of the operations against Mexico on the part of Spain. A month had almost passed since the event had been officially communicated to him by Mr. Istúriz. With all that, in his personal interview with the Spanish Ambassador, John Russell breaks no word breathing the slightest displeasure or astonishment at "the precipitate steps taken by Gen. Serrano," nor leave his utterances the faintest impression on the mind of Mr. Istúriz that all was not right, and that the Spanish proceedings were not fully approved of by the British Government. The Castilian pride of Mr. Istúriz shuns, of course, any notion of Spain being played with by her powerful allies and made a mere catspaw of. Yet, the time of the meeting of Parliament approached, and John Russell had now to pen a series of dispatches, especially intended, not for international business, but for Parliamentary consumption. Accordingly, on the 16th of January, he pens a dispatch inquiring, in rather angry tones, about the onesided initiative ventured upon by Spain. Doubts and scruples, which for longer than a month had slumbered in his bosom, and had not even matured into symptoms of existence, on the 7th of January, during his personal interview with Mr. Istúriz, all at once disturb the serene dream of that confident, sincere and unsuspecting statesman. Mr. Istúriz feels thunderstruck, and in his reply, dated January 18, somewhat ironically reminds his Excellency of the opportunities missed by him of giving vent to his posthumous spleen. He pays in fact his Excellency in his own coin, assuming in his justification of the initiative taken by Spain, the same air of *naïveté* Lord John Russell affected in his request for an explanation.

"The Captain-General of Cuba," says Mr. Istúriz, "came too early because he was fearful of arriving too late at Vera Cruz." "Besides," and here he pinches Lord John, "the expedition had been for a long time ready on every point," although the Captain-General, till the middle of December, was "unacquainted with the details of the treaty, and with the point fixed for the meeting of the squadrons."

Now, the treaty was not concluded before the 20th of November. If, then, the Captain-General had his expedition for a long time "ready in every point before the middle of December," the orders originally sent out to him from Europe for starting the expedition, had not waited upon the treaty. In other words, the original agreement between the three Powers, and the steps taken in its execution, did not wait upon the treaty, and differed in their "details" from the clauses of the treaty, which, from the beginning, were intended not as a rule of action, but only as decent formulas, necessary to conciliate the public mind to the nefarious scheme. On the 23d January, John Russell replies to Mr. Istúriz in rather a bluff note, intimating to him that "the British Government was *not entirely* satisfied with the explanation offered," but, at the same time would not suspect Spain of the fool-hardiness of presuming to act in the teeth of England and France. Lord John Russell, so sleepy, so inactive, for a whole month, becomes all life and wide awake as the Parliamentary session rapidly draws near. No time is to be lost. On the 19th of January he has a personal interview with Count Flahaut, the French Ambassador at London. Flahaut broaches to him the ill-omened news that his master considered it necessary "to send an additional force to Mexico," that Spain by her precipitate initiative had spoiled the mess; that

"the allies must now advance to the interior of Mexico, and that not only the forces agreed upon would now prove insufficient for the operation, but that the operation itself would assume a character in regard to which Louis Bonaparte could not allow the French forces to be in a position of inferiority to those of Spain, or run the risk of being compromised."

Now, Flahaut's argumentation was anything but conclusive. If Spain had overstepped the convention, a single note to Madrid from the quarters of St. James and the Tuileries would have sufficed to warn her off her ridiculous pretensions, and drive her back to the modest part imposed upon her by the convention. But no. Because Spain has broken the convention—a breach merely formal and of no consequence, since her premature arrival at Vera Cruz changed nothing in the professed aim and purpose of the expedition—because Spain had presumed to cast anchor at Vera Cruz in the absence of the English and French forces, there remained no other issue open to France but to follow in the track of Spain, break also the convention, and augment, not only her expeditionary forces, but change the whole character of the operation. There was, of course, no pretext needed for the Allied Powers to let the murder out, and, on the very outset of the expedition, set at naught the pretexts and purposes upon which it was ostensibly started. Consequently, John Russell, although he

"regrets the step" taken by France, indorses it by telling Count
Flahaut that "he had no objection to offer, on behalf of her
Majesty's Government, to the *validity* of the French *argument.*" In
a dispatch dated January 20, he forwards to Earl Cowley, the
English Ambassador at Paris, the narrative of this his interview
with Count Flahaut. The day before, on the 19th January, he had
penned a dispatch to Sir F. Crampton, the English Ambassador at
Madrid—that dispatch being a curious medley of hypocritical cant
addressed to the British Parliament, and of sly hints to the Court
of Madrid as to the intrinsic value of the liberal slang so freely
indulged in. "The proceedings of Marshal Serrano," he says, "are
calculated to produce some uneasiness," not only because of the
precipitate departure of the Spanish expedition from Havana, but
also "of the tone of the proclamations issued by the Spanish
Government." But, simultaneously, the *bon homme* suggests to the
Madrid Court a plausible excuse for their apparent breach of the
Convention. He is fully convinced that the Madrid Court means
no harm; but, then, commanders, at a distance from Europe, are
sometimes "rash," and require "to be very closely watched." Thus,
good man Russell volunteers his services, in order to shift the
responsibility from the Court at Madrid to the shoulders of
indiscreet Spanish commanders "at a distance," and even out of
the reach of good man Russell's sermonizing. Not less curious is
the other part of his dispatch. The Allied forces are not to
preclude the Mexicans from their right "of choosing their own
Government," thus intimating that there exists "no Government"
in Mexico; but that, on the contrary, not only new governors, but
even "a new form of Government," must so be chosen by the
Mexicans under the auspices of the Allied invaders. Their
"constituting a new Government" would "delight" the British
Government; but, of course, the military forces of the invaders
must not falsify the general suffrage which they intend calling the
Mexicans to for the installation of a new Government. It rests, of
course, with the commanders of the armed invasion to judge what
form of new government is or is not "repugnant to the feelings of
Mexico." At all events, good man Russell washes his hands in
innocence. He dispatches foreign dragoons to Mexico, there to
force the people into "choosing" a new Government; but he hopes
the dragoons will do the thing gently, and be very careful in
sifting the political feelings of the country they invade. Is it
necessary to expatiate one moment upon this transparent farce?
Apart from the context of good man Russell's dispatches, read *The
Times* and *The Morning Post* of October, six weeks before the

conclusion of the sham convention of Nov. 30,[a] and you will find
the English Government prints to foretell all the very same
untoward events Russell feigns to discover only at the end of
January, and to account for by "the rashness" of some Spanish
Ambassadors at a distance from Europe.

The second part of the farce Russell had to play was the putting
on the tapis of the Archduke Maximilian of Austria as the
Mexican King held in petto by England and France.

On the 24th of January, about ten days before the opening of
Parliament, Lord Cowley writes to Lord Russell that not only Paris
gossip was much busied with the Archduke, but that the very
officers going with the re-enforcements to Mexico, pretended that
the expedition was for the purpose of making the Archduke
Maximilian King of Mexico. Cowley thinks it necessary to
interpellate Thouvenel upon the delicate subject. Thouvenel
answers him, that it was not the French Government, but Mexican
emissaries, "come for the purpose, and gone to Vienna," that had
set on foot such negotiations with the Austrian Government.

Now, at last, you expect unsuspecting John Russell, who even
five days ago, in his dispatch to Madrid, had harped upon the
terms of the convention, who even later yet, in the Royal speech of
Feb. 6, had proclaimed "the redress" of wrongs sustained by
European subjects the exclusive motive and purpose of the
intervention[b]—you expect him now at last to fly into a passion and
to fret and foam at the very idea of his kind-natured confidence
having been played such unheard-of pranks with. Nothing of the
sort! Good man Russell receives Cowley's gossip on the 26th of
January, and on the following day he hastens to sit down and
write a dispatch volunteering his patronage of the Archduke
Maximilian's candidature for the Mexican throne.[c]

He informs Sir C. Wyke, his representative at Mexico, that the
French and Spanish troops will march "at once" to the City of
Mexico; that Archduke Maximilian "is said" to be the idol of the
Mexican people, and that, if such be the case, "there is nothing in
the convention to prevent his advent to the throne of Mexico."

There are two things remarkable in these diplomatic revelations:
first, the fool Spain is made of; and secondly, that there never
passes the slightest thought through Russell's mind that he cannot

---

    [a] This probably refers to the treaty signed on November 20, 1861.— Ed.

    [b] J. Russell [Speech in the House of Lords on February 6, 1862], The Times,
No. 24163, February 7, 1862.— Ed.

    [c] Presumably, a slip of the pen in the text. Russell received Cowley's report on
the 25th, Russell's dispatch was sent on the 27th.— Ed.

wage war upon Mexico without a previous declaration of war, and that he can form no coalition for that war with foreign Powers, except on the ground of a treaty binding upon all parties. And such is the people who have fatigued us for two months with their hypocritical cant on the sacredness of, and their homage to, the strict rules of international law! [186]

Written on February 15, 1862   Reproduced from the newspaper

First published in the *New-York Daily Tribune*, No. 6530, March 10, 1862

Karl Marx

AMERICAN AFFAIRS [187]

President Lincoln never ventures a step forward before the tide of circumstances and the general call of public opinion forbid further delay. But once "Old Abe"[a] realises that such a turning point has been reached, he surprises friend and foe alike by a sudden operation executed as noiselessly as possible. Thus, in the most unassuming manner, he quite recently carried out a coup that half a year earlier would possibly have cost him his presidential office and only a few months ago would have called forth a storm of debate. We mean the *removal of McClellan* from his post of Commander-in-Chief[b] of all the Union armies. Lincoln first of all replaced the Secretary of War, Cameron, by an energetic and ruthless lawyer, Mr. *Edwin Stanton*. An order of the day was then issued by Stanton to generals Buell, Halleck, Butler, Sherman and other commanders of whole areas or leaders of expeditions, notifying them that in future they would receive all orders, open and secret, from the War Department direct and, on the other hand, would have to report directly to the War Department. Finally, Lincoln issued some orders which he signed as "Commander-in-Chief of the Army and Navy", an attribute to which he was constitutionally entitled. In this "quiet" manner "the young Napoleon"[188] was deprived of the supreme command he had hitherto held over *all* the armies and restricted to the command of the army on the Potomac, although the *title* of "Commander-in-Chief" was left to him. The successes in Kentucky,

---

[a] Marx uses the English nickname.—*Ed.*
[b] Here and below Marx uses the English title.—*Ed.*

Tennessee and on the Atlantic coast propitiously inaugurated the assumption of the supreme command by President Lincoln. The post of Commander-in-Chief hitherto occupied by *McClellan* was bequeathed to the United States by Britain and corresponds roughly to the dignity of a Grand Connetable[a] in the old French army. During the Crimean War even Britain discovered the inexpediency of this old-fashioned institution. A compromise was accordingly effected by which part of the attributes hitherto belonging to the Commander-in-Chief were transferred to the War Ministry.

The requisite material for an estimate of McClellan's Fabian tactics[189] on the Potomac is still lacking. That his influence, however, acted as a brake on the general conduct of the war, is beyond doubt. One can say of McClellan what Macaulay says of Essex:

"The military errors of Essex were produced for the most part by political timidity. He was honestly, but by no means warmly, attached to the cause of Parliament; and next to a great defeat he dreaded nothing so much as a great victory."[b]

McClellan and most of the officers of the regular army who got their training at West Point[190] are more or less bound by *esprit de corps*[c] to their old comrades in the enemy camp. They are inspired by the same jealousy of the *parvenus* among the "civilian soldiers". In their view, the war must be waged in a strictly businesslike fashion, with constant regard to the restoration of the Union on its *old* basis, and therefore must above all be kept free from revolutionary tendencies and tendencies affecting matters of principle. A fine conception of a war which is essentially a war of principles. The first generals of the English Parliament fell into the same error.

"But," said *Cromwell* in his speech to the Rump on July 4, 1653, "how changed everything was as soon as men took the lead who professed a principle of godliness and religion!"[d]

The Washington *Star*,[e] McClellan's special organ, declares in one of its latest issues:

---

[a] Grand Constable.— *Ed.*

[b] Th. B. Macaulay, *Critical and Historical Essays Contributed to the Edinburgh Review*, Vol. I, *John Hampden.—Ed.*

[c] Common spirit pervading the members of a body as a whole.— *Ed.*

[d] Th. Carlyle, *Oliver Cromwell's Letters and Speeches, with elucidations*, Vol. II. Marx partly quotes in English: "a principle of godliness, etc.".— *Ed.*

[e] *Evening Star.— Ed.*

"The end and aim of all General McClellan's military combinations is the restoration of the Union *just* as it existed before the Rebellion began." [a]

No wonder, therefore, that on the Potomac, under the eyes of the general-in-chief, the army was trained to catch slaves! Only recently, by a special order, McClellan expelled the Kutchinson family of musicians from the camp because they sang anti-slavery songs.

Apart from such "anti-tendency" demonstrations, McClellan covered the traitors in the Union army with his saving shield. Thus, for example, he promoted Maynard to a higher post, although Maynard, as the papers made public by the committee of inquiry of the House of Representatives prove, was active as an agent of the secessionists. From General · Patterson, whose treachery determined the defeat at Manassas, to General Stone, who *brought about* the defeat at Ball's Bluff in direct agreement with the enemy,[191] McClellan managed to save every military traitor from court martial, and in most cases even from dismissal. The Congress committee of inquiry has revealed the most surprising facts in this respect. Lincoln resolved to prove by an energetic step that with his assumption of the supreme command the hour of the traitors in epaulets had struck and a *turning point* in the war policy had been reached. By his order, General Stone was arrested in his bed at two o'clock in the morning of February 10 and taken to Fort Lafayette. A few hours later, the order for his arrest, signed by *Stanton,* appeared; in this the charge of high treason was formulated, to be judged by court martial. Stone's arrest and putting on trial took place without any previous communication to General McClellan.

As long as he himself remained in a state of inaction and merely wore his laurels in advance, McClellan was obviously determined to allow no other general to forestall him. Generals Halleck and Pope had resolved on a combined movement to force General Price, who had already been saved once from Frémont by the intervention of Washington, to a decisive battle. A telegram from McClellan forbade them to deliver the blow. General Halleck was "ordered back" by a similar telegram from the capture of Fort Columbus, at a time when this fort stood half under water. McClellan had expressly forbidden the generals in the West to correspond with one another. Each of them was obliged first to apply to Washington whenever a combined movement was

---

[a] Quoted from an item in the *New-York Daily Tribune,* No. 6508, February 12, 1862, beginning with the words: "*The Washington Star,* in an article...".— *Ed.*

intended. President Lincoln has now restored to them the necessary freedom of action.

How advantageous to secession McClellan's general military policy was is best proved by the panegyrics that the *New-York Herald* continually lavishes upon him. He is a hero after the *Herald*'s own heart. The notorious *Bennett*, proprietor and editor-in-chief of the *Herald*, had formerly held the administrations of Pierce and Buchanan in his power through his "special representatives", alias correspondents, in Washington. Under Lincoln's Administration he sought to win the same power again in a roundabout way, by having his "special representative", Dr. *Ives*, a man of the South and brother of an officer who had deserted to the Confederacy, worm himself into McClellan's favour. Under McClellan's patronage, great liberties must have been allowed this Ives at the time when Cameron was at the head of the War Department. He evidently expected Stanton to guarantee him the same privileges and accordingly presented himself on February 8 at the War Office, where the Secretary of War, his chief secretary and some members of Congress were discussing war measures. He was shown the door. He got up on his hind legs and finally beat a retreat, threatening that the *Herald* would open fire on the present War Department in the event of its withholding from him his "special privilege" of having, in particular, Cabinet deliberations, telegrams, public communications and war news confided to him in the War Department. Next morning, February 9, Dr. Ives had assembled the whole of McClellan's General Staff at a champagne breakfast with him. Misfortune, however, moves fast.[a] A non-commissioned officer entered with six men, seized the mighty Ives and took him to Fort McHenry, where, as the order of the Secretary of War expressly states, he "is to be kept under strict watch *as a spy*".[b]

Written in late February 1862

First published in *Die Presse*, No. 61, March 3, 1862

Printed according to the newspaper

---

[a] A line from Schiller's *Lied von der Glocke*.—*Ed.*
[b] "War Department, Washington, Feb. 10, 1862", *New-York Daily Tribune*, No. 6507, February 11, 1862.—*Ed.*

Karl Marx

THE SECESSIONISTS' FRIENDS IN THE LOWER HOUSE.—RECOGNITION OF THE AMERICAN BLOCKADE[192]

London, March 8

Parturiunt montes![a] Since the opening of Parliament the English friends of *Secessia* had threatened a "motion" on the American blockade. The resolution has at length been introduced in the Lower House[b] in the very modest form of a motion in which the government is urged "to submit further documents on the state of the blockade"—and even this insignificant motion was rejected without the formality of a division.

Mr. *Gregory,* the member for Galway, who moved the resolution, had in the parliamentary session of last year, shortly after the outbreak of the Civil War, already introduced a motion for recognition of the Southern Confederacy.[c] To his speech[d] of this year a certain sophistical adroitness is not to be denied. The speech merely suffers from the unfortunate circumstance that it falls into two parts, of which the one cancels the other. One part describes the disastrous effects of the blockade on the English cotton industry and *therefore* demands removal of the blockade. The other part proves from the papers submitted by the ministry, two memorials by Messrs. Yancey and Mann and by Mr. Mason among them, that the blockade does not *exist* at all, except on paper, and *therefore* should no longer be recognised. Mr. Gregory spiced his argument with successive citations from *The Times. The Times,* for whom a reminder of its oracular pronouncements is at

---

[a] Parturiunt montes, nascetur ridiculus mus!—The mountains are in labour, a ridiculous mouse will be born! (Horace, *Art of Poetry,* 139.)—*Ed.*

[b] W. H. Gregory [Speech in the House of Commons, March 7, 1862], *The Times,* No. 24188, March 8, 1862.—*Ed.*

[c] W. H. Gregory [Speech in the House of Commons, May 28, 1861], *The Times,* No. 23945, May 29, 1861.—*Ed.*

[d] Marx gives the English word.—*Ed.*

this moment thoroughly inconvenient, thanks Mr. Gregory with a *leader*[a] in which it holds him up to public ridicule.[b]

Mr. Gregory's motion was supported by Mr. *Bentinck*,[c] an ultra-Tory who for two years has laboured in vain to bring about a secession from Mr. Disraeli in the Conservative camp.

It was a ludicrous spectacle in and by itself to see the alleged interests of English industry represented by Gregory, the representative of Galway, an unimportant seaport in the West of Ireland, and by Bentinck, the representative of Norfolk, a purely agricultural district.

Mr. *Forster,* the representative of Bradford, a centre of English industry, rose to oppose them both. Forster's speech deserves closer examination, since it strikingly proves the vacuity of the phrases concerning the character of the American blockade given currency in Europe by the friends of secession. In the first place, he said, the United States have observed all formalities required by international law. They have declared no port in a state of blockade without previous proclamation, without special notice of the moment of its commencement or without fixing the fifteen days after the expiration of which entrance and departure shall be forbidden to foreign neutral ships.

The talk of the legal "inefficacy" of the blockade rests, therefore, merely on the allegedly frequent cases in which it has been broken through. Before the opening of Parliament it was said that 600 ships had broken through it. Mr. Gregory now reduces the number to 400. His evidence rests on two lists handed the government, the one on November 30 by the Southern commissioners *Yancey* and *Mann,* the other, the supplementary list, by *Mason.* According to Yancey and Mann, more than 400 ships broke through between the proclamation of the blockade and August 20, running the blockade either inwards or outwards. According to official customs-house reports, however, the total number of the incoming and outgoing ships amounts to only 322. Of this number, 119 departed *before* the declaration of the blockade, 56 *before* the expiration of the time allowance of fifteen days. There remain 147 ships. Of these 147 ships, 25 were river boats that sailed from inland to New Orleans, where they lie idle; 106 were coasters; with the exception of three ships, all were, in

---

[a] Marx uses the English word.— *Ed.*

[b] "The demand which Mr. Gregory makes...", *The Times,* No. 24188, March 8, 1862.— *Ed.*

[c] The speeches of Bentinck and other members of the House of Commons on March 7, 1862 are cited according to *The Times,* same issue.— *Ed.*

14*

the words of Mr. Mason himself, "quasi-inland"[a] vessels. Of these
106, 66 sailed between Mobile and New Orleans. Anyone who
knows this coast is aware how absurd it is to call the sailing of a
vessel behind lagoons, so that it hardly touches the open sea and
merely creeps along the coast, a breach of the blockade. The same
holds of the vessels between Savannah and Charleston, where they
sneak between islands and narrow tongues of land. According to
the testimony of the English consul, Bunch, these flat-bottomed
boats only appeared for a few days on the open sea. After
deducting 106 coasters, there remain 16 departures for foreign
ports; of these, 15 were for American ports, mainly Cuba, and one
for Liverpool. The "ship" that berthed in Liverpool was a
schooner, and so were all the rest of the "ships", with the
exception of a sloop. There has been much talk, exclaimed Mr.
Forster, of sham blockades. Is this list of Messrs. Yancey and
Mann not a sham list? He subjected the supplementary list of Mr.
Mason to a similar analysis, and showed further that the number
of cruisers that slipped out only amounted to three or four,
whereas in the last Anglo-American war[b] no less than 516
American cruisers broke through the English blockade and
harried the English seaboard.

"The blockade, on the contrary, has been wonderfully effective from its
commencement."

Further proof is provided by the reports of the English consuls;
above all, however, by the Southern price lists. On January 11 the
price of cotton in New Orleans offered a premium of 100 per cent
for export to England; the profit on import of salt amounted to
1500 per cent and the profit on contraband of war was
incomparably higher. Despite this alluring prospect of profit, it
was just as impossible to ship cotton to England as salt to New
Orleans or Charleston. In fact, however, Mr. Gregory does not
complain that the blockade is inefficacious, but that it is too
efficacious. He urges us to put an end to it and with it to the
crippling of industry and commerce. One answer suffices:

"Who urges this House to break the blockade? The representatives of the
suffering districts? Does this cry resound from Manchester, where the factories
have to close, or from Liverpool, where from lack of freight the ships lie idle in the
docks? On the contrary. It resounds from Galway and is supported by Norfolk."

On the side of the friends of secession Mr. *Lindsay,* a large
shipbuilder of North Shields, made himself conspicuous. Lindsay

---

[a] Marx gives the English words: "quasi-inland".— *Ed.*

[b] Of 1812-14.— *Ed.*

had offered his shipyards to the Union, and, for this purpose, had travelled to Washington, where he experienced the vexation of seeing his business propositions rejected. Since that time he has turned his sympathies to the land of *Secessia*.

The debate was concluded with a circumstantial speech by Sir R. *Palmer,* the Solicitor-General,[a] who spoke in the name of the government. He furnished well grounded juridical proof of the validity of the blockade in international law and of its sufficiency. On this occasion he in fact tore to pieces—and was taxed with so doing by Lord Cecil—the "new principles" proclaimed at the Paris Convention of 1856.[193] Among other things, he expressed his astonishment that in a British Parliament Gregory and his associates ventured to appeal to the authority of Monsieur *de Hautefeuille*. The latter, to be sure, is a brand-new "authority" discovered in the Bonapartist camp. Hautefeuille's compositions in the *Revue contemporaine* on the maritime rights of neutrals[b] prove the completest ignorance or *mauvaise foi*[c] at higher command.

With the complete fiasco of the parliamentary friends of secession in the blockade question, all prospect of a breach between Britain and the United States is eliminated.

Written on March 8, 1862

First published in *Die Presse*, No. 70, March 12, 1862

Printed according to the newspaper

---

[a] Marx gives the English title.— *Ed.*

[b] L. B. Hautefeuille, "Nécessité d'une loi maritime...", "Le règlement du 31 janvier 1862 sur l'asile maritime..." and "Le droit maritime international devant le parlement britannique", *Revue contemporaine,* 2ᵉ série, Tomes 25, 27, Paris, 1862.— *Ed.*

[c] Unconscientiousness.— *Ed.*

Karl Marx and Frederick Engels
THE AMERICAN CIVIL WAR[194]

From whatever standpoint one regards it, the American Civil War presents a spectacle without parallel in the annals of military history. The vast extent of the disputed territory; the far-flung front of the lines of operation; the numerical strength of the hostile armies, the creation of which hardly drew any support from a prior organisational basis; the fabulous cost of these armies; the manner of commanding them and the general tactical and strategic principles in accordance with which the war is being waged, are all new in the eyes of the European onlooker.

The secessionist conspiracy, organised, patronised and supported long before its outbreak by Buchanan's administration, gave the South a head-start, by which alone it could hope to achieve its aim. Endangered by its slave population and by a strong Unionist element among the whites themselves, with two-thirds less free men than in the North, but readier to attack, thanks to the multitude of adventurous idlers that it harbours— for the South everything depended on a swift, bold, almost foolhardy offensive. If the Southerners succeeded in taking St. Louis, Cincinnati, Washington, Baltimore, and perhaps Philadelphia, they might then count on a panic, during which diplomacy and bribery could secure recognition of the independence of all the slave states. If this first onslaught failed, at least at the decisive points, their position must then become worse from day to day, while the North was gaining in strength. This point was rightly understood by the men who in truly Bonapartist spirit had organised the secessionist conspiracy. They opened the campaign in the corresponding manner. Their bands of adventurers overran

Missouri and Tennessee, while their more regular troops invaded eastern Virginia and prepared a *coup de main*[a] against Washington. If this coup were to miscarry, the Southern campaign was lost *from a military point of view.*

The North came to the theatre of war reluctantly, sleepily, as was to be expected considering its higher industrial and commercial development. The social machinery there was far more complicated than in the South, and it required far more time to get it moving in this unusual direction. The enlistment of volunteers for three months was a great, but perhaps unavoidable mistake. It was the policy of the North to remain on the defensive in the beginning at all decisive points, to organise its forces, to train them through operations on a small scale and without risk of decisive battles, and, as soon as the organisation had become sufficiently strong and the traitorous element had simultaneously been more or less removed from the army, to go on to an energetic, unflagging offensive and, above all, to reconquer Kentucky, Tennessee, Virginia, and North Carolina. The transformation of civilians into soldiers was bound to take more time in the North than in the South. Once effected, one could count on the individual superiority of the Northern men.

By and large, and allowing for the mistakes that arose more from political than from military sources, the North acted in accordance with those principles. The guerilla warfare in Missouri and West Virginia, while protecting the Unionist population, accustomed the troops to field service and to fire without exposing them to decisive defeats. The great disgrace of Bull Run[195] was, to a certain extent, the result of the earlier error of enlisting volunteers for three months. It was absurd to let raw recruits attack a strong position, on difficult terrain and having an enemy scarcely inferior in numbers. The panic, which seized the Union army at the decisive moment, and the cause of which has yet to be established could surprise no one who was at all familiar with the history of people's wars. Such things happened to the French troops very often from 1792 to 1795; this did not, however, prevent these same troops from winning the battles of Jemappes and Fleurus, Montenotte, Castiglione and Rivoli.[196] The *only* excuse for the silliness of the jests of the European press with regard to the Bull Run panic is the previous bragging of a section of the North American press.

The six months' respite that followed the defeat at Manassas was

---

[a] A surprise attack.— *Ed.*

utilised to better advantage by the North than by the South. Not only were the Northern ranks replenished in greater measure than the Southern ones. Their officers received better instructions; the discipline and training of the troops did not encounter the same obstacles as in the South. Traitors and incompetent interlopers were increasingly removed, and the period of the Bull Run panic is a thing of the past. The armies on both sides are naturally not to be measured by the standard of the great European armies or even of the former regular army of the United States. Napoleon could in fact train battalions of raw recruits in the depots during the first month, have them on the march during the second and during the third lead them against the enemy, but then every battalion received a sufficient reinforcement of experienced officers and non-commissioned officers, every company some old soldiers, and on the day of the battle the new troops were brigaded together with veterans and, so to speak, framed by the latter. All these conditions were lacking in America. Without the considerable amount of people of military experience who had immigrated to America in consequence of the European revolutionary unrest of 1848-49, the organisation of the Union army would have required a much longer time still. The very small number of killed and wounded in proportion to the total of the troops engaged (usually one in every twenty) proves that most of the engagements, even the most recent ones in Kentucky and Tennessee, were fought mainly with firearms at fairly long range, and that the occasional bayonet charges either soon halted in the face of enemy fire or put the adversary to flight before it came to a hand-to-hand encounter. Meanwhile, the new campaign has been opened under more favourable auspices with the successful advance of Buell and Halleck through Kentucky and Tennessee.[a]

After the reconquest of Missouri and West Virginia, the Union opened the campaign with the advance on Kentucky. Here the secessionists held three strong positions, fortified camps: Columbus on the Mississippi to their left, Bowling Green in the centre, and Mill Springs on the Cumberland River to the right. Their line stretched for 300 miles from west to east. The extent of this line prevented the three corps from rendering each other support and offered the Union troops the chance of attacking each individually with superior forces. The great mistake in the disposition of the secessionists sprang from their attempt to occupy all the ground.

---

[a] From here on the text is practically identical with that of Engels' article "The War in America" (present edition, Vol. 18).— *Ed.*

A single fortified, strong central camp, chosen as the battlefield for a decisive engagement and held by the main body of the army, would have defended Kentucky far more effectively. It was bound either to attract the main force of the Unionists or put them in a dangerous position, had they attempted to march on, disregarding so strong a concentration of troops.

Under the given circumstances the Unionists resolved to attack those three camps one after another, to manoeuvre their enemy out of them and force him to fight in open country. This plan, which conformed to all the rules of the art of war, was carried out with energy and dispatch. Towards the middle of January a corps of about 15,000 Unionists marched on Mill Springs, which was held by 10,000 secessionists. The Unionists manoeuvred in a manner that led the enemy to believe he only had to deal with a weak reconnoitring body. General Zollicoffer at once fell into the trap, sallied from his fortified camp and attacked the Unionists. He soon realised that a superior force confronted him. He fell and his troops suffered as complete a defeat as the Unionists at Bull Run. This time, however, the victory was exploited in quite another fashion. The defeated army was hard pressed until it arrived broken, demoralised, without field artillery or baggage, in its encampment at Mill Springs. This camp was pitched on the north bank of the Cumberland River, so that in the event of another defeat the troops had no retreat open to them save across the river by way of a few steamers and river boats. We find in general that almost all the secessionist camps were pitched on the *enemy* side of the river. To take up such a position is not only according to rule, but also very practical if there is a bridge in the rear. In such a case, the encampment serves as the bridgehead and gives its holders the chance of throwing their fighting forces at will on both banks of the river and so maintaining complete command of these banks. Without a bridge in the rear a camp on the enemy side of the river, on the contrary, cuts off the retreat after an unsuccessful engagement and compels the troops to capitulate, or exposes them to massacre and drowning, a fate that befell the Unionists at Ball's Bluff on the enemy side of the Potomac, whither the treachery of General Stone had sent them.[197]

When the beaten secessionists reached their camp at Mill Springs, they at once understood that an enemy attack on their fortifications must be repulsed or capitulation must follow in a very short time. After the experience of the morning, they had lost confidence in their powers of resistance. Accordingly, when the Unionists advanced to attack the camp next day, they found that the enemy had taken advantage of the night to cross the river, leaving the camp, the baggage, the artillery and stores behind him. In this way, the extreme right of the secessionist line was pushed back to Tennessee, and east Kentucky, where the mass of the population is hostile to the slaveholders' party, was reconquered for the Union.

At about the same time—towards the middle of January—the preparations for dislodging the secessionists from Columbus and Bowling Green commenced. A strong fleet of mortar vessels and ironclad gunboats was held in readiness, and the news was spread in all directions that it was to serve as a convoy to a large army marching along the Mississippi from Cairo to Memphis and New Orleans. All the demonstrations on the Mississippi, however, were merely mock manoeuvres. At the decisive moment, the gunboats were brought to the Ohio and thence to the Tennessee, up which they sailed as far as Fort Henry. This place, together with Fort Donelson on the Cumberland River, formed the second line of defence of the secessionists in Tennessee. The position was well chosen, for in case of a retreat beyond the Cumberland the latter river would have covered its front, the Tennessee its left flank, while the narrow strip of land between the two rivers was sufficiently covered by the two forts mentioned above. But the swift action of the Unionists broke through even the second line before the left wing and the centre of the first line had been attacked.

In the first week of February the Unionists' gunboats appeared in front of Fort Henry, which surrendered after a short bombardment. The garrison escaped to Fort Donelson, since the land forces of the expedition were not strong enough to encircle the spot. The gunboats now sailed down the Tennessee again, upstream to the Ohio and thence up the Cumberland as far as Fort Donelson. A single gunboat sailed boldly up the Tennessee through the very heart of the State of Tennessee, skirting the State of Mississippi and pushing on as far as Florence in northern Alabama, where a series of swamps and banks (known by the name of the Muscle Shoals) prevented further navigation. The fact that a single gunboat made this long voyage of at least 150 miles and then returned, without experiencing any attack, proves that Union sentiment prevails along the river and will be very useful to the Union troops should they push forward as far as that.

The boat expedition on the Cumberland now combined its movements with those of the land forces under generals Halleck and Grant. The secessionists at Bowling Green were deceived over the movements of the Unionists. Accordingly they remained quietly in their camp, while a week after the fall of Fort Henry, Fort Donelson was surrounded on the land side by 40,000 Unionists and threatened on the river side by a strong fleet of gunboats. Just as in the case of the camp at Mill Springs and Fort Henry, the river lay beyond Fort Donelson, without a bridge for retreat. It was the strongest place the Unionists had attacked up to the present. The works had been carried out with greater care; moreover, the place was capacious enough to accommodate the 20,000 men who occupied it. On the first day of the attack the gunboats silenced the fire of the batteries trained towards the river side and bombarded the interior of the defence works, while the land troops drove back the enemy outposts and forced the main body of the secessionists to seek shelter close under the guns of their own defence works. On the second day, the gunboats, which had suffered severely the day before, appear to have accomplished but little. The land troops, on the other hand, had to fight a long and, in places, hard battle with the columns of the garrison, which sought to break through the right wing of the enemy in order to secure their line of retreat to Nashville. However, an energetic attack by the Unionist right wing on the left wing of the secessionists and considerable reinforcements received by the left wing of the Unionists decided the victory in favour of the assailants. Various outworks had been stormed. The garrison, pressed back into its inner lines of defence, without the chance of retreat and manifestly not in a position to withstand an assault next morning, surrendered unconditionally on the following day.

[II] [a]

With Fort *Donelson* the enemy's artillery, baggage and military stores fell into the hands of the Unionists; 13,000 secessionists surrendered on the day of its capture [b]; 1,000 more the next day, and as soon as the advance guard of the victors appeared before Clarksville, a town that lies further up the Cumberland River, it opened its gates. Here, too, considerable supplies had been accumulated for the secessionists.

The capture of Fort Donelson presents only *one* riddle: the

---

[a] Here *Die Presse* has the editorial note, "Conclusion of yesterday's feuilleton".— *Ed.*

[b] February 16, 1862.— *Ed.*

flight of General Floyd with 5,000 men on the second day of the bombardment. These fugitives were too numerous to be smuggled away in steamers during the night. If certain precautions had been taken by the assailants, they could not have got away.[a]

Seven days after the surrender of Fort Donelson, Nashville was occupied by the Federals. The distance between the two places is about 100 English miles, and a march of 15 miles a day, on very bad roads and in the most unfavourable season of the year, redounds to the honour of the Unionist troops. On receipt of the news that Fort Donelson had fallen, the secessionists evacuated Bowling Green; a week later, they abandoned Columbus and withdrew to a Mississippi island, 45 miles south. Thus, Kentucky was completely reconquered for the Union. Tennessee, however, can be held by the secessionists only if they give and win a big battle. They are said in fact to have concentrated 65,000 men for this purpose. Meanwhile, nothing prevents the Unionists from bringing a superior force against them.[b]

The leadership of the Kentucky campaign from Somerset to Nashville deserves the highest praise. The reconquest of so extensive a territory, the advance from the Ohio to the Cumberland in a single month, evidence energy, resolution and speed such as have seldom been attained by regular armies in Europe. One may compare, for example, the slow advance of the Allies from Magenta to Solferino in 1859[198]—without pursuit of the retreating enemy, without endeavour to cut off his stragglers or in any way to outflank and encircle whole bodies of his troops.

Halleck and Grant, in particular, offer good examples of resolute military leadership. Without the least regard either for Columbus or Bowling Green, they concentrate their forces on the decisive points, Fort Henry and Fort Donelson, launch a swift and energetic attack on these and precisely thereby render Columbus and Bowling Green untenable. Then they march at once to Clarksville and Nashville, without allowing the retreating secessionists time to take up new positions in northern Tennessee. During this rapid pursuit the corps of secessionist troops in Columbus remains completely cut off from the centre and right wing of its army. The English papers have criticised this operation unjustly. Even if the attack on Fort Donelson had failed, the secessionists kept busy by General Buell at Bowling Green could not dispatch

---

[a] End of the passage identical with Engels's article.— *Ed.*

[b] The last two sentences are identical with the corresponding passage in Engels's article.— *Ed.*

sufficient men to enable the garrison to follow the repulsed Unionists into the open country or to endanger their retreat. Columbus, on the other hand, lay so far off that it could not interfere with Grant's movements at all. In fact, after the Unionists had cleared Missouri of the secessionists, Columbus became an entirely useless post for the latter. The troops that formed its garrison had greatly to hasten their retreat to Memphis or even to Arkansas in order to escape the danger of ingloriously laying down their arms.

In consequence of the clearing of Missouri and the reconquest of Kentucky, the theatre of war has so far narrowed that the different armies can co-operate to a certain extent along the whole line of operations and work to achieve definite results. In other words, for the first time the war is now assuming a *strategic* character, and the geographical configuration of the country is acquiring a new interest. It is now the task of the Northern generals to find the Achilles' heel of the cotton states.

Before the capture of Nashville, no concerted strategy between the army of Kentucky and the army on the Potomac was possible. They were too far apart from each other. They stood in the same front line, but their lines of operation were entirely different. Only with the victorious advance into Tennessee did the movements of the army of Kentucky become important for the entire theatre of war.

The American papers influenced by McClellan are full of talk about the "anaconda" envelopment plan. According to it, an immense line of armies is to wind round the rebellion, gradually tighten its coils and finally strangle the enemy. This is sheer childishness. It is a rehash of the so-called *cordon system*[199] devised in Austria about 1770, which was employed against the French from 1792 to 1797 with such great obstinacy and with such constant failure. At Jemappes, Fleurus and, more especially, at Montenotte, Millesimo, Dego,[200] Castiglione and Rivoli, the final blow was dealt at this system. The French cut the "anaconda" in two by attacking at a point where they had concentrated superior forces. Then the coils of the "anaconda" were cut to pieces one after another.

In densely populated and more or less centralised states there is always a centre, with the occupation of which by the enemy the national resistance would be broken. Paris is a brilliant example.[201] The slave states, however, possess no such centre. They are sparsely populated, with few large towns and all these on the seacoast. The question therefore arises: Does a military centre of gravity nevertheless exist, with the capture of which the backbone of their resistance will be broken, or are they, just as Russia still was in 1812, not to be conquered without occupying every village and every plot of land, in short, the entire periphery?[202]

Cast a glance at the geographical shape of the secessionists' territory, with its long stretch of coast on the Atlantic Ocean and its long stretch of coast on the Gulf of Mexico. So long as the Confederates held Kentucky and Tennessee, the whole formed a great compact mass. The loss of both these states drives an enormous wedge into their territory, separating the states on the North Atlantic Ocean from the States on the Gulf of Mexico. The direct route from Virginia and the two Carolinas to Texas, Louisiana, Mississippi and even, in part, to Alabama leads through Tennessee, which is now occupied by the Unionists. The *sole* route that, after the complete conquest of Tennessee by the Union, connects the two sections of the slave states goes through Georgia. This proves that *Georgia is the key to the secessionists' territory.* With the loss of Georgia the Confederacy would be cut into two sections, which would have lost all connection with one another. A reconquest of Georgia by the secessionists, however, would be almost unthinkable, for the Unionist fighting forces would be concentrated in a central position, while their adversaries, divided into two camps, would have scarcely sufficient forces to put in the field for a joint attack.

Would the conquest of all Georgia, with the seacoast of Florida, be required for such an operation? By no means. In a land where communication, particularly between distant points, depends much more on railways than on highways, the seizure of the railways is sufficient. The southernmost railway line between the States on the Gulf of Mexico and the Atlantic coast goes through Macon and Gordon near Milledgeville.

The occupation of these two points would accordingly cut the secessionists' territory in two and enable the Unionists to beat one part after another. At the same time, one gathers from the above that no Southern republic is viable without the possession of Tennessee. Without Tennessee, Georgia's vital spot lies only eight or ten days' march from the frontier; the North would constantly have its hand at the throat of the South, and, at the slightest pressure, the South would have to yield or fight for its life anew, under circumstances in which a single defeat would cut off every prospect of success.

From the foregoing considerations it follows:

The Potomac is *not* the most important position in the war

theatre. The seizure of Richmond and the advance of the Potomac army further south—difficult on account of the many rivers that cut across the line of march—could produce a tremendous moral effect. From a purely military standpoint, they would decide *nothing*.

The outcome of the campaign depends on the Kentucky army, now in Tennessee. On the one hand, this army is nearest to the decisive points; on the other hand, it occupies a territory without which secession cannot survive. This army would accordingly have to be strengthened at the expense of all the rest and the sacrifice of all minor operations. Its next points of attack would be Chattanooga and Dalton on the Upper Tennessee, the most important railway junctions of the entire South. After their occupation, the link between the eastern and western states of *Secessia* would be limited to the lines of communication in Georgia. The further problem would then be to cut off another railway line, with Atlanta and Georgia, and finally to destroy the last link between the two sections by the capture of Macon and Gordon.

On the contrary, should the anaconda plan be followed, then, despite all the successes gained at particular points and even on the Potomac, the war may be prolonged indefinitely, while the financial difficulties together with diplomatic complications acquire fresh scope.

Written between March 7 and 22, 1862

First published in *Die Presse*, Nos. 84 and 85, March 26 and 27, 1862

Printed according to the newspaper

Karl Marx

AN INTERNATIONAL *AFFAIRE* MIRÈS [203]

London, April 28

A main theme of diplomatic circles here is France's conduct on the Mexican scene. People are puzzled by the fact that Louis Bonaparte should have increased the expeditionary troops at the moment when he promised to reduce them, and that he should want to go forward whilst England draws back. Here people are well aware that the impulse for the Mexican expedition [204] came from the Cabinet of St. James and not from that of the Tuileries. It is equally well known that Louis Bonaparte likes to carry out all his undertakings, and particularly the overseas adventures, under England's aegis. As is known, the restored Empire has not yet emulated the feat of its original[a] in quartering the French armies in the capital cities of modern Europe. As a *pis aller*,[b] on the other hand, it has led them to the capital cities of ancient Europe, to Constantinople, Athens and Rome, and, over and above that, even to Peking. [205] Should the theatrical effect of a jaunt to the capital city of the Aztecs be lost, and the opportunity for military archaeological collections *à la* Montauban [206]? If, however, one considers the present state of French finance and the future serious conflicts with the United States and England to which Louis Bonaparte's actions in Mexico may lead, one is then obliged to reject without further question the foregoing interpretation of his doings which is popular with various British papers. I believe I can give you the real explanation.

At the time of the Convention of July 17, 1861,[207] when the claims of the English creditors were to be settled, but the English

---

[a] The empire of Napoleon I.— *Ed.*
[b] As a *pis aller*—here: instead.— *Ed.*

plenipotentiary simultaneously demanded that the entire register of the Mexican debts or misdeeds should be examined, Mexico's Foreign Minister[a] put the debt to France at $200,000, i.e., a mere bagatelle of some £40,000. The account *now* drawn up by France, on the other hand, does not confine itself to these modest limits by any means.

Under the Catholic administration of Zuloaga and Miramón, an issue of Mexican state bonds to the amount of $14,000,000 was contracted through the Swiss banking house of J. B. Jecker and Co. The whole sum that was realised by the first issue of these bonds came to only 5 per cent of the nominal amount or to $700,000. The sum total of the bonds issued very soon fell into the hands of prominent Frenchmen, among them relatives of the Emperor and fellow string-pullers of *"haute politique"*.[b] The house of Jecker and Co. let these gentlemen have the aforesaid bonds for far less than their original nominal price.

Miramón contracted this debt at a time when he was in possession of the capital city. Later, after he had come down to the role of a mere guerilla leader, he again caused state bonds to the nominal value of $38,000,000 to be issued through his so-called Finance Minister, Señor Peza-y-Peza. Once more it was the house of Jecker and Co. which negotiated the issue, but, on this occasion, it limited its advances to the modest sum of barely $500,000, or from one to two per cent to the dollar. Once more, the Swiss bankers knew how to dispose of their Mexican property as quickly as possible, and once more the bonds fell into the hands of those "prominent" Frenchmen, among whom were some *habitués* of the imperial court whose names will live on in the annals of the European stock exchanges as long as the *affaire* Mirès.

This debt, then, of $52,000,000, of which not even $4,200,000 have hitherto been advanced, the administration of President Juárez declines to recognise, on the one hand, because it knows nothing about it and, on the other hand, because it claims that Messrs. Miramón, Zuloaga and Peza-y-Peza were possessed of no constitutional authority to contract such a state debt. The above-mentioned "prominent" Frenchmen, however, had to carry the contrary view at the decisive place. Lord Palmerston was, for his part, opportunely instructed by some members of Parliament that the whole affair would lead to highly objectionable interpellations in the Lower House. Among other things to be feared, it was said,

---

[a] M. de Zamacona.— *Ed.*
[b] High politics.— *Ed.*

was the question whether British land and sea power might be
employed to support the gambling operations of certain *rouge-et-
noir*[a] politicians on the other side of the Channel. Accordingly,
Palmerston caught eagerly at the Conference of Orizaba[208] to
withdraw from a business that threatens us with the filth of an
international *affaire* Mirès.

Written on April 28, 1862

First published in *Die Presse*, No. 120,
May 2, 1862

Printed according to the newspaper

---

[a] Red and black, a game of chance.— *Ed.*

Karl Marx

THE ENGLISH PRESS
AND THE FALL OF NEW ORLEANS [209]

London, May 16

On the arrival of the first rumours of the fall of New Orleans,[210] *The Times, The Herald, The Standard, The Morning Post, The Daily Telegraph,* and other English "sympathisers"[a] with the Southern "nigger-drivers" proved strategically, tactically, philologically, exegetically, politically, morally and fortificationally that the rumour was one of the "canards" which Reuter, Havas, Wolff[211] and their understrappers so often let fly. The natural means of defence of New Orleans, it was said, had been augmented not only by newly constructed forts, but by submarine infernal machines of every sort and ironclad gunboats. Then there was the Spartan character of the citizens of New Orleans and their deadly hatred of Lincoln's mercenaries. Finally, was it not at New Orleans that England suffered the defeat that brought her second war against the United States (1812 to 1814) to an ignominious end? Consequently, there was no reason to doubt that New Orleans would immortalise itself as a second Saragossa or a Moscow of the "South".[212] Besides, it harboured 15,000 bales of cotton, with which it could so easily have kindled an inextinguishable fire to destroy itself, quite apart from the fact that in 1814 the duly damped cotton bales proved more indestructible by cannon fire than the earthworks of Sevastopol. It was therefore as clear as daylight that the fall of New Orleans was a case of the familiar Yankee bragging.

When the first rumours were confirmed two days later by steamers arriving from New York, the bulk of the English

---

[a] Marx uses English words: "sympathisers" and, below, "nigger-drivers", and "understrappers".— *Ed.*

pro-slavery press persisted in its scepticism. *The Evening Standard,* especially, was so positive in its unbelief that in the same number it published a first leader which proved the Crescent City's [213] impregnability in black and white, whilst its "latest news" announced the impregnable city's fall in large type. *The Times,* however, which has always held discretion for the better part of valour,[a] veered round. It still doubted, but, at the same time, it made ready for every eventuality, since New Orleans was a city of "rowdies"[b] and not of heroes.[c] On this occasion, *The Times* was right. New Orleans is a settlement of the dregs of the French *bohème,* in the true sense of the word, a French *convict colony*—and never, with the changes of time, has it belied its origin. Only, *The Times* came *post festum*[d] to this pretty widespread realisation.

Finally, however, the *fait accompli*[e] struck even the blindest Thomas. What was to be done? The English pro-slavery press now proves that the fall of New Orleans means a gain for the Confederates and a defeat for the Federals.

The fall of New Orleans allowed General Lovell to reinforce Beauregard's army with his troops; Beauregard was all the more in need of reinforcements, since 160,000 men (surely an exaggeration!) were said to have been concentrated on his front by Halleck and, on the other hand, General Mitchel had cut Beauregard's communications with the East by breaking the railway connection between Memphis and Chattanooga, that is, with Richmond, Charleston and Savannah. After his communications had been cut (which we indicated as a necessary strategical move long *before* the battle of Corinth[f]), Beauregard had no longer any railway connections from Corinth, save those with Mobile and New Orleans. After New Orleans had fallen and he was only left with the single railway to Mobile to rely on, he naturally could no longer procure the necessary provisions for his troops. He therefore fell back on Tupelo and, in the estimation of the English pro-slavery press, his provisioning capacity has, of course, been increased by the entry of Lovell's troops!

On the other hand, the same oracles remark, the yellow fever

ª Shakespeare, *King Henry IV,* Part I, Act V, Scene 4.— *Ed.*

ᵇ Marx uses the English word.— *Ed.*

ᶜ "The spirit in which the fall of New-Orleans has been met...", leading article in *The Times,* No. 24244, May 13, 1862.— *Ed.*

ᵈ Too late. From the Latin saying, "Post festum venire miserum est"—"It is a wretched thing to arrive after the feast" (Plato, *Gorgias,* 1).— *Ed.*

ᵉ Accomplished fact.— *Ed.*

ᶠ See this volume, p. 194— *Ed.*

will take a heavy toll of the Federals in New Orleans and, finally, if the city itself is no Moscow, is not its mayor[a] a Brutus? Only read (cf. New York[b]) his melodramatically valorous epistle to Commodore Farragut, "Brave words, Sir, brave words!"[c] But hard words break no bones.

The press organs of the Southern slaveholders, however, do not construe the fall of New Orleans so optimistically as their English comforters. This will be seen from the following extracts:

The Richmond *Dispatch* says:

"What has become of the ironclad gunboats, the *Mississippi* and the *Louisiana*, from which we expected the salvation of the Crescent City? In respect of their effect on the foe, these ships might just as well have been ships of glass. It is useless do deny that the fall of New Orleans is a heavy blow. The Confederate government is thereby cut off from West Louisiana, Texas, Missouri and Arkansas."

The Norfolk *Day Book* observes:

"This is the most serious reverse since the beginning of the war. It augurs privations and want for all classes of society and, what is worse, it threatens our army supplies."[d]

The Atlantic *Intelligencer* laments:

"We expected that the outcome would be different. The approach of the enemy was no surprise attack; it has long been foreseen, and we had been promised that, should he even pass by Fort Jackson, fearful artillery contrivances would force him to withdraw or ensure his annihilation. In all this, we have deceived ourselves, as on every occasion when the defences were supposed to guarantee the safety of a place or town. It appears that modern inventions have destroyed the defensive capacity of fortification. Ironclad gunboats destroy them or sail past them unceremoniously. Memphis, we fear, will share the fate of New Orleans. Would it not be folly to deceive ourselves with hope?"[e]

Finally, the Petersburg *Express*:

"The capture of New Orleans by the Federals is the most extraordinary and fateful event of the whole war."

Written on May 16, 1862

First published in *Die Presse*, No. 138, May 20, 1862

Printed according to the newspaper

---

[a] J. F. Monroe.— *Ed.*

[b] This parenthesis, added by the editors of *Die Presse,* referred the reader to the report from New York, "Des Bürgermeisters von Neuorleans Erklärung", published in the same issue of the paper.— *Ed.*

[c] Paraphrase of Falstaff's words ("Rare words! brave world!") from Shakespeare's *King Henry IV,* Part I, Act III, Scene 3.— *Ed.*

[d] Quoted from the report, "From Fortress Monroe", the *New-York Daily Tribune,* No. 6575, May 1, 1862.— *Ed.*

[e] Quoted from the report, "Washington, Thursday, May 1, 1862", the *New-York Daily Tribune,* No. 6576, May 2, 1862.— *Ed.*

Karl Marx

A TREATY AGAINST THE SLAVE TRADE[214]

London, May 18

The Treaty on the suppression of the slave trade concluded between the United States and Britain on April 7 of this year in Washington[a] is now communicated *in extenso*[b] by the American newspapers. The main points of this important document are the following: The right of search is reciprocal, but can be exercised only by such warships on either side as have received special authority for this purpose from one of the contracting powers. From time to time, the contracting powers supply one another with complete statistics concerning the sections of their navies that have been appointed to keep watch on the traffic in Negroes. The right of search can be exercised only against merchantmen within a distance of 200 miles from the African coast and south of 32° north latitude, and within 30 nautical miles of the coast of Cuba. Search, whether of British ships by American cruisers or of American ships by British cruisers, does not take place in that part of the sea which is British or American territory (therefore within three nautical miles of the coast); no more does it take place just outside the ports or settlements of foreign powers.

Mixed courts, composed half of Englishmen, half of Americans, and resident in Sierra Leone, Capetown and New York will pass judgment on the prize vessels. In the event of a ship's conviction, her crew will be handed over to the jurisdiction of the nation under whose flag the ship sailed, so far as this can be done without great cost. Not only the crew (including the captain, mate, etc.), but also the owners of the vessel will then incur the penalties customary in the country. Compensation to owners of merchantmen that have been acquitted by the mixed courts is to be paid within a year by the power under whose flag the capturing

---

a "Treaty between the United States of America and Her Majesty the Queen of the United Kingdom of Great Britain and Ireland, for the Suppression of the African Slave-Trade. Concluded at Washington, April 7, 1862".— *Ed.*

b In detail.— *Ed.*

warship sailed. Not only the presence of captive Negroes is regarded as affording legal grounds for the seizure of ships, but also special equipment in the ship for the traffic in Negroes, manacles, chains and other instruments for guarding the Negroes and, lastly, stores of provisions that greatly exceed the requirements of the ship's company. A ship on which such suspicious articles are found has to furnish proof of her innocence and even in the event of acquittal can claim no compensation.

The commander of a cruiser who oversteps the authority conferred on him by the Treaty, is liable to punishment by his respective government. Should the commander of a cruiser of one of the contracting powers harbour a suspicion that a merchant vessel under escort by one or more warships of the other contracting power is carrying Negroes on board, or was engaged in the African slave trade, or is equipped for this trade, he has then to communicate his suspicion to the commander of the escort and search the suspected ship in his presence; the latter is to be conducted to the place of residence of one of the mixed courts if, according to the Treaty, it comes under the category of suspicious ships. The Negroes found on board convicted ships are placed at the disposal of the government under whose flag the capture was made. They are to be set at liberty at once and remain free under guarantee of the government in whose territory they find themselves. The Treaty can only be terminated after ten years. It remains in force for a full year from the date of the notice given by one of the contracting parties.

A mortal blow has been dealt the Negro trade by this Anglo-American Treaty—the result of the American Civil War. The effect of the Treaty will be completed by the Bill recently introduced by Senator Sumner,[a] which repeals the law of 1808 dealing with the traffic in Negroes on the coasts of the United States and punishes the transport of slaves from one port of the United States to another as a crime.[215] This Bill does, to a large extent, paralyse the trade that the states raising Negroes (border slave states[b]) are carrying on with the states consuming Negroes (the slave states proper).

Written on May 18, 1862

First published in *Die Presse*, No. 140, May 22, 1862

Printed according to the newspaper

---

[a] A report on the Bill date-lined "Senate. Washington, May 2, 1862" appeared in the *New-York Daily Tribune*, No. 6577, May 3, 1862.— *Ed.*

[b] Here and below Marx gives the English words in brackets.— *Ed.*

Karl Marx and Frederick Engels

THE SITUATION
IN THE AMERICAN THEATRE OF WAR[216]

The capture of New Orleans, as the detailed reports now to hand show, is distinguished as an almost unparalleled act of valour on the part of the fleet. The Unionists' fleet consisted merely of wooden ships: about six warships, each having from 14 to 25 guns, supported by a numerous flotilla of gunboats and mortar vessels. This fleet had before it two forts which blocked the passage of the Mississippi. Within range of the 100 guns of these forts the river was barred by a strong chain, beyond which there was a mass of torpedoes, fire-floats and other instruments of destruction. These first obstacles had therefore to be overcome in order to pass between the forts. On the other side of the forts, however, was a second formidable line of defence, formed by ironclad gunboats, among them the *Manassas,* an iron ram, and the *Louisiana,* a powerful floating battery. After the Unionists had bombarded the two forts, which completely command the river, for six days without any effect, they resolved to brave their fire, force the iron barrier in three divisions, sail up the river and risk battle with the "ironsides".[a] The hazardous enterprise succeeded. As soon as the flotilla effected a landing before New Orleans, the victory was naturally decided.

Beauregard now had nothing more to defend in Corinth. His position there only made sense so long as it covered Mississippi and Louisiana, and especially New Orleans. He now finds himself strategically in the position that a lost battle would leave him no other choice than to disband his army into guerillas, for without a

---

[a] The authors use the English word.— *Ed.*

large town, where railways and supplies are concentrated, in the rear of his army, he can no longer hold masses of men together. McClellan has irrefutably proved that he is a military incompetent who, having been raised by favourable circumstances to a commanding and responsible position, wages war not to defeat the foe, but rather not to be defeated by the foe and thus forfeit his own usurped greatness. He bears himself like the old so-called "manoeuvring generals", who excused their anxious avoidance of any tactical decision with the plea that, by strategic flanking manoeuvres, they obliged the enemy to give up his positions. The Confederates always escape him, because at the decisive moment he never attacks them. Thus, although their plan of retreat had already been announced ten days before even by the New York papers (for example, the *Tribune*[a]), he let them retire unmolested from Manassas to Richmond. He then divided his army and flanked the Confederates strategically by establishing himself with one body of troops near Yorktown. Siege warfare always affords an excuse for wasting time and avoiding battle. As soon as he had concentrated a military force superior to the Confederates, he let them retire from Yorktown to Williamsburg and from there further, without forcing them to give battle. A war has never yet been so wretchedly waged. If the rearguard action at Williamsburg ended in defeat for the Confederate rearguard instead of in a second Bull Run[217] for the Union troops, McClellan was in no way responsible for this result.

After a march of about twelve miles (English) in a twenty-four hours' downpour and through veritable seas of mud, 8,000 Union troops under General *Heintzelman* (of *German* descent, but born in Pennsylvania) arrived in the vicinity of Williamsburg and met with only weak enemy pickets. As soon, however, as the enemy had assured himself of their numerically inferior strength, he dispatched from his picked troops at Williamsburg reinforcements that gradually increased the number of his men to 25,000. By nine o'clock in the morning, battle was being waged in earnest; at half past twelve General Heintzelman discovered that the engagement was going in favour of the foe. He sent messenger after messenger to General Kearny, who was eight miles to his rear, but could only push forward slowly since the road had been completely "dissolved" by the rain. For a whole hour Heintzelman remained without reinforcements and the 7th and 8th Jersey

---

[a] "Movements of the Manassas Rebels", *New-York Daily Tribune*, No. 6517, February 22, 1862.— *Ed.*

regiments, which had expended their stock of powder, began to run for the woods on either side of the road. Heintzelman now made Colonel Menill with a squadron of Pennsylvanian cavalry. take up positions on both edges of the forest, under the threat of firing on the fugitives. This brought the latter once more to a standstill.

Order was further restored by the example of a Massachusetts regiment, which had likewise expended its powder, but now fixed bayonets to its muskets and calmly awaited the enemy. At length, Kearny's vanguard under Brigadier *Berry* (from the State of Maine) came in sight. Heintzelman's army welcomed its rescuers with a wild "Hurrah"; he ordered the regimental band to strike up *Yankee Doodle*[a] and Berry's fresh forces to form a line almost half a mile in length in front of his exhausted troops. After preliminary musket fire, Berry's brigade made a bayonet charge at the double and drove the enemy off the battlefield to his earthworks, the largest of which after repeated attacks and counter-attacks remained in the possession of the Union troops. Thus, the equilibrium of the battle was restored. Berry's arrival had saved the Unionists. The arrival of the brigades of Jameson and Birney at four o'clock decided the victory. At nine o'clock in the evening the retreat of the Confederates from Williamsburg began; on the following day they continued it—in the direction of Richmond—hotly pursued by Heintzelman's cavalry. On the morning after the battle, between six and seven o'clock, Heintzelman ordered Williamsburg to be occupied by General Jameson. The rearguard of the fleeing enemy had evacuated the town from the opposite end only half an hour before. Heintzelman's battle was an infantry battle in the true sense of the word. Artillery hardly came into action. Musket fire and bayonet attack were decisive. If the Congress at Washington wanted to pass a vote of thanks, it should have been to General Heintzelman, who saved the Yankees from a second Bull Run, and not to McClellan, who in his wonted fashion avoided "the tactical decision" and let the numerically weaker adversary escape for the third time.

The Confederate army in Virginia has better chances than Beauregard's army, first because it is facing a McClellan instead of a Halleck, and then because the many rivers on its line of retreat flow crosswise from the mountains to the sea. However, to avoid breaking up into bands *without a battle,* its generals will sooner or later be forced to accept a decisive battle, just as the Russians were

---

[a] English title in the original.— *Ed.*

obliged to fight at Smolensk and Borodino[218] *against* the will of the generals, who judged the situation correctly. Lamentable as McClellan's manner of conducting the war has been, the constant withdrawals, accompanied by abandonment of artillery, munitions and other military stores, and simultaneously the small unsuccessful rearguard engagements, have at any rate badly demoralised the Confederates, as will become manifest on the day of a decisive battle. To sum up:

Should Beauregard or Jefferson Davis lose a decisive battle, their armies will then break up into bands. Should one of them win a decisive battle, which is most unlikely, at best the disbanding of their armies will be deferred. They are not in a position to draw the least lasting benefit even from a victory. They cannot advance 20 English miles without coming to a standstill and again awaiting the renewed offensive of the enemy.

It still remains to examine the chances of a guerilla war. But precisely in respect of the present war of the slaveholders it is most amazing how slight or rather how wholly lacking is the participation of the population in it. In 1813, the communications of the French were continually cut and harassed by Colomb, Lützow, Chernyshev and twenty other leaders of partisans and Cossacks. In 1812, the population in Russia vanished completely from the French line of march; in 1814, the French peasants armed themselves and slew the patrols and stragglers of the Allies. But here nothing happens at all. People resign themselves to the *fate of the big battles* and console themselves with *"Victrix causa diis placuit, sed victa Catoni"*.[a] The tall talk of war even with knives is going up in smoke. There can be hardly any doubt, it is true, that the *white trash*,[b] as the planters themselves call the "poor whites", will attempt guerilla warfare and brigandage. Such an attempt, however, will very quickly transform the propertied planters into *Unionists*. They will even call the Yankee troops to their aid. The alleged burnings of cotton, etc., on the Mississippi rest exclusively on the testimony of two Kentuckians who are said to have come to Louisville—certainly not on the Mississippi. The conflagration in New Orleans was easily organised. The fanaticism of the New Orleans merchants is explained by the fact that they were obliged to take a quantity of Confederate treasury bonds for hard cash. The conflagration at New Orleans will be repeated in other towns;

---

[a] "The conquering cause pleased the gods, but the conquered one pleased Cato" (Lucan, *Pharsalia*, I, 128).— *Ed.*

[b] Here and below the English phrase is used.— *Ed.*

assuredly, also, there will be a lot more burning; but theatrical coups like this can only bring the dissension between the planters and the "white trash" to a head and therewith—*finis secessiae!*[a]

Written on May 23-25, 1862

First published in *Die Presse*, No. 148, May 30, 1862

Printed according to the newspaper

---

[a] The end of secession.— *Ed.*

Karl Marx

ENGLISH HUMANITY AND AMERICA[219]

London, June 14

Humanity in England, like liberty in France, has now become an export article for the traders in politics.[a] We recollect the time when Tsar Nicholas had Polish ladies flogged by soldiers and when Lord Palmerston found the moral indignation of some parliamentarians over the event "impolitic". We recollect that about a decade ago a revolt took place on the Ionian Islands[220] which gave the English governor[b] there occasion to have a fairly considerable number of Grecian women flogged. *Probatum est,*[c] said Palmerston and his Whig colleagues who at that time were in office. Just a few years ago proof was furnished to Parliament from official documents that the tax collectors in India employed means of coercion against the wives of the ryots,[221] the infamy of which forbids giving further details. Palmerston and his colleagues did not, it is true, dare to justify these atrocities, but what an outcry they would have raised, had a *foreign* government dared to publicly proclaim its indignation over these English infamies and distinctly indicate that it would step in if Palmerston and colleagues did not at once disavow the Indian tax officials. But Cato the Censor himself could not watch over the morals of the Roman citizens more anxiously than the English aristocrats and their ministers over the "humanity" of the war-waging Yankees!

The ladies of New Orleans, yellow beauties, tastelessly bedecked with jewels and comparable, perhaps, to the women of the old Mexicans, save that they do not devour their slaves *in natura,*[d] are

---

[a] Marx gives the English words: "traders in politics".— *Ed.*
[b] G. Colborne.— *Ed.*
[c] Approved.— *Ed.*
[d] Alive.— *Ed.*

this time—previously it was the harbours of Charleston—the occasions for the British aristocrats' display of humanity. The English women who are starving in Lancashire (they are, however, not ladies, nor do they possess any slaves), have inspired no parliamentary utterance hitherto; the cry of distress from the Irish women, who, with the progressive eviction of the small tenant farmers in green Erin,[a] are flung half naked on the street and driven from house and home quite as if the Tartars had descended upon them, has hitherto called forth only one echo from the Lords, the Commons, and Her Majesty's government[b]— homilies on the absolute rights of landed property.[222] But the ladies of New Orleans! That, to be sure, is another matter. These ladies were far too enlightened to participate in the tumult of war, like the goddesses of Olympus, or to cast themselves into the flames, like the women of Saguntum.[223] They have invented a new and safe mode of heroism, a mode that could have been invented only by female slaveholders and, what is more, only by female slaveholders in a land where the free part of the population consists of shopkeepers by vocation, tradesmen in cotton or sugar or tobacco, and does not keep slaves, like the cives[c] of the ancient world. After their men had run away from New Orleans or had crept into their back closets, these ladies rushed into the streets in order to spit in the faces of the victorious Union troops or to stick out their tongues at them or, like Mephistopheles, to make in general "an unseemly gesture",[d] accompanied by insulting words. These Magaeras imagined they could be ill-mannered "with impunity".

This was their heroism. General Butler issued a proclamation[e] in which he notified them that they should be treated as street-walkers, if they continued to act as street-walkers. Butler has, indeed, the makings of a lawyer, but does not seem to have undertaken the requisite study of English statute law.[224] Otherwise, by analogy with the laws imposed on Ireland under Castlereagh,[225] he would have prohibited them from setting foot on the streets at all. Butler's warning to the "ladies" of New Orleans has aroused

---

[a] Old name of Ireland.—Ed.
[b] Marx gives the English words: "Lords," "Commons" and "Her Majesty's government".—Ed.
[c] Citizens.—Ed.
[d] Cf. Goethe, Faust, Der Tragödie erster Teil, "Hexenküche".—Ed.
[e] B. F. Butler, A Proclamation [May 15, 1862], The Times, No. 24272, June 14, 1862.—Ed.

such moral indignation in Earl Carnarvon, Sir. J. Walsh (who played so ridiculous and odious a role in Ireland) and Mr. Gregory, who was already demanding recognition of the Confederacy a year ago,[a] that the Earl in the Upper House, the knight and the man "without a handle to his name"[b] in the Lower House, interrogated the Ministry to learn what steps it intended to take in the name of outraged "humanity". Russell and Palmerston both castigated Butler, both expected that the government at Washington would disavow him; and the so very tender-hearted Palmerston, who behind the Queen's[c] back and without the foreknowledge of his colleagues recognised the *coup d'état* of December 1851 [226] (on which occasion "ladies" were actually shot dead, whilst others were violated by Zouaves[227]) merely out of "human admiration"—the same tender-hearted Viscount declared Butler's' warning to be an "infamy".[d] Ladies, indeed, who actually own slaves—such ladies were not even to be able to vent their anger and their malice on common Union troops, peasants, artisans and other rabble with impunity! It is "infamous".

Among the public here, no one is deceived by this humanity farce. It is meant partly to call forth, partly to fortify the feeling in favour of intervention, in the first place on the part of France. After the first melodramatic outbursts, the knights of humanity in the Upper and Lower House, as if by word of command, discarded their emotional mask. Their declamation served merely as a prologue to the question whether the Emperor of the French[e] had communicated with the English government in the matter of mediating, and whether the latter, as they hoped, had received such an offer favourably. Russell and Palmerston both declared they did not know of the offer. Russell declared the present moment extremely unfavourable for any mediation. Palmerston, more guarded and reserved, contented himself with saying that at the *present* moment the English government had no intention of mediating.

---

[a] W. Gregory [Speech in the House of Commons, May 28, 1861], *The Times*, No. 23945, May 29, 1861.— *Ed.*

[b] Marx gives the English phrase.— *Ed.*

[c] Victoria's.— *Ed.*

[d] The reference is to the speeches of H. Carnarvon and J. Russell in the House of Lords and of J. Walsh, W. Gregory and H. Palmerston in the House of Commons on June 13, 1862 published in *The Times*, No. 24272, June 14, 1862.— *Ed.*

[e] Napoleon III.— *Ed.*

The plan is that during the recess of the English Parliament France should play her role of mediator and, in the autumn, if Mexico is secure, should open her intervention. The lull in the American theater of war has resuscitated the intervention speculators in St. James and the Tuileries from their marasmus. This lull is itself due to a strategic error on the part of the North. If, after its victory in Tennessee, the Kentucky army had rapidly advanced on the railway junctions in Georgia, instead of letting itself be drawn South down the Mississippi on a side track, Reuter and Co. would have been cheated of their business in "intervention" and "mediation" rumours. However that may be, Europe can wish nothing more fervently than that the *coup d'état*[a] should attempt "to restore order in the United States" and "to save civilisation" there too.

Written on June 14, 1862

First published in *Die Presse*, No. 168, June 20, 1862

Published according to the newspaper

---

[a] An allusion to Napoleon III.— *Ed.*

Frederick Engels

THE AMERICAN CIVIL WAR
AND THE IRONCLADS AND RAMS[228]

About three and a half months ago, on March 8, 1862, the naval battle between the *Merrimac* and the frigates *Cumberland* and *Congress* in Hampton Roads ended the long era of wooden men-of-war. On March 9, 1862, the naval battle between the *Merrimac* and the *Monitor* in the same waters opened the era of war between ironclad ships.[a]

Since then the Congress in Washington has approved considerable sums for building various ships armoured with iron and completing the large iron floating battery of Mr. Stevens (in Hoboken, near New York). In addition, Mr. Ericsson is engaged in completing six ships built on the pattern of the *Monitor,* but larger and with two mobile turrets, each flanked with two heavy cannons. The *Galena,* a second ironclad, not constructed by Mr. Ericsson, and of different design to the *Monitor,* has been completed and has joined the *Monitor,* at first to watch the *Merrimac* and then to clear the banks of the James River of rebel forts; this task has been performed to within seven or eight miles of Richmond. The third ironclad in the James River is the *Bengaluche,* first named the *Stevens* after its inventor and former owner.

A fourth ironclad, the *New Ironsides,* is being built in Philadelphia and should be ready to go to sea in a few weeks. The *Vanderbilt* and another large steamer have been converted into rams; a large number of other wooden men-of-war, such as the *Roanoke,* are to be reborn as ironclads. In addition, the Union government had 4 or 5 ironclad gunboats built on the Ohio, which did good service at Fort Henry, Fort Donelson and Pittsburg

---

[a] See this volume, pp. 289-95.— *Ed.*

Landing. Finally, Colonel *Ellet* and his friends fitted out various rams by levelling down and ironcladding the bows of old steamships at Cincinnati and other places on the Ohio. He did not arm them with cannons but with sharpshooters, in which the West abounds. He then offered the rams, the crews and his own services to the Union government. We shall come back later to the first feat of arms of these improvised rams.

On the other side, the Confederates did not remain inactive. They began to build new iron ships and remodel old ones at Norfolk. Before they had finished their work there, Norfolk fell to the Union troops and all those ships were destroyed. In addition, the Confederates built three very strong iron rams at New Orleans, and a fourth ironclad of enormous size with excellent armament was nearing completion when New Orleans fell. According to Union naval officers, the last-named ship, when ready for battle, would have exposed the entire Union navy to the greatest peril, since the government in Washington had nothing equal to opposing this monster. Its cost came to two million dollars. As we know, the rebels themselves destroyed the ship.

At *Memphis,* the Confederates had built no fewer than eight rams, each of which carried four or six guns of large caliber. It was at Memphis that the first *"battle of the rams"* took place on the Mississippi on June 6. Although the Union flotilla, coming down the Mississippi, had five ironclad gunboats, it was two of Colonel *Ellet's rams,* the *Queen* and the *Monarch,* that essentially decided the combat. Of the eight enemy rams, four were destroyed, three were captured and one escaped. After the gunboats of the Union flotilla had opened a lively cannonade against the rebel ships and kept it up for some time, the *Queen* and the *Monarch* sailed into the midst of the enemy squadron. The fire of the gunboats ceased almost completely, since Colonel Ellet's rams were tied up in such a knot with the enemy ships that the gunners could not distinguish friend from foe.

Ellet's rams, as already mentioned, carried no cannons but a host of sharpshooters. Their engines and boilers were protected only by timber work. Powerful steam engines and a sharp oak bow covered with iron constituted the entire equipment of these rams. Men, women and children streamed out of Memphis by the thousands to the steep banks of the Mississippi, at some points hardly half an English mile from the scene of battle, to watch the "battle of the rams" in anxious suspense. The conflict lasted little more than an hour. While the rebels lost 7 ships and 100 men, about 40 of them by drowning, only one Union ship was seriously damaged, only one man wounded and none killed.

Apart from the one iron ram that escaped from the naval engagement at Memphis, the Confederates may still have a couple of rams and ironclads at Mobile. Except for these, and the few gunboats at Vicksburg, which are, simultaneously, threatened by Farragut, sailing up the river, and Davis, sailing down it, their navy has already seen the end of its days.

Written at the end of June, 1862

First published in *Die Presse*, No. 181, July 3, 1862

Printed according to the newspaper

Published in English for the first time

Karl Marx

CHINESE AFFAIRS

A little while before tables started to dance,[229] *China,* that living fossil, began to revolutionise.[230] In itself, there was nothing extraordinary about this phenomenon, for the Oriental empires demonstrate constant immobility in their social substructure, with unceasing change in the persons and clans that gain control of the political superstructure. China is dominated by a foreign dynasty.[231] Why should not a movement to overthrow this dynasty make its appearance after 300 years? The movement had a religious tinge right from the outset; but it had this in common with all the Oriental movements. The immediate causes giving rise to the movement were evident: European intervention, the opium wars,[232] the resultant undermining of the existing regime, outflow of silver abroad, disturbance of the economic equilibrium by the importation of foreign goods, etc. To me it seemed a paradox that opium, instead of lulling, stimulated. Actually, the only thing novel about this Chinese revolution are those who are making it. They are aware of no task except changing the dynasty. They have no slogans. They are an even greater abomination for the masses of the people than for the old rulers. They seem to have no other vocation than, as opposed to conservative stagnation, to produce destruction in grotesquely detestable forms, destruction without any nucleus of new construction. The following excerpts from a letter of Mr. *Harvey* (English consul at Ningpo) to Mr. *Bruce,* the English ambassador in Peking,[a] may help to give one an idea of these "scourges of God".

---

[a] Harvey [Letter to Mr. Bruce], *The Times,* No. 24274, June 17, 1862.— *Ed.*

For three months, Mr. Harvey writes, Ningpo has been in the hands of the revolutionary *Taipings*. Here, as everywhere else where these robbers had extended their domination, devastation has been the only result. Have they any other aims? In point of fact, the power of unbridled and boundless licentiousness seems to be as important to them as the destruction of other people's lives. This view of the Taipings is, of course, at odds with the illusions of English missionaries, who fabricated stories about the "salvation of China", the "rebirth of the empire", the "saving of the people", and the "introduction of Christianity" by the Taipings. After ten years of tumultuous pseudo-activity they have destroyed everything and produced nothing.

At any rate, Mr. Harvey says, the Taipings show to advantage, as compared to the mandarins, in their official dealings with foreigners because of a certain openness of conduct and energetic crudeness; but that is their entire catalogue of virtues.

How do the Taipings pay their troops? They receive no pay but live off booty. If the captured cities are rich, they swim in plenty. If they are poor, the soldier holds out with exemplary patience. Mr. Harvey asked a well-dressed Taiping soldier how he liked his trade. "Why shouldn't I like it?" he answered. "I take what I like; if there is any resistance, then—" and he made the gesture with his hand of cutting off a head. And this is his manner of speech. A human head means no more than a head of cabbage to a Taiping.

The revolutionary army has a core of regular troops, old, veteran and tested partisans. The rest consists of younger recruits or peasants drafted for service on raids. The leaders systematically send conscripts from a conquered province into a different province far off. Thus, at the present time, forty different dialects are spoken among the rebels in Ningpo, while the Ningpo dialect is now being heard for the first time in remote districts. All the riffraff, vagabonds and bad characters in a district join up voluntarily. Discipline extends only to obedience in the service. Marriage and opium smoking are forbidden to the Taipings under penalty of death. Marrying will only come "when the empire has been established". As compensation, the Taipings get *carte blanche* for the first three days after capturing a city whose inhabitants did not flee in good time, to perpetrate every conceivable act of violence on women and girls. At the end of the three days all females are driven out of the cities by force.

To produce terror is the entire tactics of the Taipings. Their success is based solely on the operation of this mechanism. The means of producing the terror are: first of all, the overwhelming masses in which they appear at a given point. Emissaries are sent out first to feel the way out in secret, spread alarming rumours, start some fires. If these emissaries are seized by the mandarins and executed, others follow immediately, until either the mandarins flee with the population of the city or, as was the case at Ningpo, the demoralisation that has set in makes the victory of the insurgents much easier.

One important means of causing terror is the variegated clownish attire of the Taipings. They would make a comical impression on Europeans. On the Chinese they work like a talisman. This buffoon-like clothing gives the rebels a greater advantage in battle than rifled cannons would afford them. Added to this is their long, unkempt hair, black or dyed black, their wild looks, their melancholy howls and an affectation of anger and raving, enough to frighten to death the polite, tame, ordinary Chinese, moving within the pale of his traditional way of life.

If the emissaries have spread panic, they are followed by purposely chased fugitive villagers, who exaggerate the number and power and frightfulness of the advancing army. While the flames rise inside the city and, perhaps, its troops take the field under the impression of these scenes of terror, they see in the distance, dizzying their minds, a few of the harlequin hellhounds, whose appearance has a magnetic effect. Then, at the right moment a hundred thousand Taipings, armed with knives, spears and fowling-pieces, rush wildly at their half-dismayed adversaries and overrun everything, unless, as was recently the case at Shanghai, they meet with resistance.

"The essence of the Taipings," says Mr. Harvey, "is a huge mass of nothingness.[a]"

Obviously, the Taiping represents the devil *in persona,* as the Chinese fantasy must represent him. But also, only in China was this sort of devil possible. It is the product of a fossil social life.

Written between June 17 and early July, 1862

First published in *Die Presse,* No. 185, July 7, 1862

Printed according to the newspaper

Published in English for the first time

---

[a] Marx uses the English word and gives the German translation in brackets.— *Ed.*

Karl Marx

A SCANDAL

At the moment London is absorbed in one of those characteristic scandals that are only possible in a country where old aristocratic tradition flourishes in the midst of the most modern bourgeois society. The *corpus delicti* is a Blue Book of the Parliamentary committee set up to report on the embankment of the Thames and a road to be built along its bank within the city, which is to connect Westminster Bridge with Blackfriars Bridge.[a] The project, very costly, kills several birds with one stone — making London more attractive, cleaning up the Thames, creating more salubrious conditions, a splendid promenade, and finally a new way of communication intended to free the Strand, Fleet Street, and the other streets running parallel to the Thames from the flood of traffic overwhelming them and becoming more dangerous every day, a flood that almost reminds us of the satire of Juvenal's in which a Roman makes his will before leaving the house, because he is almost sure of being run over or knocked down.[b] Now, on the section of the bank of the Thames which is to undergo this metamorphosis, on the north bank, east of Westminster Bridge and at the end of Whitehall there are the city residences of some major aristocrats, with their palaces and gardens stretching down to the Thames. Naturally, these gentlemen welcome the project by and large, because it would improve

---

[a] *Correspondence relating to the Works under the Thames Embankment Bill...,* London, 1862.— *Ed.*

[b] Juvenal, *Satires,* III, 270-74.— *Ed.*

the immediate surroundings of their mansions^a at *government expense* and raise their value. They have only one reservation. The projected construction should be *interrupted* at those points where it would directly cause the public road to run along their own estates and thus bring them into contact with the *"misera contribuens plebs"*.^b The Olympian seclusion of the *"fruges consumere nati"*^c should not be disturbed by the sight, or the noise or the breath of the busy world of commoners. At the head of these noble Sybarites is the *Duke of Buccleuch,* who, as the richest and most powerful, went furthest in his "modest" demands. And lo and behold, the Parliamentary committee draws up its report in the spirit of the wishes of the Duke of Buccleuch! The new constructions are to be *interrupted*—where they would *inconvenience* the Duke of Buccleuch. On that committee of the Lower House are *Lord Robert Montagu,* a *relative* of the Duke, and *Sir John Shelley,* member for a part of London, Westminster. He may as well start looking for a suit of armour to protect him from the Armstrong bombs in the shape of rotten apples and eggs full of hydrogen sulphide that he is already threatened with at the coming elections.

On the committee's report itself, *The Times* says:

"That Blue Book is a maze of ravellings. It consists of eight lines of Report, the rest being a chaos of, for the most part, worthless partisan opinions of members of the public and experts. There is no index, no analysis, no argument. We wander through a wishy-washy, everlasting flood of twaddle, without meeting with facts which we can test or estimates in which we can confide. When we think we are coming at last to some real expert testimony, the Committee suddenly interposes and refuses to hear any evidence discordant with the wishes of the Duke of Buccleuch. The book is a vast and ponderous *suppressio veri*.^d It has obviously been compiled with the object of making any substantive Parliamentary debate impossible. For this purpose, even the plan drawings have been suppressed, and are to be published *post festum*,^e probably *after* the debate." ^f

In the wake of this scandal, the Londoner has raised two questions. First, who is this *Duke of Buccleuch,* this mighty man whose private caprices run counter to the interests of three million people? Who is this giant who single-handed challenges all of

---

^a Here and below Marx uses the English word.— *Ed.*

^b Wretched taxpaying rabble.— *Ed.*

^c Those born to eat the fruits of the field. (Horace, *Epistles,* Book I, II, 27.)— *Ed.*

^d Suppression of the truth.— *Ed.*

^e Literally: after the feast. From the Latin saying "Post festum venire miserum est"—"It is a wretched thing to arrive after the feast" (Plato, *Gorgias,* 1).— *Ed.*

^f "That Blue Book which has just emanated...", *The Times,* No. 24287, July 2, 1862, leading article.— *Ed.*

London to a duel? Nobody knows the name of this man from any parliamentary battle. He sits in the Upper House but takes as little part in its work as a eunuch in the joys of the seraglio. The answers he gave before the committee suggest an abnormal lack of phosphorus in the substance of his brain. And so who is "that man Buccleuch",[a] as the London cockney says in his unceremonious manner? Answer: A descendant of the bastards that the "merry monarch" Charles II gave to the world with Lucy *Parsons,* the most shameless and notorious of his mistresses. That is "that man Buccleuch"! The second question that the Londoner raised was: How did this Duke of Buccleuch come to own his "mansion" on the Thames? For the Londoner remembers that the land on which this "mansion" is built belongs to the crown and only eight years ago was managed by the royal Department of Lands and Woods.

The answer to this second question was not long in coming. In these matters the press here does not mince words. To characterise not only the case itself but also the manner in which the English press handles such delicate subjects I quote *verbatim* from last Saturday's *Reynolds's Newspaper:*[b]

"The Duke of Buccleuch's privilege of obstructing the proposed improvements in London is not seven or eight years old. In 1854, the duke became the lessee of Montagu House, Whitehall, by a stroke of sharp practice which in all probability would have brought a poor man face to face with a criminal judge at the Old Bailey.[233] But the duke has a yearly income of 300,000*l* and, in addition, the advantage of being the descendant of Lucie Parsons, the brazen paramour of the Merry Monarch. Montagu House was Crown property, and it was well known in 1854 that the site on which it stood would be required for public improvements. For this reason, Mr. *Disraeli,* who was then Chancellor of the Exchequer, refused to sign the lease drawn up for the duke. But, *d'une manière ou d'une autre,*[c] the lease was signed. Mr. Disraeli was indignant at this, and denounced his successor, Mr. Gladstone, in the House of Commons for sacrificing the interests of the public to the private interests of a duke. Mr. Gladstone, in his usual ironically suave manner, owned that it was wrong to sign the duke's lease, but thought there must be some special reason for it. A Parliamentary investigation ensued, when, lo! it was discovered that the signer of the lease was none other than—Mr. *Disraeli himself.*

"Here, then, comes the above-mentioned sharp practice, reeking of the criminal gang at the Old Bailey, by the noble descendant of Lucie Parsons. Mr. Disraeli declared that he was utterly unconscious of *his* having signed the lease. But he admitted the genuineness of his signature. No one doubts Mr. Disraeli's veracity. What then is the explanation of the mystery? The noble descendant of Lucie Parsons used some tool or friend of his to *smuggle in* the lease for Montagu House

---

[a] Here and below Marx uses the English phrases "that man Buccleuch", "cockney" and "lands and woods". He also uses the English nickname "Merry Monarch" and gives the German translation in brackets.— *Ed.*

[b] *Reynolds's Newspaper* appeared on Sundays.— *Ed.*

[c] Somehow or other.— *Ed.*

among the mass of papers submitted to Mr. Disraeli for signature as part of his routine duties. Thus he signed it, not having the slightest idea of its contents. And thus Lucie Parsons' descendant obtained the power to oppose his whims to the welfare of 3 million Londoners. The Parliamentary Committee has become the servile tool of his arrogance. If the dwellings of a thousand workmen, instead of the ill-gotten mansion of *one* Duke of Buccleuch, had been in the way, they would be instantly and remorselessly razed to the ground and their owners bundled out, without one farthing of compensation." [a]

Written not earlier than July 2, 1862

First published in *Die Presse*, No. 189, July 11, 1862

Printed according to the newspaper

Published in English for the first time

---

[a] "The Duke of Buccleuch Stops the Way", *Reynolds's Newspaper*, No. 620, June 29, 1862.— *Ed.*

Karl Marx

A SUPPRESSED DEBATE ON MEXICO AND THE ALLIANCE WITH FRANCE[234]

London, July 16

One of the most curious of English parliamentary devices is the count out.[a] What is the count out? If less than 40 members are present in the Lower House, they do not form a *quorum,* that is, an assembly competent to adopt resolutions. If a motion is introduced by an independent parliamentarian, which is equally irksome to *both* oligarchical factions, the *Ins* and the *Outs*[b] (those in office and those in opposition), they then come to an agreement that on the day of the debate parliamentarians from both sides will gradually slip off, *alias* absent themselves. When the emptying of the benches has reached the necessary maximum, the government whip,[c] that is, the parliamentarian entrusted with party discipline by the ministry of the day, then tips the wink to a brother previously chosen for this purpose. The brother parliamentarian gets up and quite nonchalantly requests the chairman to have the house counted. The counting takes place and, behold, it is discovered that there are less than 40 members assembled. Herewith the proceedings come to an end. The obnoxious motion is *got rid of* without the government party or the opposition party having put itself in the awkward and compromising position of being obliged to vote it down.

At yesterday's sitting the count out was brought up in an interesting manner. Lord *R. Montagu* had given notice of a motion for that day which dealt with the communication of new

---

[a] Marx uses the English term "count out", and gives the German translation in brackets.— *Ed.*

[b] Here and below Marx uses the English terms "Ins" and "Outs".— *Ed.*

[c] Marx uses the English terms "government whip" and, below, "chairman", giving the German translation in brackets.— *Ed.*

diplomatic documents on *intervention in Mexico.* He began his speech[a] with the following words:

"Last Saturday the latest Blue Book on Mexico[b] was presented to the House, which therefore ought to be in a position to debate the Mexican question. I *know* that Government and Opposition have agreed to dispose of my motion by means of a count out. I expect that the House, conscious of its duty, will not tolerate such a manoeuvre in so important a matter."

But Lord R. Montagu had reckoned without his host. After he himself had spoken, *Layard* had replied to him on behalf of the government and *Fitzgerald* had delivered himself of some official chatter on behalf of the Tories, *Kinglake* (a Liberal member) rose. The *exordium* of his speech concluded with the following words:

"The whole series of negotiations disclosed by the papers presented is a striking illustration of the way in which the French government uses its relations with this country as a means to prop the Imperial throne.

"It is of decisive moment to the French government to divert the attention of the French people from affairs at home by causing it to be seen that the French government is engaged in great transactions abroad, and it is still more important for it to show that it is engaging in them in concert with one of the great respectable powers."

Hardly had *Kinglake* uttered these words when an *"honourable"* member of the House moved that the House be *"counted."* And behold! The House had dwindled to just 33 members. Lord *Montagu's* motion had been killed by the same count out against which he had protested at the beginning of the debate.

Apart from Kinglake's interrupted speech, only that of Lord Montagu was of any material interest. Lord R. Montagu's speech contains the following important analysis of the facts of the case:

"Sir Charles Wyke had concluded a treaty with Mexico. Out of servility to Louis Bonaparte, this treaty was not ratified by Lord John Russell. Sir Charles Wyke concluded the said treaty after France, through her connection with Almonte, the leader of the reactionary party, had entered upon a path that abrogated the joint convention between England, France and Spain.[c] Lord John Russell himself declared in an official dispatch that that treaty satisfied all England's legitimate demands. In his correspondence with Thouvenel, however, he promised, in compliance with Bonaparte's wish, *not* to ratify the treaty for the time being. He allowed Thouvenel to communicate this decision to the *Corps législatif.* Indeed, Lord John Russell lowered himself so far as to promise Thouvenel that he would break off all communication with Sir Charles Wyke until July 1, 1862—a date that gave Thouvenel time to answer. Thouvenel answered that Bonaparte did not

---

[a] The deputies' speeches in the House of Commons on July 15, 1862, are cited according to the reports published in *The Times,* No. 24299, July 16, 1862.—*Ed.*

[b] *Correspondence Respecting the Affairs of Mexico,* London, 1862.—*Ed.*

[c] *Convention, conclue à Londres, le 31 octobre 1861, entre l'Espagne, la France et la Grande-Bretagne pour combiner une action commune contre le Mexique.—Ed.*

contest England's right to act in isolation, but disapproved of the Anglo-Mexican treaty concluded by Sir Charles Wyke. Thereupon Russell ordered Wyke to withhold the ratification of the treaty."

England, added Lord Montagu, lends her influence to enforce the fraudulent claims on the Mexican Treasury with which *Morny* "and *perhaps persons of higher standing* in France" have provided themselves per medium of the Swiss bourse-swindler *Jecker*.

"The whole Mexican business," he continued, "was launched without the foreknowledge of Parliament. The first extra-Parliamentary war was waged in 1857.[235] Palmerston defended that on the ground that it was an Asiatic war.[a] The same principle is now being applied to America. It will ultimately be applied to Europe. The Parliamentary system thus becomes a mere farce, for, in losing control over wars, the people's representatives lose control over their purse."

Lord *Montagu* wound up with the words:

"I accuse the Ministry of having made us accomplices in the murder of liberty in France and of enabling that unscrupulous adventurer[b] to plant despotism in a foreign country. It ties our future to that of one doomed to the abhorrence of man and the vengeance of Heaven."

Written on July 16, 1862

First published in *Die Presse*, No. 198, July 20, 1862

Printed according to the newspaper

---

[a] H. J. Palmerston [Speech in The House of Commons on July 16, 1857], *Hansard's Parliamentary Debates*, Third series, Vol. CXLVI, London, 1857.— *Ed.*

[b] Napoleon III.— *Ed.*

Karl Marx

A CRITICISM OF AMERICAN AFFAIRS[236]

The crisis, which at the moment reigns in the United States has been brought about by two causes: military and political. Had the last campaign been conducted according to a *single* strategic plan, the main army of the West was then bound, as previously explained in these columns,[a] to exploit its successes in Kentucky and Tennessee to make its way through north Alabama to Georgia and to seize the railway junctions there at Decatur, Milledgeville, etc. The link between the Eastern and Western armies of the secessionists would thereby have been broken and their mutual support rendered impossible. Instead of this, the Kentucky army marched south down the Mississippi in the direction of New Orleans and its victory near Memphis had no other result than to dispatch the greater part of Beauregard's troops to Richmond, so that the Confederates, with a superior army in a superior position, here now suddenly confronted McClellan, who had not exploited the defeat of the enemy's troops at Yorktown and Williamsburg and, moreover, had from the first split up his own forces. McClellan's generalship, already described by us previously,[b] was in itself sufficient to ensure the ruin of the biggest and best disciplined army. Finally, War Secretary Stanton committed an unpardonable error. To make an impression abroad, he suspended recruiting after the conquest of Tennessee and so condemned the army to be constantly weakened, just when it was most in need of reinforcements for a rapid, decisive offensive. Despite the strategic blunders and despite McClellan's generalship, with a steady influx of recruits the war, if not

---

a See this volume, pp. 194, 212.— *Ed.*
b See this volume, pp. 179-81, 205-08.— *Ed.*

decided, had hitherto been rapidly nearing a victorious end. Stanton's step was all the more disastrous since the South had at that precise moment enlisted every man from 18 to 35 years old and therefore staked everything on a *single* card. It is those men, who have been trained in the meantime, that give the Confederates the upper hand almost everywhere and secure them the initiative. They held Halleck fast, dislodged Curtis from Arkansas, beat McClellan, and under Stonewall Jackson gave the signal for the guerilla raids that are now already pushing forward as far as the Ohio.

In part, the military causes of the crisis are connected with the political ones. It was the influence of the Democratic Party that elevated an incompetent like McClellan to the position of Commander-in-Chief [a] of all the military forces of the North, because he had been a supporter of Breckinridge. It is anxious regard for the wishes, advantages and interests of the spokesmen of the *border slave states* [b] that has so far broken off the Civil War's point of principle and deprived it of its soul, so to speak. The "loyal" slaveholders of these border states saw to it that the fugitive slave laws [c] dictated by the South [237] were maintained and the sympathies of the Negroes for the North forcibly suppressed, that no general could venture to put a company of Negroes in the field and that slavery was finally transformed from the Achilles' heel of the South into its invulnerable horny hide. Thanks to the slaves, who do all the productive work, all able-bodied men in the South can be put into the field!

At the present moment, when secession's stocks are rising, the spokesmen of the border states are making even greater claims. However, Lincoln's appeal [d] to them, in which he threatens them with inundation by the Abolition party, shows that things are taking a revolutionary turn. Lincoln knows what Europe does not know, that it is by no means apathy or giving way under pressure of defeat that causes his demand for 300,000 recruits [e] to meet

---

[a] Marx uses the English term.— *Ed.*

[b] Marx gives the English designation in brackets after the German equivalent.— *Ed.*

[c] Marx uses the English words "fugitive slave laws" and gives the German translation in brackets.— *Ed.*

[d] A. Lincoln [Address to the Representatives and Senators of the Border Slaveholding States, July 12, 1862], *New-York Daily Tribune*, No. 6643, July 19, 1862.— *Ed.*

[e] A. Lincoln, *Executive Mansion*. Washington, July 1, 1862. Ordinance on the enlistment of 300,000 recruits, *New-York Daily Tribune*, No. 6628, July 2, 1862.— *Ed.*

with such a cold response. New England and the Northwest, which have provided the main body of the army, are determined to force on the government a revolutionary kind of warfare and to inscribe the battle-slogan of "Abolition of Slavery!" on the star-spangled banner. Lincoln yields only hesitantly and uneasily to this pressure from without,[a] but he knows that he cannot resist it for long. Hence his urgent appeal to the border states to renounce the institution of slavery voluntarily and under advantageous contractual conditions. He knows that only the continuance of slavery in the border states has so far left slavery untouched in the South and prohibited the North from applying its great radical remedy. He errs only if he imagines that the "loyal" slaveholders are to be moved by benevolent speeches and rational arguments. They will yield only to force.

So far, we have only witnessed the first act of the Civil War—the *constitutional* waging of war. The second act, the *revolutionary* waging of war, is at hand.

Meanwhile, during its first session Congress, now adjourned, decreed a series of important measures that we shall briefly summarise here.

Apart from its financial legislation, it passed the Homestead Bill,[b] which the Northern masses had long striven for in vain; in accordance with this Bill, part of the state lands is given gratis to the colonists, whether indigenous or new-comers, for cultivation.[238] It abolished slavery in Columbia and the national capital, with monetary compensation for the former slaveholders.[239] Slavery was declared "forever impossible" in all the *Territories* of the United States.[c] The Act, under which the new State of West Virginia is admitted into the Union, prescribes abolition of slavery by stages and declares that all Negro children born after July 4, 1863, are born free. The conditions of this emancipation by stages are on the whole borrowed from the law that was enacted 70 years ago in Pennsylvania for the same purpose.[240] By a fourth Act all the slaves of rebels are to be emancipated, as soon as they fall into the hands of the republican army.[d] Another law, which is now being put into effect *for the first time,* provides that these emancipated

---

    [a] Marx uses the English words: "pressure from without".— *Ed.*
    [b] Marx gives the English name.— *Ed.*
    [c] *An Act to secure Freedom to all Persons within the Territories of the United States.*— *Ed.*
    [d] *An Act to suppress insurrection, to punish treason and rebellion, to seize and confiscate the property of Rebels, and for other purposes.*— *Ed.*

Negroes may be militarily organised and put into the field against the South. The independence of the Negro republics of Liberia and Haiti[241] has been recognised and, finally, a treaty on the abolition of the slave trade has been concluded with Britain.[a]

Thus, no matter how the dice may fall in the fortunes of war, even now it can safely be said that Negro slavery will not long outlive the Civil War.

Written in early August, 1862   Printed according to the news-

First published in *Die Presse*, No. 218,   paper
August 9, 1862

---

[a] "Treaty between the United States of America and Her Majesty the Queen of the United Kingdom of Great Britain and Ireland, for the Suppression of the African Slave-Trade".— *Ed.*

Karl Marx

RUSSELL'S PROTEST AGAINST AMERICAN RUDENESS.—
THE RISE IN THE PRICE OF GRAIN.—
ON THE SITUATION IN ITALY[242]

London, August 20

Lord John Russell is known as a "letter writer"[a] among the English. In his last missive to Mr. Stuart[b] he complains of the insults to "Old England"[c] in the North American papers. *Et tu, Brute!*[d] It is impossible to speak privately with a respectable Englishman who will not throw up his hands in astonishment at this *tour de force.*[e] It is well known that from 1789 to 1815 English journalism broke all records in its scurrilous hate attacks on the French nation. And yet it has broken its own record this past year by its "malignant brutality"[f] against the United States! A few recent examples may suffice.

"We owe all our moral support," says *The Times,* "to our kin" (the Southern slaveholders), "who are fighting so bravely and staunchly for their freedom, against a mixed race of robbers and oppressors."

To this the New York *Evening Post* (the Abolitionist organ) remarks:

"Are these English lampoon-writers, these descendants of Britons, Danes, Saxons, Celts, Normans and Dutchmen, of such *pure* blood that all other peoples are mixed races as compared with them?"

---

[a] Marx uses the English phrase and gives the German translation in brackets.— *Ed.*

[b] J. Russell [Letter to W. Stuart], "Foreign-office, July 28, 1862", *The Times,* No. 24323, August 13, 1862.— *Ed.*

[c] Marx uses the English phrase.— *Ed.*

[d] Caesar's exclamation at seeing Marcus Brutus, his relative and favourite, among his assassins (Shakespeare, *Julius Caesar,* Act III, Scene I).— *Ed.*

[e] Feat of strength or skill.— *Ed.*

[f] Marx uses the English phrase and gives the German translation in brackets.— *Ed.*

Shortly after the foregoing passage was published, *The Times,* in bold Garamond type, called President Lincoln "a respectable buffoon", his cabinet ministers "a gang of rogues and riffraff", and the army of the United States "an army whose officers are Yankee swindlers and whose privates are German thieves". And Lord John Russell, not content with the laurels of his epistles to the Bishop of Durham and Sir James Hudson in Turin,[a][243] dares to speak, in his letter to Stuart, of the "insults of the North American press" to England.

Yet there is a limit to everything. In spite of malignant impertinence and nasty rancour, official England will keep the peace with the "Yankee swindlers" and confine its deep sympathies with the high-minded vendors of human blood in the South to blotting-paper phrases, and isolated smuggling ventures, for a rise in the price of grain is no joke, and any conflict with the Yankees would now add a food famine to the cotton famine.

England has long since ceased to live off its own grain production. In 1857, 1858 and 1859 it imported grain and flour to the amount of 66 million pounds sterling, and in 1860, 1861 and 1862 for 118 million pounds sterling. As for the quantity of grain and flour imported, it was 10,278,774 quarters[b] in 1859, 14,484,976 quarters in 1860 and 16,094,914 quarters in 1861. In the last five years alone, therefore, grain imports have risen by 50 per cent.

England is now in fact already satisfying half of its grain requirements with imports. And there is every probability that next year will add at least 30 per cent to this importation, we mean 30 per cent to the cost price, since the very large harvest in the United States will prevent any excessive rise in grain prices. The extensive reports from all the farming districts that the *Mark Lane Express*[c] and *The Gardeners' Chronicle and Agricultural Gazette* have just published virtually prove that the grain harvest of this year will be from $1/4$ to $1/5$ below the average harvest. Just as after the peace treaty of 1815 Lord Brougham said that England, by its national debt of a thousand million, gave Europe a pledge of

---

[a] J. Russell, "To the Right Reverend the Bishop of Durham. Downing Street, Nov. 4", *The Times,* No. 20640, November 7, 1850; [Despatch addressed to the British Minister at Turin], "Foreign-office, Oct. 27", *The Times,* No. 23769, November 5, 1860.— *Ed.*

[b] A quarter is 12.7 kilograms.— *Ed.*

[c] "Review of the British Corn Trade, during the Past Week", *The Mark Lane Express and Agricultural Journal,* No. 1599, August 18, 1862.— *Ed.*

"good behaviour",[a] so this year's grain deficit gives the United States the best security that England "will not break the Queen's peace".[b]

I have been shown a letter from one of Garibaldi's best friends in Genoa, from which I give some excerpts. Among other things, it says:

"The last letters of Garibaldi and various officers in his camp arrived here yesterday (August 16). They are dated August 12. All of them breathe the unshakable determination of the general to keep to his programme: 'Rome or death!' and contain peremptory orders to this effect to his friends. On the other side, *positive* orders went out yesterday from Turin to General Cugia to proceed to the ultimate acts of violence, i.e. to attack the volunteers with guns and bayonets and to capture Garibaldi and his friends, if he should refuse to lay down his arms in twenty-four hours. If the troops obey orders, a grave catastrophe is imminent. The decision to resort to extreme measures was taken as the result of a telegram from Paris, whose tenor is: 'The Emperor will not condescend to negotiation with the Italian Government until Garibaldi is disarmed.' If Rattazzi had loved his country more than his office, he would have resigned and let Ricasoli or some other less unpopular minister take his place. He would have considered the fact that taking Louis Bonaparte's side against Italy, instead of Italy's side against Bonaparte, means endangering the monarchy he professes to serve. If Italian blood is shed at Italian hands in Sicily, that is not Garibaldi's fault, for his slogan is: 'Long live the Italian army!', and the enthusiastic manner in which this army is received everywhere proves what obedience there is to Garibaldi. But, if the army should shed the blood of the volunteers, who would dare to count on quiet tolerance on the part of the people?"

Written on August 20, 1862

First published in *Die Presse,* No. 233, August 24, 1862

Printed according to the newspaper

Published in English in full for the first time

---

    [a] Marx uses the English phrase and gives the German translation in brackets.— *Ed.*
    [b] Marx gives the quoted passage in English and supplies the German translation in brackets.— *Ed.*

Karl Marx

ABOLITIONIST DEMONSTRATIONS
IN AMERICA[244]

It was previously observed in these columns[a] that President *Lincoln,* legally cautious, constitutionally conciliatory, by birth a citizen of the border slave state of *Kentucky,* is escaping only with difficulty from the control of the "loyal" slaveholders, seeking to ,avoid any open breach with them and precisely thereby provoking a conflict with the parties of the North which are consistent in point of principle and are being pushed more and more into the foreground by events. The speech that *Wendell Phillips* delivered at Abington, *Massachusetts,*[b] on the occasion of the anniversary of the slaves' emancipation in the British West Indies,[245] may be regarded as a prologue to this conflict.

Together with *Garrison* and *G. Smith, Wendell Phillips* is the leader of the Abolitionists in New England. For 30 years he has without intermission and at the risk of his life proclaimed the emancipation of the slaves as his battle-cry, regardless alike of the persiflage of the press, the enraged howls of paid rowdies[c] and the conciliatory representations of solicitous friends. Even his opponents acknowledged him as one of the greatest orators of the North, as combining iron character with forceful energy and purest conviction. The London *Times*—and what could characterise this magnanimous paper more strikingly—today *denounces* Wendell Phillips' speech at Abington to the government in Washington. It says it is an "abuse" of freedom of speech.

"Anything more violent it is impossible to imagine," says *The Times,* "and anything more daring in a time of Civil War was never said in any country by any

---

[a] See pp. 178-79, 227-28 of this volume.— *Ed.*
[b] On August 1, 1862. The source from which Marx quotes is unknown.— *Ed.*
[c] Marx uses the English word.— *Ed.*

sane man who valued his life or liberty. In reading the speech it is scarcely possible
to avoid coming to the conclusion that the speaker's object was to force the
government to prosecute him."[a]

And *The Times,* in spite of, or perhaps because of, its hatred of
the Union government, appears not at all disinclined to assume
the role of public prosecutor!

In the present state of affairs Wendell Phillips' Abington speech
is of greater importance than a battle bulletin. We therefore
summarise its most striking passages.

"The government," he says among other things, "is fighting for the
preservation of slavery, and therefore it is fighting in vain. Lincoln is waging a
political war. Even now he is more afraid of Kentucky than of the entire North. He
believes in the South. The Negroes on the Southern battlefields, when asked
whether the rain of cannon-balls and bombs that tore up the earth all round and
split the trees asunder did not terrify them, answered: 'No, massa; we know that
they are not meant for us!' The rebels could speak of McClellan's bombs in the
same way. They know that they are not meant for them, to do them harm. I do not
say that McClellan is a traitor; but I say that, if he were a traitor, he would have
had to act exactly as he has done. Have no fear for Richmond; McClellan will not
take it. If the war is continued in this fashion, without a rational aim, then it is a
useless squandering of blood and gold. It would be better were the South
independent today than to hazard one more human life for a war based on the
present execrable policy. To continue the war in the fashion prevailing hitherto,
requires 125,000 men a year and a million dollars a day. But you cannot get rid of
the South. As Jefferson said of slavery:

"The Southern states have the wolf by the ears, but they can neither hold him
nor let him go." In the same way, we have the South by the ears and can neither
hold it nor let it go. Recognise it tomorrow and you will have no peace. For 80
years it has lived with us, in fear of us the whole time, with hatred for us half the
time, ever troubling and abusing us. Made presumptuous by a concession of its
present claims, it would not keep within an imaginary border-line a year—nay, the
moment that we speak of conditions of peace, it will cry victory! We shall never
have peace until slavery is uprooted. So long as you retain the present tortoise[b] at
the head of our government, you make a hole with one hand in order to fill it with
the other. Let the entire nation endorse the resolutions of the New York Chamber
of Commerce[246] and then the army will have something for which it is worth while
fighting. Had Jefferson Davis the power, he would not capture Washington. He
knows that the bomb that fell in this Sodom would rouse the whole nation.

"The entire North would thunder with one voice! 'Down with slavery, down
with everything that stands in the way of saving the republic!' Jefferson Davis is
quite satisfied with his successes. They are greater than he anticipated, far greater!
If he can continue to swim on them till March 4, 1863, England will then, and this
is in order, recognise the Southern Confederacy.... The President has not put the
Confiscation Act[c] into effect. He may be honest, but what has his honesty to do
with the matter? He has neither insight nor foresight. When I was in Washington, I

---

[a] "New York, Aug. 8", *The Times,* No. 24331, August 22, 1862.— *Ed.*

[b] An allusion to Abraham Lincoln.— *Ed.*

[c] *An Act to confiscate the property of Rebels for the payment of the expenses of the
present rebellion, and for other purposes [1862].—Ed.*

ascertained that three months ago Lincoln had written the proclamation for general emancipation of the slaves and that McClellan bullied him out of his decision and that the representatives of Kentucky bullied him into the retention of McClellan, in whom he places no confidence. It will take years for Lincoln to learn to combine his legal scruples as an attorney with the demands of the Civil War. This is the appalling state of a democratic government and its greatest evil.

"In France a hundred men, convinced of the righteousness of their cause, would carry the nation with them; but in order that our government may take a step, 19 million people must previously put themselves in motion. And to how many of these millions has it been preached for years that slavery is an institution ordained by God! With these prejudices, with paralysed hands and hearts, you entreat the President to save you from the Negro! If this theory is correct, then only slaveholding despotism can bring a temporary peace.... I know Lincoln. I have taken his measure in Washington. He is a first-rate second-rate man.[a] He waits honestly, like a new broom, for the nation to take him in hand and sweep away slavery through him.... In past years, not far from the platform from which I now speak, the Whigs[247] fired small mortars in order to smother my voice. And what is the result?

"The sons of these Whigs now fill their own graves in the marshes of Chickahominy![248] Dissolve this Union in God's name and replace it with another, on the corner-stone of which is written: 'Political equality for all the citizens of the world'... During my stay in Chicago I asked lawyers of Illinois, among whom Lincoln had practised, what sort of man he was. Whether he could say No. The answer was: 'He lacks backbone. If the Americans wanted to elect a man absolutely incapable of leadership, of initiative, then they were bound to elect Abraham Lincoln.... Never has a man heard him say No!' I asked: 'Is McClellan a man who can say No?' The manager of the Chicago Central Railroad, on which McClellan was employed, answered: 'He is incapable of making a decision. Put a question to him and it takes an hour for him to think of the answer. During the time that he was connected with the administration of the Central Railroad, he never decided a single important controversial question.'

"And these are the two men who, above all others, now hold the fate of the Northern Republic in their hands! Those best acquainted with the state of the army assure us that Richmond could have been taken five times, had the do-nothing at the head of the army of the Potomac allowed it; but he preferred to dig up dirt in the Chickahominy swamps, in order to ignominiously abandon the locality and his dirt ramparts. Lincoln, out of a cowardly fear of the border slave states, keeps this man in his present position; but the day will come when Lincoln will confess that he has never believed in McClellan.... Let us hope that the war lasts long enough to make men of us, and then we shall soon triumph. God has put the thunderbolt of emancipation into our hands in order to crush this rebellion..."

Written on August 22, 1862

First published in *Die Presse*, No. 239, August 30, 1862

Printed according to the newspaper

---

[a] Marx gives the English phrase in brackets after its German equivalent.— *Ed.*

Karl Marx

A MEETING FOR GARIBALDI

Preparations are being made for a Garibaldi meeting in London[249]; another was held yesterday in Gateshead, a third one in Birmingham is announced, while *Newcastle* began the cycle of these popular demonstrations last Tuesday.[a] A brief report on the Newcastle meeting may serve to indicate the characteristic mood prevailing here. Such a meeting is always a curious event. The one in question took place in Newcastle Town Hall. Mr. *Newton* (a town councillor) opened the proceedings with a speech in which he said, among other things:

"As long as Italy is not free, no freedom is possible in Europe. As long as France keeps a great army in the heart of Europe, there is no guarantee even of the freedoms we now boast. It should not be forgotten for an instant that the true cause of the disaster that has befallen Garibaldi is to be found not so much in Italy as in Paris. The French ruler[b] is the true author of that misfortune. *(Loud applause.)* It is the same force that has silenced the press and the rostrum, that has suffocated, gagged, and unmanned the whole of France. I do not doubt that a day of reckoning will come, that the *coup d'état*[c] will be punished, that Providence will demand atonement for its sins and crimes! Great self-control is needed to speak calmly of France's behaviour towards Italy. Ever since the time of Charles VIII it has made it its business to destroy Italy and make Italy the pretext for breaking the peace of Europe.[250]... I have read somewhere that the old Romans did not dare to proceed with the trial of Manlius in view of the Capitol.[251] Is there an inch of Italian soil that could bear a trial of Garibaldi?..."

Jos. Cowen moved that a memorandum be sent to Lord Russell demanding that the British government should urge the French Emperor to evacuate Rome.

---

[a] September 9, 1862.— *Ed.*
[b] Napoleon III.— *Ed.*
[c] Of December 2, 1851.— *Ed.*

"Rome," he said, "is the old and honourable capital of Italy.... How does this ancient seat of civilisation come to be held prisoner by the troops of a foreign despot? What more right do French troops have to Rome than to Naples, Turin or London? *(Loud applause.)* The Pope[a] had fled, refused to return, and left Rome without a government for three months. At that point, the Romans elected their own government. While they were still engaged in setting up the new organisation, they were attacked by the same French who had set them an example a year earlier.[252]

"Inconsistency is too weak an expression to describe such conduct. It was infamous *(furious applause)*, and history will brand every Frenchman who took part in this nefarious deed.... With the possible exception of the partition of Poland,[253] there has never been a more shameless violation of every principle of national independence and the law of nations than that committed by the French bands of pretorians[254] in murdering the Roman Republic! Rome fell in June 1849, and Louis Bonaparte holds it to this day, a full 13 years!... When his ministers explained to the French National Assembly that the expedition was due to anarchy in Rome, they were lying. (Hear, hear![b]) When his officers explained to the troops in Toulon, who objected to the annihilation of a sister republic, that the struggle was not against Rome but against Austria, they were lying. After the army had landed in Civitavecchia, they lied again, proclaiming to the people that they came not as enemies but as friends, and deceitfully interweaving French and Italian flags! The French plenipotentiary and his underlings lied when they gained admission to the triumvirs[c] on the pretext of negotiations but actually for the purpose of studying the state of the defences. General Oudinot lied when he promised not to attack the city before June 4 but actually attacked it on the 2nd, and thus took the Romans by surprise. The entire conduct of the French in this infamous action was deliberate and hypocritical guile. *(Loud applause.)*

"From Louis Bonaparte down to his lowest agents, they all deceived Rome, the French people and Europe. Louis Bonaparte never wanted a free Italy. What he wants is a Sardinian kingdom in the north, another kingdom in the south under Murat, and a third in the centre for cousin Plon-Plon. *(Applause and laughter.)* These three small monarchies, all linked to the house of Bonaparte by family ties, all seeking their inspiration in the Tuileries, would assure Louis Bonaparte of a great increase of his power in Europe. The plan was not a bad one, and its execution would have done honour to his dexterity, but Garibaldi thwarted it. *(Storm of applause.)* For the moment Garibaldi is disarmed. This makes it all the more the duty of the English people to put an end to the encroachments of French despotism and to close the gates of Rome to the pretorian hordes of the *coup d'état*.... Bonapartism is the source of all the evil in Europe. But the days of its power are numbered.... An implacable will, hundreds of thousands of soldiers, all the deadly instruments of war in profusion, a senate packed full of servile place-seekers, a house of representatives drummed up by gendarmes and prefects—but on the other side stands human nature, which has to defend its eternal rights!" *(Storm of applause.)*

Mr. *Cowen* then argued in favour of and read the memorandum to Lord Russell, which was adopted unanimously, after the attempt of a certain Mr. Rule to take the part of "our noble ally

---

[a] Pius IX.—*Ed.*
[b] Marx gives the English phrase.—*Ed.*
[c] G. Mazzini, A. Saffi and C. Armellini.—*Ed.*

across the Channel" was buried under a storm of hisses, yells, catcalls and laughter.

Mr. *Rutherford* (A Protestant minister) then made the second motion, to this effect:

"This meeting invites General Garibaldi to take up residence in England and assures him of the constant and growing admiration of the English people."

In supporting his motion Mr. Rutherford remarked, among other things:

"If the Pope should find Rome too hot, he too will find asylum in England. We will even welcome him, not as a secular prince but as the head of an enormous church."

The motion was adopted unanimously. The chairman closed the proceedings with a violent apostrophe against "the despot of Paris".

"Let him remember ancient Italy with its Brutus and Cassius; let him remember the Nemesis that dogs his heels; let him reflect, like Macbeth, that an armed hand and a helmeted head can spring from the earth,[a] and let him not forget that not all the Orsinis have had their heads cut off."

Thus spoke Town Councillor Mr. *Newton*.

The present language of English newspapers and meetings is reminiscent of the first days after the *coup d'état,* in such vivid contrast to the later hymns to the "saviour of society".[b]

Written on September 11, 1862

First published in *Die Presse*, No. 256, September 17, 1862

Printed according to the newspaper

Published in English for the first time

---

[a] Shakespeare, *Macbeth*, Act II, Scene I, and Act IV, Scene I.— *Ed.*
[b] Napoleon III.— *Ed.*

Karl Marx

WORKERS' DISTRESS IN ENGLAND

*

For the last two months a polemic has been going on in the local press whose records should be of much more interest to the future historian of English society than all the catalogues of the Great Exhibition,[255] illustrated or not illustrated.

It will be recalled that shortly before the closing of Parliament a bill was rushed through both houses in great haste, at the insistence of the big industrialists, which raises the tax for the poor in the municipalities of Lancashire and Yorkshire.[a] This measure, very limited in itself, in the main affects the lower middle classes in the factory districts, while it hardly touches the landlords and the cotton lords.[b] During the debate on the Bill, Palmerston used harsh language towards the cotton lords, whose workers were starving in the streets while they themselves were heaping up riches by speculative buying and selling of cotton.[c] He explained their "masterly inaction" during the crisis likewise on "speculative" grounds. Even at the opening of the session, Lord Derby had declared that the cotton shortage had been like a *deus ex machina*[d] for the manufacturers, since an enormous flooding of the markets would have caused a frightful crisis if the American Civil War had

---

[a] *An Act to enable Boards of Guardians of certain Unions to obtain temporary Aid to meet the extraordinary Demands for Relief therein.*—*Ed.*

[b] Here and below Marx uses the English words "landlords", "cotton lords" and "masterly inaction", and gives the German translation in brackets.—*Ed.*

[c] Palmerston's speech in the House of Commons on July 30, 1862 (*The Times*, No. 24312, July 31, 1862).—*Ed.*

[d] Literally: "a deity from a machine" (in the ancient Greek and Roman theatre, the intervention of a god, brought in suddenly by stage machinery, to resolve an apparently insoluble conflict).—*Ed.*

not suddenly cut off imports of raw materials.[a] Cobden, as spokesman for the industrialists, answered with a three-day diatribe against Palmerston's foreign policies.[b]

After the prorogation of Parliament, the fight went on in the press. Appeals to the English public for relief for the suffering working population, and the constantly growing dimensions of impoverishment in the factory districts, gave new occasions daily for continuing the fight. The *Morning Star* and other organs of the industrial press recalled that the Earl of Derby and a whole gang of aristocrats owed their yearly rents of 300,000 and more pounds sterling on their real estate holdings in the factory districts solely to industry, in which they had never invested anything, and which had given their previously worthless land its present price. The *Morning Star* went so far as to set a figure for the charitable contributions that Derby and other big landlords should give. It set Derby's contribution, e.g., at 30,000 pounds. In fact, Lord Derby called a meeting in Manchester shortly after Parliament adjourned, to collect charitable contributions. He taxed himself at 1,000 pounds and the other large landholders signed for corresponding amounts. The result was not brilliant, but the landed aristocracy had done something at least. They beat their breasts with a *"salvavi animam meam".*[c]

The high dignitaries of the cotton industry, meanwhile, persisted in their "stoic" attitude. They are nowhere to be found, neither in the local committees that were formed to alleviate the distress nor in the London committee. "They are neither here nor there, but they are on the Liverpool market",[d] says a London paper. The Tory journals and *The Times* fulminate daily against the cotton despots who have sucked millions "out of the flesh and blood of the workers" and now refuse even to contribute a few pennies to preserve "the source of their wealth".[e] *The Times* has sent its reporters into the factory districts; their highly detailed reports are in no way calculated to make the "cotton lords" popular.[f] On the other hand, the industrial organs of the

---

[a] E. G. Derby's speech in the House of Lords on February 6, 1862 (*The Times*, No. 24163, February 7, 1862).— *Ed.*

[b] Cobden spoke about foreign policy on August 1, 1862, i.e. on the third day of his long House of Commons address (*The Times*, No. 24314, August 2, 1862).— *Ed.*

[c] "I have delivered my soul" (cf. *Ezekiel*, 3:19, 33:9).— *Ed.*

[d] Marx gives this sentence in English and supplies the German translation in brackets.— *Ed.*

[e] "It must tend to relieve...", *The Times*, No. 24333, August 25, 1862.— *Ed.*

[f] Reports from Blackburn, Wigan, Stockport and Ashton-under-Lyne published in *The Times* on August 30 and September 2, 5, 12 and 16, 1862.— *Ed.*

press—the *Morning Star, Economist,*[a] *Manchester Guardian,* etc.—
accuse *The Times* of fomenting the class struggle in order to cover
up the guilt of the government, its mismanagement in India, etc.
Indeed, *The Times* is even charged with "communist tendencies".
The Times, obviously much pleased at this chance to win back its
popularity, replies with biting sarcasm: While the "cotton lords"
·act in a highly economistic manner, on the one hand, in that they
take speculative advantage of the present cotton shortage, on the
other hand, they are hardened communists, and indeed "communists òf the most loathsome kind". These rich gentlemen
demanded that England open its pockets in order to preserve the
most valuable portion of their capital, without any cost to
themselves, whatsoever. For their capital does not consist solely of
factories, machinery and bank balances, but, to an even greater
extent, of the well-disciplined armies of workers in Lancashire and
Yorkshire. And while the gentlemen close down their factories in
order to sell the raw material at 500 per cent profit, they
demanded that the English people keep their discharged armies
going!

During this strange dispute between the landed aristocracy and
the industrial aristocracy, as to which of them grinds the working
class down the most, and which of them is least obliged to do
something about the workers' distress, things are happening to the
patients themselves that the continental admirers of the "Great
Exhibition"[b] have no inkling of. The incident that I describe in the
following lines is officially confirmed.

In a small cottage[c] at Gauxholme, near Todmorden (West
Riding of Yorkshire), there lived a father and his two daughters;
the father was old and feeble, and the girls earned their living as
workers at the Halliwells' cotton mill. They lived in a miserable
room on the ground floor, a few feet from a filthy little brook,
and past their window a staircase, used by the people who lived
upstairs, cut off the light from their dreary habitation. At the best
of times, they earned just enough to "keep body and soul
together", but for the last 15 weeks they had lost the only source
of their livelihood. The factory had been closed down; the family
could no longer earn the means to buy food. Step by step, poverty
dragged them into its abyss. Every hour brought them nearer to
the grave. Their pitiful savings were soon exhausted. Next came

---

[a] See, e.g., "Distress and Relief in Lancashire", *The Economist,* No. 994,
September 13, 1862.— *Ed.*

[b] Marx uses the English name.— *Ed.*

[c] Marx uses the English word.— *Ed.*

their few sticks of furniture, clothing, linen, and whatever could be sold or pawned—to be converted into bread. It is a fact that during the 14 weeks in which they did not earn a farthing, they never asked for help from the parish.

To add to their troubles, the old man had been sick for a month and unable to leave his bed. The tragedy of Ugolino and his sons[a] was repeated, without their cannibalism, in the cottage at Todmorden. In desperation, about a week ago (on the 12th) the stronger of the two girls pulled herself together, went to the head of the poorhouse and told him the pitiful story. This gentleman, hard though it may be to believe, told her he could do nothing for the family until the following Wednesday. The three poor sufferers would have to perish for five more days until the mighty bailiff would condescend to give them some help. The family waited—there was nothing else they could do. When the appointed Wednesday finally arrived on which official charity was to throw a crumb to the starving family, the village was horrified by the report that one of the sisters had died of starvation. The terrible news was all too true. Stretched out on a wretched plank bed, among the signs of the most terrible poverty, lay the corpse of the starved girl, while her father, worn and helpless, sobbed on his bed and the surviving sister had just enough strength to tell the story of her woe. We know, by experience, where this horrible case, by no means an exception today, will lead. An inquest will be held. The coroner[b] will dwell at length on the charitable spirit of the English poor law; he will again adduce the excellence of the machinery for administering it as *prima facie*[c] proof that the law cannot possibly be responsible for the deplorable event. The head of the poorhouse will be whitewashed, and if not warmly complimented by the court, will at any rate learn, to his comfort, that there is not the slightest stain on him. Finally, the jury will crown the solemn comedy by the verdict: "Died by the visitation of God."[d]

Written about September 20, 1862

First published in *Die Presse*, No. 266, September 27, 1862

Printed according to the news-paper

Published in English for the first time

---

[a] Dante, *La Divina Commedia*. Inferno, Canto XXXIII.— *Ed.*
[b] Marx uses the English word and gives the German translation in brackets.— *Ed.*
[c] Self-evident.— *Ed.*
[d] Marx uses the English phrase and gives the German translation in brackets.— *Ed.*

Karl Marx

A NOTE ON THE AMNESTY[256]

Wilhelm Wolff, former editor of the *Neue Rheinische Zeitung* and at present a teacher in Manchester, sent an application to the Breslau[a] authorities on January 4, 1862. In it he requested the restoration of his Prussian citizenship in accordance with the recently proclaimed amnesty.[257] Nine months later he received the following piece of writing in reply:

"In response to your applications of January 4 and June 4 of this year,[b] we have to inform you that since you have by your flight withdrawn from the further continuation of the judicial proceedings brought against you in 1845 and 1848, we are not in a position to accede to your request to be reinstated in your rights as a Prussian subject (!). Furthermore, if you believe that the Royal Decree of January 12 renders the case against you *null and void*, this rests on a false interpretation of that Decree, according to which it is your duty to *present* yourself (!) to the authorities in *these states* so that the proceedings against you may be resumed and whose outcome you must await.

"Breslau, September 5, 1862

H. M. Government,
Ministry of the Interior,
(signed) *Stich*

"To Mr. Johann Friedrich Wilhelm Wolff, student of philosophy, in Manchester."

We may note in passing the curious circumstance that, although Wolff has lost his citizenship "in these states", his status as "student" lives on in them for ever. But to the matter in hand.

Since the Breslau authorities took three months to compose the document we have just cited, might we not have expected, at the very least, *factual accuracy* in the justification of their refusal?

---

[a] Wrocław.— *Ed.*
[b] See this volume, p. 335.— *Ed.*

However, the Breslau authorities appear to "believe" that the administration shares with the law the privilege of *"fictiones juris"*.[a]

Wolff became a refugee in *1846* (not 1845), after the press trial launched against him had gone through *all the stages of investigation,* after he had himself undergone all the interrogations and not long before judgment was due. He withdrew by his flight, therefore, from the *judgment,* and not from "the further continuation of the judicial *proceedings* brought against him".

Furthermore, in 1848 the people wrested from the authorities a general amnesty as a result of which Wolff returned in the first place to Breslau. In April 1848 he was summoned to appear before the criminal court in Breslau in order to declare in writing—which he actually did—that he accepted the amnesty on his own behalf.

The Breslau authorities appear to "believe", therefore, that the amnesty of 1848 and the *rights obtained* in consequence of it have been *annulled* by the amnesty of 1861. This type of "retroactive" legislation would certainly inaugurate a new era in the annals of law.

It is no less a "fiction" on the part of the Breslau authorities that Wolff "withdrew by his flight from the further continuation of the judicial proceedings brought against him in 1848". Wolff became a refugee not in 1848 but in 1849 and this was in fact *before* any proceedings against him had begun. The latter related to his participation in the Rump Parliament.[258] In the summer of 1849 Wolff made his way to Switzerland. At that time, no proceedings against him were in progress and he could not therefore "withdraw" from them. The *warrant for his arrest* was issued in the autumn of 1849, long after he had been abroad. Judicial proceedings that *precede* the flight and a warrant that *follows* it seem to be identical things in the eyes of the Breslau authorities.

What do government bodies pay a legal adviser[259] for, if such crude schoolboy violations of the simplest and most ordinary rules in interpreting the law are possible?

Written in mid-September 1862

First published in the *Barmer Zeitung,* No. 226, September 27, 1862

Printed according to the newspaper

Published in English for the first time

---

[a] Legal fictions.— *Ed.*

Karl Marx

GARIBALDI MEETINGS.—
THE DISTRESSED CONDITION OF COTTON WORKERS

London, September 30

After the Garibaldi meeting in Newcastle which I described in a previous letter,[a] similar meetings were held in Sunderland, Dundee, Birmingham, London, and other places. The tone of the meetings was the same everywhere and their last word was always: "Removal of the French from Rome". At this moment, it is intended to choose delegates in every London district and send them *en masse* to Lord John Russell to compel him to take steps against the continuing occupation of Rome by French troops. "Pressure from without"[b] is the *ultima ratio*[c] of the Englishman against his government.

In the meanwhile, the Tuileries cabinet[d] neither feels easy about nor is indifferent to the demonstrations of the British people, as the following excerpt from the *Newcastle Journal* will show:

"The Emperor of the French has called the attention of the English government to the language prevailing at the last Garibaldi meeting in Newcastle. It was emphasised that two speakers, including the chairman, Town Councillor Newton, alluded to plots to assassinate the Emperor and, in the most unmistakable way, threatened him with death because of his Italian policy. The government therefore felt itself obliged to take steps in this matter and to declare that the laws of England are to be applied rigorously to prevent and punish any such conspiracies, like those of Orsini, Dr. Bernard, and others, particularly since a repetition of Orsini's attempt at assassination was announced so openly at the meeting. This warning by the government is based on the fact that in Mazzini circles speeches have recently been made, threats uttered and dark hints dropped

---

[a] See this volume, pp. 236-38.— *Ed.*
[b] Marx uses the English phrase and gives the German translation in brackets.— *Ed.*
[c] Last resort.— *Ed.*
[d] The government of Napoleon III.— *Ed.*

similar to those that foreshadowed the Orsini conspiracy. Finally, we are able to inform the public that the first legal steps arising out of the Newcastle meeting have already been taken."

This is what the *Newcastle Journal* had to say about it. Anyone who has the slightest knowledge of English conditions and the attitude prevailing here knows, in addition, that any interference on the part of the present cabinet with the popular demonstrations can only end in the fall of the government, as at the time of the Orsini attempt.[260]

As winter approaches, the conditions in the factory districts grow more menacing every day. *The Morning Star* warns today that, if the present method of "official charity" is continued, next winter will see the violent scenes of 1842-43[261] far exceeded. The immediate occasion for its Cassandra cry is a declaration, which appeared in all the English papers, of a Manchester worker previously employed at a machine (cotton) weaving mill and now out of a job. In order to understand this declaration, which I will summarise briefly further on, it is necessary to know what the "labour test"[a] is. The English poor law of 1834,[b] which aimed at eliminating pauperism by punishing it as a disgraceful crime, requires the applicant for help to prove his "willingness to work", before his application is granted, by breaking stones or "picking oakum",[c] useless operations with which criminals condemned to "hard labour" are punished in English prisons. After this "labour test", the applicant receives a shilling a week for each member of his family, that is, half a shilling in cash and half a shilling in bread per capita.

Now to the "declaration" of the English weaver. His family consists of six persons. Previously he earned good wages. For 18 weeks, however, he had been cut down to half-time and quarter-time. During this period the weekly income of the family hardly came to 8 shillings. Last week the factory he worked at was closed down completely. His rent is 2 sh. 3d. a week. He had pawned everything that was not nailed or riveted down; he had nothing more to sell, not a penny in his pocket; hunger was staring him and his family in the face. He was therefore forced to

---

[a] Marx uses the English term and gives the German translation in brackets.— *Ed.*

[b] *An Act for the amendment and better administration of the laws relating to the poor in England and Wales* [1834].— *Ed.*

[c] Marx uses the English expression and gives the German translation in brackets.— *Ed.*

look for help from the poor board. Early last Monday[a] he went to the "guardians".[b]

After "pointed questioning", they gave him a note to the relief officer of his district. It took an hour for the official to allow him into his august presence. Then he underwent questioning again— and was denied relief on the grounds that he had earned 3 shillings in the preceding week, although "the patient" had given a detailed accounting of the way in which this "fortune" had been spent. He and his family had to go hungry until the following Wednesday. He went back to the office of the "guardians". There he learned that he had to go through the "labour test" before help could be given him. And so he marched to the workhouse (a Bastille for the poor) and there, on an empty stomach, he had to pick oakum until half past five, packed in together with 300 other workers in a narrow room about 30 yards [long]. There, squeezed tightly together on benches, in the stifling summer heat, choking with smoke and dust, the "patients of the labour test", skilled workers, pillars of England's national wealth, had to perform the meanest operations that can be imposed on a human being. One could just as well require a watchmaker to hammer horseshoes, or an organist to blow his own bellows. At the end of this operation, he received exactly 5 shillings, half in bread, half in money. After paying the rent, there was hardly 2 pence (about 2 Prussian silbergroschen) for the daily consumption of 6 persons. And the following Wednesday he would have to go through the "ordeal" again, since it is repeated every week. The "weaver" now declares publicly that he would rather starve to death with his family than have that ignominy repeated.

Written on September 30, 1862

First published in *Die Presse*, No. 273, October 4, 1862

Printed according to the newspaper

Published in English for the first time

---

[a] September 22, 1862.— *Ed.*

[b] Here and below Marx uses the English word. He also uses, further on, the English words "workhouse", "oakum" and "labour test".— *Ed.*

18*

Karl Marx

COMMENTS ON THE NORTH AMERICAN EVENTS[262]

The short campaign in Maryland[263] has decided the fate of the American Civil War, however much the fortune of war may still vacillate between the opposing parties for a shorter or longer time. As we have already stated in this newspaper, the fight for the possession of the border slave states is a fight for the domination over the Union,[a] and the Confederacy has been defeated in this fight, which it started under extremely favourable circumstances that are not likely ever to occur again.

Maryland was rightly considered the head and Kentucky the arm of the slaveholders' party in the border states. Maryland's capital, Baltimore, has been kept "loyal" up to now only by martial law. It was a dogma not only in the South but also in the North that the arrival of the Confederates in Maryland would be the signal for a popular rising *en masse* against "Lincoln's satellites". Here it was not only a question of a military success but also of a moral demonstration which was expected to electrify the Southern elements in all the border states and to draw them forcefully into the vortex.

With Maryland Washington would fall, Philadelphia would be menaced and New York would no longer be safe. The invasion of Kentucky,[264] the most important of the border states owing to the size of its population, its situation and its economic resources, which took place simultaneously, was, considered in isolation, merely a diversion. But supported by decisive success in Maryland,

---

[a] See pp. 43-52, 226-29 of this volume.— *Ed.*

it could have crushed the Union party in Tennessee, outflanked Missouri, protected Arkansas and Texas, threatened New Orleans, and above all shifted the theatre of war to Ohio, the central state of the North, whose possession spells the subjugation of the North just as the possession of Georgia spells that of the South. A Confederate army in Ohio would cut off the West of the Northern states from the East and fight the enemy from his own centre. After the fiasco of the rebels' main army in Maryland, the invasion of Kentucky which was not pressing ahead with sufficient drive and was nowhere supported by popular sympathy, was reduced to an insignificant guerilla attack. Even the occupation of Louisville would now only unite the "Great West",[265] the legions from Iowa, Illinois, Indiana and Ohio, so that they would form an "avalanche" similar to that which crashed down on the South during the first glorious Kentucky campaign.[266]

The Maryland campaign has thus proved that the waves of secession lack the power to roll over the Potomac and reach the Ohio. The South has been reduced to the defensive, but *offensive operations* were its *only* chance of success. Deprived of the border states and hemmed in by the Mississippi in the west and the Atlantic in the east, the South has conquered nothing—but a graveyard.

One must not forget even for a moment that, when the Southerners hoisted the banner of rebellion, they held the border states and dominated them politically. What they demanded were the Territories. They have lost both the Territories and the border states.

Nevertheless, the invasion of Maryland was risked at a most favourable conjuncture. The North had suffered a disgraceful series of quite unprecedented defeats, the Federal army was demoralised, Stonewall Jackson the hero of the day, Lincoln and his government a universal laughing-stock, the Democratic Party, strong again in the North and people expecting Jefferson Davis to become president, France and England were openly preparing to proclaim the legitimacy—already recognised at home—of the slaveholders. "*E pur si muove.*"[a] Reason nevertheless prevails in world history.

Lincoln's proclamation[b] is even more important than the

---

[a] "But it does move"—the words Galileo is supposed to have said after recanting his theory on the rotation of the Earth.— *Ed.*

[b] A. Lincoln, *A Proclamation* [September 22, 1862], *New-York Daily Tribune*, No. 6699, September 23, 1862.— *Ed.*

Maryland campaign. Lincoln is a *sui generis*[a] figure in the annals of history. He has no initiative, no idealistic impetus, no cothurnus, no historical trappings. He gives his most important actions always the most commonplace form. Other people claim to be "fighting for an idea", when it is for them a matter of square feet of land. Lincoln, even when he is motivated by an idea, talks about "square feet". He sings the bravura aria of his part hesitatively, reluctantly and unwillingly, as though apologising for being compelled by circumstances "to act the lion". The most redoubtable decrees—which will always remain remarkable historical documents—flung by him at the enemy all look like, and are intended to look like, routine summonses sent by a lawyer to the lawyer of the opposing party, legal chicaneries, involved, hidebound *actiones juris.*[b] His latest proclamation, which is drafted in the same style, the manifesto abolishing slavery,[267] is the most important document in American history since the establishment of the Union, tantamount to the tearing up of the old American Constitution.

Nothing is simpler than to show that Lincoln's principal political actions contain much that is aesthetically repulsive, logically inadequate, farcical in form and politically contradictory, as is done by the English Pindars of slavery, *The Times, The Saturday Review* and *tutti quanti.*[c] But Lincoln's place in the history of the United States and of mankind will, nevertheless, be next to that of Washington! Nowadays, when the insignificant struts about melodramatically on this side of the Atlantic, is it of no significance at all that the significant is clothed in everyday dress in the new world?

Lincoln is not the product of a popular revolution. This plebeian, who worked his way up from stone-breaker to Senator in Illinois,[268] without intellectual brilliance, without a particularly outstanding character, without exceptional importance—an average person of good will, was placed at the top by the interplay of the forces of universal suffrage unaware of the great issues at stake. The new world has never achieved a greater triumph than by this demonstration that, given its political and social organisation, ordinary people of good will can accomplish feats which only heroes could accomplish in the old world!

Hegel once observed that comedy is in fact superior to tragedy

---

[a] Unique.— *Ed.*
[b] Juridical acts.— *Ed.*
[c] The rest.— *Ed.*

and humourous* reasoning superior to grandiloquent reasoning.[a] Although Lincoln does not possess the grandiloquence of historical action, as an average man of the people he has its humour. When does he issue the proclamation declaring that from January 1, 1863, slavery in the Confederacy shall be abolished? At the very moment when the Confederacy as an independent state decided on "peace negotiations" at its Richmond Congress.[b] At the very moment when the slave-owners of the border states believed that the invasion of Kentucky by the armies of the South had made "the peculiar institution"[c] just as safe as was their domination over their compatriot, President Abraham Lincoln in Washington.[d]

Written on October 7, 1862

First published in *Die Presse*, No. 281, October 12, 1862

Printed according to the newspaper

---

[a] Marx presumably refers to Hegel's *Vorlesungen über die Aesthetik*, Bd. III, Theil III, Abschnitt III, Kapitel III "Das Princip der Tragödie, Komödie und des Drama".— *Ed.*

[b] On September 19, 1862.— *Ed.*

[c] Marx uses the English phrase and gives the German translation in brackets.— *Ed.*

[d] Lincoln was born in Kentucky, a border state.— *Ed.*

Karl Marx

BREAD MANUFACTURE

Garibaldi, the American Civil War, the revolution in Greece, the cotton crisis, Veillard's bankruptcy [269]—everything is overshadowed for the moment in London by the—*question of bread,* but the question of bread in the literal sense. The English, who are so proud of their "ideas in iron and steam", have suddenly discovered that they have been making the "staff of life" [a] in the same antediluvian manner as at the time of the Norman Conquest. The only essential progress consists in the adulteration of the foodstuffs that modern chemistry has facilitated. It is an old British proverb that every man, even the best, must eat "a peck of dirt" in his lifetime. This was meant in the moral sense. John Bull has not the slightest suspicion that he is eating, in the coarsest physical sense, an incredible *mixtum compositum* [b] of flour, alum, cobwebs, black beetles, and human sweat. Being the Bible reader he is, he knew, of course, that man earns his bread in the sweat of his brow [c]; but it was something brand-new to him that human sweat must enter into bread dough as a seasoning.

The sequence of steps in which big industry appropriates the various territories in which it finds handiwork, artisanship and manufacture established seems preposterous at first sight. Producing wheat, for example, is a rural occupation, and baking bread an urban one. Should it not be expected that industrial production would take over the urban trade earlier than the rural one? And

---

[a] Marx uses the English phrase and gives the German translation in brackets. Further on he uses the English phrases "a peck of dirt" and "black beetles" and giving the German translation in the first case.— *Ed.*

[b] Hodge-podge.— *Ed.*

[c] *Genesis,* 3:19.— *Ed.*

yet things have gone in the opposite direction. Wherever we look, we shall find that the most immediate needs have thus far avoided the influence of large-scale industry, with more or less obstinacy, and their satisfaction depends upon the hopelessly detailed craft methods of ancient tradition. It is not England but North America that first made a breach in this tradition, and that only in our times. The Yankee was the first to apply machinery to tailoring, bootmaking, etc., and even transferred them from the factory into the private house. The phenomenon can easily be explained, however. Industrial production calls for mass production, on a large scale, for commerce, instead of for private consumption, and by the nature of things raw materials and semi-manufactured goods are the *first* things it takes over, and finished goods destined for immediate consumption the *last.*

Now, however, the hour of the downfall of the *master* bakers and of the rise of the bread *manufacturer* seems to have struck in England. The disgust and loathing evoked by Mr. *Tremenheere*'s disclosures as to the "mysteries of bread"[a] would not by themselves have been sufficient to produce such a revolution if it were not for the added circumstance that capital, in large amounts driven by the American crisis out of domains it has long monopolised, is anxiously looking around for new fields to settle down in.

The journeymen at the London bakeries had flooded Parliament with petitions protesting their exceptionally wretched condition. The Home Secretary[b] appointed Mr. Tremenheere investigator and a kind of examining magistrate into these complaints. Mr. Tremenheere's report was the signal for the storm to begin.

Mr. Tremenheere's report is divided into two main sections. The first describes the wretched state of the workers in the bakeries; the second reveals the disgusting mysteries of breadmaking itself.

The first part portrays the journeymen in the bakeries as "the white slaves of civilisation". Their usual working hours begin at 11 in the evening and last until 3 or 4 in the afternoon. The work increases towards the weekend. In most London bakeries it continues without a break from 10 o'clock Thursday evening till Saturday night. The average life-span of these workers, most of whom die of consumption, is 42 years.

---

[a] This refers to the *Report Addressed to Her Majesty's Principal Secretary of State for the Home Department, Relative to the Grievances Complained of by the Journeymen Bakers.* London, 1862.— *Ed.*

[b] G. Grey.— *Ed.*

As for the breadmaking itself, it takes place for the most part in cramped underground vaults either ventilated badly or not at all. In addition to lack of ventilation, there are the pestilential vapours from bad outlet ducts, "and the fermenting bread gets impregnated with the noxious gases surrounding it". Cobwebs, black beetles, rats and mice are "incorporated with the dough".

"It was with the utmost reluctance," says Mr. Tremenheere, "that I came to the conclusion that a batch of dough is rarely made without having more or less of the perspiration, and often of the more morbid secretions, of the men who make it mixed up with it."

Even the finest bakeries are not free from these revolting abominations, but they reach an indescribably low point in the holes where the bread of the poor is baked, and where too the adulteration of the flour with alum and bone-earth is practised most freely.

Mr. Tremenheere proposes stricter laws against adulteration of bread, as well as putting the bakeries under government supervision, limiting the working hours for "young people" (i.e., those who have not reached the age of 18) from 5 in the morning to 9 at night, and so forth, but very reasonably does not expect the elimination of the abuses, which arise out of the old method of production itself, to come from Parliament, but from large-scale industry.

As a matter of fact, the Stevens machine for preparing dough has already been installed in certain places. There is another, similar machine at the industrial exhibition. Both still leave too much of the baking process to manual work. On the other hand, Dr. Dauglish has revolutionised the entire process of making bread. From the moment the flour leaves the hopper to the time the bread goes into the oven, no human hand touches it in this system. Dr. Dauglish does away with yeast entirely and effects fermentation by the use of carbonic acid. He reduces the entire operation of making bread, including the baking, from eight hours to 30 minutes. Night work is entirely done away with. The employment of carbonic acid gas interdicts any admixture of adulterants. A great saving is made by the changed method of fermentation, and also in particular by combining the new machinery with an American invention, by which the gritty coating of the grain is removed without, as previously, destroying three-fourths of the bran, which is the most nutritious part of the grain, according to the French chemist, Mége Mouriès. Dr. Dauglish calculates that his process would save England 8 million pounds sterling in flour every year. Another saving is in coal consumption. The cost of coal, including the steam engine, for the oven is reduced from 1 shilling to 3 pence. The carbonic acid gas, prepared from the best sulfuric acid, costs about 9 pence per sack, while at the present time the yeast comes to over a shilling for the bakers.

A bakery on the now much improved method of Dr. Dauglish was installed some time ago in a part of London, at Dockhead, Bermondsey, but went out of business because of the unfavourable location of the shop. At the present time, similar plants are operating in Portsmouth, Dublin, Leeds, Bath, and Coventry, and, it is said, with very satisfying results. The plant recently installed in Islington (a suburb of London) under Dr. Dauglish's personal supervision is aimed more at training the workers than at sales. Preparations for introducing the machinery on a large scale are being made at the municipal bakery of Paris.

General adoption of the Dauglish method will turn most of today's English master bakers into mere agents of a few large bread manufacturers. They will only be engaged in retail selling thereafter, not with production; and for most of them that will not be a particularly painful metamorphosis, since in point of fact they are already only agents of the large millers. The triumph of machine-made bread will mark a turning point in the history of large-scale industry, the point at which it will storm the hitherto doggedly defended last ditch of medieval artisanship.

Written on October 26, 1862

First published in *Die Presse*, No. 299, October 30, 1862

Printed according to the newspaper

Published in English for the first time

Karl Marx

THE SITUATION IN NORTH AMERICA[270]

London, November 4

General Bragg, who commands the Southern army in Kentucky—the other fighting forces of the South there are restricted to guerilla bands—on invading this border state issued a proclamation which throws considerable light on the latest combined moves of the Confederacy.[a] Bragg's proclamation, addressed to the states of the Northwest, presupposes his success in Kentucky as a matter of course, and obviously reckons on the eventuality of a victorious advance into Ohio, the central state of the North. In the first place, he declares the readiness of the Confederacy to guarantee freedom of navigation on the Mississippi and the Ohio. This guarantee only makes sense the moment the slaveholders are in possession of the border states. At Richmond, therefore, it was assumed that the simultaneous invasions of Lee in Maryland and Bragg in Kentucky would secure possession of the border states at one sweep. Bragg then goes on to vindicate the South, which is only fighting for its independence, but, for the rest, wants peace. The real, characteristic point of the proclamation, however, is the offer of a separate peace with the Northwestern states, the invitation to them to secede from the Union and join the Confederacy, since the economic interests of the Northwest and the South coincide just as much as those of the Northwest and the Northeast are inimically opposed. The following can be seen: No sooner did the South fancy itself safely in possession of the border states, than it officially boasted of its ulterior motive of reconstructing the Union but without the states of New England.

---

[a] B. Bragg, "Address to the People of the Northwest...", September 26, 1862.— Ed.

Like the invasion of Maryland, however, that of Kentucky came to grief: just like the former in the battle of Antietam Creek, so it happened to the latter in the battle of Perryville, near Louisville.[271] The Confederates were on the offensive here, just as they were there, having attacked the advance guard of Buell's army. The Federals owe their victory to General McCook, the commander of the advance guard, who held his ground against the enemy's considerably superior forces long enough to give Buell time to bring his main body into the field. There is not the slightest doubt that the defeat at Perryville will entail the evacuation of Kentucky. The most considerable guerilla band, formed of the most fanatical partisans of the slave system in Kentucky and led by General Morgan, was annihilated at Frankfort (between Louisville and Lexington) at almost the same time.[272] Finally, there comes the decisive victory of Roseccrans at Corinth, which makes imperative the hastiest retreat of the beaten invasion army commanded by General Bragg.[273]

Thus, the Confederate campaign for the reconquest of the lost border slave states which was undertaken on a large scale, with military skill and with the most favourable chances, has come utterly to grief. Apart from the immediate military results, these battles contribute in another way to the removal of the main difficulty. The hold of the slave states proper on the border states naturally rests on the slave element of the latter, the same element that enforces diplomatic and constitutional considerations on the Union government in its struggle against slavery. However, in the border states, the principal theatre of the Civil War, this element is in practice being destroyed by the Civil War itself. A large section of the slaveholders, with their "black chattels",[a] are constantly migrating to the South, in order to bring their property to a place of safety. With each defeat of the Confederates this migration is renewed on a larger scale.

One of my friends, a German officer, who fought under the star-spangled banner in Missouri, Arkansas, Kentucky and Tennessee in turn,[b] writes to me that this migration is wholly reminiscent of the exodus from Ireland in 1847 and 1848.[274] Furthermore, the energetic sections of the slaveholders, the young people, on the one hand, and the political and military leaders, on the other, separate themselves from the bulk of their class, since they either form guerilla bands in their own states and, as guerilla

---

a Here and below Marx uses the English phrase. In the first instance he gives the German translation in brackets.— *Ed.*

b Joseph Weydemeyer.— *Ed.*

bands, are annihilated, or they leave home and join the army or the administration of the Confederacy. Hence the result: on the one hand, a tremendous dwindling of the slave element in the border states, where it had always to contend with the "encroachments"[a] of its competitor, free labour; on the other hand, removal of the energetic section of the slaveholders and its white following. Only a sediment of "moderate" slaveholders is left, who will soon grasp greedily at the pile of money offered them by Washington for the redemption of their "black chattels", whose value will in any case be lost as soon as the Southern market is closed to their sale. Thus, the war itself brings about a solution by, in fact, radically changing the form of society in the border states.

For the South the most favourable season for waging war is over; for the North it is beginning, since the inland rivers are now navigable once more and the combination of land and sea warfare already attempted with so much success is again possible. The North has used the interval to good advantage. "Ironclads", ten in number, for the rivers of the West, are rapidly nearing completion; to which must be added twice as many semi-armoured vessels for shallow waters. In the East many new armoured vessels have already left the yards, whilst others are still under the hammer. All will be ready by January 1, 1863. Ericsson, the inventor and builder of the *Monitor*,[b] is directing the building of nine new ships after the same model. Four of them are already "afloat".

On the Potomac, in Tennessee and Virginia, as well as at different points in the South—Norfolk, New Bern, Port Royal, Pensacola and New Orleans—the army daily receives fresh reinforcements. The first levy of 300,000 men, which Lincoln announced in July, has been fully provided and is in part already at the theatre of war. The second levy of 300,000 men for nine months is gradually being raised. In some states conscription has been replaced by voluntary enlistment; in none does it encounter serious difficulties. Ignorance and hatred have decried conscription as an unheard-of occurrence in the history of the United States. Nothing can be more mistaken. Large numbers of troops were conscripted during the War of Independence[275] and the second war with England (1812-15),[276] indeed, even in sundry small wars with the Indians, without this ever encountering opposition worth mentioning.

[a] Marx uses the English word and gives the German translation in brackets.— *Ed.*

[b] See this volume, p. 213.— *Ed.*

It is a noteworthy fact that during the present year Europe supplied the United States with an emigrant contingent of approximately 100,000 souls and that half of these emigrants consist of Irishmen and Britons. At the recent congress of the English Association for the Advancement of Science[a] at Cambridge, the economist Merivale was obliged to remind his countrymen of a fact that *The Times, The Saturday Review, The Morning Post* and *The Morning Herald,* not to mention the *dii minorum gentium,*[b] have so completely forgotten, or want to make England forget, namely, that the majority of the English surplus population finds a new home in the United States.

Written on November 4, 1862

First published in *Die Presse,* No. 309, November 10, 1862

Printed according to the newspaper

---

[a] Marx gives the English name.— *Ed.*

[b] Literally: "gods of humbler lineage", i.e., in this context, less important newspapers.— *Ed.*

Karl Marx

SYMPTOMS OF DISINTEGRATION
IN THE SOUTHERN CONFEDERACY[277]

The English press is more Southern than the South itself. While it sees everything black in the North, and everything white in the land of the "nigger",[a] people in the slave states themselves do not by any means lull themselves with the "certainty of victory" that *The Times* celebrates.

The Southern press, with one voice, raises cries of dismay at the defeat at Corinth and accuses Generals Price and Van Dorn of "incompetence and conceit".[278] The *Mobile Advertiser* speaks of a regiment, the 42nd Alabama, that went into battle on Friday[b] 530 men strong, numbered 300 men on Saturday and consisted of only 10 men on Sunday evening. The rest were killed, captured, wounded or otherwise lost in the meantime.[c] The Virginia papers use similar language.

"It is clear," says the *Richmond Whig*, "that the immediate purpose of our Mississippi campaign has not been attained." "It is to be feared," says the *Richmond Enquirer*, "that the outcome of this battle will have the most harmful effect on our campaign in the West."

This foreboding has come true, as the evacuation of Kentucky by Bragg and the defeat of the Confederates at Nashville (Tennessee) show.[279]

From the same source, the newspapers of Virginia, Georgia and Alabama, we are getting interesting disclosures concerning the conflict between the central government in Richmond and the governments of the individual slave states. The occasion for the conflict arose out of the last Conscription Act, in which the

---

[a] Marx uses the English word.— *Ed.*
[b] October 3.— *Ed.*
[c] *Mobile Advertiser and Register*, October 10, 1862.— *Ed.*

Congress extended military service far beyond the normal age.[a] A certain Levingood was enrolled in Georgia under this Act and arrested by an agent of the Confederacy, J. P. Bruce, because he refused to serve. Levingood appealed to the highest court of Elbert County (Georgia), which ordered his immediate release. The extensive substantiation of the ruling says inter alia:

"The preamble to the constitution of the Confederacy is careful to emphasise explicitly that the individual states are sovereign and independent. How can this be said of Georgia if any militiaman can be forcibly removed from the control of his commander? If the Congress in Richmond can pass a conscription act with exceptions, what is to prevent it from passing a conscription act without exceptions and thus enrolling the Governor, the Legislature, the judges, and thereby putting an end to the entire state government?... For these and other reasons, it is hereby ordered and decreed that the Conscription Act of the Congress is null and void and has no force of law..."

Thus, the State of Georgia has forbidden conscription within its borders, and the Confederate government did not dare to revoke the prohibition.

Similar friction occurred in Virginia between the "individual state" and the "league of individual states". The source of the dispute is the refusal of the state government to grant the agents of Mr. Jefferson Davis the right to conscript the militiamen of Virginia and enrol them in the Confederate army. The incident led to an exchange of caustic letters between the Secretary of War[b] and General J. B. Floyd, the notorious character who as Secretary of War of the Union under President Buchanan prepared the secession and in the process managed to "secede" notable portions of the Treasury funds into his private coffers. This chief of the secession, known in the North as "Floyd the thief",[c] now appears as the champion of the rights of Virginia as against the Confederacy. The *Richmond Examiner* comments, among other things, on the correspondence between Floyd and the Secretary of War:

"The entire correspondence is a good illustration of the resistance and hostility that our state (Virginia) and its army have to suffer at the hands of those who abuse the power of the Confederacy in Richmond. Virginia has been plagued with endless burdens. But everything has limits, and the state will no longer tolerate the repetition of injustice.... Virginia supplied almost all the arms, ammunition and military supplies that won the battles of Bethel and Manassas.[280] It gave the

---

[a] The Conscription Act was an amendment to the earlier Act to provide further for the public defence.— *Ed.*

[b] E. M. Stanton.— *Ed.*

[c] Marx uses the English nickname and gives the German translation in brackets.— *Ed.*

Confederate service, out of its own armouries and arsenals, 75,000 rifles and muskets, 233 pieces of artillery and a magnificent arms factory. Its manpower capable of bearing arms has been drained to the dregs in the service of the Confederacy; it had to drive the enemy from its western frontier unaided, and is it not a cause for indignation if the creatures of the Confederate government now dare to make sport of it?"

In Texas, too, the repeated drawing-off of its adult male population to the east has aroused antagonism towards the Confederacy. On September 30, Mr. Oldham, the Texas representative, protested to the Congress in Richmond:

"In the wild-goose expedition of Sibley, 3,500 picked troops were sent out from Texas to perish in the arid plains of New Mexico. The result was to bring the enemy to our borders, which he will cross in the winter. You have transported Texas' best troops east of the Mississippi, dragged them to Virginia, used them at the points of greatest danger, where they were decimated. Three-fourths of every Texas regiment sleep in the grave or have had to be discharged because of illness. If this government continues to draw the able-bodied men out of Texas in this manner in order to keep those regiments up to normal strength, Texas will be ruined, irrevocably ruined. This is unjust and impolitic. My constituents have families, property and their homeland to defend. I protest in their name against transporting men from west of the Mississippi to the east and thus laying their own country open to invasion by enemies from the north, east, west and south."

Two things emerge from the foregoing quotations taken from Southern journals. The coercive measures of the Confederate government to swell the ranks of the army have gone too far. The military resources are giving out. Secondly, and this is even more decisive, the doctrine of the "states' rights",[a] (the sovereignty of states) with which the usurpers in Richmond gave the secession a constitutional colouring,[281] is already beginning to turn against itself. That is how little Mr. Jefferson Davis has succeeded in "making a nation of the South",[b] as his English admirer Gladstone boasted.

Written on November 7, 1862

First published in *Die Presse*, No. 313, November 14, 1862

Printed according to the newspaper

---

[a] Marx uses the English phrase.— *Ed.*

[b] This refers to Gladstone's speech in Newcastle on October 7, 1862, reported in *The Times*, No. 24372, October 9, 1862.— *Ed.*

Karl Marx

[THE ELECTION RESULTS IN THE NORTHERN STATES] [282]

The elections have in fact been a defeat for the Washington government.[283] The old leaders of the Democratic Party have skilfully exploited the dissatisfaction over the financial clumsiness and military ineptitude, and there is no doubt that the State of New York, officially in the hands of the Seymours, Woods and Bennetts, can become the centre of dangerous intrigues. At the same time, the practical importance of this reaction should not be exaggerated. The existing Republican House of Representatives continues, and its recently elected successors will not replace it until December 1863. For the time being, therefore, the elections are nothing more than a demonstration, so far as the Congress in Washington is concerned. No gubernatorial elections have been held except in New York. The Republican Party thus retains the leadership in the individual states. The electoral victories of the Republicans in Massachusetts, Iowa, Illinois and Michigan more or less balance the losses in New York, Pennsylvania, Ohio and Indiana.

A closer analysis of the "Democratic" gains leads to an entirely different result than the one trumpeted by the English papers. New York *City,* strongly corrupted by Irish rabble, actively engaged in the slave trade until recently, the seat of the American money market and full of holders of mortgages on Southern plantations, has always been decidedly "Democratic", just as Liverpool is still Tory. The *rural districts* of New York State voted Republican this time, as they have since 1856, but not with the same fiery enthusiasm as in 1860. Moreover, a large part of their men entitled to vote is in the field. Reckoning the urban and rural districts together, the Democratic majority in New York State comes to only 8,000-10,000 votes.

In Pennsylvania, which has long wavered, first between Whigs[284] and Democrats, and later between Democrats and Republicans, the Democratic majority was only 3,500 votes. In Indiana it is still smaller, and in Ohio, where it numbers 8,000, the Democratic leaders known to sympathise with the South, such as the notorious Vallandigham, have lost their seats in Congress. The Irishman sees the Negro as a dangerous competitor. The efficient farmers in Indiana and Ohio hate the Negro almost as much as the slaveholder. He is a symbol, for them, of slavery and the humiliation of the working class, and the Democratic press threatens them daily with a flooding of their territories by "niggers".[a] In addition, the dissatisfaction with the miserable way the war in Virginia is being waged was strongest in those states which had provided the largest contingents of volunteers.

All this, however, is by no means the main thing. At the time Lincoln was elected (1860) there was no civil war, nor was the question of Negro emancipation on the order of the day. The Republican Party, then quite independent of the Abolitionist Party, aimed its 1860 electoral campaign solely at protesting against the extension of slavery into the Territories, but, at the same time, it proclaimed non-interference with the institution in the states where it already existed legally.[b] If Lincoln had had *Emancipation of the Slaves* as his motto at that time, there can be no doubt that he would have been defeated. Any such slogan was vigorously rejected.

Matters were quite different in the latest election. The Republicans made common cause with the Abolitionists. They came out emphatically for immediate emancipation, whether for its own sake or as a means of ending the rebellion. If this circumstance is taken into account, the majority in favour of the government in Michigan, Illinois, Massachusetts, Iowa and Delaware, and the very significant minority vote it obtained in the states of New York, Ohio and Pennsylvania, are equally surprising. Before the war such a result would have been impossible, even in Massachusetts. All that is needed now is energy, on the part of the government and of the Congress that meets next month, for the Abolitionists, now identical with the Republicans, to have the upper hand everywhere, both morally and numerically. Louis

----

a Marx uses the English word.— *Ed.*

b "The Platform", *New-York Daily Tribune*, No. 5950, May 19, 1860.— *Ed.*

Bonaparte's hankering to intervene[285] strengthens the Abolitionists' case "from abroad". The only danger lies in the retention of such generals as McClellan, who are, apart from their incompetence, avowed pro-slavery men."[a]

Written on November 18, 1862

First published in *Die Presse*, No. 321, November 23, 1862

Printed according to the newspaper

---

[a] Marx uses the English words "pro-slavery men".— *Ed.*

Karl Marx

THE DISMISSAL OF McCLELLAN[286]

McClellan's dismissal! That is Lincoln's answer to the election victories of the Democrats.[a]

The Democratic journals had stated with the most positive assurance that the election of *Seymour* as Governor of New York State would entail the immediate revocation of the *proclamation* in which Lincoln declared slavery abolished in *Secessia* from January 1, 1863.[b] The paper that took this prophetic imprint had hardly left the press when their favourite general—their favourite because "next to a great defeat he most dreaded a decisive victory"[c]—was deprived of his command and went back to private life.

We recall that McClellan replied to this proclamation of Lincoln with a counter-proclamation, an order of the day to his army, in which he indeed forbade any demonstration against the President's measure, but at the same time let slip the fatal words: "...It is the task of citizens through the polls to remedy the government's errors or to pass judgement on its actions."[d] McClellan, at the head of the main army of the United States, therefore appealed from the President to the impending elections. He threw the weight of his

---

a See this volume, pp. 263-65.— *Ed.*

b A. Lincoln, *A Proclamation* [September 22, 1862], *New-York Daily Tribune,* No. 6699, September 23, 1862.— *Ed.*

c Th. B. Macaulay, *Critical and Historical Essays Contributed to the Edinburgh Review,* Vol. I, John Hampden.— *Ed.*

d G. B. McClellan [Order, Enjoining on his Officers and Soldiers Obedience to the President's Proclamation of Freedom], *Headquarters Army of the Potomac. Camp near Sharpsburg, Md. Oct. 7, 1862, New-York Daily Tribune,* No. 6713, October 9, 1862.— *Ed.*

position into the scales. A *pronunciamento* in the Spanish manner aside, he could not have demonstrated his hostility to the President's policy more strikingly. Accordingly, after the election victory of the Democrats the only choice left to Lincoln was either to sink to the level of a tool of the pro-slavery compromise party or with McClellan to remove from under it its point of support in the army.

McClellan's dismissal at *this* moment is accordingly a political demonstration. In any case, however, it had become indispensable. *Halleck,* the Commander-in-Chief,[a] in a report to the Secretary of War,[b] had charged McClellan with direct insubordination.[c] For, shortly after the defeat of the Confederates in Maryland, on October 6, Halleck ordered the crossing of the Potomac, particularly as the low water-level of the Potomac and its tributaries favoured military operations at the time. In defiance of this order, McClellan remained immobile, under the pretext of his army's inability to march due to lack of provisions. In the report mentioned, Halleck proves that this was a hollow subterfuge, that, compared with the Western army, the Eastern army enjoyed great privileges in respect of the commissariat and that the supplies still lacking could have been received just as well south as north of the Potomac. A second report links up with this report of Halleck's; in it the committee appointed to inquire into the surrender of Harper's Ferry[287] to the Confederates accuses McClellan of having concentrated the Union troops stationed near that arsenal in an inconceivably slow fashion—he let them march only six English miles (about one and a half German miles) a day—for the purpose of its relief.[d] Both reports, that of Halleck and that of the committee, were in the President's hands *before* the election victory of the Democrats.

McClellan's generalship has been described in these columns so repeatedly[e] that it is sufficient to recall how he sought to substitute strategic envelopment for tactical decision and how indefatigable he was in discovering considerations of general-staff discretion which forbade him either to take advantage of victories

---

[a] Marx gives the title in English.— *Ed.*

[b] E. M. Stanton.— *Ed.*

[c] H. W. Halleck [Report to E. M. Stanton, Secretary of War], *Headquarters of the Army, Washington, October 28, 1862, New-York Daily Tribune,* No. 6740, November 10, 1862.— *Ed.*

[d] [Report of the Investigating Commission...], *New-York Daily Tribune,* same issue.— *Ed.*

[e] See this volume, 179-81, 205-08, 226-27, 234-35.— *Ed.*

or to anticipate defeats. The brief Maryland campaign cast a false halo about his head. Here, however, we have to consider the fact that he received his general marching orders from General *Halleck,* who also drew up the plan of the first Kentucky campaign, and that the victory on the battlefield was due exclusively to the bravery of the subordinate generals, in particular, of General *Reno,* who fell, and of *Hooker,* who has not yet recovered from his wounds. Napoleon once wrote to his brother Joseph that on the battlefield there was danger at all points and one ran into its jaws most surely when one sought to avoid it. McClellan seems to have grasped this axiom, but without giving it the practical application that Napoleon suggested to his brother. During the whole of his military career McClellan has *never* been on the battlefield, has *never* been under fire, a peculiarity that General *Kearny* strongly stresses in a letter, which his brother published, after Kearny, fighting under Pope's command, fell in one of the battles near Washington.[a]

McClellan understood how to conceal his mediocrity under a mask of restrained earnestness, laconic reticence and dignified reserve. His very defects secured him the unshakable trust of the Democratic Party in the North and the "loyal acknowledgement" of the secessionists. Among the higher officers of his army he gained supporters through the formation of a general staff of dimensions hitherto unprecedented in the annals of military history. Some of the older officers, who had belonged to the former army of the Union and had received their training at West Point Academy, found in him a point of support for their rivalry with the newly-sprung-up "civilian generals" and for their secret sympathies with the "comrades" in the enemy camp. The soldiers, finally, knew of his military qualities only by hearsay; for the rest they ascribed to him all the merits of the commissariat and could tell many a glorious tale of his reserved affability. McClellan possessed one single gift of the supreme commander—that of assuring himself of popularity with his army.

McClellan's successor, *Burnside,* is too little known to pronounce a judgement on him. He belongs to the Republican Party. *Hooker,* on the other hand, who is assuming command of the army corps serving specifically under McClellan, is incontestably one of the best warriors in the Union. "Fighting Joe",[b] as the troops call him,

---

[a] Ph. Kearney [Letter to O. S. Halstead, Jr., August 4, 1862], *New-York Daily Tribune,* No. 6719, October 16, 1862.— *Ed.*

[b] Marx gives the English nickname, and the German translation in brackets.— *Ed.*

played the biggest part in the successes in Maryland. He is an *Abolitionist.*

The same American papers which bring us the news of McClellan's dismissal, contain utterances of Lincoln in which he resolutely declares that he will not deviate a hair's breadth from his proclamation.

"[*Lincoln*]," *The Morning Star*[a] observes quite justly, "has taught the world to know him as a slow, but solid man, who advances with exceeding caution, but does not go back. Each step of his administrative career has been in the right direction and has been stoutly maintained. Starting from the resolution to exclude slavery from the Territories, he has at last arrived at the ultimate purpose of all 'anti-slavery movements'—the uprooting of this evil from the soil of the Union—and has already reached the high vantage point on which the *Union* has ceased to be responsible in any way for the continuance of slavery."

Written on November 24, 1862

First published in *Die Presse*, No. 327, November 29, 1862

Printed according to the newspaper

---

[a] Of November 22, 1862.— *Ed.*

Karl Marx

ENGLISH NEUTRALITY.—
THE SITUATION IN THE SOUTHERN STATES [288]

London, November 29

The negotiations between the Cabinet here and the government at Washington on the corsair *Alabama*[289] are still pending, whilst fresh negotiations on the renewed fitting out of Confederate warships in English ports have already begun. Professor *Francis W. Newman,* one of the theoretical representatives of English radicalism, publishes a letter in today's *Morning Star* in which, among other things, he says:

"After the American Consul at Liverpool[a] had been assured by an English lawyer that the *Alabama* affair was illegal, he directed a formal protest to Lord John Russell. The law officers of the Crown[b] were consulted on the matter and likewise declared the fitting out of the *Alabama* illegal; but so much time was lost in the process that the pirate meanwhile escaped. At this moment a flotilla of more or less ironclad ships is ready at Liverpool, prepared to break through the American blockade. Apart from this, a swarm of pirate ships is waiting to follow the *Alabama* in its infamous progress any moment. Is our government a second time going to wink at the successors of the *Alabama* escaping? I fear that it is. Mr. *Gladstone,* in his speech at Newcastle,[c] said he had been informed that the rebel President,[d] whom he panegyrised, *was soon to have a navy.* Did this allude to the navy his Liverpool friends have built?.. Lord Palmerston and Lord Russell, as much as the Tory Party, are animated by a hatred of republicanism strong enough to overbear all scruples and doubts; while Mr. Gladstone, a probable future Prime Minister, avows himself an admirer of the perjured men who have leagued together to perpetuate and extend slavery."[e]

---

[a] T. H. Dudley.— *Ed.*

[b] W. Atherton and R. Palmer.— *Ed.*

[c] W. E. Gladstone [Speech in Newcastle on October 7, 1862], *The Times,* No. 24372, October 9, 1862.— *Ed.*

[d] J. Davis.— *Ed.*

[e] F. W. Newman [To the editor of the *Morning Star*], *The Morning Star* November 29, 1862.— *Ed.*

Of the papers that arrived from America today, the *Richmond Examiner,* an organ of the Confederates, is perhaps the most interesting. It contains a detailed article on the situation, the most important features of which I summarise in the following extract:

"The extraordinary and sudden increase in the enemy's sea power threatens to make our prospects gloomy. This weapon has acquired such a range that in many respects it seems more dangerous to us than the power of the enemy on land. The Yankees now command 200 more warships than at the outbreak of the war. Great preparations have been made for naval operations during the coming winter and, apart from the vessels already fit for service, some 50 ironclad warships are in process of construction. We have every reason to believe that, in the armament and .construction of its ships, the Yankee fleet, which will descend upon our coast this winter, far surpasses its predecessors. The objectives of the forthcoming expeditions are of the greatest importance. It is intended to capture our last seaports, complete the blockade and, finally, open up points of invasion in Southern districts, in order to put the Emancipation Acts into practical operation from the beginning of the new year. It would be foolish to deny the advantages which must accrue to our enemy from the capture of our last seaports, or to dismiss such misfortune lightly with the consoling thought that we can still always beat the foe by waging war in the interior.... With Charleston, Savannah and Mobile in the enemy's hands, the blockade would be carried out with a severity of which even our sufferings hitherto have given no idea. We would have to give up all thought of building a fleet on this side of the Atlantic Ocean and submit anew to the humiliation of surrendering our shipbuilding to the 'enemy or destroying it ourselves. Our great system of railroad connections in the cotton states would be more or less broken through, and, perhaps too late, we would make the discovery that the land warfare, on which such great hopes are built, would have to be continued under circumstances which forbade the maintenance, provisioning and concentration of great armies.... These disastrous results arising from the capture of our seaports became insignificant, however, before a greater danger, the greatest danger of this war—the occupation of points in the cotton states from which the enemy can carry out his emancipation plan. Great efforts are naturally being made to safeguard this pet measure of the Abolitionists from falling through and to prevent the spirit of revenge, which Mr. Lincoln has corked in a bottle till January 1,[290] from fizzling out in the harmless hissing of soda-water.... The attempt is now being made on our most defenceless side; the heart of the South is to be poisoned.... Prediction of future misfortune sounds bad to the ears of the masses, who blindly believe in the government and consider boasting to be patriotism.... We do not assert that *Charleston, Savannah* and *Mobile* are in no state to defend themselves. In the South there are naturally scores of military authorities, asserting that these ports are more impregnable than Gibraltar; but military men and their mouthpieces have too often lulled our people into false security.... We heard the same story with regard to New Orleans. According to their description, its defences surpassed those of Tyre against Alexander.[a] Nevertheless, the people woke up one fine morning to see the enemy's flag flying over its harbour.... The state of our ports' defences is a secret of the official circles. But the indications of the immediate past are not comforting. A few weeks ago, *Galveston* fell into the enemy's hands almost without a struggle. The local newspapers had been forbidden to write about the town's means of defence. No cry for help resounded, save that

---

[a] Alexander of Macedon.— *Ed.*

which fell on the deaf ear of the government. The people were not stirred to action. Their patriotism was requested to remain in ignorance, to trust the leaders and to submit to the decrees of providence. In this way, another prize fell into the lap of the enemy.... The method of wrapping all military matters in a mantle of secrecy has borne bad fruit for the South. It may have reduced criticism to dead silence and drawn a veil over the mistakes of the government. But it has not blinded the foe. He always seems thoroughly instructed on the state of our defences, whilst our people first learn of their weakness when they have fallen into the hands of the Yankees.

Written on November 29, 1862

First published in *Die Presse*, No. 332, December 4, 1862

Printed according to the newspaper

Karl Marx

[LETTER TO THE EDITORS
OF THE *BERLINER REFORM*][291]

The anecdote related in No. 83 of your paper referring to my stay in Berlin in 1861[a] has only "one drawback", that it is a fabrication. This is just to keep the record straight.

Karl Marx

London, April 13, 1863

First published in *Berliner Reform*, No. 89, April 17, 1863

Printed according to the manuscript and checked with the text in the newspaper

Published in English for the first time

---

[a] "Wie wir hören, ist Lassalle...", *Berliner Reform*, No. 83, April 10, 1863.— *Ed.*

Frederick Engels

KINGLAKE ON THE BATTLE OF THE ALMA[292]

Kinglake's book on the Crimean War has caused a great stir in England and outside, and deservedly. It contains a great deal of valuable, new material, and it could hardly be otherwise, since the author was able to use the papers of the English headquarters, many notes by senior English officers, and not a few memoirs prepared especially for him by Russian generals.[293] Nonetheless, so far as the military presentation is concerned, this is not a history but a novel; its hero is Lord Raglan, the English commander-in-chief, its ultimate aim is glorification, carried to absurdity, of the English army.

Kinglake's account is likely to produce a great effect in Germany; while it reduces the share of the French in the victory on the Alma to a minimum, it treats the Russians with ostensible respectful impartiality, refers to the already known sources of all three nations involved, and steers clear of the specifically French variety of bragging that we find as offensive in Thiers and his consorts as it is laughable. At the same time, our friends the English can brag, too, and, although they are slightly more accomplished in praising themselves than the French are, the colours are laid on at least as thick. If for no other reason, this makes it worthwhile to strip off the fictional cover from the description of the only military event in the two volumes which have appeared up to now, the battle of the Alma, and to separate the real new historical material from the embellishments, rodomontades and conjectures with which Mr. Kinglake fills out his picture.

An additional factor is that the battle of the Alma is of very special tactical interest, an aspect that has been inadequately appreciated thus far. In this battle, for the first time since Waterloo,[294] two different tactical formations clashed, one of them practised by preference by all the armies of Europe, the other rejected by all but one—the English. On the Alma, the English line advanced against the Russian columns and routed them without any particular difficulty. This is at least an indication that the old line is not yet as obsolete as the continental textbooks on tactics assert, and it is at least worth the trouble of looking a little more closely into the matter.

I

Kinglake lists the forces engaged on the two sides very carelessly. For the English he had the official data at his disposal and from them establishes the number of combatants as 25,404 infantrymen and artillerymen, something more than 1,000 cavalrymen and 60 guns. This may be regarded as authentic. He gives a round number for the French, 30,000 men and 68 cannons; there were also 7,000 Turks. In round numbers, this makes 63,500 allies with 128 guns, which may be fairly correct by and large. But Mr. Kinglake begins to have difficulties with the Russians. Now, we have in Anichkov's *Feldzug in der Krim* (German translation, Berlin, Mittler, 1857, first part) an account that is obviously based on official sources and that has never been contested until now in any essential point, with the names and numbers of the regiments, battalions, squadrons, and batteries. According to this account, the Russians had 42 battalions, 16 squadrons, 11 Cossack squadrons,[a] and 96 guns in ten and a half batteries on the Alma, 35,000 men in all. But this does not satisfy Mr. Kinglake at all. He puts together a special reckoning, constantly referring to Anichkov as his authority, but arriving at quite different conclusions, without however thinking it worth the trouble to cite evidence in favour of his divergent data. In general, it is characteristic of the entire book that it constantly cites authorities when reporting notorious facts but carefully avoids doing so when making new and risky assertions.

The two accounts differ little with respect to the infantry. Anichkov gives 40 battalions of the line, 1 battalion of skirmishers and $1/2$ battalion of marine sharpshooters; Kinglake transforms this last half-battalion into two battalions and, to support this, refers to Chodasiewicz (major in the Tarutino infantry regiment), who is said to have seen them.[b] The point is unimportant, since Kinglake

---

[a] Engels uses the Russian word "Sotnien" (hundreds).—*Ed.*

[b] R. Hodasevich, *A Voice from within the Walls of Sebastopol*, London, 1856, pp. 59-60.—*Ed.*

himself concedes that the Russians themselves think very little of these troops. He also transforms the 2 companies of engineers that appear in Anichkov into an entire battalion and always counts them as infantry.

In the case of the cavalry, however, Kinglake's exaggeration is more marked. Throughout the account of the battle it is emphasised on every occasion that the Russians had "3,400 lances" in the field, and on every map there appears an enormous column behind the Russian right wing with a note that the Russian cavalry, 3,000 strong, was held in this region. We are reminded continually of the remarkable inactivity of these 3,000 men and the danger their proximity constituted for the English, who had only just over 1,000 horsemen. Kinglake is very careful not to call our attention to the fact that over a third of this cavalry consisted of Cossacks, of whom everyone knows that they are incapable of fighting in close order against regular cavalry. Given the great ignorance of all military matters that pervades the entire book, this gross blunder should be attributed to a lack of knowledge rather than to malice.

Kinglake's critical judgement fails him completely, when he comes to the artillery. Anichkov, as has been said, gives 96 guns in all, in 10 specified light and heavy field batteries, supplemented by 4 horse-drawn naval guns. He knows exactly where each of these batteries was located during the battle. All these batteries appear in Kinglake (with a few minor discrepancies in the numbers), but three additional ones are given. The 5th battery of the 17th brigade, which Anichkov also lists, figures *twice* in Kinglake in the original position, once on the left wing (p. 231[a]) and immediately thereafter again in the main reserve (p. 235)! Similarly, the 3rd battery of the same 17th brigade, which, according to Anichkov, *was not there at all*, appears *twice* in Kinglake, once on the left wing (p. 231) and again—but as a "fixed battery"—in the centre! The fact that, in accordance with the well-known organisation of the Russian artillery at the time of the Crimean War (cf. Haxthausen, *Studien über Russland*[b]) there was only one heavy battery of 12 guns in every artillery brigade, and that later, when the batteries were set up with 8 guns each, there could therefore be a 1st and a 2nd heavy battery in a brigade *but never a 3rd*

---

[a] Here and below the references are to pages in the second volume of Kinglake's book.— *Ed.*

[b] A. F. Haxthausen, *Studien über die innern Zustände, das Volksleben und insbesondere die ländlichen Einrichtungen Russlands*, Dritter Theil, Berlin, 1852, S. 255-92.— *Ed.*

heavy battery—all this does not disturb our historian. What he is concerned with is presenting the heroic deeds of the English on the Alma as prodigiously as possible; and for that he required as many Russian cannons as possible. Hence, wherever he finds a battery listed in Russian reports (all of which, with the exception of Anichkov's, are more or less useless in terms of such details) that Anichkov does not mention, he assumes Anichkov forgot it and calmly adds it to the batteries listed by Anichkov. If he finds the same battery listed in different sources at two different points on the battlefield, he calmly counts it twice and at best assumes that a light battery is meant in one case and a heavy battery in the other.

All this sleight of hand notwithstanding, Kinglake can only scrape up $13\frac{1}{2}$ batteries with 8 guns each, a total of 108 guns, and since he fails to see that, according to Anichkov, the three batteries of the 16th brigade were still organised on the old basis of 12 guns (we see how superficially the man works), that still gives, as against Anichkov, only an addition of 12 guns. Hence, Kinglake must make an extraordinary effort in order to stud the heights of the Alma with Russian cannons. He is helped in this task by the fieldworks which the English bombastically call "the great redoubt". Of this Anichkov says simply:

"To the right of the road, Battery No. 1 of the same (16th) brigade was drawn up in an advantageous position and protected by an epaulement."

Kinglake describes this insignificant work quite correctly, but cannot imagine that simple twelve-pounders would be stationed behind it; he asserts they were heavy guns from Sevastopol. Chodasiewicz states, to be sure, that the guns of the 2nd battery of the 16th brigade were emplaced there (he confuses the 1st and 2nd battery), but the calibre of the cannon and *howitzer*, which, he said, are still in Woolwich, proved that these guns were not part of the regular field artillery (p. 233). Kinglake is even better informed. He says very definitely (p. 229):

"They were 32-pounders and 24-pound *howitzers*."

In 1849, during the uprising in the Palatinate,[295] some officers of the volunteers always justified the continual backwards movements of their units by claiming that they had been under fire from "red-hot 24-pound bombshot". This writer certainly never expected that the howitzer from which these terrible balls were shot would be captured by Mr. Kinglake on the Alma. As for these 24-lb. balls....[a]

---

[a] The next two pages of the manuscript are missing.— *Ed.*

[II]

...guns separated by a distance of 1,500 paces from Canrobert, whose division was neutralised by the Russian cannons while his own artillery tried to reach him by a circuitous route of at least half a German mile [a]; finally, Prince Napoleon was held down in the valley, 1,200 paces away from Canrobert and hesitating to cross the river. This scattering of his troops on a front of 6,000 paces and especially Bosquet's exposed position finally caused Marshal Saint-Arnaud such anxiety that he resorted to the desperate measure of sending his entire reserve forward. Lourmel's brigade was sent to Bouat, while d'Aurelle's brigade reinforced Prince Napoleon. By sending both of his reserves precisely into the two defiles that were already choked with troops, Saint-Arnaud completed the scattering of his forces. If this were not all stated in the official French report (the *Atlas historique de la guerre d'Orient*), it would be hard to believe.

What was it like on the Russian side, and what saved the French from this perilous situation?

The Russian left wing was commanded by Kiryakov. Over against Canrobert and Prince Napoleon he had in the first line 4 reserve battalions (Brest and Bialystok regiments), indifferent troops; in the second line the 4 battalions of the Tarutino regiment, in reserve the 4 Moscow battalions and the 2nd battalion of the Minsk regiment, which with 4 guns (4th battery of 17th art. brigade) was detached to the left to observe the seacoast. The 4 Borodino battalions, which were also under his command, were placed further east, right by the Sevastopol road, and when they

---

[a] The German mile is 7.420 km.— *Ed.*

were not engaged as skirmishers, they fought almost exclusively against the English. All in all, the French were therefore opposed by 13 battalions with 8 guns.

When Bosquet's flanking column appeared on the plateau south of the Alma, Prince Menshikov himself came to the left wing, bringing with him from the main reserve the remaining 3 battalions of the Minsk regiment, one foot- and two horse-batteries, and 6 squadrons of hussars. Up to that point the fighting had been limited to skirmishing and cannonade; the main bodies of Russians had pulled back somewhat, for the most part, and the French—Napoleon and Canrobert—had not yet appeared on the plateau at all or were so far off (Bosquet, Bouat, Lourmel) that they could not for the moment enter into combat. Now since the troops of Prince Napoleon had got stuck in the defile so thoroughly that they had not yet debouched, the Russians had no other point to attack than the Canrobert division covered beyond the edge of the plateau. Against him, Menshikov now formed a monster column of the 8 Minsk and Moscow battalions—two battalions in the front and four battalions deep, all in attack columns against the middle. Called away to his centre, he turned this unwieldy mass over to Kiryakov with the order to attack at once. When the column came to within gunshot range of the French, the latter

"no longer bore up under the weight that is laid upon the heart of a Continental soldier by the approach of a great column of infantry" (p. 400).

They withdrew a little further down the slope. At this moment, however, Canrobert's two batteries, along with those of Bosquet, came up rapidly a little further to the right through a depression in the terrain; they positioned their cannons quickly and opened fire against the left flank of the massive Russian force, with such effect that the latter quickly took cover. The French infantry did not follow them up.

Kiryakov's four reserve battalions had "dissolved", as Chodasiewicz puts it, under the skirmisher and artillery fire; the four Tarutino battalions had also suffered heavy losses; the eight battalions of the monster column were certainly not in any shape to renew the attack too soon. The French infantry of d'Aurelle and Canrobert now deployed on the plateau under cover of their artillery, and Bosquet had come close to them; Prince Napoleon's troops (whose 2nd Zouave regiment [296] had already joined Canrobert) finally began to climb the heights. The superiority had grown out of all proportion; the Russian battalions, concentrated on Telegraph Hill, melted away under the crossfire of the French artillery; finally, the Russian right wing had "entered into a very definite movement of withdrawal", as Kiryakov himself says. In these circumstances, it retreated, "not pursued by the enemy" (Kiryakov's manuscript memoir).

In French accounts the general forward rush of the French that followed at this point is crowned by an alleged storming of the telegraph tower in hand-to-hand combat, which gives the fray a neatly melodramatic conclusion. The Russians are unaware of this combat, and Kiryakov flatly denies that it took place. It is indeed likely that the tower was occupied by sharpshooters and had to be taken by storm, and there may also have been some other Russian skirmishers in the vicinity who had to be driven off; but that did not, of course, require the storming, or rather the race, of an entire division, and even the account given in the *Atlas historique* is grossly exaggerated anyway.

This marked the end of the battle, and Saint-Arnaud declined to pursue when Raglan called on him to do so, on the grounds that

"the troops had left their knapsacks on the other side of the river" (p. 492).

The heroic deeds recounted to us by Saint-Arnaud after the battle, and by Bazancourt later,[a] shrink considerably according to this description. The entire French army, 37,000 strong with the Turks, and with 68 guns, had....[b]

---

[a] The reference is to Saint-Arnaud's reports of September 21 and 22, 1854, published in the *Moniteur universel*, Nos. 280 and 281, October 7 and 8, 1854, and to C. L. Bazancourt's *L'expédition de Crimée jusqu'à la prise de Sébastopol.—Ed.*

[b] The next page of the manuscript is missing.—*Ed.*

III

The English advanced on the allied left flank. Their first battle-line consisted of the Evans division and Brown's light division; the second line was made up of the England and Duke of Cambridge divisions. The Cathcart division, from which one battalion had been detached, and the cavalry brigade followed on the left as reserve behind the left wing which was dangling in the air. Each division had 6 battalions in two brigades. The attack front of the English, which linked up with Prince Napoleon's left wing at the village of Burliuk, was about 3,600 paces long, so that each of the 12 battalions of a line had a front of 300 paces.

After reaching the gentle slope down to the Alma, the columns came under the fire of the Russian batteries positioned opposite, and, in conformity with English custom, the first line deployed at once. However, because the width of the front had been too narrowly reckoned, it came about that the right wing of the light division was overlapped by the left of the Evans division; in this way an entire battalion (7th regiment) was forced out of the line of battle. The artillery was placed before the front. In the second line, the Cambridge division likewise deployed, and since its battalions (Guards and Highlanders) were stronger, by themselves they formed an almost adequately extended second line; the England division remained out of range of the artillery fire in columns, as did the reserve. The Russians began to fire at about half past one. Until the French attack developed, the English lay flat on the ground to minimise losses from the fire. The skirmishers were engaged in the thickets and vineyards in the valley, pressing the Russians back slowly; as the Russians were withdrawing, they set the village of Burliuk on fire, thereby making the English attack front still narrower.

The English faced all the rest of the Russian army, i.e. $25\,^1/_2$ (Anichkov) or 27 battalions (Kinglake), and 64 guns. They attacked with 29 battalions and 60 guns; their battalions were stronger than the Russian ones. The Russians had, in their first line, the Suzdal (extreme right wing) and Kazan (or Grand Duke Mikhail Nikolayevich, right centre) regiments, to which the Borodino regiment was added. In the second line was the Vladimir regiment, in the special reserve the Uglich regiment; the Volhynia regiment remained available in the main reserve; each of these regiments had 4 battalions, besides a skirmisher battalion and the marine skirmishers.

Towards three o'clock the French attack had developed to such an extent that the Bosquet and Canrobert columns had come to a halt on the plateau, and Prince Napoleon's were halted in the valley; the reserves, as we saw, had already been ordered forward. Now Raglan had the English go forward. The first line stood up and moved down into the valley in the line it had formed. The vineyards and thickets soon disrupted the order of the troops, even where they formed into double-file columns in squads, as is prescribed in England for such conditions. Evans's division sent two battalions and a battery to the right around the burning village, while the rest went to the left of it alongside the Sevastopol road. Here they soon came under the fire at close range of the two Russian batteries protecting the road; the two batteries, although under fire from 18 English guns, brought the English troops to a halt. The Russian infantry opposite them were the 4 Borodino battalions and the 6th skirmisher battalion; we learn nothing of their action.

The light division advanced further to the left. Facing it were the 4 Kazan battalions to the right and left of the 1st battery of the 16th artillery brigade emplaced behind an epaulement; in the second line were the 4 Vladimir battalions, all in column formation, and, according to Kinglake's data, in columns of two battalions each. The English crossed the river by the numerous fords, as best they could, and found on the south bank a natural ledge fifteen paces wide protected by a steep drop 8 to 10 feet high, under whose cover they could reform. Beyond the drop, the terrain rose gently and was open to the battery some 300 paces away. Here they were bothered by skirmishers only at a few points; their own thinly scattered skirmishers had gone far off to the left and cleared the entire front. But they did not send skirmishers forward themselves nor did they reform; Brown himself abandoned the attempt and ordered the advance, "relying on the courage of the troops" (p. 315). While the brigadier of the left flank kept two battalions in hand to meet any possible flank attacks by the Russian cavalry, the other four, with a battalion of Evans's division that joined them (95th regiment), advanced on the battery, half in line, half in irregular bunches.

They had hardly climbed the slope, when the two columns of the Kazan regiment marched on them. And here our author begins one of his most glowing dithyrambs on the inimitability of the British troops.

"Here it came to be seen that now, after near forty years of peace, our soldiery were still gifted with the priceless quality which hinders them from feeling the weight of an infantry column in the same way as foreigners ... In their English way, ... they began half jesting, half annoyed, shooting easy shots into the big, solid mass of infantry which was solemnly marching against them. The column was not unsteady, but it was perhaps an over-drilled body of men, unskilfully or weakly handled. At all events, their chiefs were unable to make its strength tell against clusters of English lads,[a] who marched on it merrily and vexed it with bullets. Soon the column came to a halt, retreated and lapsed out of sight behind an undulation of the terrain" (p. 325).

We will not go any further into this bragging and boasting than to point out that these "lads" and "young troops", as Kinglake likes to call them, and whom we saw often enough (the 33rd regiment, which fought here, only a short time before it left for the Crimea), were at that time at least 27 years old on average, given the 12-year enlistment period in England and the frequent reenlistments for 9 years more, and that since the Crimean War and the East Indian mutiny,[297] where these fine regiments were wiped out, every English officer wishes in vain that he had such old "lads" under his command again. Suffice it to say that this column (the one to the east, on the Russians' right wing) seems, after a weak attempt at a bayonet attack, to have been forced to give way by the fire even of the irregular line. The other column advanced against the 7th regiment, soon was engaged in immobile musketry combat, and persisted in that for a long time without deploying, naturally suffering enormous losses in the process.

The three English battalions in the middle advanced on the battery, whose fire seems to have been slow and did not hold up the attackers. When they were close enough to rush the guns, the battery fired a salvo, limbered up and went off. A 7-pounder howitzer was found in the trench; a 32-pounder with only three

---

[a] Engels gives the English word "lads" in brackets after the corresponding German word.— Ed.

horses harnessed to it was stopped by Captain Bell of the 23rd regiment and brought back. The English occupied the outer breastwork of the epaulement and remained assembled to the right and the left. The Vladimir regiment now approached, but, instead of driving into the confused mass with the bayonet, they let themselves get into a firefight again and came to a halt. Under the fire of the English, who were still extended along a much longer front, the dense column would probably have shared the fate of the Kazan regiment—when the signal to retreat was sounded twice in succession among the English and repeated twice all along the line; the troops began the retreat at some points, and then generally, in part calmly but in part in complete disorder. The four battalions engaged here lost 46 officers and 819 men altogether.

The second line (Cambridge) had been slow in coming up and during this entire action had just crossed the river and stayed under the cover of the above-mentioned ledge. Now it went forward for the first time. The centre battalion of the brigade on the right, the Royal Scots Fusiliers, advanced at first, but its left wing was overrun by the fugitives of the light division pressing back, its right wing could not resist the fire of the Vladimir regiment, and this battalion too, left without any timely support, fell back in disorder. It was at about the same time that the French attack had come to a standstill and the column of eight battalions was forming against Canrobert.

This instant, when everything was going badly for the allies, is just the right moment for Mr. Kinglake to treat us to a miracle that can only find a parallel in the 1001 Nights, and lets Lord Raglan appear in hitherto unsuspected glory. We would pass this circumstance by if it had not in point of fact had a certain effect on the course of the battle and if it had not been given a certain significance by the fact that Kinglake is speaking here as an *eyewitness,* though an extremely inexpert one.

As the English line started moving to cross the river, Raglan rode across the Alma with his staff at the point where the English and French lines met and up a hollow on the far side of the river, without being molested by any more than a couple of sniper shots. He soon found before him a dome-shaped hill, which he ascended and from which he could see the entire length of the Russian formation against the English, and could even detect their reserves. As strange as it may seem that the general of an attacking army should station himself, without any protection, on a hill on the enemy's flank, the fact is confirmed by many witnesses and cannot be called into doubt. But Kinglake, not content with stationing his hero just in front of or in the extension of the enemy flank, transfers the hill in question *behind* the enemy front, between the latter and the Russian reserves, and from that point has Lord Raglan paralyse the entire Russian army by his mere appearance. On this point, the text of the book is not a whit more melodramatic than the map, on which a red star representing Lord Raglan, 1,200 paces in front of the English right wing, in the midst of the green Russian columns, which immediately show him respect as "Lord Zeus of the thundercloud", directs the battle.

This hill, whose exact location we cannot be expected to clarify here, but which is in any case not where Kinglake puts it—this hill did indeed provide a good position for artillery, and Raglan sent for guns at once, as well as for infantry. Somewhat later, two guns came up, at about the same time as the battery was captured by the English. One of these guns is said to have dispersed the Russians' main reserve (which, according to Kinglake, was only 1,100 paces away!), the other attacked the flank of the battery defending the bridge on the Sevastopol road. After a few shots this battery, which had been under the frontal fire of superior artillery (18 guns) for a long time, limbered up and thus the way was opened up for Evans's division to cross [the river]. That division slowly pushed back the Russian infantry, which, for the most part, fought in dispersed order here, and, followed by the England division, whose artillery combined with Evans's, brought its guns into play on the first ridge of hills.

In the meantime, further to the left, the Cambridge division was engaged in the decisive action. Of the three Guards battalions on its right wing, the centre one, the Scots Fusiliers, had advanced too soon and had been thrown back in disorder. Now the Grenadier Guards on the right and the Coldstream Guards on the left went forward in line against the epaulement, which the Vladimir regiment had retaken; between them was the interval of the battalion front that should have been occupied by the Scots Fusiliers but was now only covered more or less by the remnants of that battalion and of the light division, now reassembling to the rear. To the left of the Coldstream, the three Highlands battalions of Colin Campbell, also in line, advanced in perfect order in echelons from the right wing.

Opposite the Grenadier Guards were the two left Kazan battalions, which had already been driven back by the fire of the 7th regiment, and the two left Vladimir battalions, which now advanced towards the gap between the Grenadiers and the

Coldstreams. The Grenadiers came to a halt, wheeled the left flank back a little, and stopped the column immediately with their fire. In a short time, of course, the column was so shaken by the fire of the line that even Prince Gorchakov, who commanded the Russian right wing, could no longer get them to attack with the bayonet. A slight change in the front by the English Grenadiers brought the column under the fire of their entire line; the column wavered and fell back, as the English advanced. The two other Vladimir battalions were exchanging fire with the Coldstreams meanwhile, after the Scottish brigade finally drew level with them. The four Suzdal battalions posted on the Russian extreme right wing now came closer to the point of decisive action, the battery breastwork, but during this flanking march suddenly came under the fire of the Scottish lines and fell back without offering any serious resistance.

General Kwizinski, chief of the 16th division, was now in command of the Russian right wing after Prince Gorchakov had withdrawn because of a fall when his horse was shot under him. The English line formation was so new to him that it deprived him of all judgment as to the strength of his enemy. In his memorandum, which Kinglake had, he says himself that he saw the English advance in three overlapping lines (these were evidently the three Scottish echelons) and had to give way before such superior forces after the attacks of the four Vladimir battalions had been repulsed. It is sufficient to say that the four Uglich battalions only advanced as far as was necessary to gather up the fugitives; the artillery and cavalry were not used any further, and the Russians went into retreat unmolested by the English, who wanted to spare their cavalry. The Cambridge division lost some 500 men.

Here then the 6 battalions of the Cambridge division, supported by the remnants of the light division, a total of 11 battalions, were in action at the decisive moment (the two left-wing battalions of the light division did not advance even later) against the twelve Kazan, Vladimir and Suzdal battalions of the Russians; and if we add the 4 Uglich battalions, whose actual participation in the fight is highly problematical, they engaged 16 Russian battalions and routed them completely after a very brief combat.

The author even asserts that the entire action of the infantry in the ranks did not last more than 35 minutes; at any rate, the outcome was completely decided towards four o'clock. How are we to explain these swift successes against at least equal, perhaps stronger masses of infantry in a strong defensive position?

The English were certainly not commanded in the best possible way. Apart from the fact that Evans did not make the slightest attempt to attack the enemy's left flank but limited himself to a lustreless frontal action, it must be clear to everyone that the Duke of Cambridge did not do what he should have done as commander of the second line. When the first line had stormed the battery breastworks, the second was not there to back it up; it only arrived after the first had been thrown back, and so it had to do the work over again. But as soon as any English leader came up against the enemy and had no definite orders to the contrary, he attacked—if possible, in cooperation with adjacent troops—and that gave each of the two main assaults the decisiveness that assured success.

The Russians, on the other hand, showed great uncertainty in their leadership. It is true that Menshikov was unfortunate enough to be far away from the crucial point during the short period of decision; but neither Gorchakov nor Kwizinski, according to their own accounts, took any steps whatsoever to meet the attack with energy. The first attack was launched by the 4 Kazan battalions against five English [battalions] and failed; the second, again by 4 battalions (Vladimir), likewise failed; we do not hear of any serious attack by the 4 Uglich battalions, and the 4 Suzdal battalions allowed themselves to be surprised by enemy fire during their flanking march. The Volhynia regiment, in the main reserve, does not seem to have been ordered forward at all. The artillery soon fell silent, and the cavalry did nothing at all. Whether it was fear of responsibility, or orders not to risk the army, in any event on the English wing the Russians did not act with the energy and vigour that alone can guarantee victory to the weaker side either.

There certainly was another cause, however, that facilitated the English victory. The Russians fought in deep, thick columns, the English in line. The Russians suffered enormous losses from artillery fire, the English very little up to the grape-shot range. When the masses of infantry came close to one another, only the most vigorous pressing home of a bayonet attack could save the columns from the murderous fire of the lines, but everywhere we see the attack bog down and end as a fire-fight. What then? If one deploys under enemy fire, no one can tell how that will turn out, and if one remains in a column—one rifle firing against *four* enemy ones—the column is certain to be routed. This was the outcome in every single case on the Alma. More than that. The column, once under fire, could *never again* be brought to the decisive charge; the firing line could *in every case.* Both adversaries—Russians and English—were notoriously poor in open-order fighting; accordingly, the battle was decided exclusively by the masses; unless we wish to assume, with Kinglake, that the English are sort of demigods, we shall have to admit that in more or less open terrain the line has significant advantages over the column for both attack and defence.

The entire recent military history of the English....[a]

Written in late June 1863

First published in: Marx and Engels, *Works*, First Russian Edition, Vol. XII, Part II, Moscow, 1935

Printed according to the original

Published in English for the first time

---

[a] The manuscript breaks off here.— *Ed.*

Frederick Engels

ARTILLERY NEWS FROM AMERICA [298]

That the American Civil War, given the inventive spirit of the nation and the high technical level of engineering in America, would lead to great advances and usher in a new epoch in the technical side of warfare was only to be expected. The battle between *Monitor* and *Merrimac*,[a] to which the *Allgemeine Militär-Zeitung* again returned,[b] has justified this expectation. We now have some new facts to put on record.

I

Although the final outcome was in favour of the turret ship, the battle between the *Monitor* and the *Merrimac* still did nothing to decide the question of which class of battleships was superior: turret ships or broadside battery ships. A short while ago,[c] however, a battle took place which will, to all appearances, settle the matter once and for all, and which we are all the more pleased to examine since it is, to our knowledge, hardly known in England and France, and not at all in Germany.

The Confederates had had a commercial steamer of Scottish construction, the *Fingal,* armoured with 4-inch deal, 4-inch oak and 4-inch iron, in the harbour of Savannah. The iron plating

---

[a] See this volume, p. 213.— *Ed.*

[b] Engels probably means the article "Verlauf und Bedeutung des diesjährigen Feldzugs in Nordamerika" (*Allgemeine Militär-Zeitung*, No. 41, October 11, 1862) and the editorial note to the article "Der Angriff auf Charleston am 7. April 1863" in the *Allgemeine Militär-Zeitung*, No. 20, May 16, 1863.— *Ed.*

[c] On June 17, 1863.— *Ed.*

consisted of two layers of 6" wide and 2" thick slabs, the bottom layer horizontal and the top layer vertical, secured with strong bolts. After the fashion of the *Merrimac* the armour plating was laid aslant or roof-like over the ship, though flattened out on top, so that the ship resembled a lopped-off pyramid. It carried 4 six-inch broadside and two 7-inch pivot cannons (fore and aft).

The *Atlanta,* as the ship was called, came sailing down the Savannah River early one morning and soon ran into the two blockade ships, two turret ships, the *Weehawken* and the *Nahant,* which immediately headed for her. (For our description of the battle, we follow the report in the New York *Harper's Weekly* of July 11.[a]) The *Atlanta* opened the engagement by firing three shots at the *Weehawken,* which came closer without firing and then replied with solid shells of 440 lbs (English) from her 15-inch Dahlgren gun.* The first shot went right through *both sides* of the *Atlanta* and laid low about 40 men partly with the splinters, partly with shock. Among the latter was a lieutenant, who afterwards said that he had not been able to stand up for ten minutes. The second shot smashed through the iron cover of a gun port, killing or injuring 17 men. The third shell smashed the upper section of the armoured bridge on the upper deck, killing both pilots and knocking down the two helmsmen. The fourth hit the edge, where the side of the ship meets the deck, and seems to have bounced off without causing any damage. The fifth went through the funnel just as the *Atlanta* was hoisting the white flag to surrender,

---

* The Dahlgren gun is a comparatively short gun of some 12-14 calibre length. Its external shape was determined by Dahlgren (now admiral in command of Charleston) in the following way: at equal distances from one another, holes of rifle calibre were drilled perpendicularly on the axis of the bore from the outside, and loaded with rifle bullets, while the gun was loaded and fired as usual. The initial velocity of the individual bullets was established in the normal way and taken as a measure of the pressure of the explosion gases at the corresponding spot on the wall of the gun barrel. The corresponding abscissas were drawn on the axis of the bore as ordinates, and the curve connecting these indicated the external shape of the gun. Guns constructed on this principle are very thick at the breech and in the region of the trunnions, and only taper sharply towards the muzzle. They look rather like a soda water bottle. They are smoothbored and are cast hollow, over a hollow plug through which cold water runs during cooling. This cooling from inside gives the guns such strength—even in cast iron—that it is possible to cast guns of 15" and even 20" bore which are able to withstand 500 shots with a powerful charge without danger. Initially intended only for hollow shells, they have subsequently been strengthened so that solid shells can be fired from them, too. These reinforced guns are called *Columbiads.*

---

[a] The report was entitled "The Capture of the Rebel Iron-clad *Atlanta* by the *Weehawken* captain Rodgers".— *Ed.*

before the *Nahant,* which had just arrived on the scene, could even fire a single shot. In a quarter of an hour it was all over.

Yesterday the writer of this article visited the English Channel fleet lying in Liverpool harbour. There were the *Warrior,* the *Black Prince,* the *Royal Oak,* the *Defence,* the *Resistance*—all of them battleships with broadside guns (smoothbore 68-pounders, 8" calibre and 110 1b Armstrong, 7" calibre) armoured with 18-24" timber and $4^{1}/_{2}$-5" iron; undeniably the most beautiful and powerful armoured fleet now afloat, which, its draught permitting, could steam unmolested in between any *European coastal forts, as these are at present armed,* and into the harbour behind them. But how would the best of these ships fare against one of these American turret ships with its 440 1b gun? To judge by the trials made by the English themselves, a much smaller calibre is sufficient to pierce their sides; what havoc would a 440 1b shell not wreak in their innards? One single hit on the waterline would be bound to sink the ship, since a leak like that cannot be plugged. At the sight of these splendid ships, each one of which must have cost close on £1 million sterling, including the experiments, one cannot help thinking that all of them were already condemned and completely outdated.

Henceforth, it would seem to be an absolute necessity to equip battleships with the heaviest calibres that a ship can carry. These guns, however, cannot be broadside guns; the largest ship can only carry a few of them, and these have to be positioned *in the middle* of the ship. But this is only possible with *turret ships,* and for this reason turret ships will, from now on, constitute the decisive strength of any navy.

True, the turret ships built hitherto have only been seaworthy in a certain qualified sense. This was because they were constructed in America for a specific purpose: for operations in shallow coastal waters. If they are built bigger and given a greater draught they will certainly prove at least as seaworthy as the broadside battleships, which still leave much to be desired on this score. But, even if we restrict ourselves to the experience we have at present, the following points are quite definite:

1) Turret ships with heavy guns (10-15" calibre) are incomparably the strongest ships both for defence proper and for offensive operations on neighbouring coasts.

2) Armoured battleships with $2^{1}/_{2}$-5" iron plating and broadside guns of 8" calibre can be of great advantage for operations over a longer distance, against coasts, if one has *coaling stations,* and, above all, if one does not have to fight against turret ships.

3) For true mobile tactics on the open sea wooden ships continue to be the only ones suitable. They alone are able to hold enough provisions, coal and ammunition to carry their own base of operations around with them for several months; they alone are able to carry out the necessary repairs after a battle themselves. In India and China, for instance, armour-plated ships of any kind would be helpless, even in the hands of the English.

What are the conclusions as far as Germany is concerned?

1) Learn to cast guns of American calibre and build turret ships. Two such ships in the Elbe or Weser will keep the entire North Sea coast clear. Four of them in the Baltic will bring the sea under our control and, if necessary, force Copenhagen to capitulate; then no one will take the present Danish Navy seriously any longer.[299] Even if improvements are introduced making really seaworthy turret ships possible, the old ones will still remain the best harbour defence there is. They are cheap in any case.

2) Broadside armoured ships of 6-7,000 tons like the English and French ones each cost as much as six turret ships, while two turret ships are sufficient to beat one of them. They are not worth the money. On the other hand, *very fast* screw steamers of moderate dimensions armoured with $2^1/_2$-3″ of the very best (e.g. Styrian) iron plating and with a few guns, but heavy ones, can be of considerable service against the *existing* navies. They are able to evade the large, unwieldy armoured frigates and are well able to cope with a wooden ship of the line.

3) For long-distance operations wooden ships—both sailing vessels and screw steamers—are indispensable. We already have the Chinese station[300]; it is bound to become more important every year. As long as we have no coaling station there, sailing vessels are the only ones that can be used; for the time being, they are sufficient too. Stations in the West Indies, on the east and west coasts of North and South America and in the Levant have long been needed; everywhere German trade must be protected and respect won for the name of Germany. Twenty-five per cent steamers to seventy-five per cent sailing vessels would be enough there. At home, however, many large wooden ships are of no use; in fact, there is now no point whatever in having ships larger than 60-gun frigates, as the present-day ships of the line are outdated while those of the future have yet to be invented.

II

According to established practice, when laying siege to fortified ramparts the breach batteries were placed on the crest of the glacis, about fifty paces from the wall that was to be bombarded. When Montalembert's casemated works with uncovered stone walls were proposed,[301] and especially when such uncovered masonry was used in many places in Germany, there was much discussion whether or not such stone walls could be breached even at a distance; as far as actual experiments are concerned, however, the only one known to us is that of Wellington in 1823, when a detached wall covered by a contregarde was breached at 500 and 600 paces by indirect hits. The Crimean War only proved that stone-built coastal forts were safe against ships; Bomarsund[302] only proved that the Russian government had been dreadfully swindled by the building contractors. The Italian War[303] proved nothing, since it never came to siege operations. Until then one could assume that, with the artillery means available at the time, the uncovered stone walls of casemates could, in certain circumstances, make possible such superior firepower against siege batteries that it was worth its expense.[a] The trials at Juliers have proved that rifled guns with percussion shells, even of a light calibre, are able to breach brick fortifications at 1,200 paces, even by an indirect hit. And in America things are now happening that have quite different lessons to teach us.

During the attack on Port Pulaski (outside Savannah) General Gillmore (indisputably the foremost living American artilleryman) had only heavy Columbiads, smoothbore guns up to 15″ calibre for solid shells and powerful charges.[304] He set up his batteries 1,200 paces away and turned the casemated fortification made of strong masonry into a heap of rubble in just a few days. Nevertheless, this experiment convinced him that at greater distances his guns would not be able to knock down stone-wall fortifications. Unfortunately, we have no data as to the charges, since all American reports are framed in an extremely superficial way; but it is obvious that $1/3$ shot heavy charges are quite out of the question with such guns.

Gillmore therefore demanded rifled guns of heavy calibre for the assault on Charleston, and got them. They were so-called Parrott guns, breech-loading guns with 4-7 grooves according to the calibre. The rifling is flat and has less twist than the Armstrong guns. The guns are of *cast iron* with a wrought-iron

---

[a] Here Engels crossed out the words: "How do things stand now?"—*Ed.*

ring welded on above the breech which reaches as far as the trunnions, and are the same shape as the ordinary guns. Hundredweight for hundredweight they are said to cost exactly one quarter of what the heavy English Armstrongs cost. The shells were cylindro-ogival and had a coating of soft metal to be pressed into the rifling.

With these guns Gillmore attacked Fort Wagner [305] (see the plan of Charleston recently printed in the *Allgemeine Militär-Zeitung*[a]). But this fortification, built out of light sand from the dunes, stood up to it. The bombproof covered shelters kept the garrison safe and several assaults were repulsed. It was necessary to mount a proper attack, and for this the heavy guns were too good. Gillmore therefore had them drawn up in three new batteries which he had set up against Fort Sumter, the latter lying in the middle of the harbour entrance. These batteries, one of which was *in the swamp,* were 3,300 to 4,200 yards (4,000 to 5,000 paces) away from Fort Sumter.

Fort Sumter was built on an artificial island of special, very hard brick. The walls were 6-7' thick, at the base up to 12', the casemate arches and buttresses 8-9' thick. It had two floors of casemates and one floor of guns on the roof, which fired from the barbette. Its shape was that of a truncated lunette; it was chiefly the gorge and one of the flanks that were exposed to Gillmore's batteries. The fort contained 140 gun emplacements.

The bombardment lasted for 8 days, from 16 to 23 August; from time to time the navy joined in, though without much success. But the rifled 200-pounders did their job. The gorge and flank walls fell first, and then the fronts taken *à revers*.[b] At the end of the bombardment the fort was, as Gillmore put it, a shapeless mass of ruins.[c] All in all 7,551 shots were fired, of which 5,626 were hits (at these enormous distances!); 3,495 of these hit the outer wall area, 2,130 the inner. After the walls had been subjected to fire for a while many shells went right through both of them.

Gillmore also had a rifled 300-pounder but it burst on the seventh shot. The first six shells, however, are said to have gone through both walls and caused collapses of brickwork up to 20 feet high in places.

---

a The plan was published as a supplement to the *Allgemeine Militär-Zeitung*, No. 20, May 16, 1863.— *Ed.*

b From the other side.— *Ed.*

c Engels gives Gillmore's words in English, followed by the German translation.— *Ed.*

Understandably, the fort returned the fire on a small scale only. The batteries could not have provided any visible targets at a distance of half a German mile, even if there had been guns with such a range. As it was situated under the close fire of many Confederate batteries, no attempt was made to occupy it immediately, but now that Fort Wagner and Cunnings Point have fallen, this will probably already have happened.[306]

From the same batteries Gillmore launched 15 incendiary bombs on to the town of Charleston—over one German mile away—and only discontinued the bombardment because, after such a long journey, his percussion shells, not landing on their noses, failed to explode.

What should we in Germany make of all this shooting? What should we think of our uncovered stone-wall fortifications? What about the detached forts, 800-1,200 paces before the main rampart, which are supposed to protect the place against bombardment? What of the redoubts of the Cologne forts, the flanking gates of Coblenz, and what about Ehrenbreitstein? Our enemies, who are naval powers, will soon have enough rifled artillery of the very heaviest calibre, and railways to carry it are everywhere. On the other hand, as far as we know, the biggest rifled calibre yet introduced is that of the 24-pounder, roughly $4^1/_2''$—a veritable dwarf gun compared with what our enemies will pitch against us; and, if we had the same artillery in our casemates, it would not be possible to hit batteries 5,000 paces anyway. Our Rhine fortresses, however inadequately fortified the river line might be, have hitherto been our main strength against the first French attack; but what are they worth after experiences such as those described above?

This is no time for reflection. We must act, and straight away. Any delay may cost us a campaign. *Videant consules, ne quid respublica detrimenti capiat.*[a]

Written in late September 1863. Section I first appeared in the collection, *Friedrich Engels. 1820-1970. Referate, Diskussionen, Dokumente. Internationale wissenschaftliche Konferenz in Wuppertal vom 25.-29. Mai 1970*, Hannover, 1971; the full available text was first published in: Marx and Engels, *Works*, Second Russian Edition, Vol. 44, Moscow, 1978

Printed according to the manuscript

Published in English for the first time

---

[a] Let the Consuls see to it that the republic suffers no harm. (The traditional formula addressed by the Roman Senate to the Consuls in time of danger to the state.)— *Ed.*

Karl Marx

[PROCLAMATION ON POLAND BY THE GERMAN WORKERS' EDUCATIONAL SOCIETY IN LONDON] [307]

The *London German Workers' Educational Society,*[308] in agreement with an agent of the Polish national government,[309] has authorised the undersigned committee to organise a collection of funds for Poland among the German workers in England, Germany, Switzerland and the United States. Even if only little material help can be given Poland in this manner, great moral assistance can be rendered.

The Polish question is the German question. Without an independent Poland there can be no independent and united Germany, no emancipation of Germany from the Russian domination that began with the first partition of Poland.[310] The German aristocracy long since recognised the Tsar as secret supreme sovereign. The German bourgeoisie looks on, silent, passive and indifferent, at the slaughter of the heroic nation which alone still shields Germany from the Muscovite deluge. Part of the bourgeoisie realises the danger, but is willing to sacrifice German interests to those of the individual German states, whose existence depends on the dismemberment of Germany and the maintenance of the Russian hegemony. Another section of the bourgeoisie regards the autocracy in the east as it does the reign of the coup d'etat[a] in the west, as a necessary buttress of *order.* Finally, a third part is so absolutely obsessed by the important business of making money that it has completely lost understanding of and insight into major historical relations. The Germans of 1831 and 1832, by their open demonstration in support of Poland,[311] at least forced the Federal Diet to take strong measures. Today Poland finds its

---

[a] The reign of Napoleon III.— *Ed.*

most eager opponents, and hence Russia finds its most useful tools, among the liberal masterminds of the so-called *National Association*.[312] Everyone is free to decide for himself how far this liberal Russophilism is linked to the *Prussian upper crust*.

In this fateful moment, the German working class owes it to the Poles, to foreign countries and to its own honour to raise a loud protest against the German betrayal of Poland, which is at the same time treason to Germany and to Europe. It must inscribe the *Restoration of Poland* in letters of flame on its banner, since bourgeois liberalism has erased this glorious motto from its own flag. The English working class has won immortal historical honour for itself by thwarting the repeated attempts of the ruling classes to intervene on behalf of the American slaveholders by its enthusiastic mass meetings, even though the prolongation of the American Civil War subjects a million English workers to the most fearful suffering and privations.

If police restrictions prevent the working class in Germany from conducting demonstrations on such a scale for Poland, they do not in any way force them to brand themselves in the eyes of the whole world as accomplices in the betrayal, through apathy and silence.

The undersigned committee requests that money be sent to Mr. *Bolleter,* the occupant of the Society's premises at 2 Nassau Street, Soho, London. The expenditure of the money is controlled by the Society and public account thereof will be given as soon as the purpose of this collection permits.

Bolleter, Berger, Eccarius, Krüger,
Lessner, Limburg, Linden, Matzrath,
Tatschky, Toups, Wolff

Written in late October 1863   Printed according to the leaflet

First published as a leaflet in
London in November 1863

Frederick Engels

THE ENGLISH ARMY[313]

In a detailed review of the small work by Petrie and James, the *Allgemeine Militär-Zeitung* recently described the organisation of the English army,[a] and since then, in another article, the position of this army in the English state.[b] What remains is only to consider this army itself in its historical development in the last seventy years, its present form, its materiel, its internal service organisation, its tactical training and its characteristic forms of combat. This is the purpose of the present lines.

The English army is especially interesting to the military observer. It is the only one in the world that still keeps unbendingly to the old line tactics, at least in so far as it has never known columns within the range of infantry fire (except for actions in defiles). Not only does it fire in line, its bayonet attacks, too, are made only in line. Nonetheless—or perhaps precisely for that reason—it is undeniably the army that has suffered fewest defeats. In any event, it is worthwhile taking a closer look at the battle methods of such an army, particularly now, when, to the astonishment of the whole world, what was believed to be impossible has become possible: that England threatens to make war on us Germans.[314]

---

[a] This refers to the review of the pamphlet *Organization, composition and strength of the Army of Great Britain. (Compiled by Captain Martin Petrie and Colonel James.)* The review appeared in the literary supplement to the *Allgemeine Militär-Zeitung*, Nos. 34-39, August 22 and 29 and September 5, 12, 19 and 26, 1863, under the correspondent's sign [16.].— *Ed.*

[b] "Die englische Armee und Verfassung", *Allgemeine Militär-Zeitung*, Nos. 44-46, October 31 and November 7 and 14, 1863.— *Ed.*

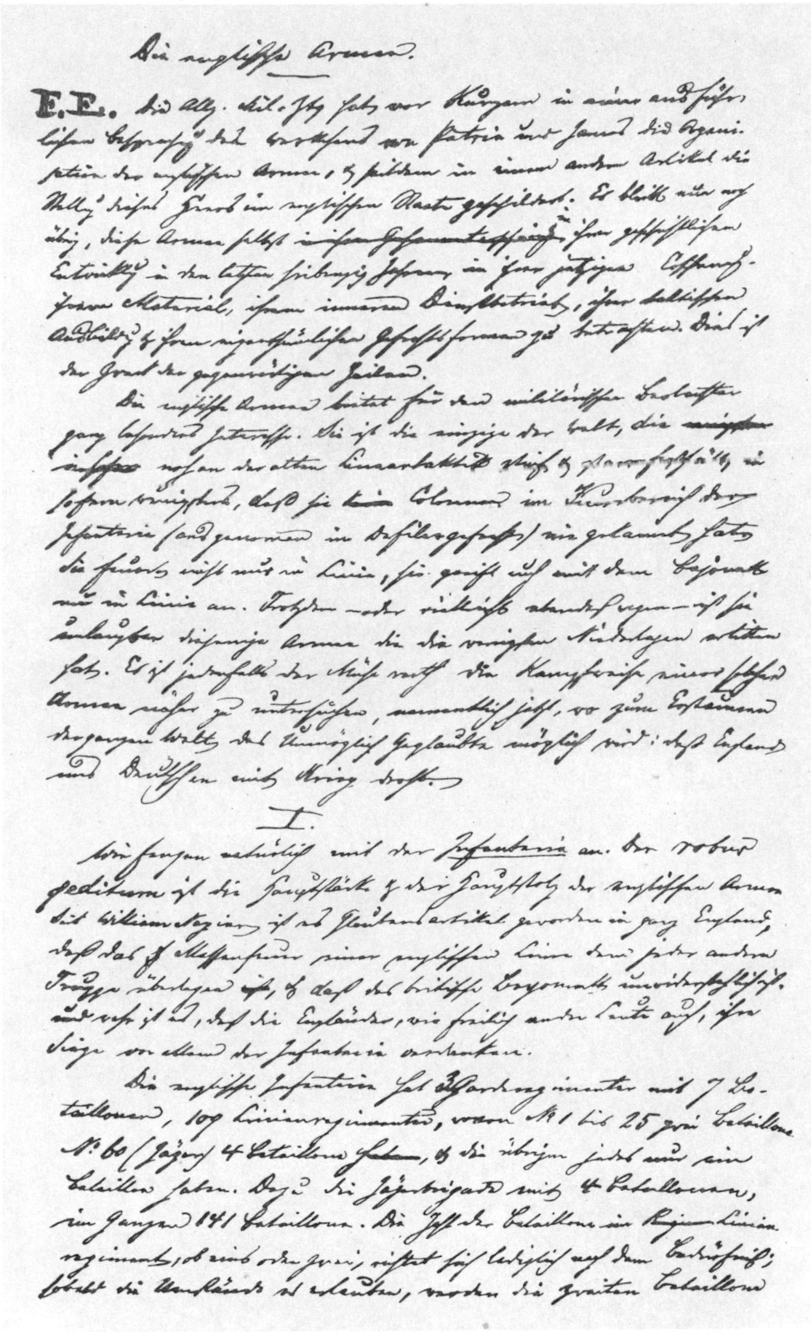

First page of Engels's manuscript of "The English Army"

I

We begin with the *infantry*, naturally. The *robur peditum*[a] is the chief strength and the pride of the English army. Ever since William Napier it has been an article of faith for all England that the massed fire of an English line is superior to that of any other troops, and that the British bayonet is irresistible, and true it is that the English, like other people, to be sure, owe their victories above all to their infantry.

The English infantry has 3 Guards regiments with 7 battalions, 109 line regiments, of which Nos. 1 to 25 have two battalions, No. 60 (Rifles) 4 battalions, and the remainder only one battalion each. In addition, there is the Rifle Brigade with 4 battalions, making a total of 141 battalions. Whether there are one or two battalions in a line regiment is determined exclusively by requirements; as soon as circumstances permit, the second battalions of the first 25 regiments will certainly be disbanded again. The promotion of the officers likewise takes place in the regiment, which often gives rise to absurd disarrangements, e.g. when, as at present, the first battalion of the 13th Regiment is stationed in Jamaica and the second in New Zealand.

The reserve and elite troops are primarily the Guards and the eight Highland regiments, who have always honoured their reputation. Nine so-called "light" and 5 "fusilier" regiments count as light infantry, but differ in only a few respects from the [regiments of the] line, and only 8 rifle battalions are true light infantry. Regiments Nos. 101 to 109, formerly European regiments of the East India Company,[315] serve only in India.

Apart from these 141 battalions of British infantry, there are also various corps in the home country, to which we shall return later, and in the colonies:

In North America: 1 battalion and 2 companies of British troops	1,350	men
In the West Indies: 4 battalions of Negroes and mulattoes	3,700	"
In St. Helena: 1 British battalion	560	"
In Malta: native fortress artillery	640	"
At the Cape of Good Hope: mounted rifles, $^5/_6$ Hottentots, $^1/_6$ Europeans, mainly Germans and Swiss	900	"
In Ceylon: 3 battalions of native rifles	1,460	"
	8,610	men

---

[a] Elite infantry.— *Ed.*

Finally, the native army in India, 151 battalions with a total of 110,000 men. With few exceptions, these troops are commanded by British officers and their entire organisation is very similar to the English line. But the Indian army still retains many characteristics from the time of the East India Company; e.g., commissions cannot be bought there,[316] at least not officially, although similar things are done indirectly there, too.

On February 5 of this year[a] there were 58 battalions of English infantry in India, 3 in China, 2 in Mauritius (Isle-de-France), 4 at the Cape, 12 in Canada and the other North American possessions, 1 in Bermuda, 2 in the West Indies, 10 in New Zealand (because of the war with the natives),[317] 5 in Gibraltar, 4 in the Ionian islands, 5 in Malta, 42 in England and on the way home. Of the latter, there were 6 in London, 9 in the Aldershot camp,[318] 10 in Portsmouth, Plymouth and Dover, 1 in Jersey, 2 in inland England, 2 in Scotland, 10 in Ireland, 2 on the way back home. We see from this what strong support the navy gives the army; without its protection and the rapid means of transportation it affords, these weak garrisons would be far from adequate. Where the navy can provide only slight protection, however, as in India and Canada, we find strong garrisons, and likewise so in the strategic positions in the Mediterranean, where it is necessary to be prepared for conflicts with European troops.

It was formerly the rule to send the Guards out of the country only in case of war; but there are now two battalions in Canada.

The total strength of the infantry on active service at the present time comes to 133,500 men; this averages 884 men per battalion, divided into 10 companies, each with a captain, a lieutenant, and an ensign[b] (equivalent to our second lieutenant). In addition, each battalion, with the exception of the Guards, has two depot companies for training recruits; 6 to 8 of these depots are combined into a depot battalion, of which there are 23, with a total strength of about 18,000 men. These depots are all in the home country, usually by or near the sea. Thus, the total strength of the English infantry is something over 150,000 men.

[a] 1863.— Ed.
[b] Engels uses the English word.— Ed.

II

The officers are recruited from all the educated classes of the nation. Not much theoretical schooling is demanded of the aspirants; the prescribed examinations pose questions that would make a Prussian ensign smile. However, increasing efforts are being made to get young men from the military school at Sandhurst[319] into the army, in particular by giving commissions as ensigns *without purchase* to those who come out top in the examinations. Not much is required by way of foreign languages, and the aspirant has great freedom of choice among a number of European and Indian languages; the mathematical requirements are extremely low; on the other hand, much more emphasis is laid on good, clear, simple expression in practical English composition than among us, where almost every German army writes its own kind of German, and not always good common sense German at that. In a country where the two principal parties are almost equally represented in the aristocracy, it goes without saying that no inquiry is made into political opinions; the greatest military family in England, the Napiers, consisted and consists almost entirely of Radicals. In general more stress is laid on manly character than on knowledge, and since the English officer can be certain that he will be sent to all corners of the world and will soon come under fire, it stands to reason that the English army cannot be, to the extent that many others can, an almshouse for people who are lacking in almost every physical and moral quality required in a soldier. This last, however, is the best guarantee of a good officer corps; for despite all the fine rules mentioned above, nowhere is there more nepotism and family influence than in the English army. No one can get into the officer corps without influential connections, and no one gets promotion without money, unless he has the good fortune to have the man ahead of him killed in action. Here, too, there are honourable exceptions, of course; a certain shoemaker's son from Glasgow died last year as Field Marshal Lord Clyde, after he had reconquered the India that had been lost; but poor Colin Campbell, to get that far, had to take part as an officer in the campaign against Buenos Aires as early as 1807,[320] and in 1854, when he went to the Crimea, he was only a colonel. And without a distant relative, who commanded a regiment, he would never have become an officer.

English officers form a very exclusive corps, especially in England itself. They even have a dialect or rather an accent of their own, as in Prussia, and have very little contact with the citizens of their garrison town. This isolation is enhanced by the circumstance that the unmarried officers live in barracks (or rather a separate building in the barracks compound) and have to eat at the officers' mess. In a country where the army is under civilian jurisdiction for all offences that are not of a strictly military nature, this living together in barracks is a necessity. Young officers are punished severely for pranks in town that could bring them into conflict with the civilian authorities; as compensation, they have fairly broad freedom in the barracks themselves. Female visitors of all sorts come and go, there is heavy drinking and gambling, and the young gentlemen play the heartiest practical jokes on one another. If a sneak gets in among them, so much the worse for him. A few years ago these practical jokes,[a] carried to excess in some regiments, led to scandalous courts martial, and since then strict orders prohibiting them have been issued; actually, however, this sort of amusement is regarded with indulgence, so long as public scandal is avoided. The government contributes 25 pounds sterling per annum per company to the officers' mess, which should be decent but economical and never place officers with limited means in a position where they are compelled to spend more money than they can afford. Nonetheless, there are occasions enough to lay out money, and the usurers ruin as many young officers with bills and I.O.U.s as elsewhere.

This way of life leaves its mark on the outward demeanor of the English officer. With civilians—although when off duty he

---

a Engels uses the English expression here: "practical jokes".— Ed.

almost always wears civilian clothes—he is usually dignified and reserved; arrogant overbearing behaviour towards the citizens occurs as exceptions in such garrison cities as Portsmouth, or in marksmanship schools, where many officers are together and set the tone. In general, the officer has to show that he is "an officer and a gentleman"; at any time he can be called up before a court martial, discharged and even cashiered "for conduct unbecoming an officer and a gentleman", and no mercy is shown if an officer has caused a scandal by his behaviour in public, unless, of course, he resigns first. Cover-ups of scandalous public incidents, such as we know have occurred in Germany, are impossible in England, and the spirit of the army can only gain from that.

The officers' right to wear civilian clothing off duty, unusual as it may seem to us Germans, has its excellent aspects, and England provides abundant proof that it has not the slightest ill effects on the military spirit of the officers. It should be noted, into the bargain, that in the main garrison towns, such as Chatham, Portsmouth, etc., where there is a good deal of military activity, the officers wear civilian clothing less frequently.

The duel has disappeared entirely from the English army. The last duel involving officers took place twenty years ago between two brothers-in-law, a major and a lieutenant; the major was killed, and the lieutenant was acquitted by the jury because of the shocking provocation leading up to the affair. The ideas of honour that have been implanted in the English officer corps— and by no one more energetically than Wellington himself—are based on the fundamental principle that anyone who insults another without cause dishonours himself, not the person he has insulted; and that he can only restore his honour by making amends for his injustice so far as he is able. Anyone who is the first to insult a comrade is therefore liable to the charge of conduct unbecoming a gentleman, unless he makes amends, or if the insult is of such a nature that it cannot be amended, a court martial soon settles the matter. This way of thinking may seem strange enough in some circles, particularly the Prussian army, but it certainly has more common sense on its side than the fantastically exaggerated duel *point d'honneur*[a] of some people. That this is thoroughly consistent with the feeling of military honour is proved by the English officers themselves, who need fear no comparison in this respect.

Advancement in the regiment is exclusively by seniority, coupled

---

[a] Point of honour.— *Ed.*

with purchase of rank, as follows: As soon as a vacancy occurs, the senior officer of the next lower rank has the choice of whether he will purchase the place or not; if he turns it down, which happens only because of lack of money, the choice goes to the next in seniority, and so forth. This purchase of commissions is without a doubt one of the worst institutions in the English army, something foreign soldiers will never reconcile themselves to. It is absurd and reprehensible, even if one allows all the mitigations that the English plead in its defence: that it enables younger officers to reach higher places more quickly, that it is an old-established custom, one hard to eradicate, etc. It is and remains a shame to the English army that it has not been able to supersede this system, and it undoubtedly does the greatest harm to the spirit of the officer corps that able officers must grow rusty in lower ranks because they have only their pay and no capital.

The price of a commission as ensign (i.e. second lieutenant) is 450 pounds sterling (3,000 thalers) in the line infantry; if the ensign wants to advance to lieutenant, he must pay a further 250 pounds (1,700 thalers); for the captain's commission, 1,100 pounds more (7,030 thalers); major's commission, 1,400 pounds more (9,030 thalers); lieutenant colonel's commission, a further 1,300 pounds (8,700 thalers). This commission is thus worth a grand total of 4,500 pounds sterling, or over 30,000 thalers, which the owner gets back from his successor when he advances to colonel. In the Guards and the cavalry the prices are still higher; there is no purchase of commissions in the artillery and the engineers. If the officer dies, all the capital invested is lost, and the next in seniority takes his place without purchase. From colonel on, purchase no longer applies; every lieutenant colonel who has been on active service in that rank for 3 years, becomes a colonel by right. It is forbidden, under penalty of being cashiered, to pay more than the set price for a position as officer, but this happens very often.

Since the requirements for the ensign's examination do not comprise any military knowledge, a special examination is set before advancing to lieutenant and captain, which is limited to practical service, service regulations, military law and drill. Theoretical attainments in tactics are *not* required.

The officers in the Guards have higher rank: the ensign that of the lieutenant, the lieutenant that of the captain, the captain that of the lieutenant colonel. This causes a great deal of resentment in the line.

Advancement of non-commissioned officers to officer rank

occurs only in exceptional cases. In every battalion the bulk of the routine work falls on three officers: the adjutant, the quartermaster, and the paymaster. Old dependable non-commissioned officers are frequently appointed to these posts, but they never get beyond the rank of lieutenant, which is granted them gratis. Otherwise, promotion to officer rank takes place rarely, for exceptional distinction in the face of the enemy. The nature of the English recruited army, which produces a very strong admixture of low and rough elements, the resulting tone prevailing among the troops and the discipline consequently required, makes it necessary for the officers to belong to a higher class of society than the soldiers, as a matter of course. Accordingly, the distance between officer and soldier is greater in England than anywhere else. And, likewise, advancement upward from the ranks is made very difficult and will always remain a rare exception so long as the purchase of commissions, on the one hand, and the recruitment system, on the other, continue. For educated young men to enlist in the army as volunteers, to serve with the prospect of advancement, as so often happens in Prussia and France, is something that cannot occur in England; the nature of the troops is such that it would be generally believed that the young man took to the soldier's trade for quite different motives, about which he would prefer to remain silent. This makes it quite understandable that the English officer corps consists almost entirely of men who have been brought up as gentlemen, and that the mass of soldiers has more respect for officers who are from the outset their "natural superiors", as the saying goes in England.

Correspondingly, the tone prevailing between officers and soldiers is cold and businesslike. The two classes are linked only by the bond of command and obedience. There are neither intimacies and jokes nor outbreaks of passion. Praise and blame are seldom communicated directly to the soldiers by the officers, and then only in the same calm businesslike voice. Naturally, this applies only to the official relationships in drilling, etc.; in private English officers can curse ... as to which their lads have plenty to say.

One very peculiar institution in the English army is that an officer can have a double rank: a lower one in his regiment and a higher one in the army. This second rank, when it is conferred permanently and unconditionally, is known as brevet rank. Thus, a captain may be a brevet major or a brevet lieutenant colonel in the army; there have even been cases (especially with commanders of Indian irregular troops) where they have been only lieutenants in their regiments but were majors in the army. Such a captain and brevet major performs the duties of a captain in his regiment, but counts as a staff officer for service in the garrison or camp. This higher rank can also be conferred for only a certain time or for a given colony or theatre of war. Thus, in the last ten years many colonels were named "brigadier generals" or even "major generals" for the duration of the Crimean War or of their stay in the Levant, and similarly in India. This system provides a way of promoting specially favoured or specially useful men to higher positions despite seniority; it is obvious, however, that it entails many unpleasantnesses and much confusion. In the Crimea, the English could never make it comprehensible to the French that a man can be a captain and a major at the same time.

One of the rules for promotion is that no one can become captain who has not had two years of full service as an ensign and lieutenant, nor can any one become a major who has not been an officer for six years.

The military training of officers who do not come from the Sandhurst school is conducted in platoon and company drill, just like that of the soldiers; it is only after examination before the battalion commander that they are released from drill and admitted to serve as officers. All the subaltern officers of a battalion are brought together into a unit under the command of a staff officer once a year before the spring training course of the battalion, and in this form, with rifle on shoulder, they go through the complete individual, platoon and company drill. No doubt this is usually done very superficially.

III

As we know, the numbers of non-commissioned officers and privates are replenished by enlistment, and exclusively in Great Britain and Ireland. Only the 100th Regiment is recruited in Canada. The recruiting is under the adjutant general of the army and is conducted in two ways: In the first place, the individual regiments and depot battalions can take enlistments in their own garrisons. Secondly, apart from this, there is an organised recruiting service throughout the country, which is divided into nine recruiting districts for the purpose (England 4, Scotland 2, Ireland 3). Each district is under a supervisory staff officer (usually a brevet colonel) and, where necessary, is subdivided into smaller regions under lieutenants or captains.—All in all, the following are employed in this service: 8 staff officers, 9 adjutants, 9 paymasters, 9 physicians, 11 recruiting subaltern officers (on half-pay), 8 sergeant-majors, 48 sergeants and an appropriate number of privates. In addition to this, the Guards also recruit, exclusively to boost their own ranks. Every recruit has the right to choose the corps he wants to join. The pious wish is expressed that every corps be recruited as far as possible in the county whose name it bears. Foreigners are to be taken in only with special permission, for which reason they are often passed through as "Scots".

In wartime the militia must serve primarily as a seedbed for the line; for a certain number of men passing over into the line from the militia (the number being set on each occasion) one officer of the militia regiment involved receives a commission in the line.

During the Indian Mutiny in 1857[321] the authorities went so far as to give a commission as lieutenant colonel to every serving or retired staff officer who brought in 1,000 recruits.

Every recruit or re-enlisted soldier receives his full equipment gratis and a bounty varying with the need for recruits but never less than 1 pound and very seldom more than 10 pounds sterling (67 thalers). It is often different for different arms; the largest amount is paid for engineers, since only the best men can be used there. The bounty is paid in part at the time of certification, but most of it is paid upon entering the regiment and after the recruit has been received by the commander of the regiment. This certification consists in having the recruit brought before the police magistrate not earlier than 24 hours after the recruitment and his stating under oath that he enlisted voluntarily and that there are no legal obstacles to his joining the army.

For the cavalry, artillery drivers, engineers, service corps, and the infantry stationed in India, China, Australia and St. Helena, recruits are accepted between the ages of 18 and 25; for the rest of the artillery and infantry, from 17 to 25. The height is set as follows:

> Cavalry: cuirassier Guards: 5' 10" to 6'
> heavy dragoon regiments: 5' 8" to 5' 11"
> medium dragoons and lancers: 5' 7" to 5' 9"
> hussars: 5' 6" to 5' 8"
>
> Artillery: cannoneers: minimum 5' 7", if under 18 years
> of age, 5' 6"
> drivers: 5' 4" to 5' 6"
> mechanics: minimum 5' 6"
>
> Infantry: minimum
> Guards: 5' 8 1/2"
> line 5' 6"

But this minimum varies greatly; any serious danger of war compels the government to lower it at once, and even the circumstance that the reduction of the length of service from 12 to 10 years will release very many soldiers in the near future was enough to induce the government a few weeks ago to reduce the minimum for the infantry to 5' 5". In general, here as elsewhere the measurements are increasingly being reduced, although, as might be expected, taller soldiers can always be obtained on average with a recruited army than with universal military service or conscription. It will be seen from the above figures that this applies in England, too; the figures can easily be converted to Rhenish measurements with sufficient accuracy if we deduct $2^1/_4$ inches from 5' to 5' 6", and $2^1/_2$" from 5' 7" to 6'.

In addition to the height, a minimum chest circumference is also set: from 5' 6" to 5' 8", 33 inches; [5'] 8" to [5'] 10", 34 inches; over 5' 10", 35 inches. Driver cannoneers, service corps soldiers and marksmen must always have 34" chest measurement. However, driver cannoneers will be accepted even if they do not fully meet these standards, provided that they are experienced in handling horses.

Boys of at least 14 are enlisted as drummers and buglers with the permission of their parents. They receive no enlistment bounty.

The length of service is 10 years for the infantry, 12 for the cavalry, artillery, engineers and service corps; at the end of the period the soldier can re-enlist for 11 years more in the infantry and 9 years in the other branches, if he is found to be still fit. At the end of this re-enlistment he can continue in the service on three months' notice. If the unit is abroad when the enlistment period expires, the officer commanding the station has the right to extend it up to two years.

Every soldier with good conduct is, as a rule, permitted to buy himself out. The redemption amount is based on the time of service already rendered and the time remaining, on the conduct, etc., and is a maximum of 30 pounds in the cavalry, 20 pounds in the infantry, and for coloured soldiers in the colonial corps 12 pounds.

After 21 years of service every soldier is entitled to a pension. The amount of the pension is based on the length of service, his conduct and the physical infirmities incurred during service; for privates and non-commissioned officers it is at least 8 pence (6 Sgr. 8 Pf.) and at most 3 shillings 6 pence (1 thaler 5 Sgr.) per diem. Under certain circumstances, pensions are granted for shorter service, too.

The recruiting sergeants, with the soldiers assigned to them, usually stay in the worst districts of the big cities and keep their eyes chiefly on the public houses. They often parade through the streets with bands on their caps, to the accompaniment of some drummers and pipers, attract a crowd and try to fish in it. If the prey they are looking for is there, he is enticed into a pub as soon as possible and every kind of trick is put into play to get the victim to accept the symbolic shilling, which seals the contract. Once the new candidate for glory has taken the shilling, he can free himself by paying "smart-money"[a] of a pound sterling before a police magistrate. The law requires that the budding hero must declare before the magistrate, at least 24 hours later, that he is enlisting voluntarily and is firm in his decision. The assumption of the law, and quite a correct one, is that the recruit is not sober, as a rule, when he takes the shilling, and the purpose is to give him a chance to sober up. But it would have to be a poor sort of recruiting sergeant that would let his prey get away from him so easily. He and his men do not let the recruit out of their sight, and before he comes before the magistrate, spirits and beer have had a chance to do their work. The best of it is that a large part of the reckoning is usually paid by the recruit himself, the sergeant advancing the money freely against the bounty. Given these circumstances, it is naive, but prudent, for the regulations to say expressly: Only unmarried soldiers and drummers should be selected for recruiting duty, and only in cases of extreme necessity married sergeants, but in any case only healthy, vigorous men. Anyone who is not a good drinker is unsuited to this duty.

One has the feeling of having been taken back quite into the eighteenth century when one sees this sort of recruiting. Despite the formal safeguards with which the law has surrounded this practice, it remains a fact that by far the largest part of the "English army entirely made up of volunteers" enters into that institution most unwillingly; whether for their own eventual good on the whole, is another question.

It is clear enough what sections of the nation come into the army in this manner. To a large extent, the army, like our recruited armies of former days, remains a *refugium peccatorum*,[b] in which the larger and better part of all the adventurous elements of the people are brought together and are restrained by an exacting course of training and very strict discipline. As a result, the English army, so far as its moral and intellectual character is concerned, is far below all those that are formed by conscription (even with substitution) or by universal military service without substitution. Only the French Foreign Legion [322] and those other French corps formed chiefly from substitutes, such as the Zouaves,[323] can be put on anything like a par with it; although it cannot be denied that the entire French army, by the increasing preference shown for the career soldier in the rank and file, is

---

a Engels gives the term "smart-money" in brackets after the corresponding German word.— *Ed.*

b Refuge of sinners.— *Ed.*

coming closer and closer to the character of the English army. But even the French remplaçant^a is far better educated and has better manners than the rough, wild lads from the dregs of the big cities who set the tone in English barracks. An educated young man can still enter the French army as a volunteer to serve for advancement, without the training time as common soldier being too intolerable for him; in England, a man would have to be out of his mind to do that. As proud as the Englishman is of his army as a whole, he is equally contemptuous of the individual common soldier; even in the lower orders of society it is still rather discreditable to be enlisted or to have a soldier as a relative. In general, the quality of the recruits has undoubtedly improved a great deal in the last ten years. An effort is made to get as much information as possible on the antecedents of the recruits and steer clear of definitely bad characters. The heavy enlistments that were made necessary by the Crimean War and the Indian Mutiny soon exhausted the degenerate class from which the army had filled its ranks as a rule during the long period of peace. Not only had the height requirements to be reduced (down to 5' 3" for the infantry at one point), but the soldier's life had to be made more attractive and steps had to be taken to improve the tone in the barracks, so that the more reliable members of the working class could also be drawn into the sphere of recruitment. An additional factor was the shortage of suitable candidates for the many new positions as non-commissioned officers (in the Crimean War the battalions were raised to almost double strength). It was also realised that warfare like Wellington's in Spain,[324] with the inevitable looting of all the captured fortresses, is no longer suitable in the Europe of today. The press took up the cause of the soldiers, and it soon became the rule among senior officers to extend philanthropy to the troops. Steps were taken to make life more agreeable for the soldiers, to provide them with facilities for recreation and activities in the barracks or camp, and to keep them away from the pubs. Thus, especially in the last seven years and for the most part by private subscription, libraries, reading rooms, clubrooms with all kinds of games, soldiers' clubs, etc., have been set up. In the camps some land has been assigned to the soldiers for gardens, where possible, as the French do; experiments have been made with theatrical performances and lectures; and from time to time exhibitions have been arranged of various small pieces of art works, etc., that they have produced. All

---

^a Substitute.— *Ed.*

these things are still in their infancy but are becoming more and more general. They are extremely necessary. During the campaigns in the Crimea and in India the recruits were undoubtedly of a much higher level than previously, since both wars were very popular among the masses of people. The tone of the army hàs improved considerably. Contact with the French soldiers in the Crimea also played a part. The job now is to keep that spirit up, so that even during a long period of peace it will be possible to obtain recruits of a similar high level and not be limited again exclusively to the disorderly elements of the population which are always the first to apply in peacetime.

These last, nonetheless, still constitute the larger part of the army, and all the arrangements are made accordingly. An English barracks with its auxiliary buildings and courtyard is surrounded by high walls on all sides, usually with only one gate. There is a separate building for the officers' quarters, and one or more for the soldiers. Where the soldiers' quarters have windows on the street, this part of the building is usually secured, in recent installations, by a deep ditch with a strong iron fence along its outer edge. In large cities, especially in the case of militia barracks, which include an armoury (the militia is called into service for only 4 weeks in the year), the entire street front of the building has loopholes instead of windows, and the corners of the wings are provided with turrets for flanking fire — proof that uprisings of workers are not considered as so unlikely. The soldier spends his life in this huge barracks prison, with the exception of his time off. The admission of civilians is strictly supervised and the entire structure is carefully guarded against view from the outside, so that the soldier may be kept under maximum control and separated from civilians. Here there is none of the easy association between citizens and soldiers that is so common in Germany, or ease of entry into the barracks for all people, and to ensure that no lasting relationships are formed, the garrisons are shifted every year, as a rule.

The most common disciplinary offences can be readily inferred from the character of the army. They are drunkenness, absence without leave after roll-call, theft from comrades, fighting, insubordination and actual acts of violence against a superior. Minor offences are punished summarily by the battalion commander. He has the exclusive power of punishment but can delegate the power to company commanders, up to three days detention in barracks. His own power of punishment extends to: 1) imprisonment up to 7 days, with or without solitary confinement, with or without hard labour; soldiers given this sentence have the *right* to appeal from the battalion commander to a court martial: 2) imprisonment in a dark cell (black-hole[a]) for up to 48 hours; 3) detention in barracks for up to a month, during which the prisoner must perform all his service and in addition any extra work imposed on him by the commander; confinement to barracks also entails punitive drill with full pack for up to 14 days; the punitive drill must not last for more than an hour at a time but may be repeated up to four times daily. In cases 2) and 3) the commander *may* grant an appeal to a court martial. Solitary confinement or the black-hole are to be reserved, so far as possible, for cases of drunkenness, brawling and insolence towards superiors, and in serious cases may be combined with confinement to barracks, but in such a way that the entire period of arrest does not exceed one month.

As we can see, an English battalion commander has means enough at his disposal to keep order among his wild young fellows. If these means do not suffice, a court martial provides the remedy, the rebellious fellow getting the cat-o'-nine-tails as a last resort. This is one of the most barbarous instruments of punishment that exists: a short-handled whip with nine long, hard, knotted thongs. The offender, stripped to the waist, is tied to a three-cornered frame and the strokes are delivered with the utmost force. Even the first stroke breaks the skin and draws blood. After a few strokes the whip and the flogger are changed in order not lo let up on the delinquent. The doctor is of course always present. Fifty strokes of this kind always make a long recovery in hospital necessary. And yet there are often men who endure these fifty strokes without a cry of pain, since it counts as more shameful to show pain than to earn the strokes.

Twelve years ago the cat was still used very frequently, and up to 150 strokes were ordered. If I am not mistaken, the regimental commander could hand out a certain number of strokes summarily until that time. Then the number was limited to 50 strokes and the power to order them given exclusively to courts martial. Finally, after the Crimean War, and particularly at the urging of Prince Albert, the Prussian division of the soldiers into two classes was introduced and it was decided that only soldiers who had already been put into the second class for *previous* offences and had not got back into the first class by virtue of a year of faultless service could be given corporal punishment for a fresh

---

[a] Engels gives the English term.— *Ed.*

offence. This distinction does not apply in the face of the enemy; there any common soldier is subject to flogging. In 1862, 126 men were flogged in the army, 114 of them being given the highest legal number of 50 strokes.

In general, it will be seen that both the need and the desire to use the whip have greatly declined, and since the same causes are still operative in the army, it is to be presumed that this will continue to be the case and that the cat will be used increasingly as an exceptional, extreme method of deterrence, reserved for the worst cases in the face of the enemy. For it has been realised that appeals to the soldiers' feeling of honour are more effective than degrading punishments, and on that subject the entire English army says with one voice that a flogged soldier is never worth anything after that. Nonetheless, complete abolition of the cat will not come so soon in England. We all know how strong the prejudices in favour of corporal punishment have been and, to some extent, still are, even in armies that are made up of much better elements of society than the English; and in a recruited army such an extreme instrument of terror is still more excusable than elsewhere. However, the English are certainly right in holding that, if there is to be corporal punishment, it should be used only as a last resort, but in that case very severely. The eternal mild canings that are still given in many armies, including German armies, unfortunately, and which can only have the effect of weakening the fear of that punishment...[a]

First published in: Marx and Engels, *Works*, First Russian Edition, Vol. XII, Part II, 1935

Printed according to the manuscript

Published in English for the first time

---

[a] The manuscript breaks off here.— *Ed.*

Frederick Engels

THE STRENGTH OF THE ARMIES IN SCHLESWIG

TO THE EDITOR OF THE *MANCHESTER GUARDIAN*

Sir,

There are most absurd reports afloat as to the relative strength of the contending armies in the Danish war.[325] It is generally supposed that the Danes are outnumbered in the proportion of one Dane to at least three Germans. To show how little this is in accordance with facts, I propose to give a detailed statement of the strength of each army, as far at least as its infantry is concerned; for as to cavalry and artillery it would at present be very difficult to get precise information.

Before the outbreak of hostilities, the Danes had the following troops in Schleswig, viz.:

	Battalions
First Division; Commander, Lieutenant-General Gerlach:	
1st Brigade, 2nd and 22nd Infantry Regiments	4
2nd Brigade, 3rd and 18th Infantry Regiments	4
3rd Brigade, 17th and 19th Infantry Regiments	4
Second Division; Major General Du Plat:	
4th Brigade, 4th and 6th Infantry Regiments	4
5th Brigade, 7th and 12th Infantry Regiments	4
6th Brigade, 5th and 10th Infantry Regiments	4
Third Division; Major General Steinmann:	
7th Brigade, 1st and 11th Infantry Regiments	4
8th Brigade, 9th and 20th Infantry Regiments	4
9th Brigade, 16th and 21st Infantry Regiments	4
Total Battalions	36

Or, at 800 men for a battalion (the full complement is
870 men and officers), say .... 28,800 men
Cavalry, 4 1/2 regiments, at 560 men .... 2,500 ”
Artillery, about .... 3,000 ”

Total Danish forces .... 34,300 men

Exclusive of several battalions, both of line and reserve, which
were sent to Schleswig in the first days of February, but as to
which it has been impossible to ascertain any particulars.

The Austrians have sent to the seat of war the sixth army corps,
consisting of the following troops:

	Battalions
General Gondrecourt's Brigade:	
Infantry Regiment, King of Prussia	3
Ditto Baron Martini	3
Chasseur Battalion, No. 18	1
General Nostitz's Brigade:	
Infantry Regiment, King of the Belgians	3
Ditto Grand Duke of Hesse	3
Chasseur Battalion, No. 9	1
General Thomas's Brigade:	
Infantry Regiment, Count Coronini	3
Ditto Prince Holstein	3
A Chasseur Battalion, number not stated	1
General Dormus's Brigade:	
Two Infantry Regiments and one battalion of Chasseurs, numbers and names not stated	7
Total battalions	28

Or at 800 men per battalion (which is a high estimate
for the present organisation of the Austrian army) .... 22,400 men
Cavalry, about .... 2,000 ”
Artillery, about .... 2,600 ”

Total, about .... 27,000 men

The Prussians have sent the following contingent:

I.—Combined army corps of Prince Frederick Charles

Sixth Division:	Battalions
11th Brigade, 20th and 60th Regiments	6
12th Brigade, 24th and 64th Regiments	6
Besides the 35th Light Infantry Regiment	3

Thirteenth Division:	
25th Brigade, 13th and 53rd Regiments	6
26th Brigade, 15th and 55th Regiments	6
7th Chasseur Battalion	1

2.—Division of Guards; General Mulbe:

1st Brigade, 3rd and 4th Foot Guards	6
2nd Brigade, 3rd and 4th Grenadier Guards	6
Chasseurs of the Guard	1

Total	41

Or at 800 men per battalion..	32,800 men
Cavalry	3,000 "
Artillery	3,000 "
	38,800 "
With Austrians	27,000 "
Total allied army	65,800 men

Or less than two allied soldiers to one Dane. If the strength of the Danish defences at the Dannevirke, at Düppel, and at Fridericia is taken into account, such a numerical superiority is not more than required to ensure success. It is almost precisely the same proportion of superiority which Wellington and Blücher, in 1815, had over Napoleon.[326]

Written after February 7, 1864

First published in the *Manchester Guard-ian*, February 16, 1864
Signed: *F. E.*

Karl Marx and Frederick Engels

OBITUARY

On May 9 of this year

WILHELM WOLFF,

of Tarnau, near Schweidnitz, Silesia, died in Manchester of a brain hemorrhage at the age of almost 55 years. He was Associate-Editor of the *Neue Rheinische Zeitung* in Cologne and deputy to the German National Assembly in Frankfurt and Stuttgart in 1848 and 1849, and a private tutor in Manchester from 1853.

Manchester, May 13, 1864

> *Karl Marx, Frederick Engels, Ernst Dronke,*
> *Louis Borchardt, M.D.,*
> *Eduard Gumpert, M.D.*

Written on May 13, 1864

First published in *Allgemeine Zeitung*, No. 144, May 23, 1864, Supplement

Printed according to the newspaper

Published in English for the first time

Frederick Engels

ENGLAND'S FIGHTING FORCES AS AGAINST GERMANY

Manchester, June 27

The incredible is taking place: England is threatening Germany with war.[327] According to the *United Service Gazette* orders have already gone out to the depot in Pimlico (London) and the Arsenal at Woolwich to have the equipment and arms needed for thirty thousand men ready for immediate use, and we may expect to hear in a few days' time that the Channel fleet has sailed for the Sound or the Belts.[a]

The *Army and Navy Gazette* informs us of the fighting forces available to England at the moment. It says, in its June 25 issue:

"The naval force which we have at hand and which can weigh anchor immediately is as follows:

	Horse-power	Guns	Tonnage	Men
Edgar, wooden ship	600	71	3,094	810
Warrior, ironcased	1,250	40	6,109	705
Black Prince, ironcased	1,250	41	6,109	705
Prince Consort, ironcased	1,000	35	4,045	605
Hector, ironcased	800	28	4,089	530
Defence, "	600	16	3,720	457
Aurora, wooden frigate	400	35	2,558	515
Galatea, "	800	26	3,227	515
Wolverene, wooden corvette	400	21	1,703	275
Research, ironcased	200	4	1,253	135
Enterprise, "	160	4	993	121

---

[a] The Great Belt and the Little Belt straits.— *Ed.*

Geyser,   paddle-wheel
wooden steam vessel	280	6	1,054	175
Assurance,   wooden
steam vessel	200	4	681	90
Salamis,   paddle-wheel
wooden steam vessel	250	2	?	65
Trinculo,   wooden
gunboat	60	2	268	24

"In addition, in order to have special vessels of smaller draught for the shallow and narrow waters of the Baltic and the Danish coasts, the Admiralty has ordered the following ships to be made ready for sea:

| | Horse-
power | Guns | Tonnage | Men |
|---|---|---|---|---|
| *Cordelia,* wooden corvette | 150 | 11 | 579 | 130 |
| *Fawn,*   " | 100 | 17 | 751 | 175 |
| *Racer,*   " | 150 | 11 | 579 | 130 |

"Moreover, the following new-built ships will be ready shortly:

| | Horse-
power | Guns | Tonnage | Men |
|---|---|---|---|---|
| *Achilles,* ironcased | 1,250 | 30 | 6,121 | 705 |
| *Royal Sovereign,* cupola
    ironcased ship | 800 | 5 | 3,963 | 500 |
| *Caledonia,* ironcased | 1,000 | 35 | 4,125 | 605 |
| *Ocean,*   " | 1,000 | 35 | 4,047 | 605 |

"In addition there are the numerous ships of the steamer reserve, and finally those of the Coast Guard, including 15 gunboats of 60 horsepower and mounting two heavy pieces of ordnance."

The latter, the *Army and Navy Gazette* believes, would be as troublesome to an enemy as blow flies to a horse; it would be impossible to shake them off. (As if the Prussians did not have 22 such blow flies in the Baltic, too!)

So much for the *Army and Navy Gazette* on the fleet. We were on board several ships of the ironclad fleet last year[a] and in addition have carefully followed their ups and downs and their test cruises. These have shown that none of these ironclads can hold the high seas in stormy weather; last winter the *Prince Consort* almost foundered in the Irish Channel during a storm, which all the wooden ships easily rode out. Thus, these ships are only usable in definite previously planned undertakings (sea battles or attacks against land fortifications), and will then have to return to port

---

[a] See this volume, pp. 289-95.— *Ed.*

each time. They are of no use for blockades, etc. Their armour is usually a $4^1/_2$-inch rolled iron of varying quality and applied in varying ways; in every case with a wood backing two feet thick, even in the ships otherwise made entirely of iron. None of this armour resists the seventy-pound flat-nosed steel Whitworth shell, most of them not even the seventy-pound steel Whitworth bomb of the same form as the shell. Rifled guns are now being cast in Prussia with the bore of the old 48-pounders, which are more or less equivalent to the above-mentioned Whitworth cannon. Flat-nosed cylindrical steel shells (*without a conical point*) from such guns will penetrate this armour, even if their rear half is hollow and carries an explosive charge. These explosive shells *do not require a fuse* (as Whitworth's tests have shown) when they are fired against iron armour; penetrating the armour produces so much heat that the shells become white-hot and the powder inside them is ignited.

The armament of the ironclads usually consists of smooth-bore sixty-eight-pounders (eight-inch calibre) as broadside cannons and hundred-ten-pound Armstrongs (seven-inch calibre) as pivoted cannons on the bow and the stern. Some of these ships also had Armstrong forty-pounders and seventy-pounders on the broadside, but it may be that these are being replaced by sixty-eight-pounders. The old sixty-eight-pounder is a very respectable, solid and, for its calibre, manageable cannon, very effective up to at least two thousand paces and certainly the best cannon of the entire English fleet. On the other hand, the Armstrong breech-loading guns are very unreliable, since the rifling grooves soon become obstructed with lead by reason of the faulty attachment of the lead coating of the shell, and in particular because the breech block is useless. It consists of a quadrilateral piece of iron inserted from above extending to somewhat below the bottom of the bore, and screwed into place and secured from behind. If we consider that in the seven-inch calibre the shell weighs 110 pounds and the breech block only 135 pounds, we shall see that, after a few shots, the powder residues will prevent the block from fitting closely and it must fly out and high in the air as soon as the explosion gases work on it from below. This happens regularly, so that these Armstrong guns, despite their otherwise good effectiveness, have a very bad reputation in the navy.

The *Royal Sovereign* will carry five very heavy guns in her four cupolas or turrets; the nature of the ordnance is not yet known. Her armour has no wood backing. It remains to be seen whether this ship is of any value on the high seas.

The smaller ships, and the wooden ships in general, have as broadside guns mainly smooth-bore thirty-two-pounders 9 feet 6 inches and 10 feet in length, very good cannon which can take charges of up to $^1/_3$ the weight of the shell, which the sixty-eight-pounders do not, and which therefore have very sure aim, for their length. Still, even on heavy ships there are some light eight-inch bomb-shell guns on the broadsides. The pivot guns are either eight-inch smooth-bore of lighter or heavier construction or Armstrong guns firing long shells weighing 40, 70 or 110 pounds.

The draught of the large ironclads is at least 25 feet, so that they are on a par with ships of the line and very heavy frigates in this respect. This makes them useless in narrow and shallow waters, but they could serve in the deep channels of narrow creeks and estuaries to attack shore batteries and coastal forts. There they are dangerous if the cannon of the defence are too light and their shells are not made of steel. It is doubtful whether the Prussian rifled twenty-four-pounder could penetrate their armour with steel shells. The rifled forty-eight-pounder can do it, in any event, if its shell is of steel and flattened at the nose, if it has a charge of a sixth to a fourth of the shell weight and if the shot can be fired at from six to eight hundred paces. Rifled guns of from seven to eight inches, which we could have made so easily of Krupp cast steel, if emplaced at suitable points, even in small numbers, would soon enough make the heavy English ironclads narmless to our coasts. Only, the shell must be of steel and cylindrical, and must not have a conical or rounded nose so that it will catch the iron armour with its sharp edge even if the impact is oblique. Whitworth has penetrated the armour with such shells even at an angle of incidence of over fifty degrees. Further, with such heavy guns it is best to leave any experiments with breech-loading quite out of consideration; beyond a certain calibre they are certainly worthless, and there is no more time for protracted tests.

So much concerning the navy; now let us hear what the *Army and Navy Gazette* can tell us about the available land forces:

"*Cavalry*. 4th, 5th, 6th regiments of Guards Dragoons; 1st and 2nd (Dragoon); 3rd, 4th, 8th (Hussar); 9th (Lancer); 10th, 11th, 12th, 13th, 14th, 15th, 16th (Hussar) regiments. Each has 650 men, including officers, a total of 10,700 men.

"*Artillery*. Ten batteries of horse-artillery (six guns each), 26 field batteries (horse-borne) also of six guns each and 25 fortress batteries. In all, 216 field guns and 13,700 men.

"*Engineers*. 20 companies and two train companies, in all 2,700 men.

"*Infantry*. The first battalions of the 2nd, 3rd, 5th, 6th, 8th, 10th, 11th, 13th, 14th, 24th, 26th, 29th, 31st, 32nd, 37th, 41st, 45th, 49th, 53rd, 58th, 59th, 60th,

61st, 64th, 69th, 73rd, 74th, 75th, 83rd, 84th, 85th, 86th, 87th regiments; the second battalions of the 1st, 12th and 60th regiments. To this should be added the first battalions of the 21st, 39th, and 62nd regiments, now on the way from America, making a total of 39 battalions. Excluding the depot companies, about 780 men per battalion are left ready to turn out, or a total force of 30,000 trained men. In addition, there are the depots of the entire army, a total of 18,000 men as first reserves, and finally the Guards (1,300 men of the cavalry and 6,000 infantry).

"In all: cavalry 12,000; artillery 13,700; engineers 2,700; infantry 54,000. Grand total: 82,000 men. But in estimating the number of troops we could send into the field, we must first deduct the depots with 18,000 men and a further 25% for those not available for service, and those who must be employed at home. We should then have some 48,000 well-drilled and well-seasoned troops, ready to go anywhere and do anything, if properly aided by the auxiliary and administrative departments. A first reserve of recruits would come to about half this number. We do not know the actual strength of the *militia* assembled at the training which has just concluded, but it should be a larger number than in 1863, when it turned out 102.000 strong for inspection. Finally, the volunteers amount to about 160,000."

This is what the *Army and Navy Gazette* reports. These statistics may suffice for today, since we plan to give your readers an exact report on the English forces on land anyway.[328] However, your German troops should realise one thing: If they come up against Englishmen, they will be facing quite a different opponent than the brave, but badly-trained, slow Danes.

Written on June 27, 1864

First published in the *Allgemeine Militär-Zeitung*, No. 27, July 6, 1864

Signed: *F. E.*

Printed according to the newspaper

Published in English for the first time

FROM THE PREPARATORY MATERIALS

Karl Marx

GROUND RENT

1) We have already seen that
in order to understand ground rent correctly two things must be distinguished from [...] [a]
1) *Firstly*, the portion paid to the landowner for *improvements* made to the land, i.e. for the *capital* invested in and *merged* with it. This is the [...] interest. Whether I have invested 1,000 thalers in a cotton-machine or in [...] canals on the land is immaterial to the source of the income [...] I derive from these 1,000 thalers. For that is and remains the interest on capital productively used.

2) *Secondly*, the form which the ground rent [assumes] as a money rent. Supposing a plot of land brings in 20 thalers rent annually. Suppose further that the land[owner sells] this plot of land, i.e. that he sells the annual ground rent of 20 thalers. How is the purchase price of the ground rent or the plot of land [fixed?...] The land only has value in so far as these 20 thalers [...] are taken into account.

The question thus is:
How much capital must I pay the landowner [in order] to purchase an annual rent of 20 thalers? In other words the

---

[a] Here and below leaders in square brackets indicate damaged or completely faded, illegible places in the manuscript. The words in square brackets have been inserted by the Editors.— *Ed.*

question is: how large a capital is required to yield 20 thalers annually in our [...] social conditions? To answer this question I have to know the rate of interest in general and how much interest on average a capital of [...]

If the rate of interest is 5% this means that the 100 thalers I invest bring in 5 thalers interest. The question is:

If 100 thalers yield 5 thalers annually how large a capital must I have to produce 20 thalers annually? If 100 thalers bring in 5 thalers annually, then 400 thalers yield 20 thalers interest p.a.

Thus, if the rate of interest stands at 5%, the landowner will sell a plot of land that brings in 20 thalers p.a. for 400 thalers. In 20 years the purchaser would have replaced his capital. $20 \times 20 = 400$.

Thus, the farmer pays 20 thalers rent p.a., but the [purchaser] who has bought the land for 400 thalers receives 20 thalers rent p.a. In his eyes the 20 thalers which the farmer pays him are nothing but interest paid to him on the 400 thalers which he has laid out as the purchase price of the land. In many regions the capital invested in land may yield a lower interest than the capital invested in other branches of industry. It is therefore possible that capital invested in land may only bring in $2^1/_2$%, while if employed in trade or industry, it [...] In that event, a plot of land yielding [20 thalers] rent p.a. would be [sold] for 800 thalers instead of 400. [The purchaser] will then need 40 years to recover his capital. If a farmer pays out [...] rent of 20 thalers p.a. for a morgen[a] of land, it may very easily be that the landlord who receives these 20 thalers only [...] $2^1/_2$ thalers.

[A high or] low level of ground rent bears no [relation to] the high or low interest which capital [...] on the purchase of the ground rent, i.e. of the land [...]

[...] furthermore, that the land has a price, that it can be sold because there is such a thing as ground rent and not the other way round, i.e. that there is such a thing as ground rent because a price is paid for the land.

[...] in general that the price of the land is [nothing] but *capitalised ground rent*. What is meant by *capitalised ground rent*? It means that I regard ground rent as the interest on the capital invested in the purchase of the land. The rent on a morgen of land may be 20 thalers; but for the man who buys the land the 20 thalers can never be more than the 5 or 3 or $2^1/_2$%, i.e. the going

_____

[a] German measure of land varying from 0.6 to 0.9 acres.— *Ed.*

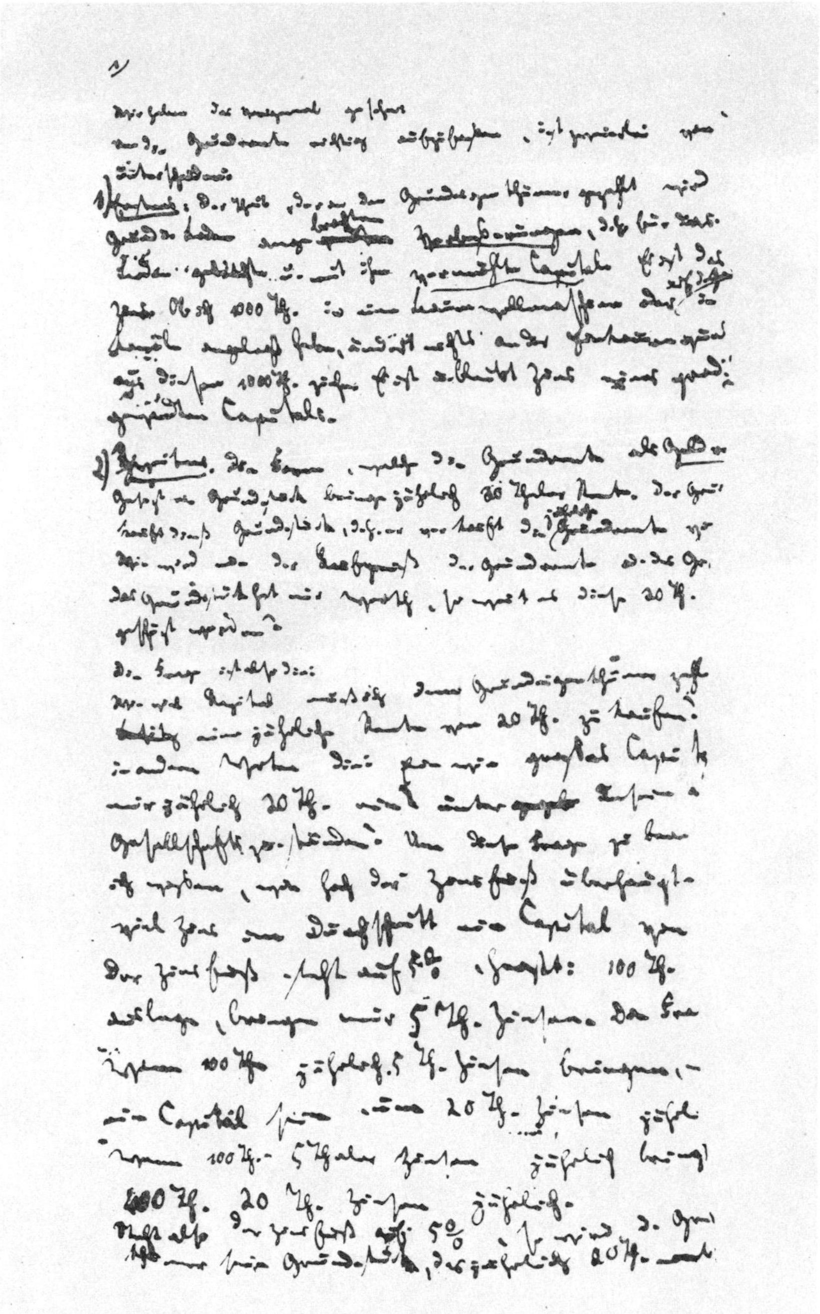

Beginning of Marx's notes for a lecture on ground rent

rate of interest on capital. If interest rates are 5%, I can recover my capital in 20 years. Thus, in order to capitalise the ground rent, i.e. to exchange it for capital, it must be multiplied by the number of years it takes, at the prevailing rate of interest, to replace the capital, to restore it to the lender.

c) The sale of land *presupposes ground rent* and hence does not explain it.

3) *Thirdly.*

Ground rent is the annual sum paid to the landowner by the farmer or the manufacturer of the products of the earth. If a manufacturer, an industrial capitalist, is to invest his money in farming, it must bring him on average the same profits as any other industry. Otherwise no capitalist would cultivate the land. If the farmer, i.e. the manufacturer of farm produce, lays out a sum of 100 thalers annually to cultivate the land, to buy seed and manure, to make good the damage caused by the wear and tear to the instruments of labour or to replace them, to pay wages, etc., he will need to obtain 110 thalers from the sale of his produce, as interest and profit. Whatever the sale of his produce yields over and above 110 thalers goes to the landowner and constitutes the ground rent. Thus, if he obtains 120 thalers, the ground rent is equal to 10 thalers. Thus, ground rent is equal to *the surplus of the market price of the produce of the land over its price of production.* The price of production here includes the farmer's interest and profit.

Where does this surplus of the market price of the produce of the land over its price of production come from? What is it that enables the manufacturer of farm produce, apart from receiving interest and profit, paying wages and meeting the other costs of production, also to pay ground rent to the man who leases the land to him? How does it come about that the selling price of farm produce is sufficiently high to yield a rent in addition to the wages, interest and profit—something which is not the case in other branches of industry?

In the first place, it cannot be argued that this arises from the special *productivity* of agriculture or of the soil itself. Nor can it be said to stem from the fact that the land is *limited* in extent. To assert that agriculture is more *productive* than any other industry might mean nothing beyond the fact that in no other industry is it possible to extract more produce at the same cost. But, since the price of a product is governed basically by the cost of its production, this would imply that the price of farm produce should be lower than that of all the other products—a fact which cannot possibly help to explain the *surplus of its market price over the price of production.*

We come now to the question of the *limited* area of land.[a]

Written in late 1861

First published in: *Marx-Engels Gesamtausgabe*, Abt. II, Bd. 2, Berlin, 1980

Printed according to the manuscript

Published in English for the first time

---

[a] The manuscript breaks off here.— *Ed.*

Karl Marx

[BIOGRAPHICAL NOTES ON WILHELM WOLFF] [329]

1809, June 21. Born in Tarnau, Schweidnitz [a] District.
1813. Russians.
1834-38. $4^1/_2$ years in *Silberberg*.[330] "*Casemate Wolf[f]*" wishes to see his dying father, even if accompanied by a gendarme. Refused.
1843-February 1846, in Breslau.[b]
1846. Wolff flees because of press prosecution. Article on uprising of Silesian weavers.[c]
1846-48. Brussels. "Bureau de Correspondance".[331] Jailed in Brussels. (Arrested between February 26 and 28.)
1848, April to June, in Breslau.
1848, September, Cologne. Lupus presents himself [for trial].[332] Warrant of arrest withdrawn.
October 22, 1848. Warrant of arrest issued by Hecker. Withdrawn March 8, 1849.
June 1848 to May 10, 1849, in Cologne. Thence to Frankfurt.
May 26, 1849. Scene in German Parliament (Frankfurt).[333]
1849, with Lupus already in Switzerland, warrant of arrest issued in connection with Rump in Stuttgart.[334]
July 5, 1849, to Basle. Thence to Berne, interned. $1^3/_4$ of year teacher in Zurich. *March 31, 1851,* written order of expulsion from Zurich. (*September 10, 1850 in Zurich.* Lupus protests against being assigned to Lucerne Canton in consequence of Federal Council decision on refugees.)

---

[a] Swidnica.— *Ed.*
[b] Wrocław.— *Ed.*
[c] Wolff, W., "Das Elend und der Aufruhr in Schlesien". In: *Deutsches Bürgerbuch für 1845*, Darmstadt, 1845.— *Ed.*

June 4, 1851-1853. Arrival[a] in London. Stays about 2 years there.

January 12, 1861. Prussian Amnesty Decree.[335] *January 4, 1862,* application to the Prussian government. No answer for 5 months. Another application on *June 4, 1862. August 1, 1862* Schweidnitz Municipal Council requires him to name his last place of residence in Prussia.

September 5, 1862. Prussian government answers that amnesty implies resumption of investigation.[b]

Written in late May and early June 1864

First published in the journal *Novaya i noveishaya istoriya,* 1959, No. 4

Printed according to the manuscript

Published in English for the first time

---

[a] Marx uses the English word.— *Ed.*
[b] See this volume, p. 243.— *Ed.*

APPENDICES

[APPLICATION BY MARX FOR RESTORATION OF HIS PRUSSIAN CITIZENSHIP] [336]

To the Royal Police President
His Excellency Baron von Zedlitz-Neukirch

Your Excellency,

I hereby respectfully inform you that, on the strength of the Royal amnesty, I have returned to Prussia from London, where I have lived as a political refugee since 1849, with the intention of taking up residence here in Berlin to begin with.

In this connection I respectfully request Your Excellency:

1. on the basis of the Royal order of the amnesty [337] and the law of December 31, 1842 (Ges. S. 15-18)[a] to issue a confirmation of my reintegration into the status of a Prussian subject, for which Your Excellency is the competent authority under § 5 of the aforesaid law, and

2. to be good enough to forward to me the certificate mentioned in § 8 of the law of December 31, 1842, on the reception of newly-arrived persons (Ges. S. 5), to the effect that I have reported my entry into this community to the Royal police authorities; and I declare with respect to the latter that, upon request, I can show that I have fully independent means of subsistence through contracts as co-editor of the *New-York Tribune,* published in New York, as well as otherwise.

To begin with, I have taken up residence with a friend of mine,

---

[a] "Gesetz über die Erwerbung und den Verlust der Eigenschaft als Preussischer Unterthan ... Vom 31. Dezember 1842", *Gesetz-Sammlung für die Königlichen Preussischen Staaten,* Berlin, 1843, No. 2.— *Ed.*

Herr F. Lassalle, 13 Bellevuestr., and request that the two documents asked for be sent to me there.

With best respects

Your Excellency's devoted
Dr Karl Marx

Berlin, March 19, 1861

First published in: Marx and Engels, *Works*, Second Russian Edition, Vol. 15, Moscow, 1959

Printed according to the manuscript

Published in English for the first time

[MARX'S STATEMENT ON THE RESTORATION
OF HIS PRUSSIAN CITIZENSHIP] [338]

To the Royal Police President
His Excellency Baron von Zedlitz

Your Excellency,

I have the honour in reply to your letter of the 21st inst. to state that I am surprised that my letter of March 19 did not seem quite clear. In the words of my application, my request was:

"on the basis of the Royal order of the amnesty and the law of December 31, 1842, to issue a confirmation of my reintegration into the status of a Prussian subject".[a]

It is this application that appears not quite clear to Your Excellency and seems to contain a contradiction insofar as I referred therein to Your Excellency's being the competent authority to issue that confirmation, pursuant to § 5 of the law of December 31, 1842.

Under the Royal order of amnesty "unimpeded return to the Prussian states" has been granted to all political refugees not condemned by military courts.[b]

Since I am one of those refugees and am a native Prussian, with reference to which I attach for Your Excellency as official proof my birth certificate in the form of an extract from the Register of Civil Status of the City of Trier (May 7, 1818), moreover as I left the fatherland in 1849, up to which time I had lived in Cologne as editor of the *Neue Rheinische Zeitung*,[339] and had not been prosecuted in actions in military courts, but only in several political press suits, which I drew upon myself in my aforesaid capacity as editor, it is clear therefore that I am included in the above-mentioned amnesty.

---

[a] See this volume, p. 339.— *Ed.*

[b] "Gesetz über die Erwerbung und den Verlust der Eigenschaft als Preussischer Unterthan... Vom 31. Dezember 1842", *Gesetz-Sammlung für die Königlichen Preussischen Staaten*, Berlin, 1843, No. 2.— *Ed.*

At the same time, the foregoing provides Your Excellency with an answer to the particular questions that you addressed to me in your rescript.

But it seems possible that another question may be raised. The Royal amnesty not only declares that pardon has been extended to those already convicted under the law and those not yet convicted, but at the same time grants refugees "unimpeded return to the Prussian states".

Does this signify, apart from remission of the criminal penalty, that the status of a Prussian citizen, which they had lost by residing abroad for more than ten years, is likewise restored to the refugees?

According to *my* interpretation and that of *all* jurists, according to the unanimous conception of public opinion and the entire press, it does. And there are two arguments that prove this incontrovertibly.

First, that the amnesty order guarantees not only remission of the penalty but also *expressly* "unimpeded return to the Prussian states".

Secondly, because the entire amnesty would otherwise be a completely *illusory* one, *only* on paper. For, since all the refugees have lived abroad since 1848 and 1849, i.e., twelve years, this would mean that all of them have lost their status as Prussians, and if that status were not reinvigorated by the amnesty, the "unimpeded return" alleged to be granted would actually be granted to no one.

Accordingly, there can be no doubt that, in spite of the loss of Prussian nationality due to an absence of ten years, this right is to be revived by the Royal amnesty.

However, although this is my interpretation and that of the jurists, in practice only the interpretation of the authorities is decisive and provides an adequate basis for practical actions.

How then will the Royal authorities please to interpret the Royal amnesty?

Will they interpret it in the sense that the amnesty is an amnesty, and unimpeded return is unimpeded return? Or will they interpret it in the sense that the granting of unimpeded return impedes return and that the refugees are to remain deprived of the fatherland despite the decree? Upon unprejudiced consideration of the circumstances, Your Excellency cannot fail to see that this scepticism can hardly be regarded as totally unfounded.

So much has been decreed in the last twelve years and so much astonishing interpretation has been referred to these decrees that by now no interpretation can any longer be regarded as positively sure nor can any interpretation be regarded as absolutely impossible.

Accordingly, the only positively sure basis remaining on which practical steps can be taken seems to be the interpretation given by the *authorities themselves* to the particular *individual.*

Will Your Excellency grant that, despite my loss of the status of a Prussian by virtue of the law, I have regained it through the Royal amnesty?

That is the very simple and clear question that I wanted to, and had to, address to Your Excellency.

I am all the more forced to do so, since I cannot bring my wife and children from London until this question is decided, for obviously I cannot be expected to undertake a problematical change of residence with my entire household and family and only *thereafter* engage in a contest which, on the contrary, I should *previously* bring to a termination, if it is to be engaged in at all, *before* I take the costly step of moving and bring my wife and children back to the fatherland.

My question is all the more justified as a very natural and simple one in view of the fact that Your Excellency yourself has raised the question in your letter of the 21st inst.: on what basis do I claim "not to have lost the status of a Prussian despite absence for ten years".

Your Excellency will have seen from the foregoing the basis on which I rest my claim.

The justification for my addressing my question to Your Excellency is found in § 5 of the law of December 31, 1842, which I have adduced. For, since, according to that, Your Excellency is the competent authority to grant naturalisation, so you are *a fortiori*[a] the competent authority to explain *interpretando*[b] whether by virtue of the amnesty I have regained the lost status of a Prussian. It is only in *this* sense that I have referred to § 5 of the law in question.

Furthermore it is particularly appropriate for me to turn to Your Excellency with this question because it is in *Berlin* that I wish to take up domicile, my ability to do so depending on that confirmation as a legal *condition,* and hence Your Excellency, as chief of the police of this city, is the person on whose view in the

---

[a] All the more certainly.— *Ed.*
[b] By interpreting the law.— *Ed.*

question posed the decision on the matter of residence will depend.

It can surely not be in Your Excellency's interest, nor can it be expected of me, that I should wait three or four months or longer in complete *uncertainty* and with no possibility of taking practical steps to achieve my end until I receive notice, along with a definitive decision as to domicile, of what interpretation you give the Royal amnesty and whether thereby you will confirm my reinstatement as a Prussian or not.

Such uncertainty, lasting for months, would *be extremely damaging to me in all my plans, arrangements and economic relationships.*

It is, of course, also my *right* to know whether the competent authority *will* or *will not* confirm that status for me, and that authority will not regard a refusal or postponement of a reply thereto as either legitimate or worthy of itself.

Accordingly, I freely, openly and loyally put this question to Your Excellency:

whether or not you confirm that the Royal amnesty restores me to the status of a Prussian?

and I look forward to an equally free, open and loyal reply.

I am all the more eager to have this answer as soon as possible since only then will it be possible for me, in the most improbable case of an unfavourable decision, to appeal to the Chambers while they are still in session, during which, in any case, a proposal for an amnesty law evoked by doubts as to the interpretation of the amnesty order will be discussed, and since, on the other hand, I can stay here only for *a short time* now, as family affairs call me back to London.

I therefore request Your Excellency kindly to let me have the requested open and definite answer by return of post, for *only then* will I be able to submit, in due form, my application for settlement in this city.

I have the honour to remain,

Your Excellency's obedient servant,
Dr Karl Marx

Berlin, March 25, 1861

First published in: Marx and Engels, *Works*, Second Russian Edition, Vol. 15, Moscow, 1959

Printed according to the manuscript

Published in English for the first time

[MARX'S STATEMENT ON THE REJECTION OF HIS APPLICATION FOR RESTORATION OF HIS PRUSSIAN CITIZENSHIP] [340]

Berlin, April 6, 1861

To His Excellency the Royal Police President
Baron von Zedlitz, Knight p.p.

Your Excellency,

I have the honour to reply to your letter dated March 30 and received yesterday that the facts, referred to by Your Excellency, relating to my discharge from my Prussian citizenship in 1845 cannot be fully known to Your Excellency, since otherwise Your Excellency's decision of March 30 would certainly not have been taken.

The following facts and legal grounds will convince Your Excellency that the status of a Prussian cannot be denied me at the present time.

1. In 1844, during my residence in Paris, an order for my arrest was issued by the Royal Governor of the Rhine Province, on the grounds of the *Deutsch-Französische Jahrbücher* edited by me, and was sent to the border police authorities to be carried out as soon as I set foot on Prussian soil.

This placed me in the position of a political refugee from that time on.

But the Royal Prussian government was not content with that. In January 1845 it obtained my expulsion from France from the Guizot ministry.[a]

I went to Belgium. But the persecution of the Royal Prussian government followed me there too. Still on the pretext that I was a Prussian, which entitled the Prussian government to take steps concerning me via their embassies abroad, here too my expulsion was demanded by the Prussian government.

---

[a] Marx left Paris for Brussels on February 3, 1845.— *Ed.*

Prevented from returning to my fatherland by the order of arrest, the only thing left me of my nationality as a Prussian was the capacity for being persecuted; the only thing left me was to be persecuted and expelled everywhere abroad at the instance of the Prussian government.

This made it necessary for me to deprive the Prussian government of that period of the possibility to persecute me further, and for this reason I asked in 1845 for that discharge from Prussian citizenship.

Even at that time, it was not in the least my intention to give up my Prussian nationality. This *can be formally proved.* Anyone who gives up his nationality can only do that with the intention of getting himself admitted to another nationality. I have *never* done this. I have not had myself naturalised anywhere, and, when the provisional government of France *offered* me naturalisation in 1848, I refused it.[341]

That application in 1845 for discharge from Prussian citizenship was therefore not, as Your Excellency writes in error, a surrender, "by my own free will", of my status as a Prussian, but merely a device, *forced* on me by extreme persecution, to free myself from the continuing device of this persecution. It was a *pretext* employed against another pretext, not at all a serious intention to give up my status as a Prussian.

Your Excellency will see from the foregoing that it is impossible for you to rely on that proceeding in 1845.

To try to rely on it would mean supporting the era of the worst absolutist persecutions of German writers, perpetuating them in their effects, and trying to take advantage of them. It would mean trying, on the basis of the political oppression of that period and the means thereby forced on me of saving myself from unbounded persecution, to deprive me of my Prussian nationality, which I never seriously intended to give up.

Finally, with reference to the expulsion in 1849 mentioned by Your Excellency, I will remark by way of supererogation that I returned to Prussia immediately after March 1848[a] and took up my domicile in Cologne and was admitted as a citizen by the municipality of Cologne without further ado. To be sure, the Manteuffel ministry ordered my expulsion in 1849 as an alleged foreigner. But this action is one of the most illegal deeds of violence of that ministry and hence cannot in any way be adduced

---

[a] Marx and Engels left Paris and returned to Germany about April 6, 1848.— *Ed.*

as a decisive precedent, and even at that time I would not have yielded to it had not a number of political press prosecutions forced me to go abroad as a refugee, quite apart from that expulsion.

After the foregoing explanations, I regard Your Excellency as just as unable to wish to rely on those facts as it is objectively impossible to deduce from them anything against me.

However, this is also

2. quite impossible because of the Royal decree on the amnesty. By it "unimpeded return to the Prussian states" is assured all political refugees. That is, unimpeded return even if they had in the meantime legally lost their status as Prussians. Unimpeded return, whatever the way in which they might have lost that status, whether by the law itself[a] as the result of absence for ten years or by reason of an added verbal declaration of withdrawal from Prussian citizenship. The amnesty *does not distinguish* between these two modes of loss of the status of a Prussian. Neither does it distinguish between the refugees of 1848-49 and those of an earlier period; it does not distinguish between those who lost the rights of native-born Prussians as a result of the conflicts in 1848 and those who lost them as a result of the political conflicts of earlier years.

"Unimpeded return" is assured all political refugees, from whatever time their political conflicts and the resulting loss of their rights as native-born [Prussians] may date; all these are thereby restored to their previous rights as native-born.

Since the Royal amnesty does not distinguish whether those rights were lost by virtue of the law itself because of absence for ten years or because of an added declaration, it is absolutely impermissible to try, by *interpretation,* to introduce a limitation and a distinction into the Royal amnesty which it never makes itself.

Your Excellency will be aware of this firmly-established principle, that an amnesty *may never be interpreted restrictively.* This principle has been consecrated by the jurisprudence of all times and all countries with unanimity like no other principle. If this has been the inviolable principle of every tribunal that has had to apply and interpret amnesty decrees, it must equally be the principle of administrative authorities when it behoves them to make this interpretation. Any restrictive interpretation would

---

[a] This refers to the "Gesetz über die Erwerbung und den Verlust der Eigenschaft als Preussischer Unterthan... vom 31. Dezember 1842".— *Ed.*

signify: *abbreviating the amnesty after the event and repealing it in part.*

This will certainly not be Your Excellency's intention. If I refrain from adducing the juridical materials on this matter that are at my disposal, the reason is that it will suffice to call Your Excellency's attention to the fact that any other interpretation of the Royal amnesty than mine would contain a restriction thereof.

Your Excellency will see from the foregoing that in fact everything comes down to whether, as I stated in my latest memorandum,[a] the refugees are reintegrated into the status of native-born Prussians by the Royal amnesty, although all of them had lost the same under the law in view of their staying abroad for ten years without permission. If this is conceded, and Your Excellency yourself accepts this in your rescript dated March 30, it is a matter of total indifference if there has been, in addition to this legal loss of native-born status, which is set aside by the amnesty, a declaration by the individual in question in the past, and posing such a distinction would constitute an impermissible restriction of the amnesty.

But this is the case not only because of the *wording* of the amnesty and of the favourable *spirit* in which amnesties must always be interpreted, but likewise

3. in conformity with the legal nature of the situation under consideration. For in fact, what difference should it make to the Royal amnesty whether the rights as native-born, which the amnesty restores, as Your Excellency yourself does not dispute, were lost under the law itself or by reason of an added declaration on the part of the individual? As little as an individual declaration by a refugee of unwillingness to lose his status as a native-born Prussian, despite the law, would change his losing it under the law, just so little could that declaration either set this losing aside or reinforce it. The declaration by an individual that something should take place which would have taken place in any event by virtue of the law—discharge from Prussian citizenship—remains a *déclaration surérogatoire*,[b] a totally indifferent, superfluous declaration, whose absence is no hindrance and whose presence is ineffectual.

Your Excellency seems to wish to see a distinction in that the status of a Prussian was allegedly given up by me "of my own free will", whereas for the other refugees it was brought about

---

a See this volume, pp. 341-44.— *Ed.*
b Supererogatory declaration.— *Ed.*

involuntarily by a ten-year absence. But this too is incorrect. Formally, the refugee's remaining out of the country for ten years likewise constitutes a *voluntary* abandonment of the status of a Prussian, for as a matter of fact none of the refugees was prevented from returning before this time had elapsed and presenting himself before the Prussian courts. Inasmuch as he did not do this, he voluntarily preferred to lose the status of a Prussian. The *last day* of the ten-year stay abroad without permission is thus completely the equivalent of a written declaration to the Prussian government of a desire to relinquish Prussian citizenship. Since this absence is *just as free an act of the will* as a document addressed to the government, the same declaration was submitted by *voluntas tacita*[a] on the last day of this ten-year absence by all the refugees as the one that you have in your files submitted by me in 1845.

So far as *form* is concerned, there is just as voluntary a surrender of the rights of the native-born on the part of all the refugees as there is on mine.

It is true that in point of fact those refugees were prevented from returning unless they wanted to expose themselves to the harm of arrest and a criminal procedure, and hence they were, *in point of fact,* under compulsion. But the same *real* compulsion was present in my case as well, as Your Excellency will have seen from Point 1. I too was, *in point of fact,* prevented in the same way from returning by the warrants of arrest that had been issued and I gave up the status of a Prussian only under exactly the same compulsion as that under which the other refugees surrendered it on the last day of their ten-year absence. Indeed, I was also compelled to this ostensible surrender by the persecution extending into foreign countries.

Thus, whether Your Excellency takes the formal or the real side of the question into consideration, that affects me in precisely the same way as it does all other refugees, and if, as Your Excellency does not deny, the native-born status lost by ten-year absence has been restored to the refugees by the amnesty, it is equally restored to me despite the enforced disavowal, which is completely equivalent to this loss under the law.

As has been shown, my having declared in writing that I desired to lose the status of a Prussian, which I had lost anyway by virtue of the law, this declaration, which is totally without effect after the

---

[a] Tacit consent.— *Ed.*

loss incurred *lege ipsa*,[a] is not the essential point. It could at best only be seen as constituting a difference, although not a valid one, if I had assumed a new nationality elsewhere. This and only this would have been a *voluntary* action. The mere surrender of Prussian citizenship was enforced and would have taken place anyway *lege ipsa*. But I have never and nowhere had myself naturalised. Very many refugees did in fact do this. If even for these cases the Royal amnesty must be regarded as unconditionally sufficient grounds for granting them renaturalisation, in the event that they desire it, then in the case of myself, who have never taken out naturalisation in any other state, the restoration of the status of a native-born [Prussian] must of necessity be recognised as effected by the amnesty itself.

4. In the foregoing I have explained to Your Excellency that I have undoubtedly[b] regained my status as a native-born Prussian, even if I had lost it in 1845, by virtue of the Royal amnesty. But an equally decisive ground for my claim is the circumstance that I have already *won back my rights as a Prussian citizen by the decision of the Federal Diet dated March 30, 1848*.[c]

That decision declared that all the political refugees *had the right to vote* and to be elected to the German National Assembly who were to return to Germany and declare that they desired to regain the rights as citizens of the state. By this decision, which is binding on Prussia and towards which the Prussian government contributed, all political refugees were thus restored to their rights as citizens of the state in the state to which they had previously belonged or in the one in which they now wished to take it out.

As a consequence of this decision I went from Paris to Cologne at once, there reassumed my rights as a citizen of the Prussian state, obtained permission without difficulty from the Cologne City Council to take up domicile there and hence was undoubtedly *in lawful possession from then on of the status of a native-born Prussian*, which cannot in any way be altered by the unlawful coup, in violation of the Federal Diet's decision, of the expulsion attempted by the Manteuffel ministry.

This fact of law is so decisive that it would be superfluous to add even a single word to it.

---

[a] By the law itself.— *Ed.*

[b] The word "undoubtedly" *(jedenfalls)* has been underlined in the manuscript, obviously by von Zedlitz. The margin has a note "not at all" *(keineswegs)*.— *Ed.*

[c] Cf. *Protokolle der Deutschen Bundesversammlung vom Jahre 1848*, Frankfurt am Main, 1848.— *Ed.*

Your Excellency will be as convinced of this as I am and will equally regard it as not in the interest of the Prussian government to force me to appeal to the Federal Diet against a violation of its decisions by the Prussian government. It would be too contradictory a position if Prussia, which continues to recognise the *reactivated* Federal Diet, should wish to change over to refusing to recognise the few scattered decisions of the *old, original Federal Diet* that were issued in the interest of the people and in a liberal direction.

Such a procedure would be, juridically and politically, too exorbitant a monstrosity to be taken into consideration even tentatively.

As Your Excellency will see, it is not even necessary for me to refer to the decision, independent of the Federal Diet decision, of the Preparliament,[342] likewise recognised de facto by the Prussian government, according to which even those German refugees who had been *naturalised* in other countries in the interim were also entitled to reassume their previous rights as citizens.

Pursuant to the decision of the Federal Diet dated March 30, 1848, to my removal to Cologne as a consequence thereof, and my declaration to the Prussian ministry dated August 22, 1848,[343] which is in Your Excellency's files, I have therefore been once more in possession of the rights of a native-born Prussian since 1848, even if I did lose them in 1845.

Accordingly, I am still in possession thereof today since, as Your Excellency yourself does not deny, the loss thereof which ensued by reason of the subsequent ten-year absence has been cancelled again by the present amnesty.

Although the foregoing demonstration that I already am in possession of the rights of a native-born Prussian and require only recognition of that status is so clear and irrefutable I have, in returning to my fatherland, only a practical purpose in mind and not that of a fruitless juridical-theoretical conflict.

If Your Excellency should, as it seems, conceive the relevant situation in such a way that I must first obtain a new naturalisation, that can and should be a matter of indifference to me provided that Your Excellency, since you are the competent authority to do this pursuant to § 5 of the law of December 31, 1842, declares your willingness to grant the naturalisation. Only *then* and only *insofar* can I yield up my already existing full right, *if* and *insofar as* Your Excellency prefers to issue a new naturalisation without difficulties. Up to that point I must maintain my rights and therefore request you, in this sense and reserving all rights, to treat this letter, in that case, also as a possible request to obtain a new naturalisation.[a]

Your Excellency's obedient servant,

Dr Karl Marx

First published in: Marx and Engels, *Works*, Second Russian Edition, Vol. 15, Moscow, 1959

Printed according to the manuscript
Published in English for the first time

---

[a] The rest is written in Marx's hand.— *Ed.*

[ANSWER TO MARX'S APPLICATION FOR RESTORATION OF HIS PRUSSIAN CITIZENSHIP][a]

In reply to your request dated April 6 of this year,[b] I inform you that the conviction that you are to be regarded as a foreigner is not in any way refuted even by the considerations stated therein. § 20 of the law of December 31, 1842, on the acquisition and loss of the status of a Prussian subject rules that that status is lost at the issuance of the document waiving it.[c] Accordingly, neither the motive for your seeking that waiver nor whether you have obtained citizenship elsewhere is relevant. Further, you have not regained the status of a Prussian either in virtue of the Federal Diet's decision of March 30, 1848,[d] or by His Majesty's act of grace of January 12 cr.[e] What is determinant for the elections to the German National Assembly is not that decision but the order of April 11, 1848, which is not in your favour in any way. His Majesty's decree of January 12 cr. is an act of grace and hence relates only to remission or reduction of punishment (Art. 49 of the Constitution[f]). But the loss of the status of a Prussian is never incurred by a conviction and is therefore not cancelled by acts of grace.

---

[a] Text on the envelope of the letter: "815. To Dr Carl Marx, Esq., Here, 13 Bellevuestr. *Today, immediately!*".— *Ed.*

[b] See this volume, pp. 345-52.— *Ed.*

[c] "Gesetz über die Erwerbung und den Verlust der Eigenschaft als Preussischer Unterthan... Vom 31. Dezember 1842".— *Ed.*

[d] In *Protokolle der Deutschen Bundesversammlung vom Jahre 1848*, Frankfurt am Main, 1848.— *Ed.*

[e] *Currentis*—of this year.— *Ed.*

[f] "Verfassungsurkunde für den Preussischen Staat. Vom 31. Januar 1850", in *Preussischer Staats-Anzeiger*, No. 32, February 2, 1850.— *Ed.*

Consequently, the Police Presidium can only regard you as a foreigner. If you intend to apply for Prussian citizenship, it will be necessary for you, in order to meet the requirements prescribed in § 7 of the law of December 31, 1842, to make your application in the customary manner at the suitable police precinct, and no assurance can be given you in advance as to the prospects of success.

Royal Police Presidium
von Zedlitz

Berlin, April 10, 1861

First published in: Marx and Engels, *Works*, Second Russian Edition, Vol. 15, Moscow, 1959

Printed according to the manuscript

Published in English for the first time

[MARX'S APPLICATION FOR NATURALISATION AND RIGHT OF DOMICILE IN BERLIN][344]

Official Opinion of the 33rd Police Precinct

Done at Berlin, April 10, 1861

Dr *Karl Marx* arrived here on *March 1, 1861*.[a] After *he* had declared that *he* wished to settle here and obtain the status of a Prussian citizen by *naturalisation, he* gave the following information as to *his* personal situation:

I was born on *May 5, 1818*, at *Trier* in *the Prussian Rhine Province*, profess the Evangelical religion and am legally competent according to the laws of my previous homeland. I have resided in *England* for the last *twelve* years, supported myself there by *literary work* and have *not* been aided by public relief funds. I have *several times* been under investigation because of *political press prosecutions* and *refer to the existing files* for my conduct. I have not applied to any other Prussian authority for naturalisation or domiciliation and have never been rejected in this respect. In this connection, I have been notified that failure to report an investigation made of me or my dependents as well as incorrect data concerning my situation in general, or failure to report an application for naturalisation made to another Prussian authority will entail the cancellation and the withdrawal of the certificate of naturalisation, that the decision as to my application for domiciliation regardless of the declaration of the municipal authorities and acceptance of the filing fees, is made *exclusively* by the Royal Police Presidium, and I am therefore to refrain before obtaining the naturalisation and domiciliation certificates from any steps whatsoever to establish myself.

---

[a] The document is obviously incorrect here: Marx came to Berlin on March 17, 1861.— *Ed.*

I have *not yet* rented any dwelling place *of my own* here—I have found lodging with *Dr Lassalle, Bellevuestr. No. 13*—and will support myself and my family *by my literary work.*

My income comes to *about 2,000 reichsthaler;* neither I nor my wife have any property.

With respect to my military status, I am already exempt from all service in the army because of my age.

I have no decorations.

I request:

that the certificate of naturalisation be issued me and that I be permitted to take up residence here.

Read aloud, accepted, signed.

Dr Karl Marx[a]

First published in: Marx and Engels, *Works,* Second Russian Edition, Vol. 15, Moscow, 1959

Printed according to the manuscript

Published in English for the first time

---

[a] Marx's authentic signature is followed by the illegible signature of an official.— *Ed.*

[LETTER FROM MARX
TO POLICE PRESIDENT VON ZEDLITZ]

To His Excellency Herr von Zedlitz
Royal Police President

Your Excellency,

I received your esteemed letter of April 10[a] last evening. Although in Your Excellency's last letter[b] you were of the opinion that because of the application in 1845 it would be of no effect in my case even if the amnesty should have cancelled the loss of the status of a Prussian due to absence for ten years, Your Excellency now, in view of my latest arguments, takes rather the opposite opinion that the amnesty, because as such it allegedly can only contain a pardon of penalties, cannot cancel the *loss* of the status of a Prussian, *no matter for what reason that loss has ever been incurred.*

In order not to prejudice my rights, I am forced to remark that this letter, according to the legal opinion of the undersigned, would present 1) a partial annulment of the Royal amnesty, 2) a non-recognition of the Federal Diet and its decisions and hence a violation of the German constitutional principles, as laid down in the Federal Act,[345] 3) finally, an equally emphatic negation of all public law in Prussia.

Mindful, however, of the practical purpose by which I am guided, *I will not weary* Your Excellency by a demonstration of these three legally unassailable theses, but agree, in the sense in which I expressed it to Your Excellency at the end of my last

---

[a] See this volume, pp. 353-54.— *Ed.*
[b] Of March 30, 1861.— *Ed.*

memorandum,[a] to receive what is my right and what I must hold fast as such, even in the form of a new naturalisation from Your Excellency.

Being compelled to leave here in haste because of news from my family, I applied early yesterday in this sense *in omnem eventum*[b] for the new naturalisation at the police precinct of my district.[c]

At the same time, I respectfully inform Your Excellency that because of my departure I empower Mr. F. Lassalle, of this city, to receive the naturalisation certificate for me, to make and take note on my behalf of all the necessary applications and steps in this matter, and in general to exercise my rights to the same extent as is in my power.

Respectfully requesting Your Excellency to kindly address the final decision to Mr. F. Lassalle, of this city, I remain,

Your Excellency's obedient servant

Dr Karl Marx[d]

Berlin, April 11, 1861

First published in: Marx and Engels, *Works*, Second Russian Edition, Vol. 15, Moscow, 1959

Printed according to the manuscript

Published in English for the first time

---

[a] See this volume, p. 351.— *Ed.*

[b] In any event.— *Ed.*

[c] See this volume, pp. 355-56. At this point there is a note in the margin of the manuscript, in an unknown hand: "This request of Marx has been refused."— *Ed.*

[d] The signature is in Marx's hand.— *Ed.*

[POWER OF ATTORNEY GIVEN BY MARX
TO FERDINAND LASSALLE FOR THE RESTORATION
OF HIS PRUSSIAN CITIZENSHIP][a]

I hereby empower Mr. Ferdinand Lassalle of Berlin, on my departure from that city, to vindicate my rights in the matter, now pending before the Royal Police Presidium, relating to the recognition of my status as a Prussian, restored to me under the Royal Amnesty of January 12 of this year or, alternatively, the possible granting of new naturalisation and permission to reside in Berlin. I further empower him to submit applications, to lodge petitions and appeals with the Royal Prussian Government as also with the German Federal Diet,[346] and to avail himself of every right to which I am entitled, in the same measure to which I myself am entitled thereto.

Dr Karl Marx

Berlin, April 12, 1861

First published in: Marx and Engels, *Works*, First Russian Edition, Vol. XXV, Moscow, 1934

Printed according to the manuscript

Published in English for the first time

---

[a] The whole manuscript is written in Marx's hand.— *Ed.*

25*

Frederick Engels

TO THE DIRECTORATE OF THE SCHILLER INSTITUTE [347]

[Draft]

I have the honour to enclose as Appendix I a copy of a communication from the Librarian which was handed to me not long since.[348] When I took the liberty of making a few observations to Mr Stössel regarding certain expressions used therein, his reply, as I had expected, was that the communication was merely a copy of the set form laid down by the Literary Section of the Directorate.

If, therefore, I now feel compelled to bring the said observations to the attention of the Directorate, I should first of all emphasise that these do not in any way apply to the substance of the communication as such. Everyone will, no doubt, subscribe to this last, to a strict adherence to the time limit prescribed for the loan of books, to the levying of "fines" should that limit be exceeded, and to the observance of the Institute's rules and regulations generally. What I am concerned with here is merely the tone of this document. That tone is so very different from that customary in correspondence between educated persons that I must confess I am not used to receiving such letters, nor, from what Mr. Stössel tells me, am I the first to have been struck by this, to put it mildly, uncouth form of address.

Indeed, when I had read this missive, it was as though I had been suddenly transported home. It was as though, instead of a communication from the Librarian of the Schiller Institute, I were holding a peremptory summons from a German inspector of police ordering me, on pain of a heavy penalty, to make amends for some kind of violation "within 24 hours". The otherwise very innocuous uniform of the beadle who served this writ on me could not on this occasion but help to complete the illusion.

Immediately after this incident I took occasion to reread the manifesto dated November 12, 1859, and issued, so to speak, as the programme of the incipient Schiller Institute. Seen alongside the afore-mentioned communication from the Librarian, that programme now appears in a somewhat peculiar light. In it we read that the Schiller Institute was intended to be such

"that a young German ... should at once feel *more at home* here... find himself *better looked after and provided for*, both morally and intellectually ... and, above all, should return to the fatherland *in no way estranged from it*".

No doubt, the bureaucratic style of such official communications is the very thing to make the recipient instantly feel that he is on his *home* ground, and to instil in him the belief that he is just as well if not "better looked after *and provided for*" than he would be at home, in the dear, old patriarchal police state, that great institution looking after and making provision for little children; nor, so long as such official communications continue to flourish, can there possibly be the remotest danger of any member of the Schiller Institute's becoming *estranged from the fatherland.* Indeed if, once in a way, there should happen to be some member of the Schiller Institute who had not had occasion to become acquainted at home with the forms of bureaucracy and the imperious language of officialdom, the Schiller Institute would seem to offer him an excellent opportunity to do so; again, this presumably is the construction to be put upon the programme's undertaking that the Schiller Institute will help ensure

"that even he of advanced years, who decides to return home and settle down there again, should, along with the German language and culture, *also preserve and even develop to a higher degree*, his capacity for *public service as a German man and citizen*".

Indeed, it would hardly have occurred to many members that "the German spirit in the fullest sense of the term", for the nurturing of which the Schiller Institute was to be a rallying-point, should *inter alia* also comprise that spirit of bureaucracy in whose hands, alas, almost all political power at home is still vested but against which the whole of Germany is fighting and over which, at this very moment, it is scoring victory after victory. This hectoring tone, these categorical demands that an order be obeyed within 24 hours are, at all events, out of place here, and if they entail, not a fortnight's imprisonment on a diet of bread and water, but the fearsome threat of a half-crown fine, then the effect is comical into the bargain.

Among its members the Schiller Institute numbers not only

Germans, but also Englishmen, Dutchmen and Danes, for whom this tone will certainly not have the ring of "home". I permit myself to ask what such members are likely to think of the "German spirit" upon receiving missives of this kind?

It so happens that I myself do at present belong to the Literary Section of another society [349] here which does not boast a librarian and, in similar cases, it often falls to me to send out circulars to members. I enclose herewith the customary form (Appendix II), [350] not because of any pretence it might have to serve as a model, but rather because it may, perhaps, show that the same object can be attained without infringing on that deference which one educated person owes another.

I repeat that while *fortiter in re*[a] is certainly most commendable, members would also seem to me to be entitled to some *suaviter in modo*.[b] By all means, let the iron hand of the Literary Section descend on the head of every member, but let it also wear a velvet glove. And that is why I would request the Directorate to be so kind as to ensure that the Literary Section's official correspondence with members should be modelled, not so much on orders issued by German administrative offices to those they administer, as on what is proper in correspondence between educated persons.

Written about May 3, 1861

First published in: Marx and Engels, *Works*, First Russian Edition, Vol. XXV, Moscow, 1934

Printed according to the manuscript

Published in English for the first time

---

a Firmness in doing what is to be done.— *Ed.*
b Inoffensiveness in manner.— *Ed.*

[POWER OF ATTORNEY ISSUED BY MARX TO ENGELS TO TAKE OVER WILHELM WOLFF'S ESTATE][a]

23 May, 1864
1, Modena Villas, Maitland Park,
Haverstock Hill, London, N.W.

My dear Sir,

I hereby request you and give you full power to act as my representative at, and take all the necessary steps for, the execution of the will of our common friend, Wilhelm Wolff.

KARL MARX, Dr. Ph.

First published in: *Marx-Engels Gesamtausgabe*, Dritte Abteilung, Bd. 3, 1930

Printed according to the manuscript

---

[a] The whole manuscript is written in Marx's hand. The address on the envelope reads: "Fr. Engels, Esq. 6, Thorncliffe Grove, Oxford Street, *Manchester*."— *Ed.*

NOTES
AND
INDEXES

NOTES

1 Marx and Engels began to contribute to the *New-York Daily Tribune* in 1851 (see Vol. 11, Note 2). 1861 and 1862 were the last two years of their work for the *Tribune*. With the outbreak of the US Civil War interest in European affairs in America declined. The *Tribune* cancelled its contracts with all its European correspondents except Marx, who was asked to reduce the number of his contributions from two to one a week. Between February 1861 and March 1862 the paper published ten items by Marx and one by Engels. One appeared as a leading article, nine were marked "From an Occasional Correspondent" and one was marked "From Our Own Correspondent". Marx's final break with the newspaper occurred in the spring of 1862 (see Vol. 12, Note 1 and Vol. 39, Note 4).

The theme and basic content of this article were suggested to Engels by Marx, who in a letter dated January 22, 1861 (Vol. 41 of the present edition) asked Engels to write on the Schleswig-Holstein question for the *NYDT*. Engels wrote the article on January 23. On the following day Marx sent it to New York by the steamer *Anglo-Saxon*. p. 3

2 This refers to the secession of the Southern slave states from the North American Union in late 1860 and early 1861. The armed rebellion of the secessionist States in April 1861 marked the beginning of the US Civil War (1861-65).

In 1850 popular disturbances occurred in several southern provinces of China and developed into a large-scale peasant war. The rebels (called Taipings) established a state of their own embracing a considerable part of China's territory. Its leaders put forward a utopian programme for the transformation of feudal China into a military-patriarchal state based on the egalitarian principle in production and consumption. The movement, which was also anti-colonial, was weakened by inner divisions and the rise of an aristocracy among the Taipings. The rebellion was suppressed in 1864, mainly as a result of British and French intervention. p. 3

3 Construction of the *Suez Canal* was begun in 1859 and completed in 1869.

The Fortress of *Gaëta*, the last stronghold of Francis II, King of the Two Sicilies (the Kingdom of Naples), was seized by the Piedmont troops on February 12, 1861, as a result of which the Kingdom of the Two Sicilies became part of the united Kingdom of Italy. p. 3

⁴ In July 1860 a pamphlet entitled *MacMahon, King of the Irish* appeared in France, where an anti-British campaign was in full swing. The pamphlet urged the Irish to end British rule and set up the French Marshal MacMahon, a descendant of Irish emigrants, as King of Ireland. Engels is probably referring to this pamphlet.   p. 3

⁵ The three preceding stages of the Danish-Prussian war of 1848-50 were: the period from the outbreak of hostilities on March 23, 1848 to the truce of August 26, 1848; the period from this truce to that of July 10, 1849, and finally the period from the second truce to the signing of the peace treaty in Berlin on July 2, 1850.   p. 3

⁶ This refers to the "liberal" course proclaimed by William, Prince of Prussia (King of Prussia from 1861), in October 1858 when he assumed the regency. Actually, not one of the reforms expected by the bourgeoisie was carried out. William's policy aimed at consolidating the Prussian monarchy and Junkerdom.
                                                                                 p. 5

⁷ At *Magenta* and *Solferino* the decisive battles of the 1859 Austro-Italo-French war were fought on June 4 and June 24 respectively. The Austrians were defeated on both occasions.   p. 6

⁸ On September 9, 1861 *The Times* (No. 24033) published a letter by the US Abolitionist writer Harriet Beecher Stowe to Lord Shaftesbury, the English philanthropist politician, urging Britons to give moral support to the North.
                                                                                 p. 7

⁹ The US Republican Party was formed in the north-eastern States in 1854 by a broad coalition of industrial and commercial bourgeoisie, farmers, workers and handicraftsmen in opposition to the Democratic Party. Its establishment reflected the antagonistic contradictions between the capitalism developing in the North and the system of slave labour prevalent in the South. The Republican Party, controlled by the Northern bourgeoisie, advocated the restriction of slavery to the Southern States, the free settlement of the Western Territories, and protectionist tariffs to stimulate the development of national industry. In 1860 Abraham Lincoln, the Republican candidate, was elected US President. He polled 1,866,352 votes as against 1,375,157 votes obtained by S. A. Douglas, the Democratic candidate (see Note 13).   p. 8

¹⁰ This refers to the *Constitution of the Confederate States of America*, adopted in Montgomery, Alabama, on March 11, 1861 at a congress of the seven secessionist states (Alabama, Florida, Georgia, Louisiana, Mississippi, South Carolina and Texas). The full text of the Constitution appeared in the *New-York Daily Tribune*, No. 6206, March 16, 1861.   p. 8

¹¹ *The Constitution, as formed for the United States, by the Federal Convention, held at Philadelphia, in the year 1787...* consolidated the rule of the bourgeoisie and planters in the form of a federal bourgeois republic.   p. 8

¹² The *Crittenden compromise,* a project for the peaceful settlement of the North-South conflict, was submitted by Kentucky Senator Crittenden to the US Congress on December 18, 1860. It envisaged six amendments to the US Constitution calling, in particular, for a ban on slavery in states north of the 36°30' boundary line fixed by the Missouri Compromise (see Note 14) and the legalisation of slavery south of that line. The project denied the Congress the right to abolish or alter the slave system in the Southern States. A special

Senate committee rejected the Crittenden compromise on December 22, 1860.

p. 9

[13] In the mid-1850s, following the adoption of the Kansas-Nebraska Bill (see Note 15), the US Democratic Party (founded in 1828) split up into two factions, Northern and Southern. Basically, both favoured the preservation and spread of slavery, but the Northern faction took a more flexible stand, declaring that the issue should be submitted to the US Supreme Court. The Southern faction urged the right of the Territories to make their own decisions on the matter, and pressed for the free importation of slaves into the Territories. The most reactionary among the Southern Democrats prepared the ground for the rebellion and the establishment of the separatist slaveholding Confederacy.

p. 9

[14] The *Missouri Compromise,* embodied in the Act to Authorise the People of the Missouri Territory to Form a Constitution and State Government, was reached in 1820, after a period of bitter struggle waged in the US Congress and throughout the country between the supporters and opponents of slavery. The Missouri agreement laid down a boundary between the free and slaveholding states, outlawing slavery north of the 36°30' N line. The agreement was superseded by the Kansas-Nebraska Bill, adopted by the US Congress in 1854 (see Note 15).

p. 10

[15] The *Kansas-Nebraska Bill* (An Act to Organise the Territories of Nebraska and Kansas), passed by the US Congress in May 1854 after a fierce debate, granted the white population of Kansas and Nebraska, which were being admitted to the Union, the right to permit or prohibit slavery within their boundaries. The Bill abolished the frontier line laid down by the Missouri Compromise between the free and slaveholding states (see Note 14) and allowed every state to introduce slavery, regardless of geographical position. The adoption of the Bill gave rise to an armed struggle in Kansas between the supporters and opponents of slavery (see Note 18).

p. 10

[16] This refers to a memorandum drawn up in October 1854 at the Belgian resort of Ostend by the US Minister to London Buchanan jointly with US diplomatic representatives in France and Spain. It recommended the US government to purchase or seize the island of Cuba, then in Spanish possession, with a view to extending slavery to it. It was not until March 1855 that the memorandum became public knowledge, causing indignation in the United States and abroad.

p. 10

[17] The Black slave Dred Scott had lived for four years in the non-slave States of Illinois and Wisconsin. In 1848 he brought a lawsuit, claiming freedom. In 1857 it was turned down by the US Supreme Court. The ruling implied that a slave remained the property of his master even in the free States—an example of the slaveholders' efforts to have slavery legalised throughout the country.

p. 10

[18] Marx means the armed struggle in Kansas (1854-56) between the supporters and opponents of slavery sparked off by the Kansas-Nebraska Bill (see Note 15). Despite the successes of the anti-slavery forces, Kansas fell under the sway of the pro-slavery faction, supported by the Federal government. However, the majority of the population continued the struggle and secured the admission of Kansas to the Union as a free state in 1861.

p. 10

[19] At the 1856 Presidential election, Buchanan, the Democratic candidate, polled 1,838,169 votes, as against the 1,341,264 votes for Frémont, put up by the Republican Party, which was contesting a Presidential election for the first time (see Note 9).   p. 10

[20] An ironical reference to the London press. The *Illuminati* were members of a secret Masonic society in Bavaria (1776-84).   p. 10

[21] A street in London, in which the Central Criminal Court is situated.   p. 12

[22] In October 1859 an 18-strong group of insurgents (including five Blacks), led by John Brown, seized a government arsenal in Harper's Ferry, Virginia, in an attempt to provoke a slave uprising in the Southern states. The group was encircled and almost totally wiped out by regular troops. Brown was severely wounded. He was tried and hanged in Charleston.   p. 13

[23] This refers to the protectionist tariff tabled in Congress by the Republican Justin Smith Morrill and passed by the Senate on March 2, 1861. It raised customs duties considerably.   p. 14

[24] In November 1832 the South Carolina Convention nullified the 1828 and 1832 Federal tariff acts, which imposed high import duties. The Ordinance of Nullification adopted by the Convention on November 24 proclaimed the resolve of the State's citizens to uphold their independence vis-à-vis the Federal government and threatened South Carolina's secession from the Union. President Andrew Jackson, with Congressional approval, sent troops to South Carolina, but, under pressure from the slaveholding planters, endorsed a compromise lower tariff on March 2, 1833. South Carolina soon repealed the Ordinance of Nullification.   p. 14

[25] In this article Marx probably used data he had received from Engels while staying in Manchester in the first half of September 1861.   p. 17

[26] President Lincoln's blockade of the ports of the rebel States was imposed on April 19, 1861 and lifted in August 1865. During this period, the Northern navy detained 1,500 enemy vessels and seized 31 million dollars' worth of property.   p. 17

[27] Between 1845 and 1847 potato blight was the óccasion of widespread famine in Ireland. The poverty of the small tenants ruthlessly exploited by the big landowners made the mass of the population almost entirely dependent on a diet of potatoes grown on their own little patches. About one million people starved to death, and the wave of emigration caused by the famine swept away another million. Large areas of Ireland were depopulated. The deserted land was turned by English and Irish landlords into pastures.   p. 20

[28] The *New-York Daily Tribune* carried the following editorial note on this article in the same issue: "An occasional correspondent in London furnishes us with a most interesting letter, printed this morning, concerning the London *Times* and the influence upon it of Lord Palmerston".   p. 21

[29] *Catholic Emancipation*—in 1829 the British Parliament, under pressure of a mass movement in Ireland, lifted some of the restrictions curtailing the political rights of the Catholic population. Catholics were granted the right to be elected to Parliament and hold certain government posts. Simultaneously the property qualification for electors was raised fivefold. The British ruling classes hoped that this manoeuvre would bring the élite of the Irish bourgeoisie and Catholic

landowners to their side and cause a split in the Irish national movement.

The *Reform Act* passed by the British Parliament in June 1832 was directed against the political monopoly of the landed and finance aristocracy and enabled the industrial bourgeoisie to be duly represented in Parliament. The proletariat and the petty bourgeoisie, the main forces in the struggle for reform, remained disfranchised.

The Bill repealing the *Corn Laws* was passed in June 1846. The English Corn Laws imposed high import duties on agricultural products in order to maintain high prices on the home market for the benefit of the landowners. Their repeal marked a victory for the industrial bourgeoisie, who favoured free trade. At the same time it had an adverse effect on Irish grain exports, aggravating Ireland's economic plight.

The *Stamp Tax* was imposed on newspapers in Britain in 1711 as a means of raising state revenue and combating the opposition press. It made newspapers exceedingly expensive, thus placing them beyond the reach of the mass reader and reducing their circulation. In 1836 Parliament was forced to reduce the Stamp Tax, and in 1855 to abolish it.

The *Paper Duty*, introduced in Britain in 1694, evoked widespread public protests in the mid-19th century as an obstacle for the reduction of the price of printed matter. It yielded the state about £1,400,000 annually. A campaign against the Paper Duty, waged over a number of years, led to its repeal in 1861.   p. 21

30 *Glorious Revolution*—the term used by bourgeois historians for the coup d'état of 1688-89 that established a constitutional monarchy in Britain based on a compromise between the landed aristocracy on the one hand, and the bourgeoisie and new nobility on the other.   p. 21

31 This refers to John Aberdeen's Coalition Ministry of 1852-55 (the Cabinet of All the Talents), which included Whigs, Peelites and representatives of the Irish faction in Parliament.   p. 23

32 Owing to Palmerston's patronage, *The Times'* leading observer, R. Lowe, held the posts of Vice-President of the Board of Trade and Paymaster-General between 1855 and 1858, and was Vice-President of the Committee of the Privy Council for Education from 1859 to 1864. The Editor of *The Times,* Thomas Delane, was introduced by Palmerston to London's high society.   p. 23

33 In 1839 the British Parliament issued a Blue Book on Persia and Afghanistan (*Correspondence Relating to Persia and Afghanistan*) containing, among other documents, a number of letters by A. Burnes, the British representative in Kabul, on the British-Afghan war of 1838-42 (see Note 96). The letters had been selected and presented by the Foreign Office in such a way as to conceal Britain's part in provoking the war. Shortly before his death Burnes sent duplicates of his letters to London. Those not included in the Blue Book were published by his family [A. Burnes, Cabool, Being a Personal Narrative of a Journey to and Residence in That City, in the Years 1836, 7 and 8..., London, 1842; J. Burnes' Notes on His Name and Family (Including a Memoir of Sir Alexander Burnes), Edinburgh, 1851].   p. 23

34 On May 8, 1852 representatives of Austria, Britain, France, Norway-Sweden, Prussia and Russia jointly with representatives of Denmark signed in London a protocol on the integrity of the Danish monarchy. It was based on a protocol establishing the principle of the indivisibility of the domains of the King of Denmark, including the duchies of Schleswig and Holstein, which was

adopted on July 4, 1850 and finally signed on August 2, 1850 by the above-mentioned participants in the London Conference (with the exception of Prussia). In the London Protocol the Tsar of Russia, being a descendant of Duke Karl Peter Ulrich of Holstein-Gottorp who reigned in Russia under the name of Peter III (1761-62), was referred to as one of the lawful pretenders to the throne of Denmark who had renounced their rights in favour of Duke Christian of Glücksburg, proclaimed successor to King Frederick VII. This created a precedent for the Tsar of Russia to claim the Danish throne in the event of the extinction of the Glücksburg dynasty. p. 23

[35] *In usum delphini* (édition dauphine) means, literally, "for use by the Dauphin" and, figuratively, "abridged" or "distorted". The phrase was coined in connection with the publication in 1668, in the reign of Louis XIV, of an expurgated version of Latin classics for the heir to the French throne. p. 24

[36] The Mechanics' Institute in Bradford, West Riding, Yorkshire (founded in 1825). p. 26

[37] King William I of Prussia was Napoleon III's guest at Compiègne (France) from October 6 to 8, 1861. p. 27

[38] During the period in question, *The Times* had its editorial offices in *Printing-House Square*, London.
The *Tuileries*, a palace in Paris, was the residence of French monarch. In political parlance the Tuileries meant the French government. p. 27

[39] In September 1860 Captain Macdonald of the British Army, while travelling in Germany, was detained in Bonn for six days and fined by a court on charges of insubordination to the local authorities. p. 27

[40] This refers to the polemic pamphlet by Henri d'Orléans (the Duke d'Aumale) *Lettre sur l'histoire de France*, written in reply to a speech by Prince Napoleon made in the French Senate in the spring of 1861. On Napoleon III's orders, the pamphlet was confiscated and the publisher fined and imprisoned. p. 28

[41] An allusion to Napoleon III, who in 1848, when in exile in Britain, volunteered for the Special Constabulary (a police reserve made up of civilians) which helped the police disperse a Chartist-organised workers' demonstration on April 10, 1848. p. 28

[42] During the American War of Independence (1775-83) France, in an attempt to weaken Britain, aided the latter's insurgent American colonies with money and arms. The American liberation struggle was followed with special sympathy by France's democratic and liberal sections. The Marquis de La Fayette was prominent among the French volunteers fighting on the American side. He was also active in the French revolutions of 1789 and 1830. p. 29

[43] From the mid-19th century, France, like other European powers, sought to establish itself in China and Indochina. Between 1857 and 1860, the united forces of Britain and France inflicted a series of defeats on the Chinese. The imperial government was compelled to sign several treaties reducing China to a semi-colony. In 1858 Napoleon III's government in cooperation with Spain unleashed a colonial war in Indochina. It ended in 1862, with France seizing three eastern provinces of South Vietnam (Cochin-China). p. 30

[44] On July 21, 1861 the Union army was defeated by the Confederate forces on the Bull Run river near Manassas, Virginia, in the first major battle of the US Civil War.

On August 10, 1861, the Union army, defeated at Wilson's Creek, was forced to abandon the town of Springfield, Missouri.   p. 30

[45] This is Marx's first contribution to the Viennese liberal daily, *Die Presse*. Max Friedländer, an associate editor of *Die Presse* from 1856, was previously publisher of the bourgeois-democratic *Neue Oder-Zeitung* in Breslau, to which Marx contributed in 1855 as its London correspondent. In 1859 Friedländer invited Marx to write for *Die Presse*, a welcome opening to Marx, as his collaboration with the *New-York Daily Tribune* (see Note 1) was diminishing and he badly needed another source of income. Apart from that, owing to its anti-Bonapartist stance, *Die Presse* had a fairly large readership (30,000 subscribers) which gave Marx a good opportunity for the propagation of his views in Germany and Austria. However, it was not until September 1861 that he agreed to contribute, having first made sure that in the domestic sphere the paper opposed the government of Anton von Schmerling (a Liberal) as well as the reactionary forces (see Marx's letters to Engels of 28 September and 30 October 1861 in Vol. 41 of this edition).

Marx's articles for *Die Presse*, most of which were printed with the editorial subheading "From Our London Correspondent", dealt with key issues of the foreign and home policy of Britain, France and the United States and with the condition of the working class and the democratic movement in these countries. In his articles on military matters Marx, as a rule, drew on material supplied by Engels. He contributed to *Die Presse* for somewhat over a year, during which the paper published 52 articles signed by Marx (two of these were written jointly with Engels, and one by Engels). Many of Marx's articles and reports for *Die Presse* were not published. This was the main reason why, in late 1862, he stopped contributing to the paper.

Marx presumably drafted the two articles "The North American Civil War" and "The Civil War in the United States" as early as June or July 1861, after receiving Friedländer's second request for contributions. In writing the articles Marx made use of data Engels sent him in a letter of June 12, 1861 (see Vol. 41 of this edition). The text of the articles was finalised on October 20. An introductory editorial note to the first article read: "The war, of which the great North American Republic has been the seat for more than half a year, already begins to react on Europe. France, which loses a market for her commodities through these troubles, and Britain, whose industry is threatened with partial ruin through stagnation in the export of cotton from the slave states, follow the development of the Civil War in the United States with feverish intensity. Though until recently Europe and, indeed, the Americans themselves still hoped for a peaceful solution, the war is assuming ever greater dimensions, spreading further and further over the vast territories of North America and, the longer it lasts, threatening this part of the world, too, with a crisis. It will first seize and shake Britain and France, and the panic on the British and French markets will in like manner react on the rest of the European markets. Apart from the historical aspect, we have, therefore, a very positive interest in getting our bearings with regard to the causes, the significance and the import of the transatlantic events. We have received from London a first communication on the North American Civil War from one of the leading German journalists, who knows Anglo-American relations from long years of observation. As events on the other side of the ocean develop, we shall be in a position to present communications, deriving from the same competent pen, which will outline the salient features of the war."

Marx's later articles for *Die Presse* were much shorter than "The North American Civil War" and "The Civil War in the United States". Following Friedländer's letter of October 25, 1861 asking Marx to send shorter articles, more suitable for a newspaper, his contributions did not, as a rule, exceed four handwritten pages.   p. 32

46 See Note 23.   p. 33

47 Marx means the 1831 campaign to prepare the Nullification in South Carolina, carried through in 1832 by US Vice-President John Caldwell Calhoun, an ideologist of slavery (see also Note 24).   p. 33

48 See Note 10.   p. 33

49 This refers to the fifteen slave states which, according to the plans of the secessionists, were to make up the Southern Confederacy. Initially the Confederacy included seven states: South Carolina, Mississippi, Florida, Alabama, Georgia, Louisiana and Texas. Later they were joined by Virginia, Arkansas, North Carolina and Tennessee. The remaining four—Missouri, Kentucky, Maryland and Delaware—declared themselves neutral.   p. 33

50 *Faneuil Hall* was donated to the city of Boston in 1742 by the merchant P. Faneuil. During the War of Independence (1775-83) patriotic meetings were held in the building, earning it the name of "the cradle of American liberty".
                                                                                 p. 34

51 The first *Continental Congress,* an assembly of representatives of Britain's thirteen North American colonies, was convened in September 1774. The second, convoked in May 1775, effectively was America's government until 1787.

A 1787 Congressional Ordinance stipulated that sections (Territories) of the Northwest area ceded by Virginia to the Union would be admitted to the Union as full-fledged states once their population had reached 60,000. All the US states except the original thirteen and Vermont, Kentucky, Maine, Texas, California and West Virginia initially had the status of Territories.   p. 35

52 For the *Missouri Compromise* see Note 14.   p. 35

53 See Note 17.   p. 36

54 Under the *Fugitive Slave Act,* passed by the US Congress in 1850 as a supplement to the 1793 law on the surrender of fugitive slaves, a slaveholder's evidence under oath, given to a competent official, was enough to establish his title to a runaway slave and for the latter's restitution, without a legal investigation, to his master. Every US common court of justice had special commissioners appointed for the express purpose of capturing slaves. A commissioner refusing to issue a warrant of arrest was liable to a $1,000 fine, and one responsible for a slave's escape had to pay his cost. Infringement of the Act was punishable by a $1,000 fine, six months' imprisonment and the payment of a $1,000 compensation for every fugitive. The Act caused a rise of the Abolitionist movement and became practically unenforceable even before the Civil War. It was repealed in 1864.   p. 37

55 This refers to the *free homestead* demand which became the motto of the mass anti-slavery Free Soil Party, formed in 1848 in connection with the struggle over the status of the lands seized from Mexico. The Free Soil Party later

merged with the Republican Party (see Note 9). The Free Soilers' demand was "no more slave states and no more slave territory". The Free Homestead Bill was first put to the vote in Congress in 1852, passed the House, but was rejected by the Senate. A Bill providing for the allotment of land to settlers at a moderate price (25 cents an acre) was at last adopted by Congress in 1860, but vetoed by President Buchanan. It was only after the secession of the Southern states (see Note 2) and the Republicans' victory in the 1862 election that the Homestead Act was passed. · p. 37

[56] On the *Ostend Manifesto* see Note 16. p. 37

[57] *Chihuahua, Coahuila* and *Sonora*—Northern states of Mexico that bordered on the USA. p. 37

[58] The import of slaves into the United States was banned under the 1787 US Constitution and Acts of Congress passed in 1808 and 1820. p. 37

[59] This refers to the "Old Northwest", i.e. the Northwest Territory formed by Congress in 1787 (the area north of the Ohio and west of the Mississippi). It embraced the area of what later became the states of Indiana, Illinois, Wisconsin, Michigan, Ohio and part of Minnesota. p. 38

[60] Marx means the emigrant aid companies and societies formed, with the participation of the Free Soilers (see Note 55), in several Northern states in 1854 and 1855 to promote the settlement of Kansas by free small farmers, and prevent the spread of slavery to new US Territories. They raised funds and recruited settlers, giving them financial aid and otherwise helping them start farms in Kansas. They also sent arms to keep at bay "border ruffians" from Missouri and the South.

The aid movement attained maximum scope in the summer of 1856 in connection with the intensified armed struggle in Kansas (see Note 18). In July of that year the National Kansas Committee was formed at a congress in Buffalo. The aid societies' practical activity, limited as it was, exerted a strong influence on national public opinion and contributed to the consolidation of the forces that formed the Republican Party (see Note 9). It was not until January 1861 that Kansas was granted the status of a free state. p. 38

[61] This article was prefaced in *Die Presse* with the following editorial note: "We have received another report from our London correspondent on the events in North America which presents the motives behind the policy of the secessionist South in an entirely new light. But let our reporter speak for himself."

Actually, however, as can be seen from Marx's letter to Engels of October 30, 1861 (present edition, Vol. 41), Marx sent the article to Vienna together with his previous one, "The North American Civil War" (see Note 45).

This article was first published in English in: Karl Marx and Frederick Engels, *The Civil War in the United States*, New York, 1937, London, 1937, pp. 71-83. p. 43

[62] This refers to the cessation, in 1837, of Great Britain's personal union with the Kingdom (originally, Duchy) of Hanover. Established in 1714, the union was dissolved because Victoria, who succeeded William IV on the British throne, was not eligible to the throne of Hanover as a woman. p. 43

[63] Germans accounted for 20 per cent of the white population in Texas in 1850. Most of them were political refugees who had been forced to leave Germany after the defeat of the 1848-49 revolution in Europe (they were called

"forty-eighters"). The majority of the German immigrants opposed slavery and secession, and stayed loyal to the Union government after the outbreak of the Civil War.   p. 48

64 In the winter of 1860-61 pro-Southern circles tried to wrest California from the Union by setting up a "neutral" Pacific Republic. The conspirators failed for lack of support within the state.   p. 49

65 See Note 59.   p. 50

66 *New England*—the area in the northeast of the USA (Maine, New Hampshire, Vermont, Massachusetts, Rhode Island and Connecticut) originally settled mainly by Puritans, in the seventeenth century. New England was the centre of the Abolitionist movement.   p. 50

67 The *Helots*—peasants in ancient Sparta attached to the land and obliged to perform certain services for the Spartan landowners. Unlike slaves, they were the property of the state, and the landowners were not allowed to grant them freedom, sell them separately from the land or raise their annual payments.
                                                                                    p. 50

68 The *Missouri proclamation,* issued by General Frémont on August 31, 1861 (published in the *New-York Daily Tribune,* No. 6366, September 1, 1861), called for the confiscation of the property of persons in Missouri supporting the Confederacy and proclaimed the emancipation of the rebels' slaves. Lincoln instructed Frémont to bring the proclamation into conformity with the Confiscation Act (passed by Congress on August 6, 1861, the Act only envisaged the liberation of slaves used by the rebels in the fighting) by deleting the passage on the emancipation. Frémont refused to comply and, in October 1861, was dismissed from his post as commander of the army in Missouri.
                                                                                    p. 51

69 In 1833, after an uprising of Black slaves in Jamaica, the British Parliament adopted an Act, which came into force on August 1, for the abolition of slavery throughout the British colonies. The slaveholding planters in the West Indies and other colonies were paid £20 million in compensation.   p. 51

70 First published in English in: Karl Marx and Frederick Engels, *The Civil War in the United States,* New York, 1937, London, 1937, pp. 83-87.   p. 53

71 *Quakers* (or *Society of Friends*)—a religious sect founded in England during the seventeenth-century revolution and later widespread in North America. They rejected the Established Church with its rites, preached pacifist ideas and were noted for simple living.   p. 54

72 See Note 69.   p. 54

73 In 1844, Parliament passed an Act for the regulation of railways, which placed railway companies under government control, and an Act for the registration, incorporation and regulation of joint-stock companies, which made railway projects liable to registration by the Railway Department of the Board of Trade and endorsement by Parliament. The Acts intensified competition among railway companies, causing a veritable "railway mania", with the number of projects more than trebling within a short time. To complete the drawings on time, companies lured away draftsmen and lithographers from each other, imported them by the hundred and made them work practically round the clock. Special clerks spied on rival companies and interfered with the delivery of their documents, hiring away and hiding horses and denying the competitors

railway carriage. On the last day of registration, November 30, 1845, hundreds of clerks besieged the Railway Department of the Board of Trade, even throwing documents in through the windows. As a result, more than 600 projects had been deposited by midday, when registration ceased.   p. 55

[74] Here Marx has "16,200,711", the error occurs in *The Economist,* from which Marx reproduced this table.   p. 58

[75] Marx means the attitude of the British government to the 1859-60 bourgeois revolution in Italy, which culminated in the establishment of a single Italian state. Worried by Napoleon III's hegemonic ambitions in Europe, Britain's ruling circles favoured Italian unity under the aegis of the Sardinian dynasty.
    p. 59

[76] See Note 73.   p. 59

[77] The *Société générale du Crédit Mobilier*—a big French joint-stock bank founded by the Péreire brothers in 1852. It was closely associated with Napoleon III's government and, under the latter's protection, engaged in large-scale speculation. It went bankrupt in 1867 and was liquidated in 1871 (see Marx's articles on *Crédit Mobilier* in Vol. 15 of the present edition).   p. 61

[78] First published in English in: Karl Marx and Frederick Engels, *The Civil War in the United States,* New York, 1937, London, 1937, pp. 88-91.   p. 62

[79] The *City*—the central part of London. Leading banks and industrial, commercial, transport and insurance companies have their offices there. It is a synonym for the British financial oligarchy.   p. 63

[80] An allusion to the coup d'état of December 2, 1851, which established the Second Empire in France.   p. 63

[81] See Note 75.   p. 64

[82] At the battle of *Waterloo* (June 18, 1815) the British and Prussian forces defeated the army of Napoleonic France.   p. 64

[83] *Albion*—the traditional name of the British Isles (without Ireland) since antiquity. The phrase "perfide Angleterre" (perfidious England) was coined by Bishop J.-B. Bossuet, the famous French theologian, who used it in a sermon in 1652. Napoleon quoted it when being taken into exile from Britain to St. Helena.
    p. 64

[84] See Note 23.   p. 65

[85] First published in English in: Karl Marx and Frederick Engels, *The Civil War in the United States,* New York, 1937, London, 1937, pp. 92-97.   p. 66

[86] After France had incorporated Savoy and Nice as a result of the 1859 Austro-Italo-French war (see Note 303) Napoleon III made an attempt to seize a section of Swiss territory. On October 28, 1861 a French detachment invaded the Dapp valley in Vaud Canton and occupied the village of Cressonière. The Swiss government lodged a protest, which was supported by several European powers. Under an agreement signed in December 1862, part of the Dapp valley was ceded to France in exchange for an equal section of French territory.
    p. 66

[87] See Note 38.   p. 66

[88] On October 31, 1861, the three powers concluded a convention on joint action against Mexico to overthrow the progressive Juárez government and turn the

Mexican republic into a colony of European powers. The pretext for this move was an Act of the Mexican Congress of July 17, 1861 suspending for two years the payment of interest on the country's foreign debt. The Palmerston government undertook to organise a punitive expedition.   p. 67

89 In November 1859 Spain, which was looking for colonies in Northern Africa, declared war on Morocco. The hostilities lasted until March 1860, bringing little success to the Spanish forces, which encountered stiff resistance from the freedom-loving Moroccans. Under the peace signed in April 1860 Spain received a monetary contribution and minor territorial concessions.

St. Domingo, the eastern part of the island of Hispaniola (Haiti), a Spanish colony until 1821, proclaimed the independent Dominican Republic in 1844; was re-annexed by Spain after the pro-Spanish party gained the upper hand in St. Domingo and, in March 1861, proclaimed the country's "voluntary" incorporation in Spain's West Indian possessions. The Spaniards were finally driven from the country in 1865.   p. 67

90 Marx means the British government. St. James's Palace in London used to be a royal residence.   p. 67

91 The *Holy Alliance*—an association of European monarchs formed in 1815 to suppress revolutionary movements and preserve feudal monarchies in European countries. Their famous declaration laid down that the monarchs would "on all occasions and in all places, lend each other aid and assistance", while "regarding themselves towards their subjects and armies as fathers of families" (Art. I).   p. 69

92 In 1823, French Foreign Minister Chateaubriand attempted to organise an armed intervention against a number of Latin American countries with a view to restoring Spain's colonial domination there and expanding France's colonial possessions. The Spanish colonies were to become autonomous kingdoms ruled by Bourbon princes, including members of the French line. The plan failed mainly because of opposition from Britain and the USA, both of which sought to exploit the national liberation movement in the Spanish colonies in order to establish their influence there.   p. 69

93 The *Monroe Doctrine*—a set of principles proclaimed by US President James Monroe in his message to Congress on December 2, 1823. Originally intended to prevent a restoration of Spanish colonial rule in Latin America in connection with the threat of intervention by the Holy Alliance, the message described interference by European powers in the affairs of any state in the Western Hemisphere as "a manifestation of an unfriendly disposition toward the United States". Later the Monroe Doctrine was used to justify US striving for hegemony on the American continent.   p. 69

94 See Note 91.   p. 74

95 See Note 92.   p. 77

96 This refers to the first *Anglo-Afghan war* (1838-42), in which Britain sought to establish its colonial rule in Afghanistan. Both invasions of British troops, in 1838 and 1842, failed.

On the *forged papers* see Note 33.   p. 78

97 The immediate occasion of the Anglo-Persian war of 1856-57 was an attempt by Persia's rulers, in October 1856, to capture the Herat principality. The British government exploited it as an excuse for launching an armed

intervention against Afghanistan and Persia to establish its domination in that region. It declared war on Persia and sent troops to Herat, but the national liberation uprising in India (1857-59) compelled Britain to seek an accommodation with Persia. Under the peace treaty signed in Paris in March 1857, Persia renounced its claims to Herat.   p. 78

98 This article, date-lined Paris, was written by Marx in London.   p. 79

99 The *Physiocratic school*—a trend in bourgeois classical political economy that emerged in France in the 1750s. The Physiocrats held Nature to be the only source of wealth, and agriculture the only sphere of the economy where value was created. Although they underestimated the role of industry and commerce, the Physiocrats rendered an important service by shifting the search for the origins of surplus-value from the sphere of circulation to that of production, thereby laying the basis for the analysis of capitalist production. Advocates of large-scale capitalist farming, they showed the moribund nature of the feudal economy and thus contributed to the ideological preparation of the bourgeois revolution in France. Marx gave a critical analysis of the Physiocrats' views in the second chapter of the *Theories of Surplus-Value* (see Vol. 34 of this edition).
                                          p. 80

100 The *dynastic opposition*—the group of Odilon Barrot in the French Chamber of Deputies during the July monarchy (1830-48). It spoke for the liberal industrial and commercial bourgeoisie, which favoured moderate electoral reform as a means of preventing revolution and preserving the Orleans dynasty.   p. 80

101 *Applaudite, amici!* (Applaud, friends!)—with these words actors in ancient Rome concluded their performances.   p. 81

102 *Drapeau blanc* (white flag)—France's national flag under the Bourbon monarchy (up to 1792) and during the Restoration period (1816-30). During the bourgeois revolution and the reign of Napoleon I (1792-1815), blue, white and red were France's colours. They were re-adopted in 1830 after the enthronement of the Orléans dynasty (the bourgeois July monarchy). p. 84

103 Marx's article was published in the Foreign News column under the heading "America. (The Dismissal of Frémont). Our London Correspondent writes".
      The article was first published in English in: Karl Marx and Frederick Engels, *The Civil War in the United States*, New York, 1937, London, 1937, pp. 97-100.   p. 86

104 This refers to the United States' 1846-48 war against Mexico. It was provoked by the slaveholding planters and big bourgeoisie for expansionist ends. As a result of the war, the US appropriated almost half of Mexico's territory, including Texas, Upper California and New Mexico. Frémont, who had been exploring California from the early 1840s, joined in the fighting with his team.
                                          p. 86

105 On the battle of *Bull Run* see Note 44.
      The battle of *Ball's Bluff* (northwest of Washington) was fought on October 21, 1861. The Southern forces defeated several regiments commanded by General Stone which had crossed to the right bank of the Potomac and were left without reinforcements.
      The two battles revealed serious shortcomings in the organisation and tactics of the Northern army.   p. 88

106 First published in English in: Karl Marx and Frederick Engels, *The Civil War in the United States*, New York, 1937, London, 1937, pp. 100-05.   p. 89

107 The Anglo-US war, started in 1812, was caused by Britain's refusal to recognise the United States' sovereignty and by its attempts to re-establish its domination in North America. The US was provoked to declare war on Britain by the latter's unlawful seizures of US ships and seamen. The American armed forces had the support of the people, who saw Britain poised to restore the colonial system, and regarded this struggle as another war of independence. The land fighting in 1812-14 developed unfavourably to the Americans. Their naval operations were somewhat more successful. Considerable damage was caused to the British by the numerous US privateers. The US was also benefiting by Britain's involvement in the war against Napoleonic France. Despite the temporary capture of Washington in August 1814, Britain was forced, in December of that year, to conclude the Ghent peace treaty predicated on recognition of the prewar state of affairs. News of the peace reached the troops with considerable delay. Meanwhile they continued to fight. The hostilities ceased in January 1815, after the US forces had inflicted a devastating defeat on the British at New Orleans.   p. 90

108 This refers to France's wars against the various European coalitions between 1792 and 1815, when Britain and France were involved in a bitter struggle for political and economic supremacy in Europe. In retaliation against Napoleon's Continental System (1806) which prohibited European countries from trading with Britain, the latter imposed its control over the maritime trade of the neutral states. Britain also had recourse to contraband trade and made a practice of seizing the ships of France and other countries on the high seas.   p. 91

109 *Duns Scotus controversy*—a method of pleading a case in scholastic disputes by juxtaposing a series of contradictory arguments ("pro et contra") which was widely applied by the mediaeval Scottish Nominalist philosopher Duns Scotus.   p. 91

110 Marx's article was preceded by the following editorial note: "If added proof were needed that no one would be more delighted by the *Trent* case erupting in a large-scale Anglo-American naval war than the Paris Cabinet, it is provided by the attitude of the official and semi-official Paris press. No sooner had the *Patrie* triumphantly informed its readers that the population of the Northern states was demonstrating in favour of vigorous opposition to any English demand for satisfaction, than it was able to report no less bellicose actions from London. It writes, in particular, that a council of ministers held in London on November 30 decided to recognise the Southern states and accredit a chargé d'affaires with President Jefferson Davis, if the message Lord Lyons intended to hand to the Cabinet in Washington met with an unfavourable reception. The *Patrie* is not alone in doing its utmost to foment trouble. The *Moniteur* is acting in a similar fashion. It carries the following report from Southampton: 'It is held in Southampton that this event could have the direst consequences, which is also the view held generally. There is a great deal of sympathy for the Southern states in England, and this incident cannot fail to increase further the number of their supporters.'

"So far there are no positive indications whatever as to how the French government intends to exploit the war that may arise between England and the American Union. But the Job's messages circulated from Paris at any rate prove that such a war would be most welcome to, and is indeed desired by, the Tuileries. France's attitude is a sign to the Cabinet of Saint James's and one can hardly assume that the latter is unaware of it. Significantly, too, with the exception of the *Morning Post,* the London press, particularly *The Times,* takes a very moderate and cautious stand. Our *London* correspondent, who is well informed about the state of Anglo-American relations, has sent us an article dated November 29 which makes the *Trent* case appear far less dangerous to world peace than one was bound to assume on the basis of the first dispatches from London and the statements of *Morning Post* and the semi-official Paris papers. To begin with, our London correspondent throws light on the *verdict of the law officers of the Crown.* He denies that in forcibly arresting Messrs Mason, Slidell and Co. the *San Jacinto* was, in any way, acting on the instructions of the Washington Cabinet, and brings the much discussed Liverpool indignation meeting down to its true significance. But let our correspondent speak for himself. He writes:".

The article was first published in English in: Karl Marx and Frederick Engels, *The Civil War in the United States,* New York, 1937, London, 1937, pp. 105-10.   p. 92

111 *Prize courts* are set up by belligerent countries in their ports to adjudge upon prizes, i.e. merchant ships and cargoes seized from the enemy and neutral countries. A special feature of prize jurisdiction is that the ruling is handed down by a court of the state that has captured the prize. Its principle is that the prize belongs to that state, unless the owners of ship and cargo can prove that the seizure was incorrect.   p. 93

112 *Lloyd's* is an insurance and shipping intelligence centre in London set up in the late 17th century by Edward Lloyd, the owner of a coffee-house where marine insurance deals were made.   p. 95

113 See Note 38.   p. 96

114 The *Baltic* (the Baltic Mercantile and Shipping Exchange, Limited)—an international freight and commodity market, so named after the mid-18th-century Baltic Coffee-House, which was frequented by merchants trading with Baltic ports.   p. 96

115 The *law of decisions, applied in Britain and some other countries,* regards legal precedent as a source of justice. This principle underlies the entire judicial system of the Anglo-Saxon countries.

The decision handed down by a court on a previous case is taken as an authoritative ruling in similar or analogous cases by courts of the same or lower instance.   p. 97

116 The *Temple*—two buildings, or ranges of buildings, occupied by two of the four inns of court in London (Inner Temple and Middle Temple), on the site of a monastic establishment of the Knights Templars.   p. 99

117 First published in English in: Karl Marx and Frederick Engels, *The Civil War in the United States,* New York, 1937, London, 1937, pp. 110-13.   p. 101

118 John Wilkes, whom Marx describes as a demagogue (i.e. a leader of a popular faction), was an English radical politician and journalist. In 1763, in his paper, *The North Briton,* he criticised King George III's speech from the throne, for which he was deprived of his seat in the House of Commons and outlawed. Forced to flee to France, he returned in 1768 and was four times elected to Parliament, but each time the Commons refused to recognise the vote. He was only admitted after his fifth election. Wilkes opposed the war against the North American colonies.

The Wilkes case was publicised in a series of letters that appeared between

1769 and 1772 in *The Public Advertiser* over the signature of Junius. The author, later established to be Sir Philip Francis, advocated Wilkes' rehabilitation and the democratisation of Britain's political system. In 1772 the letters appeared in book form.   p. 101

[119] At the battle of Worcester on September 3, 1651 the English troops under Cromwell inflicted a crushing defeat on the Scottish royalist army under Charles II, after which the latter fled to France. The Republicans' victory at Worcester removed the threat of a Stuart restoration for several years.

p. 102

[120] The *Privy Council* originated in England in the 13th century and initially consisted of members of the feudal nobility and higher clergy. As the King's highest consultative body, it played an important part in governing the state until the 17th century. As Parliament and the Cabinet established their ascendancy, the Privy Council's power declined, although formally it remains the supreme royal government body.   p. 102

[121] In November 1845 Slidell was sent by President James Knox Polk to Mexico to negotiate the purchase by the US of New Mexico and Upper California. After the Mexican government's refusal to receive Slidell as a Minister Plenipotentiary, the United States opened hostilities against Mexico (in April 1846) and captured the two territories.   p. 103

[122] See Note 54.   p. 103

[123] See Note 18.   p. 103

[124] On the eve of the Civil War, the pro-Southern members of Buchanan's administration abused their powers to strengthen the South and weaken the North. Secretary of the Treasury Cobb helped the secessionists (see Note 2) with money and credits. Secretary of War Floyd had weapons and equipment shipped from Northern forts and arsenals to the South, financed the arming of the Southern militia with Congressional funds and transferred pro-Northern officers to remote garrisons. Secretary of the Navy Toucey placed a large number of warships at the disposal of the Southerners, and Secretary of the Interior Thompson took the plotters under his wing.   p. 103

[125] *Die Presse* published this article with the following editorial introduction:
"The Anglo-American quarrel has plunged the European business world, as well as the public at large, into a state of frantic agitation. There is a premonition of the dangers, of the crises and catastrophes, that an armed clash between the world's two biggest commercial and industrial nations, the two nations with the greatest business experience, would bring with it, a feeling bordering on certainty that Britain's power, tied up in a transatlantic conflict, would cease to be a pillar, a guarantee of European peace, that Italy would succumb entirely to the disastrous influence, indeed the sway, of Napoleon's policy, and that the tragic duel between Faust and Valentine, who wields the sword for Mephistopheles, would be resumed, though without the certainty that Valentine would be defeated this time. The whole of Britain is clamouring about the infringement perpetrated by the Americans, and international law, the treaties, are looming large in the English papers just now. But even granted that an infringement did take place, which is by no means an established fact, must it lead to war, as almost the whole of Britain maintains? Is there no possibility of a compromise, no milder method of releasing Messrs Mason, etc.,

as demanded by Britain? Let us hope that a way out will be found. Even in Britain, the mediation party is already raising its voice; in the United States, the captain of the *San Jacinto* declares that he was acting entirely on his own responsibility when he arrested the *Trent* passengers, and as regards the message John Russell sent to Washington, we hear that it is almost begging the Washington Cabinet to display flexibility. Lastly, opinions are divided in the Ministries of London and Washington, and for all the sabre-rattling, we still believe that, unless Palmerston wants war at any price, unless he had already decided on war even before the *Trent* incident, the chances of a peaceful solution outweigh the danger of war.

"The emphasis now placed in Britain on the legal aspect impels the *Wiener Zeitung* today to draw a conclusion which suggests itself to any reader of the Palmerston papers. 'Is it not like an old fairy-tale,' the *Wiener Zeitung* says, 'when we hear people in Britain today talking of the binding principles of international law, of existing treaties, of positive Constitutional law, indeed of the word and letter of this or that stipulation which have to be upheld even with the sword! Formal right in its most immediate sense, defined by the nation's leading legal authorities, is being invoked; we can expect a reply formulated in similar terms. All of England is a party in this great lawsuit. It swears by its own good right and is prepared to avenge the infringement of that right, to stake its power and its blood for it; England appeals to the world and to history to back it with their verdict in the battle to uphold that right! With what feelings these enthusiasts of justice must have received the news from Turin that Rome has to be taken because it is essential for maintaining control over the Kingdom of the Two Sicilies, and that Venetia will be invaded as soon as the army has been brought up to 300,000 men!!"

"But is it really an established fact that international law, the letter of treaties and formal right are on Britain's side in the *Trent* affair? Weighty voices contest this view, and from our *London* correspondent we have received a communication today which exhaustively answers the above question."

The article was first published in English in: Karl Marx and Frederick Engels, *The Civil War in the United States*, New York, 1937, London, 1937, pp. 113-20.   p. 105

126 *"Last of the Englishmen"*—paraphrase of the expression "last of the Romans" (Ultimus Romanorum), the traditional description of Brutus and Cassius, who conspired against Caesar and remained loyal to the ideals of early republican Rome at a time when the Roman Republic was in decline.   p. 108

127 *Ghent peace*—see Note 107.

In 1842, Lord Ashburton and Daniel Webster conducted talks on behalf of Britain and the United States, which ended in the signing, on August 9, of a treaty laying down the frontier between the US and Britain's possessions in America, banning the slave trade and providing for the extradition of criminals. However, it contained no stipulation entitling Britain to search US ships suspected of slave trafficking.   p. 112

128 On December 6, 1861 *The Times* carried a letter on the *Trent* incident by the US General Winfield Scott. He urged a peaceful settlement of the conflict, saying the US wanted no war with Britain.

Downing Street—the official residence of the Prime Minister of Britain.

p. 114

129 First published in English in: *Political Affairs,* New York, 1959, No. 2, pp. 17-18.   p. 115

130 *Black contraband* was, during the US Civil War, a designation for runaway slaves seeking refuge at Northern army camps. Contrary to the instructions of the Washington administration, some Northern generals refused, even in the early months of the war, to hand such Blacks over to their former masters on the grounds that, being the property of rebels, they must be regarded as military contraband. In the autumn of 1861 there was a massive influx of fugitive slaves at Fort Monroe, Louisiana. General Wool used the able-bodied Blacks as free labourers and withheld part of their earnings to support disabled and sick Blacks.   p. 116

131 The *Democratic* or *Albany regency*—the leading group of the Democratic Party in New York State. With its headquarters in Albany, the capital of New York State, it existed until 1854 and was the unofficial governing body of the US Democratic Party (see also Note 13).   p. 116

132 On November 19, 1861 the *Nashville,* a Confederate privateer, attacked the Unionist merchant ship *Harvey Birch,* arrested her crew, seized her cargo and burnt the ship. On November 21, the *Nashville,* with the consent of the British authorities, took cover in the port of Southampton. She was overtaken there by the Unionist cruiser *Tuscarora,* which was watching the movements of pirate ships. Not wishing to be accused of a breach of neutrality, the British authorities on February 3, 1862 ordered both ships to leave port, but detained the *Tuscarora* for 24 hours to enable the *Nashville* to escape.   p. 117

133 At the beginning of January 1861, Fernando Wood, Mayor of New York City, proposed that in the event of disunion New York should constitute itself a free city and retain commerce with both sections.   p. 117

134 *Empire City* was a popular name for New York, the largest city in the Union. New York State, then the most populous, richest and politically most powerful State of the USA, was called the *Empire State.*   p. 118

135 During the debate on the Kansas-Nebraska Bill, May 19 and 20, 1856 (see Note 15) the Republican Senator Charles Sumner made a speech ("The Crime against Kansas") exposing the slave-owners' schemes in Kansas and deriding the pro-slavery posture of Senator A. R. Butler of South Carolina. On May 22, the latter's nephew, slave-owning Congressman P. S. Brooks, attacked Sumner in the Senate, causing him serious bodily harm. It was only in 1859 that Sumner was able to return to politics.   p. 118

136 The *Cooper Union*—a higher educational establishment in New York, founded in 1859 by the philanthropist Peter Cooper, a manufacturer and inventor.
                                                                           p. 118

137 From 1849 to 1861, the Dominican Republic (in the West Indian island of Hispaniola, or Haiti), which had freed itself from Spanish domination in 1821, was, owing to a succession of coups d'état, alternately governed by a pro-Spanish party and one favouring union with the neighbouring state of Haiti. Spain re-annexed the republic at the invitation of President P. Santa Ana in 1861, but had to withdraw its troops in 1865, following an anti-Spanish uprising.   p. 119

138 The *Court of Exchequer,* one of England's oldest courts, initially dealt mainly with financial matters. In the 19th century it became one of the country's

highest judicial bodies. In 1875 the Court of Exchequer was merged in the High Court of Judicature.   p. 120

[139] The *Lord Chief Baron* was one of the *Barons of the Exchequer*, the six judges to whom the administration of justice was committed. The title became obsolete in 1875 when the Court of Exchequer was merged in the High Court of Judicature.
                                                                    p. 123

[140] First published in English in: Karl Marx and Frederick Engels, *The Civil War in the United States*, New York, 1937, London, 1937, pp. 120-23.   p. 124

[141] Marx refers to the *Déclaration réglant divers points de droit maritime, signée ... à Paris, le 14 avril 1856,* which banned privateering and safeguarded the merchant shipping of neutral states against attack by the belligerents.
                                                                    p. 124

[142] The principles of *armed neutrality* were first formulated in a declaration by Catherine II of February 28 (March 11), 1780, during the War of American Independence. It proclaimed the right of neutral states to carry on trade with belligerent ones and the inviolability of enemy property (except war contraband) that was under a neutral flag. The declaration, supported by Austria, Denmark, Holland, the Kingdom of the Two Sicilies, Portugal, Prussia and Sweden, provided the basis for the first Armed Neutrality (1780-83).

In 1800, when Britain was at war with Napoleonic France, the second Armed Neutrality was formed by Denmark, Prussia, Russia and Sweden.
                                                                    p. 124

[143] The *Manchester School*—a trend in political economy reflecting the interests of the industrial bourgeoisie. It favoured free trade and non-interference by the state in the economy. The Free Traders' stronghold was Manchester, where the movement was led by textile manufacturers Richard Cobden and John Bright. In the early 1860s the Free Traders joined the Liberal Party. Speaking for the industrial bourgeoisie that strove to end the cotton monopoly of the Southern slave states, they opposed Britain's intervention in the US Civil War on the side of the South.   p. 125

[144] First published in English in: Karl Marx and Frederick Engels, *The Civil War in the United States,* New York, 1937, London, 1937, pp. 123-27.   p. 127

[145] Marx uses the term ironically. The *Pietists* were adherents of a mystical Lutheran trend that arose in Germany in the 17th century. It placed religious feeling above dogma and was opposed to the rationalist philosophy of the Enlightenment. Nineteenth-century pietism was distinguished by extreme mysticism and hypocrisy.   p. 128

[146] *"Truly English minister"*—an ironic reference to Lord Palmerston based on a passage from Lord Russell's speech in the House of Commons on June 20, 1850. Referring to Palmerston, he said: "So long as we continue the government of this country, I can answer for my noble friend that he will act not as the Minister ... of any other country, but as the Minister of England." On June 25, 1850, Palmerston, then Foreign Secretary, addressing the Commons, quoted the Latin phrase "civis romanus sum" ("I am a Roman citizen") saying that just as this formula ensured general respect and prestige to the citizens of ancient Rome, so British citizenship should guarantee the personal security and property of British subjects everywhere. The British bourgeoisie enthusiastically applauded this statement.   .   .   p. 128

147 *Low Churchmen*—members of the Church of England who assigned a low place to the episcopate and priesthood and to matters of ecclesiastical organisation.

p. 128

148 The *Whig war*—the Crimean war (1853-56) which was started by the Aberdeen Coalition Cabinet (see Note 31).

p. 129

149 *Penny paper*—a new type of cheap, mass-circulation daily that emerged in Britain after the lifting of the Stamp Tax (see Note 29) in 1855. The penny papers mainly carried sensational news and scandal.

p. 129

150 An allusion to the war-mongering campaign launched by Napoleon III in January 1859 in connection with the preparations for the Austro-Italo-French war. Marx and Engels described these events in detail in their articles "The War Prospect in Europe", "The Money Panic in Europe" and "Louis Napoleon's Position" (see present edition, Vol. 16, pp. 154-57, 162-70).

p. 130

151 First published in English in: Karl Marx and Frederick Engels, *The Civil War in the United States*, New York, 1937, London, 1937, pp. 128-30.

p. 131

152 See Note 107.

p. 132

153 First published in English in: Karl Marx and Frederick Engels, *The Civil War in the United States*, New York, 1937, London, 1937, pp. 130-33.

p. 134

154 The "peace party" means the Free Traders or the Manchester School (see Note 143).

p. 135

155 An allusion to Palmerston who, taking advantage of the Italian revolutionary Orsini's attempt on the life of Napoleon III, tabled a Conspiracy Bill in Parliament in February 1858 to facilitate the extradition of political refugees living in Britain. The Bill was voted down and the Palmerston Cabinet was forced to resign.

p. 135

156 This refers to an incident during the Anglo-French-Chinese war (the second Opium War) of 1856-60. In June 1859 a British squadron, reinforced by one US and two French warships, attempted to seize the Dagha fortifications on the Peiho River. The attempt was repulsed, the attackers suffering heavy losses.

p. 136

157 On December 26, 1861 the US government decided to release Mason and Slidell, the Confederate emissaries arrested on board the steamer *Trent*. In early January 1862, Mason, Slidell and their secretaries were brought to an English steamer. When informed of this, Russell declared that the British government was satisfied and considered the *Trent* incident closed.

p. 137

158 See Note 108.

p. 138

159 See Note 132.

p. 139

160 During his stay in London in 1850, Julius Haynau, an Austrian marshal notorious for his cruel repressive measures against participants in the revolutionary movement in Hungary and Italy, visited the brewery of Barclay, Perkins & Co., was physically attacked by its indignant workers and was forced to flee. The workers' action was warmly approved by the people of London.

p. 140

161 *Order in Council*—in Great Britain, an order issued by the sovereign on the advice of the Privy Council (on the latter see Note 120).

p. 141

[162] First published in English in: Karl Marx and Frederick Engels, *The Civil War in the United States*, New York, 1937, London, 1937, pp. 134-36.   p. 143

[163] The suppression of Seward's message is here compared to the tendentious selection of documents in the Blue Book on Persia and Afghanistan published in 1839, when Palmerston was Foreign Secretary (see Note 33). On the Afghan war see Note 96.   p. 144

[164] First published in English in: Karl Marx and Frederick Engels, *The Civil War in the United States*, New York, 1937, London, 1937, pp. 136-39.   p. 145

[165] See Note 38.   p. 147

[166] See Note 143.   p. 147

[167] See Note 73.   p. 149

[168] First published in English in: Karl Marx and Frederick Engels, *The Civil War in the United States*, New York, 1937, London, 1937, pp. 139-43.   p. 153

[169] *Anti-Jacobin war*—see Note 108.
Catholic Emancipation—see Note 29.
Reform Bill (Act)—see Note 29.
Corn Laws—see Note 29.
The *Ten Hours' Bill*, limiting the working day for women and children to ten hours, was passed by the British Parliament on June 8, 1847.
The *war against Russia*—the Crimean war (1853-56).
Conspiracy Bill—see Note 155.   p. 153

[170] See Note 23.   p. 154

[171] The *knife-and-fork question* was a plank of the social programme of Chartism. It was first put forward as a slogan by J. R. Stephens in his speech at a Chartist meeting in Kersall Moor, near Manchester, on September 24, 1838 (published in *The Northern Star*, No. 46, September 29, 1838).
The *People's Charter*, which contained the Chartists' demands, was published in the form of a Parliamentary Bill on May 8, 1838. It contained six points: universal suffrage (for men of 21 and over), annual parliaments, vote by ballot, equal electoral districts, abolition of the property qualification for MPs, and payment of MPs. Petitions urging the adoption of the People's Charter were turned down by Parliament in 1839, 1842 and 1848.   p. 154

[172] See Note 69.   p. 155

[173] First published in English in: Karl Marx and Frederick Engels, *The Civil War in the United States*, New York, 1937, London, 1937, pp. 144-47.   p. 157

[174] See Notes 107, 108, 127.   p. 157

[175] First published in English in: Karl Marx and Frederick Engels, *The Civil War in the United States*, New York, 1937, London, 1937, pp. 147-50.   p. 160

[176] See Note 23.   p. 161

[177] The British East India Company, founded in 1600, enjoyed monopoly rights in trade with India, China and other Asian countries for a long time. In India, it also maintained an army and performed administrative functions. It was one of the principal initiators of colonial expansion and oppression. After the 1857-59 popular insurrection in India the British government changed the form of colonial administration. In 1858 the East India Company was liquidated and the administration of India was transferred to the Crown.   p. 162

178 The *Anglo-French commercial treaty,* concluded in January 1860, envisaged the reduction and partial lifting of tariffs for British and French goods. Under the March 1860 Turin treaty, the Kingdom of Sardinia ceded *Savoy and Nice* to Napoleon III in compensation for France's help in freeing Italy from Austrian rule.   p. 162

179 *Die Presse* published this article, marked "From Our London Correspondent", in the Feuilleton section. Max Friedlander had asked Marx to write for this section, too, in his letter of January 7, 1862.   p. 163

180 First published in English in: Karl Marx and Frederick Engels, *The Civil War in the United States,* New York, 1937, London, 1937, pp. 150-55.   p. 167

181 *Magna Charta Libertatum*—the charter signed by King John of England on June 15, 1215 under pressure from his insurgent barons supported by knights and townspeople. It restricted the king's rights, mostly to the benefit of the barons, and contained certain concessions to the knights and towns. Even in the 19th century, the British bourgeoisie regarded it as the mainstay of the Constitutional system.   p. 168

182 This refers to the *Déclaration réglant divers points de droit maritime* (see Note 141).
                                                                              p. 169

183 On the intervention in Mexico see Note 88.   p. 169

184 Under the peace treaty concluded after the 1859-60 Spanish-Moroccan war (see Note 89) the town of Tetuan was to remain under Spanish occupation until Morocco had paid out the entire contribution imposed by Spain.   p. 170

185 The last article by Marx to be published in the *New-York Daily Tribune.* Engels' last contribution to the *Tribune*—an article on the progress of the US Civil War written on about March 7, 1862 at Marx's request (see Note 194)—was not published by that newspaper.   p. 172

186 An allusion to the debates on the *Trent* incident in the British Parliament and in the press (see this volume, pp. 89-114, 127-48).   p. 177

187 First published in English in: Karl Marx and Frederick Engels, *The Civil War in the United States,* New York, 1937, London, 1937, pp. 155-60.   p. 178

188 "The young Napoleon" was the name given to George McClellan by his Democratic supporters. McClellan was the first American general to become commander-in-chief at the early age of 34.   p. 178

189 *Fabian tactics*—dilatory tactics, so named after the Roman general Fabius, surnamed Cunctator ("the Delayer"), who adopted this tactic against Hannibal in 217 B.C., during the Second Punic War.   p. 179

190 *West Point,* near New York, is the site of a United States Military Academy. Founded in 1802, it was the only higher military educational establishment in the US in the mid-19th century. The complete isolation of the cadets from the external world fostered elitist and caste tendencies within the officer corps.
                                                                              p. 179

191 On the battles of Manassas and Ball's Bluff, see Notes 44 and 105.   p. 180

192 First published in English in: Karl Marx and Frederick Engels, *The Civil War in the United States,* New York, 1937, London, 1937, pp. 160-64.   p. 182

193 See Note 141.   p. 185

[194] On March 7, 1862 Engels wrote the first part of an article on the progress of the US Civil War for the *New-York Daily Tribune* at Marx's request. It is possible that on March 18 he wrote the second, concluding part (see Marx's letters to Engels of March 3 and 15, and Engels's letters to Marx of March 5 and 8, 1862 in Vol. 41 of this edition). However, the *Tribune* did not publish this article (see Note 185). Engels made use of the first part for his article "The War in America" published in *The Volunteer Journal, for Lancashire and Cheshire*, March 14, 1862 (see present edition, Vol. 18, pp. 530-34). The text intended for the *New-York Daily Tribune* was translated by Marx into German. He added more recent data and sent the text to *Die Presse*. In this volume the article is given according to *Die Presse*. The beginning and the end of the section published in *The Volunteer Journal* and included in this article are indicated in footnotes. The version from *Die Presse* was first published in English in: Karl Marx and Frederick Engels. *The Civil War in the United States*, New York, 1937, London, 1937, pp. 164-77. p. 186

[195] See Note 44. p. 187

[196] At *Jemappes* (November 6, 1792) and *Fleurus* (June 26, 1794) the French revolutionary army defeated the forces of the first coalition of European counter-revolutionary monarchies. At the battles of *Montenotte, Castiglione* and *Rivoli*, during the 1796-97 Italian campaign, the French army defeated the Austrian and Piedmontese forces. p. 187

[197] See Note 105. p. 189

[198] See Note 7. p. 192

[199] The *cordon system*, devised by the Austrian Field Marshal F. Lassy and broadly applied in Western Europe in the 18th century, called for the even distribution of the forces along the line of hostilities. p. 193

[200] At the battles of *Millesimo* and *Dego* (Northern Italy), fought between April 13 and 15, 1796, Bonaparte's army defeated an Austrian contingent attached to the Piedmontese troops, and an Austrian force sent to its relief. Following this, the French inflicted a series of defeats on the Piedmontese army, compelling the King of Piedmont to conclude a separate peace. p. 193

[201] This refers to the occupation of Paris by the troops of the Sixth Coalition (Britain, Prussia, Russia, Sweden and other states) on March 31, 1814 and the deposition of Napoleon I on April 2, 1814. p. 193

[202] A reference to Russia's war of liberation against Napoleonic France's aggression in 1812. p. 194

[203] An ironic allusion to the trial in Paris during summer 1861 of the eminent banker Jules Isaak Mirès, who was accused of fraudulent stock exchange practices. The trial revealed the complicity of high-ranking officials of the Second Empire in scandalous financial machinations.

The article was first published in English in: Karl Marx and Frederick Engels, *The Civil War in the United States*, New York, 1937, London, 1937, pp. 177-79. p. 196

[204] See Note 88. p. 196

[205] Marx means the occupation of Rome by French troops in July 1849, which continued until 1870, and the stationing of French troops in Athens and

Constantinople during the Crimean war (1853-56). In October 1860, British and French troops occupied Peking.   p. 196

206 During the second Opium War (1856-60) unleashed by Britain and France to impose crippling new terms on China, the British and French interventionist forces under General Montauban in October 1860 seized Peking, the Chinese capital, and plundered and burnt down Yüanmingyüan, the famous summer residence of the Ch'ing emperors, the greatest treasure-house of Chinese art. The plundered property was valued at tens of millions of francs. An incalculable number of valuables were barbarously destroyed.   p. 196

207 On July 17, 1861 the Mexican Congress decreed a two-year suspension of payments on foreign debts, which was exploited by Britain, France and Spain as a pretext for launching an intervention in Mexico (see Note 88). To avoid war, the Mexican government of Benito Pablo Juárez in November 1861 repealed the July 17 decree and agreed to satisfy the claims of the three powers.   p. 196

208 The conference of British, French and Spanish representatives in Orizaba, Mexico, held on April 9, 1862, was to outline a plan for the three interventionist powers' further action in Mexico. However, serious disagreements came to light, with the French representative refusing to negotiate with the Mexican government and declaring the preliminary peace treaty, concluded in La Soledad on February 19, 1862, null and void. The British and Spanish representatives declared that France was interfering in Mexico's internal affairs and their countries therefore refused to participate further in the intervention. Soon after the Orizaba conference, the British and Spanish troops were withdrawn from Mexico.   p. 198

209 First published in English in: Karl Marx and Frederick Engels, *The Civil War in the United States*, New York, 1937, London, 1937, pp. 180-83.   p. 199

210 New Orleans was surrendered on April 29, 1862, shortly after the fall of the forts protecting the approaches to the city from the Mississippi. The Northern troops entered New Orleans on May 1.   p. 199

211 *Reuter, Havas, Wolff*—news agencies in Britain, France and Germany. p. 199

212 For the Anglo-US war of 1812-14 see Note 107.
    Saragossa achieved fame with its part in Spain's national liberation struggle against Napoleon's troops. It resisted a siege in 1808, and held out for two months against another one the following year, but fell on February 21, 1809.
    Moscow was the heart of the nationwide resistance in Russia to Napoleon's invasion in 1812. The battle fought on September 7 at Borodino, near Moscow, largely predetermined the collapse of Napoleon's aggressive plans.   p. 199

213 The *Crescent City*—New Orleans, so called because the older part of the city was built within a bend of the Mississippi.   p. 200

214 First published in English in: Karl Marx and Frederick Engels, *The Civil War in the United States*, New York, 1937, London, 1937, pp. 183-85.   p. 202

215 The Act to prohibit the importation of slaves into any port or place within the jurisdiction of the United States, which came into force on January 1, 1808 (see Note 58), did not ban the slave trade within the territory of the United States. This trade, carried on between the slave states of the South and Southwest, was mostly confined to the coastal cities of the South. The ban on the importation of slaves from without was accompanied by an expansion of the internal slave trade, with

the Southern states of Maryland, Virginia and North Carolina supplying large numbers of slaves for sale. p. 203

[216] First published in English in: Karl Marx and Frederick Engels, *The Civil War in the United States*, New York, 1937, London, 1937, pp. 185-90. p. 204

[217] See Note 44. p. 205

[218] This refers to the battles fought at *Smolensk*, August 16 to 18, and *Borodino*, September 7, 1812 in the course of Russia's liberation war against aggression by Napoleonic France. p. 207

[219] First published in English in: Karl Marx and Frederick Engels, *The Civil War in the United States*, New York, 1937, London, 1937, pp. 191-94. p. 209

[220] The Ionian Islands had been a British protectorate from 1815. The 1848-49 revolt of the islands' Greek population, to which Marx refers, aimed at union with Greece. It was brutally crushed by the British. p. 209

[221] *Ryots*—hereditary lessees of state-owned lands in India. Here Indian peasants. p. 209

[222] The various *Landlord and Tenant Bills* envisaging easier terms for the tenants, first submitted to the British Parliament in the 1850s, were stubbornly resisted by the big landowners. In 1860 a half-hearted *Landlord and Tenant Act* was adopted which failed to solve the problem. Marx discussed the Act in his articles "From the Houses of Parliament.— Bulwer's Motion.— The Irish Question" and "General Simpson's Resignation.— From Parliament" (see present edition, Vol. 14, pp. 340-43 and 470-71). p. 210

[223] *Saguntum* was a town in ancient Spain. Allied with Rome, it was attacked and seized after an eight-month siege by Hannibal's troops in 219 B.C. The people of the town rejected all proposals for surrender and immolated themselves. p. 210

[224] *Statute law*—a system of legal regulations based on the statutes, or Acts, of the British Parliament. p. 210

[225] In the wake of the Irish national liberation uprising of 1798 the British Parliament, on Castlereagh's initiative, passed a series of acts in 1801 placing Ireland in a state of siege and suspending the Habeas Corpus Act, under which persons under arrest had to be brought before a court and presented with formal charges. p. 210

[226] Shortly after the December 2, 1851 coup d'état in France Palmerston, then British Foreign Secretary, approved of Louis Bonaparte's usurpation of power in a conversation with the French Ambassador to London. He did so without previously notifying the Cabinet, which led to his resignation in December 1851, although in principle the British government took a view identical to Palmerston's and was the first in Europe to recognise the Bonapartist regime. p. 211

[227] *Zouaves* was the name given to some French infantry regiments originally recruited from among the Berber tribe of the Zouaves in Algeria. p. 211

[228] The article was published with the editorial superscription "Our London correspondent writes:". p. 213

[229] An allusion to the mania for spiritualist practices that swept Europe, especially Germany, in the early 1850s. p. 216

230 See Note 2. p. 216

231 In the early seventeenth century China was invaded by the Manchu tribes, which put the country under the rule of the Ch'ing dynasty (1644-1912). p. 216

232 The *Opium wars*—aggressive wars waged against China by Britain, 1840 to 1842, and by Britain and France, 1856 to 1860. p. 216

233 See Note 21. p. 221

234 First published in English in: Karl Marx and Frederick Engels, *The Civil War in the United States*, New York, 1937, London, 1937, pp. 195-98. p. 223

235 Marx means the *1856-57 Anglo-Persian war* (see Note 97). p. 225

236 In writing this article, in early August 1862, Marx drew on factual material contained in a letter to him by Engels of July 30, 1862. At the time, Marx and Engels differed to a degree in assessing the prospects of the US Civil War. Cf. the above-mentioned letter by Engels with Marx's letter to him of August 7, 1862 (present edition, Vol. 41).

The article was first published in English in: Karl Marx and Frederick Engels, *The Civil War in the United States*, New York, 1937, London, 1937, pp. 198-201. p. 226

237 See Note 54. p. 227

238 The *Homestead Act*, adopted by the Lincoln Administration under popular pressure, was one of the revolutionary measures that turned the scales in the US Civil War in favour of the North. It provided a democratic solution to the agrarian problem by making available, for the nominal charge of $10, 160 acres of state-owned land to every US citizen and every person declaring that he wanted to become one. The land became the farmer's property after five years of cultivation, or earlier, if he paid $1.25 per acre. p. 228

239 The Federal District of Columbia, comprising the US capital Washington and its environs, is an independent administrative unit. The abolition of slavery in the US capital had been one of the principal demands of the anti-slavery forces ever since the War of Independence (1775-83). The Act for the release of certain persons held to service or labour in the District of Columbia, passed on April 16, 1862, set free 3,000 Blacks, the government undertaking to pay $300 in compensation for every released slave to the former owner. p. 228

240 Under a law passed in Pennsylvania on March 1, 1780, all slaves born there after the passage of that law were to become free at the age of 28.
p. 228

241 *Liberia*—a West African republic formed in 1847 on the basis of settlements set up by the American Colonisation Society to encourage emigration of free Blacks from the United States.

Haiti—a state in the western part of Hispaniola (Haiti) Island, a republic since 1859.

The establishment, in June 1862, of diplomatic relations with the Black republics of Liberia and Haiti, which by then had been recognised by other states, was a victory for the Abolitionists. At the same time, the Act to authorise the President of the United States to appoint diplomatic representatives to the Republics of Haiti and Liberia, respectively, aimed at encouraging the emigration of Blacks from the United States to these countries. The establishment of colonies of free Blacks outside the US, a plank of Lincoln's programme, was emphatically opposed by revolutionary Abolitionists. p. 229

242 This article, except for the passage relating to Garibaldi (p. 232), was first published in English in: Karl Marx, *On America and the Civil War*, New York, 1972, pp. 213-14. p. 230

243 In a "Letter to the Bishop of Durham" published on November 4, 1850, Russell, then Prime Minister, attacked "Papal usurpation" in connection with a Bull of Pope Pius IX in which he claimed the right to appoint Catholic bishops and archbishops in England. For details see Marx's exposé "Lord John Russell" (present edition, Vol. 14, pp. 371-93).

In a message of October 27, 1860 to Sir James Hudson, British minister in Turin, Russell, who was Foreign Secretary at the time, condemned the attitude of Austria, France, Prussia and Russia and approved of Southern Italy's union with the Kingdom of Sardinia and of the policy of Victor Emmanuel II, who exploited the Italian people's revolutionary movement for his own dynastic ends. The message also said that peoples were entitled to depose their rulers, which was a sally against Napoleon III. p. 231

244 First published in English in: Karl Marx and Frederick Engels, *The Civil War in the United States*, New York, 1937, London, 1937, pp. 201-29. p. 233

245 See Note 69. p. 233

246 *Chambers of commerce*, in the USA, are regional associations of businessmen. The Chamber of Commerce of the State of New York, set up in 1768, is the oldest. p. 234

247 The *Whig party* in the USA (1834-54) spoke for the Northern bourgeoisie and the Southern planters economically linked with it. It opposed the strengthening of Federal power and favoured protective tariffs and industrial development in the South, as well as in the North. Whig candidates won twice at Presidential elections, in 1840 (William H. Harrison) and 1848 (Zachary Taylor). Composed of motley elements, the party disintegrated in the early 1850s, the Northern Whigs flocking to the new Republican Party (see Note 9) in 1854, and the "cotton Whigs" joining the pro-slavery Democratic Party .(see Note 13). p. 235

248 A reference to the *Seven Days' Battle* (June 25-July 1, 1862) fought on the approaches to Richmond, by the river Chickahominy whose marshy banks were unsuitable for military operations. It ended in the retreat of the Northern army commanded by McClellan. p. 235

249 This refers to events connected with Garibaldi's military campaign in July-August 1862 aimed at freeing Rome from Papal rule and French occupation (see also p. 232 of this volume). Under pressure from Napoleon III, the King of Italy, Victor Emmanuel II, sent troops against Garibaldi. On August 29 Garibaldi was seriously wounded in a skirmishing action near Aspromonte and taken prisoner. He was kept under arrest for a long time. The attack on Italy's national hero caused indignation in many countries, including Britain. p. 236

250 The 1494 Italian campaign of King Charles VIII of France ushered in a series of wars for possession of Italy and hegemony in Europe between France on the one hand and Spain and the Holy Roman Empire on the other. Fought mostly on Italian soil, these wars were brought to an end in 1559 by the peace of

Cateau-Cambrésis, where two treaties were concluded. France renounced its claims to Italian possessions. Spain's supremacy in the Italian peninsula was consolidated and Italy's political fragmentation hardened.   p. 236

251 According to Roman tradition, the patrician general Manlius Capitolinus was awakened at night by the cackling of the geese sacred to Juno just in time to repulse an attack on the Capitol by the Gauls. Later he sided with the plebeians against the patricians and was accused of seeking to establish a dictatorship. For the trial, a place was chosen from which no one could see the Capitol that Manlius had saved. He was sentenced to death and hurled down from the Tarpeian rock.   p. 236

252 An allusion to the February 1848 revolution in France.   p. 237

253 There were three *partitions of Poland* (1772, 1793 and 1795) by Prussia, tsarist Russia and Austria (which did not take part in the second one). As a result of the third partition the Polish state ceased to exist.   p. 237

254 *Praetorians*—a privileged section of the army in imperial Rome, originally the generals' guards; in a figurative sense, mercenary troops propping up a system of government based on brute force.   p. 237

255 This refers to the second Great Exhibition, held in London from May to November 1862.   p. 239

256 The article is based on data sent to Marx by Wilhelm Wolff from Manchester in a letter written between September 10 and 12, 1862. It reveals the demagogic nature of the 1861 political amnesty in Prussia (see Note 257) and was rather widely read in Germany. The article appeared in the *Barmer Zeitung* and was reprinted in the *Niederrheinische Volks-Zeitung* and the *Märkische Volks-Zeitung*.
                                                                              p. 243

257 In connection with the enthronement of King William I of Prussia, an amnesty was granted on January 12, 1861 ("Supreme Decree on Amnesty for Political Crimes and Transgressions, January 12, 1861", *Königlich-Preußischer Staats-Anzeiger,* January 13, 1861) guaranteeing all political refugees unhindered return to the domains of the Prussian state.   p. 243

258 This refers to the *Frankfurt Parliament* or the German Assembly, which opened in Frankfurt am Main on May 18, 1848. It was convened to unify the country and draw up a Constitution. The liberal deputies, who were in the majority, turned the Assembly into a virtual debating club. At the decisive moment of the revolution, the liberal majority condoned the counter-revolutionary forces. In spring 1849, the liberals left the Assembly after the Prussian and other governments had rejected the Imperial Constitution that it had drawn up. The remainder of the Assembly moved to Stuttgart and was dispersed by the Württemberg forces on June 18. Marx calls it the Rump by analogy with the remainder of the Long Parliament after it had been purged by Cromwell during the English Revolution of the 17th century.   p. 244

259 Marx means legal advisers on the staff of government bodies.   p. 244

260 An allusion to the resignation of Palmerston's Cabinet in February 1858 over the Commons' rejection of his Conspiracy Bill (see Note 155).   p. 246

261 This refers to the rise of the Chartist movement in the summer and autumn of 1842 in connection with the aggravation of the economic crisis in the spring of

that year. In early August 1842, workers downed tools at a firm in Staleybridge, near Manchester, the strike soon spreading to the country's main industrial areas. The workers' initial demands were economic, but the strike rapidly grew into a political struggle for the Charter. It was only by bringing in the army that the ruling classes were able to quash the strike. Government repressions followed, and the Chartist movement subsided for a time. A slight improvement of business was a contributing factor. These events were described in detail by Engels in *The Condition of the Working-Class in England* (present edition, Vol. 4, pp. 520-23).   p. 246

262 *Die Presse* published this article with the following editorial introduction: "The defeat at Hagerstown of the Confederate forces that had invaded Maryland from Virginia across the Potomac, a defeat which compelled them to pull back to Virginia, and President Lincoln's September 22 Proclamation, which abolishes slavery as of January 1, 1863, constitute a turning-point in the North American events. Our London correspondent, whose judgment is not biased by the language of the English papers, which are almost without exception sympathetic to the South and the cause of slavery, has the following to say about the new situation in North America:".

Marx discussed the problems dealt with in the article in his letters to Engels of September 10 and October 29, 1862 (see present edition, Vol. 41).

The article was first published in English in *Political Affairs*, No. 2, 1959, pp. 18-21.   p. 248

263 The Confederates' offensive in Maryland launched on September 4, 1862 ended in their defeat at Antietam Creek near Sharpsburg on September 17.
p. 248

264 The Confederate forces that invaded Kentucky on September 12, 1862 were defeated by Unionist troops at Perryville on October 8.   p. 248

265 The *Great West*—the western states of the USA. The Western farmers decided the outcome of the struggle against slavery in the Civil War (1861-65).
p. 249

266 This refers to the Confederates' successful advance into Kentucky in early September 1861, which resulted in Kentucky's joining the Confederacy in December.   p. 249

267 Lincoln's *Emancipation Proclamation,* published on September 22, 1862, declared all Black slaves in the rebellion-ridden areas free as of January 1, 1863. All Blacks were granted the right to enrol in the army and navy. The emancipation of the Blacks, carried out under popular pressure after a series of military setbacks, marked the adoption of revolutionary methods of warfare by the North. At the same time, the Proclamation was half-hearted and inconsistent, since it withheld emancipation from slaves in areas controlled by the Federal forces.   p. 250

268 One of Lincoln's occupations as a young man was splitting fence rails, which earned him the nickname of Rail Splitter among his Republican supporters during the 1860 Presidential campaign. Lincoln was a member of the House of Representatives (not a Senator) from 1847 to 1849.   p. 250

269 The revolutionary events in Greece, from February 1862 onwards, were a reaction to the country's exceedingly grave economic position, the aftermath of the Anglo-French occupation of 1854-57. The struggle, headed by the national bourgeoisie, was directed against foreign domination of the economy and

political life. On October 22, 1862 the Athens garrison mutinied and was supported by the city's entire population. A provisional government was formed which proclaimed the deposition of King Otho (Othon) of Bavaria. However, in June 1863, Britain, France and Russia, Greece's protectors under the 1832 convention, signed a protocol enthroning Prince William of Denmark as King of Greece under the name of George I of the Hellenes.

Veillard was a French businessman connected with the organising committee of the Great Exhibition in London (see Note 255). His bankruptcy, announced in September 1862, shortly before the closure of the Exhibition, caused a sensation in the press. p. 252

270 Marx set forth the basic ideas of this article in his letter to Engels of October 29, 1862. In his reply (Nov. 5) Engels agreed with Marx's overall assessment of the Southerners' defeat in Maryland and his other statements, but was more critical of the Northerners' policy (see present edition, Vol. 41).

The article was first published in English in: Karl Marx and Frederick Engels, *The Civil War in the United States,* New York, 1937, London, 1937, pp. 206-10. p. 256

271 On the battles of *Antietam Creek* and *Perryville* see Notes 263 and 264.
p. 257

272 This passage is based on inaccurate reports published, e.g. in the *New-York Daily Tribune* of October 20, 1862. Actually, it was in July 1863 that Morgan's detachment was beaten and Morgan taken prisoner. p. 257

273 At the *battle of Corinth* (Mississippi), fought on October 3 and 4, 1862, the Unionist forces under General Rosecrans defeated the Confederates commanded by generals Van Dorn, Price and Lovell. p. 257

274 In 1845-47 there was famine in Ireland due to the ruin of farms and the pauperisation of the peasants. Although blight had caused a great shortage of potatoes, the principal diet of the Irish peasants, the English landlords continued to export food from the country, condemning the poorest sections of the population to starvation. About a million people starved to death and the new wave of emigration caused by the famine swept away another million. As a result, large areas of Ireland were depopulated and the deserted land was turned into pasture by the Irish and English landlords. p. 257

275 The *War of Independence* (1775-83)—the revolutionary liberation war against Britain of its thirteen North American colonies which culminated in the establishment of the independent United States of America. p. 258

276 See Note 107. p. 258

277 This article was published in the column "America" with the editorial note: "Our *London* correspondent writes on the 7th inst.:". Since the editors of the present publication have no access to the Confederate newspapers used by Marx, the quotations from them have been retranslated from the German.

The article was first published in English in: Karl Marx, *On America and the Civil War,* New York, 1972, pp. 227-29. p. 260

278 See Note 273. p. 260

279 This refers to the Confederates' abortive attempt, on October 20, 1862, to recapture Nashville, surrendered at the end of February. p. 260

280 At *Bethel* (near Hampton, Virginia) a five-hour battle was fought on June 10, 1861, with the Southerners carrying the day.

On the battle of *Bull Run*, near Manassas, see Note 44. p. 261

[281] As a political or constitutional principle *states' rights* may be found in the Tenth Amendment to the Constitution adopted in 1791: "The powers not delegated to the United States by the Constitution, nor prohibited by it to the states, are reserved to the states respectively or to the people." p. 262

[282] This article was included in a large editorial review, "Peace Prospects in America", published on November 23, 1862. The article was introduced by the following editorial note: "As regards the latest election in the Northern states of the Union, to which so much importance is attached in Paris and London, we present here an account from our London correspondent, who is well informed on American affairs:".

Marx outlined the basic content of this article in a letter to Engels of November 17, 1862 (see present edition, Vol. 41).

The article was first published in English in: Karl Marx, *On America and the Civil War*, New York, 1972, pp. 230-31. p. 263

[283] This refers to the Congressional elections in the Northern states and the election of the Governor of New York State, both held on November 4, 1862. The Republicans won in most states, but lost a considerable number of votes to the Democrats in New York and the Northwest. The New York governorship went to Democrat Horatio Seymour. p. 263

[284] See Note 247. p. 264

[285] Marx means the French government's message to the governments of Britain and Russia of October 30, 1862 calling for joint action by the three powers to impose a ceasefire, lift the blockade and open the Southern ports to European trade. Britain and Russia rejected this proposal for interference in the internal affairs of the United States. p. 265

[286] This article was published by *Die Presse* in the column "America", with the editorial note: "Our London correspondent writes:".

It was first published in English in: Karl Marx and Frederick Engels, *The Civil War in the United States*, New York, 1937, London, 1937, pp. 210-14. p. 266

[287] During their invasion of Maryland, the Southern troops under General T. J. Jackson on September 15, 1862, after three days' fighting, seized Harper's Ferry, an important town on the Potomac with a garrison of 10,000 and a large arsenal, burned down all the government buildings and withdrew four days later. p. 267

[288] First published in English in: Karl Marx and Frederick Engels, *The Civil War in the United States*, New York, 1937, London, 1937, pp. 214-17. p. 270

[289] The cruiser *Alabama* was built and fitted in England under a Confederacy contract. On June 23, 1862, soon after she was launched, Charles Francis Adams, the US envoy to London, lodged a protest with the British government. Nevertheless, the latter allowed the cruiser to sail to the Azores, where she was armed. Between 1862 and 1864 the cruiser destroyed about 70 North American ships. The talks with the British government on compensation for the damage caused by the *Alabama* and other privateers built in England lasted until 1872, ending in the signing of an agreement obliging Britain to pay $15.5 million to the USA. p. 270

[290] An allusion to Lincoln's Emancipation Proclamation (see Note 267). p. 271

291 Marx's letter was written in connection with the publication in the *Berliner Reform*, on April 10, 1863, of a note giving a distorted account of Marx's negotiations with Lassalle on the joint publication of a newspaper during Marx's stay in Berlin in the spring of 1861 (see his letter to Engels of May 7, 1861 in Vol. 41 of the present edition). The Editors of the *Berliner Reform* introduced the letter with the words: "We have received the following note from *Karl Marx* in *London*:".   p. 273

292 This work was intended for the Darmstadt weekly *Allgemeine Militär-Zeitung*, to which Engels contributed from August 1860 to July 1864. His articles for the weekly written between 1860 and 1862 (they were signed F. E.) dealt with the Volunteer movement in Britain. In the present edition they are in Volume 18, as are his articles written for the *Volunteer Journal, for Lancashire and Cheshire*. Of Engels's articles for the *AMZ* written in 1863 and 1864, only one, "England's Fighting Forces as against Germany", was published in the weekly (see this volume). Three more articles remained in manuscript.

The present one deals with A. W. Kinglake's book *The Invasion of the Crimea*, published in the first half of 1863. As can be seen from Engels's letters to Marx of June 11 and 24 (present edition, Vol. 41), Engels was very critical of the book, especially of Kinglake's description of the battle of the Alma. It was probably then that he decided to write a critical review of the book. Apparently, he worked on the article "Kinglake on the Battle of the Alma" until the end of the month. It exists in the form of a rough draft, which has reached us incomplete. The end of section I and the beginning and end of section II (pages 5, 6 and 9 of the manuscript) are missing. The manuscript breaks off on page 17. Page 1 bears the initials "F. E.". The article was not finished and not sent to the *AMZ*, presumably because Engels discovered in the weekly's literary supplement (Nos. 15, 23 and 24, April 11, and June 6 and 13) a critical review of Kinglake's book by another writer, marked "5" (its conclusion appeared in Nos. 30 and 31, on July 25 and August 1, 1863).

The *battle of the Alma* took place on September 20, 1854. The Russian forces were commanded by A. S. Menshikov, and the numerically superior forces of the French, British and Turks by Saint-Arnaud and Raglan. It was the first battle after the Allies' landing in the Crimea (at Eupatoria) on September 14. The defeat and withdrawal of the Russian troops opened up the way to Sevastopol for the Allies. Engels described the battle in his article "Alma" written for the *New American Cyclopaedia* (see present edition, Vol. 18).

p. 274

293 In the preface to his book Kinglake says he had, in manuscript English translation made by a Russian officer (whom he does not name), the following memoirs of Russian generals that had fought on the Alma:

O. Kwizinski, "More Details on the Alma", Letter to the Editor of the *Russki invalid* (*Russki invalid*, No. 84, April 12, 1856);

P. Gorchakov, "Remarks on the Article 'More Details on the Battle of the Alma', published in *Russki invalid*, No. 84" (*Russki invalid*, No. 101, May 8, 1856);

V. Kirjakov, "More Details on the Battle of the Alma" (*Russki invalid*, No. 136, June 21, 1856).   p. 274

294 See Note 82.   p. 274

295 In 1849, the Bavarian Palatinate, along with Saxony, Prussia and Baden, was a centre of the struggle in defence of the Imperial Constitution adopted by the

Frankfurt National Assembly on March 27, 1849 and rejected by the King of Prussia and other German monarchs. Engels fought in the ranks of the Baden-Palatinate insurgents against the Prussian troops, but sharply criticised the political and military blunders of the petty-bourgeois leaders of the uprising. He described these events in *The Campaign for the German Imperial Constitution* and *Revolution and Counter-Revolution in Germany* (present edition, Vols. 10 and 11).   p. 277

296 See Note 227.   p. 279

297 This refers to the national liberation uprising of 1857-59 against British rule in India. It flared up among the Sepoy units of the Bengal army (the Sepoys were Indian mercenaries commanded by British officers) and spread to vast regions of Northern and Central India. Peasants and poor artisans from the towns took an active part in the movement, but the leaders were, as a rule, local feudal lords. The uprising was defeated because of communal differences among the insurgents and the military and technical superiority of the British.   p. 283

298 This article, intended for the *Allgemeine Militär-Zeitung*, was not published in that paper. Each of the two sections of the manuscript bears the superscription "F. E.", in keeping with the paper's practice of giving only the contributors' initials. In all probability, Engels wrote the article in September 1863, since he mentions military events in the USA which took place in late August and news of which could not have reached Europe until the next month. In Europe, an armed conflict was brewing between the states of the German Confederation and Denmark in which other European powers could get involved, including the Bonapartist Second Empire, which was claiming the left bank of the Rhine. The first section of the article is, in content, a sequel to Engels' article "The American Civil War and the Ironclads and Rams", published in *Die Presse* at the beginning of July 1862 (this volume, pp. 213-15).   p. 289

299 Engels means the possibility of war between the German Confederation and Denmark in connection with the aggravation, in the latter half of 1863, of the German-Danish dispute over the duchies of Schleswig and Holstein which, though populated mostly by Germans, were subject to the Danish Crown. During the 1848-49 revolution, an anti-Danish national liberation movement spread in the duchies which was, however, suppressed. The London protocol of May 8, 1852 on the integrity of Denmark, signed by Austria, Britain, Denmark, France, Russia and Sweden, declared the duchies to be associated with the Danish Crown in personal union. Prussia's ruling circles were seeking the duchies' union with Germany as the first step towards establishing a united Germany under Prussia's aegis. The constant attempts of Denmark's ruling classes fully to subject the duchies by depriving them of their autonomy provided Prussia with a pretext for starting war preparations, ostensibly acting on behalf of the German Confederation. In February 1864, Prussia and Austria opened hostilities against Denmark, which ended in the latter's defeat. The Vienna peace treaty of October 30, 1864 proclaimed Schleswig, Holstein and Lauenburg co-possessions of Austria and Prussia, thus setting the stage for disputes between the two.   p. 292

300 Presumably an allusion to the rights obtained by Prussia, Mecklenburg-Schwerin, Mecklenburg-Strelitz, the Hanseatic towns and other member states of the German Customs Union under the treaty with China signed in Tientsin on September 2, 1861 and ratified in Shanghai on January 14, 1863. It granted German subjects the same privileges as had been secured by the British and

French as a result of the Anglo-Franco-Chinese war of 1856-60 (extraterritoriality, the right of trade and anchorage in a number of ports, etc.). At the time, German firms were trading in Hong Kong and other open Chinese ports.

p. 292

301 Engels discusses Montalembert's fortification system in greater detail in the article "Fortification", written for the *New American Cyclopaedia* (present edition, Vol. 18).

p. 293

302 The hostilities in the Bomarsund Strait (off the Åland Islands in the Baltic) during the Crimean war were described by Engels in the two articles "The Capture of Bomarsund" written for the *New-York Daily Tribune* (present edition, Vol. 13) and in the article "Bomarsund" written for the *New American Cyclopaedia* (present edition, Vol. 18).

p. 293

303 The *Italian war*—the war of France and the Kingdom of Sardinia (Piedmont) against Austria, which lasted from April 29 to July 8, 1859. It was unleashed by Napoleon III who, under the pretext of "liberating" Italy, sought to seize new territories and consolidate his regime at home. The Italian liberal bourgeoisie hoped in the course of the war to unify Italy under the Savoy dynasty ruling in Piedmont. Napoleon III, however, was worried by the scope of the Italian national liberation movement against the Austrian oppressors and, after several victories by the Franco-Piedmontese forces, concluded a separate peace treaty with Austria in Villafranca on July 11, behind Sardinia's back. France obtained Savoy and Nice, Lombardy was annexed to Sardinia, while Venetia remained under Austrian rule.

p. 293

304 General Gillmore bombarded Fort Pulaski, held by the Confederates, on April 10 and 11, 1862. As Engels says further in the article, the information at his disposal was unreliable. Actually, Gillmore used rifled, not smoothbore, guns at Fort Pulaski.

p. 293

305 Fort Wagner, which covered Fort Sumter, was first bombarded by the Unionists on July 10, 1863. The regular siege and bombardment of the fort began on July 18. The Confederates evacuated it on the night of September 6.

p. 294

306 Fort Sumter covered the approaches to Charleston from the sea. The Unionist forces, commanded by Dahlgren, attempted to seize it on September 8, 1863, after the bombardment described by Engels. Their landing having failed, the Unionists abandoned their plan for capturing Charleston from the sea. It was not taken until February 1865.

p. 295

307 The Proclamation on Poland was written by Marx at the request of the German Workers' Educational Society in London (see Note 308), which had set up a committee to raise funds for the participants in the Polish uprising of 1863-64.

The Proclamation was first published in English in: Karl Marx, *Surveys from Exile*, Vol. 2, Harmondsworth, 1973, pp. 354-56.

p. 296

308 The *German Workers' Educational Society* in London was founded in February 1840 by Karl Schapper, Joseph Moll and other members of the League of the Just (an organisation of German craftsmen and workers, and also of emigrant workers of other nationalities). After the League of the Just was reorganised into the Communist League in the summer of 1847, the latter's local communities played the leading role in the Society. During various periods of its activity, the Society had branches in working-class districts in London. In

1847 and 1849-50, Marx and Engels took an active part in its work, but on September 17, 1850, they and a number of their followers withdrew because the Willich-Schapper adventurist sectarian faction had temporarily increased its influence in the Society, causing a split in the Communist League. In the 1850s, Marx and Engels resumed their work in the Educational Society, which existed until 1918, when it was closed down by the British government.   p. 296

309 This refers to the Central National Committee, which in January 1863 headed the national liberation uprising in the parts of Poland held by Tsarist Russia. Though inspired by the striving to end tsarist oppression, the 1863-64 uprising also reflected the crisis of feudal relations in the Kingdom of Poland. At the beginning of the uprising the National Committee announced a programme of struggle for Poland's independence and put forward a number of democratic agrarian demands. In May 1863, the Committee assumed the name of National Government. However, its inconsistency and indecision, in particular its failure to abolish the privileges of the big landowners, alienated the peasants, the majority of whom stayed away from the uprising. This was one of the main causes of its defeat. The movement was, by and large, crushed by the Tsarist government in the autumn of 1863, though some units of the insurgents continued the struggle until the end of 1864.   p. 296

310 See Note 253.   p. 296

311 Under the impact of the July 1830 revolution in France and the 1830-31 uprising in Poland, there was an upsurge of opposition feeling almost in all the states of the German Confederation in 1831-32. On May 27, 1832, a political demonstration by members of the South German liberal and radical bourgeoisie took place at the castle of Hambach, in the Bavarian Palatinate. As well as demanding Constitutional reforms and urging German unity, the participants in the "Hambach Festival" hoisted the Polish national flag in solidarity with the fighting Poles. In retaliation, the reactionary Federal Diet, the central body of the German Confederation, in June and July 1832 adopted six articles banning political demonstrations of any kind, introducing strict censorship of the press and severer punishment for political crimes, and calling for other repressive measures. The articles evoked widespread protests.

p. 296

312 The *National Association* was formed at a congress of bourgeois liberals from different German states meeting in Frankfurt am Main on September 15 and 16, 1859. The Association's aim was the union of Germany under Prussia's aegis. It was disbanded in November 1867.   p. 297

313 Engels presumably conceived this article in late 1863, after reading a series of items on the organisation of the British army in the *Allgemeine Militär-Zeitung* published between August and November. He, for his part, intended to review the British army's development and contemporary condition. He must have started work on the article at the end of 1863 and written part of the text in early 1864. The article was not published in the paper. The manuscript consists of seven sheets covered with writing on both sides and numbered by the author. The end is missing. The first page is superscribed "F. E.", as in other manuscripts by Engels intended for the *Allgemeine Militär-Zeitung* (see Notes 292 and 298).   p. 298

314 An allusion to the demarches of the British government (its messages of November 25 and December 31, 1863) in connection with the aggravation of the German-Danish dispute after the death of King Frederick VII of Denmark

on November 15, 1863 and the promulgation of a new Constitution proclaiming the final incorporation of Schleswig and Holstein into the domains of the Danish monarch (see Note 299). p. 298

315 The British East India Company was set up at the beginning of the seventeenth century. It had the monopoly of trade with the East Indies and played a decisive part in establishing the British colonial empire. The Company was liquidated in 1858, during the 1857-59 national liberation uprising in India (see Note 297). Marx characterised the Company in his article "The East India Company.—Its History and Results" (present edition, Vol. 12). p. 301

316 The sale of officers' commissions in Britain originated at the end of the seventeenth century and was later legalised by Royal sanction. In 1719-20, an official rate was introduced, which was repeatedly modified in later years. The system existed until 1871. p. 302

317 An allusion to the wars the British had waged from 1843 against New Zealand's indigenous Maori population, who had inflicted a series of defeats on the colonial troops. It was not until 1872 that the British succeeded in pushing the Maoris back to the most infertile lands, thus dooming them to starvation. p. 302

318 *Aldershot*—a military camp about 50 miles from London set up as a drill ground in 1855, during the Crimean war. p. 302

319 The *military school at Sandhurst,* some 50 miles from London, was established in 1802. It trained officers for the infantry and cavalry. p. 303

320 In 1806, a British expedition led by General Beresford and Captain Popham was sent to capture Buenos Aires, which belonged to Spain, then an ally of Napoleonic France. Meeting with no serious resistance from the Spanish colonial forces, Beresford's detachment seized the city, but was encircled and compelled to surrender by patriotic Argentine militias. Another British expedition, sent to the mouth of the River Plate in 1807, also failed. p. 304

321 See Note 297. p. 310

322 The *French Foreign Legion,* formed in 1831, was recruited mainly from criminal and other déclassé elements of foreign extraction living in France.
The *substitution system* was for a long time practised in the French army. It was a privilege for the propertied classes, allowing them to buy themselves out of military service by hiring substitutes. The practice was banned during the French Revolution but legalised again by Napoleon I. Under a law passed in 1853, substitutes were selected mainly by the authorities and the payment for them contributed to a special "army donation" fund. The substitution system was abolished in 1872. p. 312

323 See Note 227. p. 312

324 This refers to the *Peninsular,* or *Spanish, war* (1808-14) fought by Britain against Napoleonic France on Spanish and Portuguese territory. Meanwhile, the Spanish and Portuguese peoples were fighting a war of independence against France. p. 313

325 See Note 299. p. 317

326 Engels means the battle of *Waterloo* (see Note 82). p. 319

327 See Note 314. p. 321

328 No such report by Engels appeared in the *Allgemeine Militär-Zeitung.*

p. 325

329 Marx wrote these notes in late May and early June 1864, after Wilhelm Wolff's death on May 9. He intended to write a detailed biography of Wolff, one of his closest friends and associates, and collected data on his life. However, the project failed to materialise. In 1876, Engels carried it out, in part, by writing an extensive article titled "Wilhelm Wolff", which appeared in the journal *Neue Welt*, Nos. 27, 28, 30, 31, 40-45 and 47 (see Vol. 24 of the present edition).

p. 335

330 *Silberberg* was the prison in Silesia to which Wolff was confined for being a member of a student association and for "crimes against His Majesty, the King of Prussia". He was nicknamed Casemate Wolf for his article "Die Kasematten", describing the slums of Breslau, which was published in the *Breslauer Zeitung*, No. 271, on November 18, 1843, and caused a public outcry.

p. 335

331 The *Bureau de Correspondance,* set up by the German democratic journalist Sebastian Seiler (later a member of the Communist League) in Brussels in 1845, gathered, translated and forwarded to German newspapers news items and articles from the British, French and Belgian press, giving them, as far as possible, a Social-Democratic tendency, a fact later noted by Engels in his article "Wilhelm Wolff" (present edition, Vol. 24). The Bureau maintained close links with the Brussels Communist Correspondence Committee established by Marx and Engels. In October 1847, when Seiler for unknown reasons withdrew from the Bureau, it was headed by Wolff and Louis Heilberg. p. 335

332 Following the imposition of martial law in Cologne on September 26, 1848, publication of the *Neue Rheinische Zeitung* was suspended and a number of its editors (Engels, Wolff, Bürgers and others) were charged with sedition. To evade arrest Wolff went into hiding in Dürkheim, Palatinate, but soon secretly returned to Cologne and resumed his work with the newspaper. p. 335

333 Addressing the Frankfurt National Assembly (see Note 258) on May 26, 1849, Wolff, a deputy for Silesia, demanded the outlawing of Archduke John (the Imperial Regent) and his Ministers as the worst traitors to the nation (see Engels's article "Wilhelm Wolff" in Vol. 24 of the present edition).

p. 335

334 See Note 258. p. 335

335 See Note 257. p. 336

336 In connection with the amnesty granted by the Prussian government (see Note 257) Marx, during his stay in Berlin, March 17 to April 12, 1861, submitted an application to the Prussian government requesting the restoration of his Prussian citizenship (on his earlier steps in this matter see Vol. 7, pp. 407-10). With the working-class movement on the rise and a revolutionary crisis brewing in Germany, Marx probably wished to resume his political activity in Germany when the time was ripe for it. Marx's applications, published in the Appendices to this volume, were written for him by Ferdinand Lassalle and signed by Marx. His request was refused by the Berlin Police President and, in November of the same year, by the Prussian Minister of the Interior. p. 339

337 See Note 257.   p. 339

338 This document exists in two versions: a rough draft, written in Lassalle's hand, and a clean copy written in an unknown hand. The latter bears Marx's signature and, also in his hand, the inscription "Berlin, March 25, 1861". It also bears notes by a police officer.   p. 341

339 *Neue Rheinische Zeitung. Organ der Democratie*—organ of the proletarian revolutionary democrats during the German revolution of 1848-49, published under Marx's editorship. All the editors were members of the Communist League. As a rule, Marx and Engels wrote the editorials formulating the newspaper's stand on the most important questions of the revolution.

The consistent revolutionary line of the *Neue Rheinische Zeitung*, its militant internationalism and political accusations against the government displeased its bourgeois shareholders in the very first months of the paper's existence; its editors were persecuted by the government and attacked in the feudal-monarchist and liberal-bourgeois press. Persecution by the legal authorities and police was intensified after the counter-revolutionary coup in Prussia in November and December 1848.

In May 1849, when the counter-revolution went over to the offensive throughout Germany, the Prussian government expelled Marx from Prussia on the grounds that he was not a Prussian citizen. Because of Marx's expulsion and the stepped-up repressions against other editors, the *Neue Rheinische Zeitung* had to cease publication. Its last issue (No. 301), printed in red ink, came out on May 19, 1849. In their farewell address to the workers, the editors stated that "their last word will everywhere and always be: emancipation of the working class!" (see present edition, Vol. 9, p. 467).   p. 341

340 The Statement exists in three versions: one penned by Lassalle and two others, which are copies made by an unknown person. One of the fair copies bears the words, in Marx's hand, "Your Excellency's obedient servant, Dr. Karl Marx". It also bears von Zedlitz's refusal, in his hand, which was copied by a clerk and sent to Marx (see this volume, p. 353).   p. 345

341 After the February 1848 revolution in France, F. Flocon, a member of the provisional government of the French Republic, in an official message of March 1 informed Marx that the Guizot government's January order on the expulsion of Marx from Paris had been rescinded and he invited Marx to return to France.   p. 346

342 The *Preparliament* (Preliminary Parliament), which met in Frankfurt am Main from March 31 to April 4, 1848, consisted of representatives of the German states, most of them constitutional monarchists. The Preparliament passed a resolution to convoke an all-German National Assembly and produced a draft of the "Fundamental Rights and Demands of the German People". Although this document proclaimed certain rights and liberties, including the right of all-German citizenship for the residents of all German states, it did not touch the basis of the semi-feudal absolutist system in Germany.   p. 351

343 See the article "The Conflict between Marx and Prussian Citizenship" in Vol. 7 of the present edition, pp. 407-10.   p. 351

344 This document is a handwritten form with the blanks filled in, presumably at Marx's dictation, in an unknown hand. In the present edition these insertions are indicated by italics.   p. 355

345 This refers to the German Federal Act (Bundesakte—Verordnung über die zu

bildende Repräsentation des Volks. Vom 22sten Mai 1815) adopted by the Congress of Vienna on June 8, 1815. The Act proclaimed the formation of a German Confederation consisting initially of 34 independent states and four free cities. The Federal Act hardened the political disunity of Germany and preserved the absolutist feudal regime in the German states.   p. 357

[346] The *Federal Diet* (Bundestag)—the central body of the German Confederation (see Note 345) which consisted of representatives of the German states and held its sessions in Frankfurt am Main. Having no actual power, it nevertheless served as an instrument of monarchist feudal reaction. The formation in 1867 of the North German Confederation under Prussia's hegemony put an end to the German Confederation and the Diet.   p. 359

[347] The *Schiller Institute* in Manchester was set up in November 1859 in connection with the centenary of Friedrich Schiller's birth. Its founders intended it as a cultural and social centre for Manchester's German community. Initially Engels took no part in the Institute's activities as it bore the stamp of Prussian bureaucracy and pedantic formalism. In July 1864, after the Institute's rules had been amended, Engels became a member of its Directorate, and eventually its chairman. In these capacities he gave much of his time to the Institute and exerted an important influence on its activities.   p. 360

[348] Engels means the following communication:

"Manchester, May 2, 1861

"Mr. Engels

is herewith requested, in keeping with § 34 of the Supplementary Regulations, to return No. 14, V. Vogt, *Altes und Neues,* 2ter Bd., to the Library within 24 hours.

"The fine amounts to 1/7d. Failure to comply with this request within 24 hours entails an increase of this sum by 2/6d.

Yours sincerely,
By authorisation of the Directorate,
V. Stössel, Librarian"

p. 360

[349] This may refer to the Athenaeum Club, whose members were mostly men of letters and scholars. Athenaeum clubs existed in London, Manchester and other English cities.   p. 362

[350] Appendix II has not been preserved.   p. 362

NAME INDEX

French; took part in the conquest of Algeria in the 1840s; author of anti-Bonapartist pamphlets.—28

Aurelle de Paladines, Louis Jean Baptiste d' (1804-1877)—French general; took part in the Crimean war (1853-56); in 1854-55 commanded a brigade.—278, 279

B

Ballantine, William (1812-1887)— British lawyer.—121, 164-66

Bancroft, George (1800-1891)— American historian, diplomat and politician, Democrat; author of the *History of the United States* in ten volumes; was on the side of the North during the Civil War.—118

Baring, Thomas (1799-1873)— financier, head of a banking house in London, Tory M. P.; Chancellor of the Exchequer (1852 and 1858).—30

Bazancourt, César Lécat, baron de (1810-1865)—French military writer, Bonapartist.—280

Bazley, Sir Thomas, Baronet (1797-1885)—English manufacturer and politician, Free Trader; a founder of the Manchester Anti-Corn Law League; Chairman of the Manchester Chamber of Commerce (1845-59), M.P.—160-62

Beales, Edmond (1803-1881)—English lawyer, radical; a member of the English Emancipation Society, which supported the Northerners during the US Civil War; President of the Reform League (1865-69).—155

Beauregard, Pierre Gustave Toutant (1818-1893)—American general; took part in the war against Mexico (1846-48); commanded the Southern troops in Virginia (1861-beginning of 1862) and Mississippi (1862), later in Charleston (September 1862-April 1864); bombarded and captured Fort Sumter on April 12-13, 1861.—33, 200, 204-06, 207, 226

Bell, Sir George (1794-1877)—British army officer; in 1854-55 fought in the Crimean War (1853-56).—284

Bennett, James Gordon (1795-1872)— American journalist; adhered to the Democratic Party; founder and publisher of the newspaper *New-York Herald;* during the Civil War came up for a compromise with Southern slave-owners.—181, 263

Bentinck, G. W. P.—British parliamentary figure, Tory.—183

Berger—German refugee in Britain; a member of the German Workers' Educational Society in London; was on the committee raising funds for Polish insurgents during the Polish uprising of 1863-64.—297

Berkeley, George Cranfield (1753-1818)— British admiral, Tory M. P.—141

Bernard, Simon François (1817-1862)— French politician, Republican; emigrated to Britain after the defeat of the revolution (1848); was accused by the French Government of being an accomplice in Orsini's attempt on the life of Napoleon III; acquitted by the British Court.—245

Berry, Hiram Gregory (1824-1863)— American general; fought in the US Civil War on the side of the Northerners; commanded a brigade (1862-beginning of 1863), and then a division of the Potomac Army.—206

Bethell, Richard, 1st Baron Westbury (1800-1873)—British lawyer and politician, Liberal; Lord Chancellor (1861-65).—167

Billault, Augustin Adolphe Marie (1805-1863)—French politician and lawyer; an Orleanist and after 1849 a Bonapartist; Minister of the Interior (1854-58 and 1859-60).—79, 80

Birney, David Bell (1825-1864)— American general, Abolitionist; commanded a brigade of the Army on the Potomac during the Civil War (1862).—206

South; Secretary of War in the Confederacy (1861); general of the Southern army.—34

Walker, Timothy (1806-1856)— American lawyer, author of works on law.—106

Walsh, Sir John Benn, 1st Baron Ormathwaite (1798-1881)—British politician, Tory M.P.—211

Washington, George (1732-1799)— American statesman; Commander-in-Chief of the American Army during the War of Independence (1775-83), first President of the USA (1789-97).—8, 34, 101, 155, 250

Webster, Daniel (1782-1852)—American statesman, a leader of the Whigs, State Secretary (1841-43 and 1850-52).—112, 157

Wellington, Arthur Wellesley, 1st Duke of (1769-1852)—British general and statesman, Tory; commanded the British forces in the wars against Napoleon I (1808-14, 1815); Commander-in-Chief (1827-28, 1842-52); Prime Minister (1828-30).—305, 313, 319

Weydemeyer, Joseph (1818-1866)— prominent figure in the German and American working-class movement; adopted scientific communism under the influence of Marx and Engels and became a member of the Communist League; took part in the 1848-49 revolution in Germany; emigrated to the USA after the defeat of the revolution; Colonel of the Northern army during the Civil War; was the first to propagate Marxism in the USA.—257

Wheaton, Henry (1785-1848)— American lawyer and diplomat, author of works on international law.—106, 108

White, James—British parliamentary figure, Liberal; took part in the anti-interventionist meeting in Brighton in December 1861.—134, 136

Whitney, Eli (1765-1825)—American inventor of a ginning machine.—54

Whitworth, Joseph (1803-1887)—English manufacturer and military inventor.—323, 324

Whynne—participant in the anti-interventionist workers' meeting in London (January 1862)—155

Wilberforce, William (1759-1833)— British public figure and politician, philanthropist, M.P.; campaigned against slave-trade and slavery, in British colonies.—157

Wilkes, Charles (1798-1877)—American navy officer and traveller; took part in the Civil War on the side of the Northerners; captain of the battleship *San Jacinto* (1861), captured J. M. Mason and J. Slidell from the British ship *Trent.*—92, 93, 99, 101, 107, 110, 112, 139, 141, 146

Wilkes, John (1727-1797)—British journalist and politician, radical M.P.; author of pamphlets against the absolutist regime of George III.—101

Wilkes, Washington (c. 1826-1864)— English radical journalist, an editor of *The Morning Star.*—137

William I (Wilhelm I) (1797-1888)— King of Prussia (1861-88), German Emperor (1871-88).—5, 6, 27

Williams—English navy officer, representative of the Admiralty on board the *Trent* in 1861.—92, 95, 96

Wilson, Henry (1812-1875)—American politician, Senator (1855-73), supported the policy pursued by President Lincoln.—118

Wilson, James (1805-1860)—British economist and politician, Free Trader, founder and editor of *The Economist.*—162

Wolff, Wilhelm (Lupus) (1809-1864)— German proletarian revolutionary,

INDEX OF LITERARY AND MYTHOLOGICAL NAMES

INDEX OF QUOTED
AND MENTIONED LITERATURE

WORKS BY KARL MARX AND FREDERICK ENGELS

Marx, Karl

Abolitionist Demonstrations in America (this volume, pp. 233-35)
— Abolitionistische Kundgebungen in Amerika. In: *Die Presse*, No. 239, August 30, 1862.—267

American Affairs (this volume, pp. 178-81)
— Amerikanische Angelegenheiten. In: *Die Presse*, No. 61, March 3, 1862.— 226, 233, 267

[*Application by Marx for Restoration of His Prussian Citizenship*] (this volume, pp. 339-40)
— [Antrag von Marx auf Wiederherstellung seiner preussischen Staatsbürgerschaft,] Berlin, March 19, 1861, manuscript.—341

The British Cotton Trade (this volume, pp. 17-20)
In: *New-York Daily Tribune*, No. 6405, October 14, 1861.—59

The Civil War in the United States (this volume, pp. 43-52)
— Der Bürgerkrieg in den Vereinigten Staaten. In: *Die Presse*, No. 306, November 7, 1861.—42, 248

The Conflict Between Marx and Prussian Citizenship (present edition, Vol. 7, pp. 407-10)
— Der Konflikt zwischen Marx und der preussischen Unterthanenschaft. In: *Neue Rheinische Zeitung*, No. 94, September 5, 1848.—350-51

The Crisis in England (this volume, pp. 53-56)
— Die Krise in England. In: *Die Presse*, No. 305, November 6, 1861.—63

A Criticism of American Affairs (this volume, pp. 226-29)
— Zur Kritik der Dinge in Amerika. In: *Die Presse*, No. 218, August 9, 1862.—233, 248, 267

English Humanity and America (this volume, pp. 209-12)
— Englische Humanität und Amerika. In: *Die Presse*, No. 168, June 20, 1862.—226

[*Marx's Statement on the Restoration of His Prussian Citizenship*] (this volume, pp. 341-44)

— [Erklärung von Marx zur Frage der Wiederherstellung seiner preussischen Staatsbürgerschaft], Berlin, March 25, 1861, manuscript.—348

A *Meeting for Garibaldi* (this volume, pp. 236-38)
— Ein Meeting für Garibaldi. In: *Die Presse,* No. 256, September 17, 1862.—245

The News and its Effect in London (this volume, pp. 95-100). In: *New-York Daily Tribune,* No. 6462, December 19, 1861.—112

The Opinion of the Newspapers and the Opinion of the People (this volume, pp. 127-30)
— Die Meinung der Journale und die Meinung des Volkes. In: *Die Presse,* No. 359, December 31, 1861.—105

Marx, Karl and Engels, Frederick

The American Civil War (this volume, pp. 186-95)
— Der amerikanische Bürgerkrieg. In: *Die Presse,* Nos. 84, 85, March 26, 27, 1862.—226

The Situation in the American Theatre of War (this volume, pp. 204-08)
— Die Lage auf dem amerikanischen Kriegsschauplatze. In: *Die Presse,* No. 148, May 30, 1862.—226, 267

WORKS BY DIFFERENT AUTHORS

Anitschkof, [V. M.] *Der Feldzug in der Krim. Erster Theil. Die Schlachten an der Alma, bei Balaklawa und bei Inkerman,* Berlin, 1857.—274-77, 282

Ariosto, L. *L'Orlando furioso.*—64, 114, 274

Atlas historique et topographique de la guerre d'Orient, en 1854, 1855 et 1856, Paris, 1859.—278, 280

Bazancourt, C. L. de. *L'expédition de Crimée jusqu'à la prise de Sébastopol. Chroniques de la guerre d'Orient.* The first edition in two volumes appeared in Paris in 1856.—280

Beecher Stowe, H. E. [Letter to Lord Shaftesbury.] In: *The Times,* No. 24033, September 9, 1861.—7

Bentinck, G. W. [Speech in the House of Commons on March 7, 1862.] In: *The Times,* No. 24188, March 8, 1862.—183

Bible
  The Old Testament
    Genesis.—252
    The Lamentations of Jeremiah.—65
    Ezekiel.—240

Bragg, B. *Address to the People of the Northwest,* Head-Quarters C. S. Army in Kentucky, Bardstown, Ky., September 26, 1862.—256

Burdett, F. [Speech in the House of Commons on February 12, 1811.] In: *Hansard's Parliamentary Debates,* First Series, Vol. XVIII, London, 1812.—168

Calhoun, J. C. [Speech in the Senate on February 19, 1847.] In: *Congressional Globe: New Series: Contaning Sketches of the Debates and Proceedings of the Second Session of Twenty-Ninth Congress,* Washington, 1847.—13

Cameron, S. [Speech to Soldiers.] "Washington, Thursday, Nov. 14, 1861". In: *New-York Daily Tribune*, No. 6433, November 15, 1861.—115

Carlyle, Th. *Oliver Cromwell's Letters and Speeches, with elucidations.* The first edition in three volumes appeared in 1845.—179

Carnarvon, H. H. M. [Speech in the House of Lords on June 13, 1862.] In: *The Times*, No. 24272, June 14, 1862.—211

Cecil, R. A. T. [Speech in the House of Commons on March 7, 1862.] In: *The Times*, No. 24188, March 8, 1862.—185

Cobden, R. [Address to the House of Commons on August 1, 1862.] In: *The Times*, No. 24314, August 2, 1862.—239-40

Cochrane, J. [Message to Soldiers.] "Washington, Thursday, Nov. 14, 1861". In: *New-York Daily Tribune*, No. 6433, November 15, 1861.—115

Cooper, J. F. *The Pathfinder.*—88

Croswell, E. [Open Letter.] "New York, Nov. 20, 1861". In: *New-York Daily Tribune*, No. 6441, November 25, 1861.—116

Dante Alighieri. *La Divina Commedia.*—242

Derby, E. G. [Speech in the House of Lords on February 6, 1862.] In: *The Times*, No. 24163, February 7, 1862.—168-71, 239-40

Disraeli, B. [Speech in the House of Commons on February 6, 1862.] In: *The Times*, No. 24163, February 7, 1862.—168-69

Douglas, S. A. [Statement made at a reception in Washington on August 19, 1859.] In: *New-York Daily Tribune*, No. 5720, August 23, 1859.—37-38

Dunlop, A. M. [Speech in the House of Commons on March 19, 1861.] In: *The Times*, No. 23885, March 20, 1861.—23, 24

Fitzgerald, W. R. [Speech in the House of Commons on July 15, 1862.] In: *The Times*, No. 24299, July 16, 1862.—224

Forster, W. E. "On the Civil War in America." In: *The Times*, Nc. 24054, October 3, 1861 [a lecture].—26
— [Speech in the House of Commons on March 7, 1862.] In: *The Times*, No. 24188, March 8, 1862.—183, 184

Fould, A. "Mémoire à l'Empereur, lu en séance du Conseil privé et du Conseil des ministres, aux Tuileries, le 12 novembre 1861". In: *Le Moniteur universel*, No. 318, November 14, 1861.—79, 83
— *Pas d'assignats!* Paris, 1848.—80

Gladstone, W. E. [Speech in Newcastle on October 7, 1862.] In: *The Times*, No. 24372, October 9, 1862.—262, 270

Goethe, J. W. von. *Faust.*—158, 210

Gorchakov, P. "Remarks on the Article 'More Details on the Battle of the Alma' published in the *Russki invalid*, No. 83." In: *Russki invalid*, No. 101, May 8, 1856.—274, 287

Gregory, W. H. [Speeches in the House of Commons:]
— May 28, 1861. In: *The Times*, No. 23945, May 29, 1861.—182, 211

— March 7, 1862. In: *The Times*, No. 24188, March 8, 1862.—182, 183
— June 13, 1862. In: *The Times*, No. 24272, June 14, 1862.—211

Harvey. [Letter to Mr. Bruce.] In: *The Times*, No. 24274, June 17, 1862.—216-18

Hautefeuille, L. B. *Le droit maritime international devant le parlement britannique*. In: *Revue contemporaine*, 2ᵉ série, tome 27, Paris, 1862.—185

— *Nécessité d'une loi maritime pour régler les rapports des neutres et des belligérants*. In: *Revue contemporaine*, 2ᵉ série, tome 25, Paris, 1862.—185

— *Le règlement du 31 janvier 1862 sur l'asile maritime dans les ports de la Grande-Bretagne*. In: *Revue contemporaine*, tome 25, Paris, 1862.—185

Haxthausen, A. *Studien über die innern Zustände, das Volksleben und insbesondere die ländlichen Einrichtungen Russlands*, Dritter Theil, Berlin, 1852.—276

Hegel, G. W. F. *Vorlesungen über die Aesthetik*. The first edition in three volumes was published by H. G. Hotho in Berlin in 1835.—250-51

Heine, H. *Neuer Frühling*.—105

Hennessy J. P. [Speech in the House of Commons on July 2, 1861.] In: *The Times*, No. 23975, July 3, 1861.—24

Hodasevich, R. *A Voice from within the Walls of Sebastopol: A Narrative of the Campaign in the Crimea, and of the Events of the Siege*, London, 1856.—275, 277, 279

Horace (Quintus Horatius Flaccus). *De Arte Poetica*.—128, 182
— *Epistolarum*.—220

[Jefferson, Th.] *Memoirs, Correspondence, and Private Papers of Thomas Jefferson, Late President of the United States*, Vols. I-IV, London, 1829.—10, 91

Jennison, [C. R.] [Speech to Soldiers.] "Camp Jennison. Kansas City, Tuesday, Nov. 12, 1861". In: *New-York Daily Tribune*, No. 6441, November 25, 1861.—116

Johnson, S. *A Dictionary of the English Language, in which the words are deduced from their originals and illustrated in their different significations by examples from the best writers. To which are prefixed a history of the language and an English grammar*. The first edition in two volumes appeared in London in 1755.—107-08

Junius [Francis, Sir Philip]. *Letters*. In: *The Public Advertiser*, 1769-1772.—101

Justitia. "To the Editor of *The Times*". In: *The Times*, No. 24104, November 30, 1861.—99

Juvenalis. *Satirae*.—83, 84, 219

Kearney, Ph. [Letter to O. S. Halstead, Jr., August 4, 1862.] In: *New-York Daily Tribune*, No. 6719, October 16, 1862.—268

Kent, J. *Commentaries on American Law*. The first edition in four volumes appeared in New York in 1826-30.—90, 106

Kinglake, A. W. *The Invasion of the Crimea; its Origin, and an Account of its Progress down to the Death of Lord Raglan*, Edinburgh and London, 1863, Vols. I-II. The book came out in eight volumes.—274-88

— [Speech in the House of Commons on July 15, 1862.] In: *The Times*, No. 24299, July 16, 1862.—224

Kiryakov, V. "More Details on the Battle of the Alma". In: *Russki invalid*, No. 136, June 21, 1856.—274, 280

Kvitsinsky, O. "More Details on the Battle of the Alma" (Letter to the Editor of the *Russki invalid*). In: *Russki invalid*, No. 84, April 12, 1856.—274, 287

Layard, A. H. [Speeches in the House of Commons:]
— March 31, 1854. In: *Hansard's Parliamentary Debates*, Third Series, Vol. CXXXII, London, 1854.—135
— July 15, 1862. In: *The Times*, No. 24299, July 16, 1862.—224

Leibniz, G. W. *Nouveaux essais sur l'entendement humain.* The first edition appeared in Amsterdam and Leipzig in 1765.—163

Lincoln, A. [Letter to Frémont of September 11, 1861.] In: *New-York Daily Tribune*, No. 6380, September 15, 1861.—51

Lindsay, W. S. [Speech in the House of Commons on March 7, 1862.] In: *The Times*, No. 24188, March 8, 1862.—184-85

A Liverpool Merchant. "To the Editor of *The Economist*". In: *The Economist*, No. 957, December 28, 1861.—132

Lovejoy, O. [Speech in the House of Representatives on January 14, 1862.] In: *The Times*, No. 24153, January 27, 1862.—155.

Lowe, R. "The Part of *The Times* in the Government of the Country." In: *The Free Press*, No. 8, August 7, 1861.—21

Lucan (Marcus Aeneus Lucanus). *Pharsalia* (*De bello civili*). Libri I-X.—207

Macaulay Th. B. *Critical and Historical Essays Contributed to the Edinburgh Review.* The first edition in three volumes appeared in 1843.—179, 266

Mason, J. M. [Statement urging the separation of the South.] In: *New-York Times*, October 14, 1856.—103
— [Speech in the Senate on March 11, 1861.] In: *New-York Daily Tribune*, No. 6202, March 12, 1861.—103

Monroe, J. F. [Epistle to Commodore Farragut, D. G. of April 26, 1862.] In: *New-York Daily Tribune*, No. 6576, May 2, 1862.—201

Montagu, R. [Speeches in the House of Commons:]
— June 18, 1861. In: *The Times*, No. 23963, June 19, 1861.—23-24
— July 15, 1862. In: *The Times*, No. 24299, July 16, 1862.—224-25

Mozart, W. A. *Don Giovanni.* Opera in two acts. Libretto by Lorenzo Da Ponte.—43

Napoleon III (Charles Louis Napoléon Bonaparte) [Message to A. Fould.] In: *Le Moniteur universel*, No. 318, November 14, 1861.—79

Newman, F. W. [To the editor of *The Morning Star*.] In: *The Morning Star*, November 29, 1862.—270

Orléans, H. d'. *Lettre sur l'histoire de France adressée au prince Napoléon*, Bruxelles, 1861.—28

Palmer, R. [Speech in the House of Commons on March 7, 1862.] In: *The Times*, No. 24188, March 8, 1862.—185

Palmerston, H. J. [Speeches in the House of Commons:]
— July 16, 1857. In: *Hansard's Parliamentary Debates,* Third Series, Vol. CXLVI, London, 1857.—78, 225

— February 6, 1862. In: *The Times*, No. 24163, February 7, 1862.—170
— June 13, 1862. In: *The Times*, No. 24272, June 14, 1862.—211
— July 30, 1862. In: *The Times*, No. 24312, July 31, 1862.—239

Petrie, M., James, H. *Organization, composition and strength of the Army of Great Britain*, London, 1863.—298

Phillimore, R. *Commentaries upon International Law*. The first edition in four volumes appeared in London in 1854-1861.—106, 107

Plato. *Gorgias.*—200, 220

Pratt, F. Th. *Law of Contraband of War: with a Selection of Cases from the Papers of the Right Hon. Sir Geo. Lee... and an Appendix, containing Extracts from Treaties, Miscellaneous Papers, and Forms of Proceedings. With the Cases to the Present Time.* The first edition appeared in London in 1856.—91

Roselius, C. [Speech in the State Convention of Louisiana at New Orleans on March 21, 1861.] In: *New-York Daily Tribune*, No. 6217, March 29, 1861.—48, 49.

Russell, J. [Despatch addressed to the British Minister at Turin.] "Foreign-Office, Oct. 27". In: *The Times*, No. 23769, November 5, 1860.—231
— [Letter to W. Stuart.] "Foreign-office, July 28, 1862". In: *The Times*, No. 24323, August 13, 1862.—230
— "To the Right Reverend the Bishop of Durham. Downing Street, Nov. 4". In: *The Times*, No. 20640, November 7, 1850.—231
— [Speech in Newcastle on October 14, 1861.] In: *The Times*, No. 24064, October 15, 1861.—43
— [Speeches in the House of Lords:]
— February 6, 1862. In: *The Times*, No. 24163, February 7, 1862.—169
— June 13, 1862. In: *The Times*, No. 24272, June 14, 1862.—211

Saint-Arnaud, A. de. *Au quartier général à Alma. Champs de bataille d'Alma, le 21 septembre 1854.* In: *Le Moniteur universel*, No. 280, October 7, 1854.—280
— *Au quartier général à Alma. Champs de bataille d'Alma, le 22 septembre 1854.* In: *Le Moniteur universel*, No. 281, October 8, 1854.—280

Schiller, Fr. von. *Das Lied von der Glocke.*—181
— *Don Carlos, Infant von Spanien.*—81

Scott, W. [Letter on the *Trent* affair.] "Hôtel Westminster, Paris, Dec. 2". In: *The Times*, No. 24109, December 6, 1861.—114

Seward, W. H. [Speech at Rochester on October 25, 1858.] In: *New-York Daily Tribune*, No. 5466, October 28, 1858.—87

Shakespeare, W. *Julius Caesar.*—230
— *King Henry IV.*—200, 201
— *Macbeth.*—238

Singleton, O. [Speech in the House of Representatives on December 19, 1859.] In: *New-York Daily Tribune*, No. 5822, December 20, 1859.—13

Sophocles. *Oedipus Rex.*—79

Spence, J. *The American Union; its Effect on National Character and Policy, with an Inquiry into Secession as a Constitutional Right, and the Causes of the Disruption*, London, 1861.—93, 95

Stephens, A. H. [Speech in Savannah on March 21, 1861.] In: *New-York Daily Tribune*, No. 6215, March 27, 1861.—8, 34

Stephens, J. R. [Speech at the Chartist meeting of September 24, 1838, at Kersall Moor.] In: *The Northern Star*, No. 46, September 29, 1838.—153-54

Sumner, C. [Speech before the Young Men's Republican Union of New York, November 27, 1861.] In: *New-York Daily Tribune*, No. 6444, November 28, 1861.—118

Thackerey, W. M. *The Yellowplush Papers.*—138-41

Thomas, L. [Report on the investigation of General Frémont's activity, September 21, 1861.] In: *New-York Daily Tribune*. No. 6419, October 30, 1861.—88

Thousand and One Nights.—284

Vattel, [E.] de. *Le Droit des gens ou principes de la loi naturelle. Appliqués à la Conduite et aux Affaires des Nations et des Souverains. Ouvrage qui conduit à developer les véritables Intérêts des Puissances.* The first edition in two volumes appeared in Leyden in 1758.—108

Véron, L. *Mémoires d'un bourgeois de Paris,* Vols. I-VI, Paris, 1853-1855.—79

Virgil (Publius Vergilius Maro). *Aeneid.*—28, 129

Walker, J. *A critical pronouncing dictionary, and expositor of the English language... To which are prefixed principles of English pronunciation; rules to be observed by the natives of Scotland, Ireland, and London, for avoiding their respective peculiarities: and directions to foreigners for acquiring a knowledge of the use of this dictionary: the whole interspersed with observations, etymological, critical and grammatical...,* London, 1861.—108

Walker, T. *Introduction to American Law: designed as a First Book for Students.* The first edition appeared in Philadelphia in 1837.—106

Walsh, J. B. [Speech in the House of Commons on June 13, 1862.] In: *The Times,* No. 24272, June 14, 1862.—211

Wheaton, H. *Elements of International Law,* Boston, 1857.—106, 108

Wilkes, Ch. *Narrative of the United States Exploring Expedition During the Years 1838, 1839, 1840, 1841, 1842.* Vols. I-V, Philadelphia, 1845.—101
— *Western America, including California and Oregon, with Maps of those Regions, and of "The Sacramento Valley",* Philadelphia, 1849.—101

William I. [Speech to the Chambers on January 14, 1861.] In: *The Times,* No. 23832, January 17, 1861.—5

Wolff, W. "Das Elend und der Aufruhr in Schlesien". In: *Deutsches Bürgerbuch für 1845,* Darmstadt, 1845.—334

Yankee Doodle (popular American song).—206

DOCUMENTS

Accounts relating to Trade and Navigation for the Nine Months ended September 30, 1860. In: *The Economist,* No. 897, November 3, 1860, Supplement.—59

Accounts relating to Trade and Navigation for the Nine Months ended September 30,

1861. In: *The Economist*, No. 949, November 2, 1861, Supplement.—58-59, 63-64

An Act for amending and further continuing, until the 24th day of June, 1801, two acts, passed in that part of the United Kingdom called Ireland, in the thirty-ninth and fortieth years of the reign of his present majesty, for the suppression of the rebellion which still exists within that kingdom, and for the protection of the persons and properties of his majesty's faithful subjects within the same [1801].—210

An Act for the amendment and better administration of the laws relating to the poor in England and Wales [1834].—246

An Act for the release of certain persons held to service or labor in the District of Columbia [1862].—228

An Act to amend an act, entitled, "An Act to provide further for the public defence" [1862].—261

An Act to Amend the Laws Relating to the Importation of Corn [1846].—53, 160

An Act to amend, and supplementary to, the Act entitled "An Act respecting Fugitives from Justice, and Persons escaping from the Service of their Masters", approved February twelfth, one thousand seven hundred and ninety three [1850].—37-38, 103, 227

An Act to authorize the people of the Missouri territory to form a constitution and state government, and for the admission of such state into the Union on an equal footing with the original states, and to prohibit slavery in certain territories [1820].—10, 36, 37

An Act to authorize the President of the United States to appoint diplomatic representatives to the Republics of Hayti and Liberia, respectively [1862].—229

An Act to confiscate the property of Rebels for the payment of the expenses of the present rebellion, and for other purposes [1862].—234

An Act to continue, until the 24th day of June, 1801, an act, made in the last session of parliament of Ireland, intituled "An act to empower the lord lieutenant, or other chief governor or governors of Ireland, to apprehend and detain such persons as he or they shall suspect for conspiring against his majesty's person and government" [1801].—210

An Act to enable Boards of Guardians of certain Unions to obtain temporary Aid to meet the extraordinary Demands for Relief therein [1862].—239

An Act to Organize the Territories of Nebraska and Kansas [1854].—10, 35-37, 38-39

An Act to prohibit the importation of Slaves into any port or place within the jurisdiction of the United States, from and after the first day of January, in the year of our Lord one thousand eight hundred and eight.—202-03

An Act to provide for the government of the territory north west of the River Ohio [1789].—35-36

An Act to secure Freedom to all Persons within the Territories of the United States [1862].—228

An Act to Secure Homesteads to Actual Settlers on the Public Domain, and to Provide a Bounty for Soldiers in lieu of Grants of the Public Lands [1862].—228

An Act to suppress insurrection, to punish treason and rebellion, to seize and confiscate the property of Rebels, and for other purposes [1862].—228

Allerhöchster Gnaden-Erlass wegen politischer Verbrechen und Vergehen, 12. Januar 1861.

In: *Königlich-Preussischer Staats-Anzeiger*, January 13, 1861, Zweite Ausgabe.— 243, 334, 339-44, 347-51, 353, 357, 359.

The Boundary Treaty to settle and define the Boundaries between the Territories of the United States and the Possessions of her Britannic Majesty in North America, for the final suppression of the African Slave Trade, and for giving up of Criminals, fugitives from justice, in certain cases [1842].—112

Buchanan, J., Mason, J. Y., Soulé, P. "Aix La Chapelle, October 18, 1854" [Message to W. L. Marcy, US Secretary of State.].—10, 37-38

Butler, B. F. *A Proclamation* [May 15, 1862]. In: *The Times*, No. 24272, June 14, 1862.—210

The Constitution, as formed for the United States, by the Foederal Convention, held at Philadelphia, in the year 1787, with the resolves of Congress, and of the Assembly of Pennsylvania thereon, Philadelphia, 1787.—8, 36-37, 41, 102, 250.

Constitution of the Confederate States of America. In: *New-York Daily Tribune*, No. 6206, March 16, 1861.—8, 48, 50, 260-61

Convention, conclue à Londres, le 31 octobre 1861, entre l'Espagne, la France et la Grande-Bretagne pour combiner une action commune contre le Mexique.—67, 169, 224

Convention entre la Grande-Bretagne et le Maroc relative à un emprunt à faire à Londres par le Maroc; signée à Tanger, le 24 octobre 1861.—170

Correspondence Relating to Persia and Afghanistan, London, 1839.—23, 78

Correspondence relating to the Works under the Thames Embankment Bill, and to plans for facilitating the passage and traffic or opening better communication between Whitehall and Bridge Street, London, 1862.—219, 220

Correspondence Respecting the Affairs of Mexico. Presented to both Houses of Parliament by Command of Her Majesty, 3 parts, London, 1862.—172, 224

Davis, J. *To the Congress of the Confederate States*. "Richmond. Nov. 18, 1861". In: *New-York Daily Tribune*, No. 6441, November 25, 1861.—114

Déclaration réglant divers points de droit maritime, signée par les Plénipotentiaires d'Autriche, de France, de la Grande-Bretagne, de Prusse, de Russie, de Sardaigne et de la Porte Ottomane, à Paris, le 16 avril 1856.—124-26, 168, 185

Frederik, R. *Proclamation du roi de Danemark relative à l'organisation de la monarchie danoise y compris les Duchés de Schleswig, de Holstein et de Lauenbourg, signée le 28 janvier 1852*.—3

Frémont, J. C. *Proclamation*. "Headquarters of the Western Department, St. Louis, Aug. 31, 1861". In: *New-York Daily Tribune*, No. 6366, September 1, 1861.—51, 86, 115

Fugitive Slave Act—see *An Act to Amend, and supplementary to, the Act entitled "An Act respecting Fugitives from Justice..."*.

Gesetz über die Erwerbung und den Verlust der Eigenschaft als Preussischer Unterthan, so wie über den Eintritt in fremde Staatsdienste. Vom 31. Dezember 1842. In: *Gesetz-Sammlung für die Königlichen Preussischen Staaten*, Berlin, 1843, Nr. 2.—339, 341, 343-44, 347, 348, 350, 351, 353

Halleck, H. W. [Report to E. M. Stanton, Secretary of War.] "Headquarters of the Army, Washington, October 28, 1862". In: *New-York Daily Tribune*, No. 6740, November 10, 1862.—267

Homestead Act—see *An Act to Secure Homesteads...*

[Jackson, A.] *President Jackson's proclamation against the Nullification Ordinance of South Carolina*, December 11, 1832, N.p. [1832].—14, 33

Joint Resolution for annexing Texas to the United States [1845].—48

Kansas Nebraska Bill—see *An Act to Organize the Territories of Nebraska and Kansas*

Lincoln, A. *The Inaugural Address* [March 4, 1861]. In: *New-York Daily Tribune*, No. 6196, March 5, 1861.—34
— *A Proclamation* [April 15, 1861]. In: *New-York Daily Tribune*, No. 6231, April 15, 1861.—34
— "Executive Mansion, Washington, July 1, 1862." [Ordinance on the Enlistment of 300,000 recruits.] In: *New-York Daily Tribune*, No. 6628, July 2, 1862.—227
— [Address to the Representatives and Senators of the Border Slaveholding States, July 12, 1862.] In: *New-York Daily Tribune*, No. 6643, July 19, 1862—227
— *A Proclamation* [September 22, 1862]. In: *New-York Daily Tribune*, No. 6699, September 23, 1862.—249, 251, 266, 269

Madison, J. *To the Senate and House of Representatives of the United States* [Washington, June 1, 1812].—112

Magna Charta Libertatum.—168

McClellan, G. B. [Order, Enjoining on His Officers and Soldiers Obedience to the President's Proclamation of Freedom.] "Headquarters Army of the Potomac. Camp near Sharpsburg, Md., Oct. 7, 1862." In: *New-York Daily Tribune*, No. 6713, October 9, 1862.—266

Missouri Compromise—see *An Act to authorize the people of the Missouri territory...*

Order in Council. At the Court at the Queen's Palace, the 11th of November, 1807, present, the King's most Excellent Majesty in Council.—141

An Ordinance for the government of the territory of the United States, north-west of the river Ohio, New York, 1787.—35

Ostend Manifesto—see Buchanan, J., Mason, J. Y., Soulé, P. "Aix La Chapelle..."

Papers relating to the foreign relations of the United States, transmitted to Congress, with the annual message of the President..., Washington, 1861.—125-26.

Papers Relating to Mexican Affairs. In: *The Times*, No. 24168, February 13, 1862.—172-77

Population of the United Kingdom according to the Census of 1861. In: *The Times*, No. 23992, July 23, 1861.—53

The Portfolio; Diplomatic Review (new series), London, 1844, Vol. III, No. XI: Annexation of the Texas, a Case of War between England and the United States.—75-76

Protokolle der Deutschen Bundesversammlung vom Jahre 1848, Frankfurt am Main, 1848.—350-51, 353

Report Addressed to Her Majesty's Principal Secretary of State for the Home Department, Relative to the Grievances Complained of by the Journeymen Bakers; with Appendix of Evidence, London, 1862.—253-55

[Report of the Investigating Commission called by the Government to investigate the conduct of certain officers connected with, and the circumstances attending the abandonment of Maryland Hights and the surrender of Harper's Ferry.] In: *New-York Daily Tribune*, No. 6740, November 10, 1862.—267

Traité de commerce entre la France et la Grande-Bretagne, signé à Paris, le 23 janvier 1860; suivi de deux articles additionnels signés à Paris, le 25 février et le 27 juin de la même année.—162

Traité signé à Londres, le 8 Mai 1852, entre le Danemark d'une part, et l'Autriche, la France, la Grande-Bretagne, la Russie et la Suède de l'autre part, relatif à l'ordre de succession dans la monarchie danoise.—23

Treaty between the United States of America and Her Majesty the Queen of the United Kingdom of Great Britain and Ireland, for the Suppression of the African Slave-Trade. Concluded at Washington, April 7, 1862. In: *New-York Daily Tribune*, No. 6572, April 28, 1862.—202-03, 229

A Treaty of Peace and Amity between his Britannic Majesty and the United States of America; signed at Ghent, December 24, 1814.—112

Verfassungsurkunde für den preussischen Staat. Vom 31. Januar 1850. In: *Preussischer Staats-Anzeiger*, No. 32, February 2, 1850.—353

Verhandlungen des Deutschen Parlaments, Frankfurt am Main, 1848.—350

Verordnung über die zu bildende Repräsentation des Volks. Vom 22sten Mai 1815. In: *Gesetz-Sammlung für die Königlichen Preussischen Staaten*, No. 9 (Ausgegeben zu Berlin den 8ten Juni 1815).—357

Victoria, R. A Proclamation [May 13, 1861]. In: *The Times*, No. 23933, May 15, 1861.—92, 105, 106-07, 126, 138
— A Proclamation [December 4, 1861]. In: *The Times*, No. 24108, December 5, 1861.—112
— [Speech from the Throne on the opening of Parliament, February 6, 1862.] In: *The Times*, No. 24163, February 7, 1862.—167.

ANONYMOUS ARTICLES AND REPORTS PUBLISHED IN PERIODIC EDITIONS

Allgemeine Militär-Zeitung
— No. 41, October 11, 1862: *Verlauf und Bedeutung des diesjährigen Feldzugs in Nordamerika.*—289
— No. 20, May 16, 1863: *Der Angriff auf Charleston am 7. April 1863.*—289
— No. 20, May 16, 1863: *Charleston Hafen.*—294
— Nos. 34-39, August 22, 29, September 5, 12, 19, 26, 1863 (Literaturblatt): [review of the pamphlet] Petrie, M., James, H. *Organization, composition and strength of the Army of Great Britain*, London, 1863.—298

INDEX OF PERIODICALS

Intelligencer—see *The Daily Intelligencer*.

Journal des Débats politiques et littéraires—a daily published in Paris from 1789 to 1944; spoke for the moderate Orleanist opposition after the 1851 coup d'état.—73-74

Lloyd's Weekly Newspaper—a liberal paper founded in 1842; appeared in London under various titles in 1843-1931.—121, 123

The London Gazette—British government newspaper published twice a week since 1665; appeared under the title of *The Oxford Gazette* in 1665-66.—145, 146

Macmillan's Magazine—a liberal magazine published in London in 1859-1907.—130

The Manchester Guardian—Free Traders' newspaper founded as a weekly in Manchester in 1821; a daily since 1857; organ of the Liberal Party since the middle of the 19th century.—241, 317, 319

The Mark Lane Express and Agricultural Journal, etc.—British weekly voicing the views of the commercial bourgeoisie; appeared under various titles in London in 1832-1929.—231

Mobile Advertiser and Register—American newspaper published in Mobile (Alabama) in 1862-63.—260

Le Moniteur universel—a daily published in Paris in 1789-1901; appeared under this title from 1811 and was an official government publication in 1799-1869.—67, 73, 79, 83, 280

The Morning Advertiser—a daily published in London from 1794; it voiced the views of the radical bourgeoisie in the 1850s.—96, 128-29

The Morning Chronicle—a daily published in London in 1770-1862; Whig in the 1840s, Peelite in the early 1850s, and Conservative afterwards.—96, 97, 129

The Morning Herald—a conservative daily published in London in 1780-1869.—90, 96, 113, 129, 139, 199, 259

The Morning Post—a daily founded in London in 1772; in the mid-19th century, organ of the pro-Palmerston Right-wing Whigs; merged with *The Daily Telegraph* in 1937 to form *The Daily Telegraph and Morning Post*.—67, 71, 73, 74, 89, 91, 95-98, 113, 114, 128, 138-40, 143-44, 146, 175, 199, 259

The Morning Star—a daily of the English Free Traders published in London in 1856-69.—96, 97, 130, 139, 143, 144, 240, 246, 269, 270

Neue Rheinische Zeitung. Organ der Democratie—a daily newspaper of the German revolutionary-proletarian democrats during the 1848-49 German revolution; it was published in Cologne under Marx's editorship from June 1, 1848 to May 19, 1849 with an interval between September 27 and October 12, 1848; Engels was also one of its editors.—243, 320, 341-42

Newcastle Daily Journal—British conservative paper founded in 1832; it came out under this title from 1861 to 1920.—245-46

Newcastle Journal—see *Newcastle Daily Journal*.

New-York Daily Tribune—newspaper founded by Horace Greeley, published in 1841-1924; organ of the US Left-wing Whigs till the mid-1850s, later voicing

SUBJECT INDEX